Ken Sakamura (Ed.)

TRON Project 1990

Open-Architecture Computer Systems

Proceedings of the Seventh TRON Project Symposium

With 176 Figures

Springer-Verlag
Tokyo Berlin Heidelberg
New York London Paris
Hong Kong Barcelona

KEN SAKAMURA
Leader, TRON Project
Department of Information Science
Faculty of Science
University of Tokyo
Hongo, Tokyo, 113 Japan

ISBN-13: 978-4-431-68131-1   e-ISBN-13: 978-4-431-68129-8
DOI: 10.1007/978-4-431-68129-8

© Springer-Verlag Tokyo 1990
Softcover reprint of the hardcover 1st edition 1990

Foreword

I wish to extend my warm greetings to you all on behalf of the TRON Association, on this occasion of the Seventh International TRON Project Symposium.

The TRON Project was proposed by Dr. Ken Sakamura of the University of Tokyo, with the aim of designing a new, comprehensive computer architecture that is open to worldwide use. Already more than six years have passed since the project was put in motion. The TRON Association is now made up of over 140 companies and organizations, including 25 overseas firms or their affiliates.

A basic goal of TRON Project activities is to offer the world a human-oriented computer culture, that will lead to a richer and more fulfilling life for people throughout the world. It is our desire to bring to reality a new order in the world of computers, based on design concepts that consider the needs of human beings first of all, and to enable people to enjoy the full benefits of these computers in their daily life.

Thanks to the efforts of Association members, in recent months a number of TRON-specification 32-bit microprocessors have been made available. ITRON-specification products are continuing to appear, and we are now seeing commercial implementations of BTRON specifications as well. The CTRON subproject, meanwhile, is promoting standardization through validation testing and a portability experiment, and products are being marketed by several firms. This is truly a year in which the TRON Project has reached the practical implementation stage.

Application projects, such as the Intelligent House, Intelligent Building, Intelligent Automobile and Computer City projects, are also attracting considerable attention. A new addition to these projects this year is the start up of a research group on human/machine interface in home electronics products.

It is my sincere hope that this TRON Project Symposium will be a worthwhile experience for all of you who have favored us with your attendance.

AKIO TANII
Chairman, TRON Association
President, Matsushia Electric Industrial Co., Ltd.

Preface

The last 12 months have seen application-oriented developments in the TRON Project as exemplified by the TRON Intelligent House which was completed on December 1st 1989. Three more application projects began in 1989 and 1990 which means the application projects now in existence are TRON House, TRON Intelligent Building, TRON Intelligent City Development, TRON Intelligent Automobile, BTRON Multimedia Communication Research, and TRON Electronics HMI.

The TRON Project aims at creating an ideal computer architecture which takes into account the proliferation of computers in today's society. In order to establish the architecture, we need to anticipate the investigations of the future and this is the motivation behind the application projects.

I would venture to say that older computer systems were often created with the developer's interests in mind, perhaps to the disadvantage of the user. We now see many products on the market that cause many problems or inconveniences due to this design approach. The TRON Project aims at establishing computer systems that are truly user-friendly which means we need to proceed with our projects in a way that involves the system developers from the beginning while bearing the user in mind.

We are aiming to incorporate the user's requirements that we learn from the application-oriented projects into the basic subprojects of the TRON Project such as ITRON, BTRON, CTRON, TRON-specification CPU. The feedback from application developments is an indispensable part of the Project.

We regard these application projects as essential in order to prevent us from making the same mistakes that society made in coping with environmental problems; we failed to anticipate environmental problems by neglecting a vigorous assessment of the impact of human activity on the environment. Those involved with the TRON Project do not intend to produce unwelcome surprises when advanced computer systems are in wide circulation. Now is the time to anticipate and resolve the problems before mass installation.

Today, we see real applications being added to the capabilities of ITRON, BTRON, CTRON and TRON-specification CPU and we are receiving active cooperation from application developers. With this support the MTRON subproject will become the basis of a fully computerized society in the future. As the leader of the Project, I hope that this volume conveys our enthusiasm to all readers.

KEN SAKAMURA

Table of Contents

Appendix: Additional Contributions

Key Note Address

Programmable Interface Design in HFDS

Ken Sakamura

Department of Information Science, Faculty of Science, University of Tokyo

ABSTRACT

A programming/communication model on a shared memory base is proposed as a framework for devising standard interface specifications, in a large-scale, loosely coupled distributed environment. Although this model assumes a shared memory base, it is designed to allow different access mechanisms, structures, and a diversity of practical restricting conditions to be introduced at the model level to account for specific applications. The model integrates common data spaces found in a variety of applications, making it possible to realize compact interface specifications optimized to each application.

The aim behind this model is to realize programmable interfaces, as required in implementing the highly functionally distributed systems (HFDS) that are an ultimate objective of the TRON Project. By realizing programmable interfaces on this model, it will be possible to achieve commonality among each of the interfaces in HFDS, and at the same time to allow interface expansion to adapt to technological advances and to application differences.

Keywords: uniformity, extensibility, distributed environment, shared memory, communication model, programming paradigm, programmable interface

1. INTRODUCTION

The ultimate aim of the TRON Project is to build highly functionally distributed systems (HFDS). To this end the concept of programmable interfaces has been introduced. A programming model is specified as the basis of programmable interfaces. When programming is performed in a TRON environment, this programming model represents the system as it is seen from the programmer's standpoint, regardless of the language specifications used. In a broad sense, this model is the TRON architecture itself.

In TRON, a shared memory-based programming model has been adopted, since it is semantically close to the sequential programming approach in a von Neumann computer, to a window-based user interface, to file systems, and other basic aspects. The shared memory concept in TRON, however, differs from the conventional notion, in that a framework is provided from which shared memory systems can be derived that are optimized to specific applications. This optimization is done by choosing access methods and memory space configurations suited to each application.

The thinking that led to development of this model is outlined below. The paper describes the resulting programming and communication model based on shared memory, which is proposed as the direction for future design work. The features of this design policy are then discussed as realized in TULS (TRON Universal Language System), an actual TRON system programming environment.

2. BACKGROUND

In an HFDS, many thousands or even millions of computer systems of all scales, from embedded microcontrollers to huge database servers, will be loosely coupled, forming a network that is vast and diverse, both quantitatively and qualitatively. Moreover, the network will undergo constant reconfiguration as nodes are added or removed, or replaced by different systems. In order to assure that the nodes in this network operate in harmony with each other, a flexible network architecture is required featuring both compatibility and extensibility.[1] This is the purpose of the programmable interface concept introduced in the TRON Project.

2.1 Programmable Interface

Cooperative interaction among elements in an HFDS is possible only if standard interfaces are provided on all communication paths in the network. If, however, such standardization means that all the interfaces in a vast and open network are to have the same fixed specifications, this will stifle the incorporation of future advances in computer technology. For this reason fixed specifications are not desirable. On the other hand, if version updates are allowed, inconsistency in versions throughout the network will soon become a problem. And if strict adherence to upward compatibility is made mandatory, many systems will become overweighted with nonstandard and unneeded aspects.

Similar problems apply not only between networks but also to system calls, which are interfaces between systems and application programs, as well as to data formats, which are interfaces between application programs. In the HFDS system as a whole there are many more interfaces, in the broad sense, that need to be specified, including network protocol, printer control codes, and also data coding formats and human/machine interfaces. Here, too, it is desirable to allow changes in the interface specifications in order to incorporate new technology and adapt to different applications; but at the same time, interface changes can lead to compatibility problems.

The programmable interface concept approaches this dilemma in the following way. A system with which communication is made can be programmed, and in this way interface specifications can be changed dynamically as needed. When communication takes place between systems, first of all the interface specifications on both sides are compared with each other, and if necessary, the side requiring higher-level specifications sends a program to the other party, thus establishing the necessary communication.

Perhaps the simplest example is the problem of user-defined characters. TRON already offers a character code that includes nearly all the characters in use today,[2] but there is no end to the symbols that could be devised which are not supported in the character code. If a user defines such a symbol, there are numerous cases where it will not be recognized, such as when it is transferred between different systems, between application programs, or between an application program and window system. In the programmable interface concept, however, the file containing the symbol can define the symbol in a "program section" at the head of the file, using graphical data, and thereafter this definition can be referred to by a code wherever the symbol appears in the file. The system receiving the file first receives this program section and programs itself accordingly, so that it can interpret the data following.(*Fig. 1*)

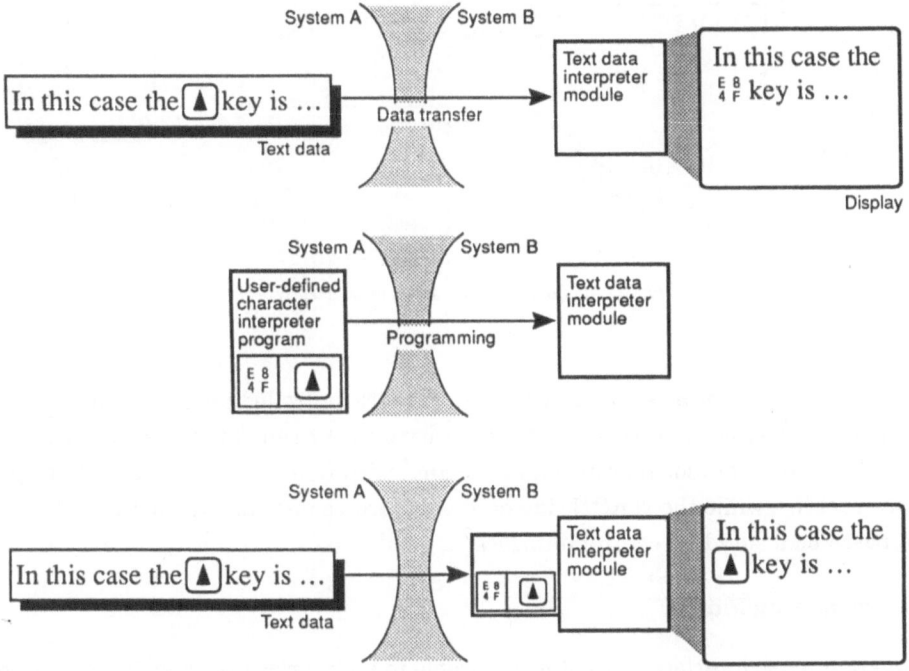

Fig. 1   Handling of user-defined characters in a programmable interface

Likewise, user expansions such as defining new character formats (outline, for example) can be handled in a similar fashion. This ensures that other systems will reproduce the character format in the same way as intended.[3] In the language processing environment, as well, an extension of this capability is used. For example, if mail is received by a system lacking the environment for interpreting the language in which the contents are expressed, the necessary language processing environment is requested and used to program the receiving system. The mail contents can then be interpreted and displayed. Similarly, where data are in a format specific to an application, the section of the application for interpreting and displaying data in that format can be made non-proprietary (even if other parts of the program are proprietary) and can be sent along with the data.

This concept also means that, besides maintaining interface compatibility, the specifications of interfaces in an HFDS can be changed flexibly at execution, resulting in an ideal load distribution and efficient communication between systems linked via a programmable interface. Moreover, by distinguishing between design guidelines and implementation, both diversity and compatibility can be achieved at the system level.(*Fig. 2*)

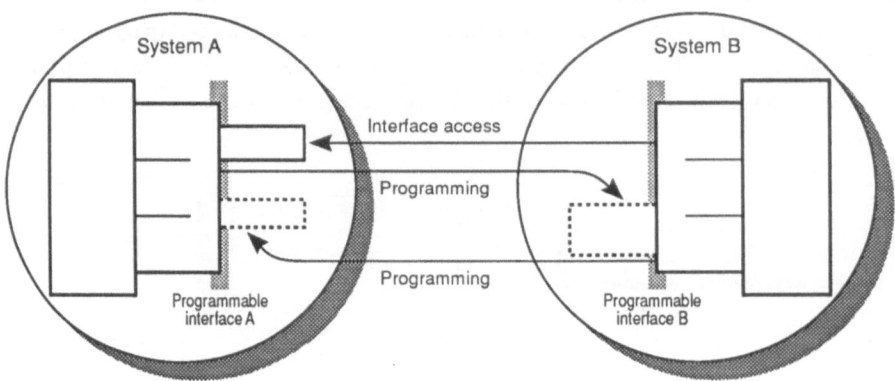

Fig. 2 Interface programming in distributed system

As an example, consider a system in which an ITRON-controlled air conditioner is operated by a BTRON machine in an HFDS. If the air conditioner sends to the BTRON machine a dialog window program for its control, interaction with human beings can be left up to the BTRON machine, while the ITRON side need only receive instructions that have been determined based on a standard control interface.

2.2 Programming Model

The programmable interface concept is applicable to all interface specifications that are conceivable in a TRON system, and in application fields it applies to BTRON as well as to ITRON and CTRON fields. This concept is not simply one in which each interface has in common the ability to be programmed; it also means that this programming takes place in a standard way for all interfaces. In other words, this is not a programmable interface that is valid only between the systems assumed by specific application programs; rather, standard provision is to be made of this capability at the system level, independently of application programs. Only in this way will it be possible for interfaces to interact on communication links between any two systems, and in this way for dynamic standardization of interfaces to be achieved.

Looking once more at the air conditioner example, dialog with the air conditioner does not have to be limited to the BTRON machine's window system, but could also use an ITRON-specification programmable remote controller, or many other combinations of communication. In this sense, as long as a display and pointing device are provided and a system is given

GUI (graphical user interface) capability for dialog with human beings, all kinds of systems can be used for communication.

The problem here comes down once again to whether such a standard programming environment is possible. That is, if a programmable interface is applied to the problem of interface specifications that defy standardization, can standard specifications be devised that fit the object of programming? Further, it is a question of whether the same programming language and environment can be provided for applications as different as window servers and file servers, or to operating systems as diverse as those of a BTRON machine and an ITRON programmable remote controller.

An answer proposed in TRON, based on the von Neumann resource model, is the macro-based programming language/environment design guideline TULS,[4] which has been made specific to programming for BTRON systems in the TACL language and environment.[3] This twofold structure of specifications arises from the judgment that, from the standpoints both of efficiency and programming ease, and for programming of interfaces for the diversity of applications and system scales noted above, relying fully on one programming language and environment would not be feasible. Instead, in this scheme, programming languages and environments are designed in accord with the guidelines (TULS), but can be tailored to specific applications and scales, as in the case of TACL. The programming languages and environments, in other words, do not have to be the same but must have similar specifications.

In subsequent studies it was decided to go beyond mere guidelines and to provide rather a framework for devising very primitive programming languages and environments, like the relation between microprograms and programs. A mechanism could then be provided for putting together programming languages and environments geared to each application and scale, through a process of specializing or fleshing out that framework. This specialization process can be described objectively.

This approach assures that two languages and environments intended for quite different applications or system scales will have sufficient similarity in specifications in the parts where similarity is possible. Even when these parts are viewed from another system, it is only necessary to be familiar with the general coding rules for the specialization process. This will enable programming of the other system without knowing the detailed internal specifications. This abstraction is necessary for a programmable interface in an open network.

This framework for devising programming languages and environments is here called a "programming model."

2.3 Programming Model Requirements, and Direction of Studies

Next a summary will be given of what is required in a programming model of the type described above. These requirements determine the direction to be taken in studies on the programming model.

A programming model for programmable interfaces must be universal enough to be usable in all the systems of different purposes that make up an HFDS. At the same time it must be sufficiently abstract so as to allow programming without detailed knowledge of the interface specifications of the other system.

Ease of programming in the languages and environments based on that model is the next requirement. This is of course important when human beings do the programming directly, but is also desirable in systems with automatic programming capability, which will no doubt be a key feature in future HFDS subsystems that operate autonomously and cooperatively.

Another obvious requirement for this programming model is achievement of execution efficiency and compactness, so as not to impose a burden on the many small-scale hardware resources included in an HFDS.

The need to realize the seemingly irreconcilable objectives of universality and efficiency leads to adoption of a policy of strict adherence to von Neumann architecture, as was the case in TULS studies. The von Neumann model, as it turns out, is simulated in all computer environments, from window systems to file systems. Any model, so long as it properly represents the basic qualities of a von Neumann computer environment, is capable of better efficiency than a purpose-specific interface that ignores those qualities. In this sense, a universal model does not necessarily have to be inefficient.

The model, in other words, expresses the von Neumann architecture at as low a level as possible, and as abstractly as possible. The object of continuing studies is to devise a universal mechanism for specializing this model to fit the needs of various applications. Further, this specialization should achieve a high level of communication between interfaces so that programming can be simplified.

2.4 Communication Model Requirements, and Direction of Studies

In an HFDS, programming must be possible while a system is operating. With a programmable interface, programming takes place without distinguishing between ordinary programming using an interface and dynamic programming. To this end, the programming model must also be a communication model between network-transparent systems, processes, and layers.

The discussion up to now has focussed on the programming model aspect, but the same requirements must be satisfied in terms of use as a communication model. That is, when application programs are programmed in a distributed environment, it must be possible to code programs simply, on a communication model that integrates communication programs that are complex and distributed for each of the diverse objects of communication.

This aim of simplifying programming of application programs by means of an integrated communication model is realized in UNIX by means of a byte stream file model. Integration in this model, however, is performed in a classic environment in which the file is a flat byte stream, the user interface is a teletype, and communication between processes is by message passing only.

Communication model integration that meets the needs of future high-level applications must take into account the emergence of a variety of files, ranging from hash files to hypertext and other types of high-level files. It must also be premised on memory shared among processes, for the sake of real-time performance, and on user-friendly window systems that display application programs independently.

In addition to uniformity, there are of course such general requirements as network transparency, extensibility, security, reliability, maintainability, and real-time performance.

When it comes to guidelines, extensibility can be achieved by means of programmable interfaces, whereas performance needs are met by the policy of "strict adherence to a von Neumann architecture." Network transparency, extensibility, security, reliability, and maintainability can be realized by increasing the degree of abstractness of communication so that when communication takes place, the necessary processing is performed at the system end, independently for each application program.

3. Two Communication Models

Integrated communication models for the sake of simplified programming can be classified as below into message passing and shared memory types.

3.1 Message Passing Model

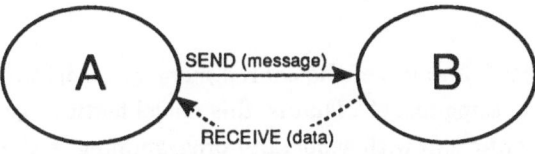

Fig. 3 Message passing model

An advantage of a message passing model is first of all the high degree of abstractness. Thus, even when rather complex communication is realized, there is little need to be concerned about side effects, and in that sense the burden on programmers is lessened. For similar reasons, network transparency, extensibility, security, reliability, and maintainability are high; and the semantic gap with network configuration is small, so that this model is suited to loosely coupled distributed systems.

On the other hand, a disadvantage of message passing is that the message issuer must know the recipient of a message. A further restriction is that the recipient must exist when messages are sent. Moreover, FIFO is the only possible form of access to messages. When messages arrive at random time intervals, they must be tracked from the head of the queue, with their states determined dynamically; and measures must be taken to assure mutual consistency.

When complex communication is attempted, there is the added burden of having to decide data format and protocols, etc. between the sender and receiver; and the problem of consistency noted above must also be taken into account, as a result of which the communication-related aspects of a program can become quite unwieldy.

Even if the programmer's burden is to be reduced by greater abstractness, when it comes to complex communication — especially in applications with severe needs for real-time control — the programming burden will still be considerable. Real-time applications are a basic assumption in TRON, and in that sense the message passing model can be seen as too abstract.

3.2 Shared Memory Model

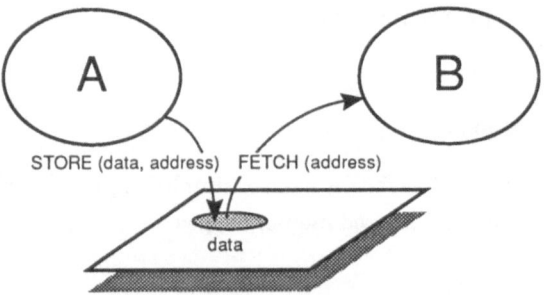

Fig. 4 Shared memory model

The advantages and disadvantages of the shared memory model are the converse of those noted for the message passing model. That is, this model features good execution efficiency due to the narrow semantic gap with sequential programming in the von Neumann model. Moreover, random access is possible, and communication is not restricted by the need for existence of a recipient when sending takes place. In addition, common data are located in shared memory, so that changes in data are inevitably reflected in the data of all those possessing it. This removes the need for concern about data consistency. This model, moreover, is best for exchanging data with complicated structures. For these reasons, programming is generally easy.

Where the shared memory model suffers in comparison with message passing is the low level of abstractness. For this reason, when complex communication is realized, the programmer's burden for those aspects is large. This is because, with programming in a conventional shared memory model, passing of control is treated as a completely separate event from access to shared memory, as a result of which changes in shared memory take place as side operations.

Along with the low degree of abstractness, a fully shared memory model, in which even non-shared data that should be kept separate are all located in the same memory space, would hardly be desirable from the standpoints of network transparency, extensibility, security, reliability, and maintainability.

In addition, when a distributed environment is configured by joining together heterogeneous systems, and especially when systems are linked whose memory structures use different endians, the shared memory model is disadvantageous.[5]

3.3 Shared Memory Object Model

A system that is simply a faithful rendition of one of the conventional models described above would thus be impractical. Instead, loosely coupled distributed systems today adopt what can be called a shared memory object model, in which a general message passing model is put into practice along the lines of a shared memory system.(*Fig. 5*)

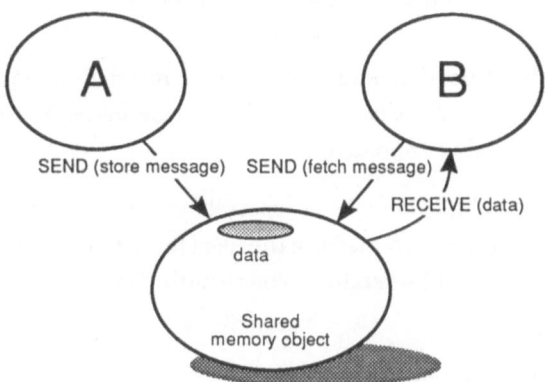

Fig. 5 Shared memory object model

In these systems, data that require sharing are stored in objects, to which those sharing the data (users) request access by means of messages. The users need only be aware of the shared memory objects as message receivers, and the only protocol necessary is that with the shared memory objects. Besides, the existence of message receivers is guaranteed at all times, and random access is possible with this approach. These added qualities also have the effect of reducing the programmer's load.

3.4 Advanced Shared Memory Model

Similarly, by devising a mechanism for triggering high-level processing involved in access to shared memory, it is possible to conceive of a model based on shared memory but which incorporates the advantages of message passing.

If the shared memory access primitives are made more advanced, it is possible to realize functions for abstraction of communication, for objectification of shared memory, for distributed memory and replication, and for distributed atomic transaction.(*Fig. 6*)

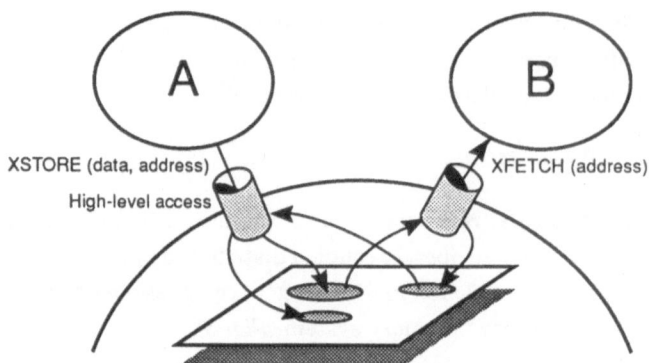

Fig. 6 Advanced shared memory model

Moreover, by means of objectification, and by imposing a restriction requiring FIFO access to shared memory that is used only between certain specific users, the model can be implemented using a message passing approach.

This expansion of the original model makes it possible to overcome the disadvantages of the shared memory model noted earlier, satisfying the need for network transparency, extensibility, security, reliability, and maintainability. The resulting model can be called an advanced shared memory model.

3.5 Consideration as Access Method

The more realistic approaches described above are the result of bringing the two basic models closer together, in the process of which many of the differences between the two are resolved. In deciding whether to adopt a model based on message passing or one based on memory sharing, it is first necessary to consider the essential differences that derive from having started out from one model or the other.

The essence of those differences is in the overhead arising from the method of access to shared data. The shared memory object model, inasmuch as it is a development out of the message passing model, realizes its access method by using messages. For this reason, it is not possible to improve efficiency beyond the message access overhead.

The advanced shared memory model, on the other hand, raises the level of memory access primitives. As for the important question of how the level is to be raised, the model must be tuned sufficiently to the particular application, so that even if overhead becomes greater than that of the pure memory access model, it will still be possible to ensure greater efficiency than message access overhead.

There is a close resemblance here to the relation between process and lightweight process. From the standpoints both of independence and of overhead size, if a message is like a process then advanced memory access is like a lightweight process.

At the same time, in the advanced shared memory model, abstraction of communication is a matter of how the model is put into operation. As with lightweight processes, the degree of independence is low and violations occur rather easily. This is the price paid for efficiency.

In considering which of these to apply as the communication model in TRON (the remaining requirements can be considered on a par in the two models), priority was given to use with small-scale systems and to the need for real-time processing. As a result, the advanced shared memory model was judged to be preferable.

4. PROGRAMMING PARADIGM

The programming model is a framework from which actual programming languages and environments can be derived through a process of objective specialization. Quite naturally, this framework includes a programming paradigm, which is a guideline for designing abstract programming languages and environments.

As noted earlier, in a loosely coupled distributed environment premised on programmable interfaces, there is a close correspondence between the communication model and the programming model or paradigm. That is, the message passing model corresponds to an object-oriented programming (OOP) paradigm, whereas the shared memory model corresponds to a general procedure-based programming paradigm.

Another programming paradigm, incidentally, is the function type, but it would be difficult to come up with a communication model that corresponds to this paradigm in its pure form. For whatever reason, a pure mapping would necessitate that all network states be handled as function values, which would be impossible from the standpoint of simultaneity in the network.

4.1 "Field" Paradigm

Although it was decided to adopt an advanced shared memory model as the TRON communication model, its essence is not simply memory access, but rather a diversity of processing can take place in the access process. When it comes to programming, naturally there will be those wanting to program also the processing that takes place in the access process. In this way it will become possible to specialize the shared memory access method itself, and this becomes another important function for deriving from the same framework different programming languages and environments suited to specific applications. Not only that, but the same mechanism can be used also for programming of general programs.

The programming model or paradigm on which this sort of concept is premised — that of a shared data space which is semantically like a program evaluation environment, and which allows programming of advanced-level processing in the very act of accessing — will be called a "field" paradigm. This name is based on a quality observed in classifying the interaction among systems, processes, and objects. Whereas the classical theory of gravity ever since Newton saw gravity in terms of interaction between two masses, Einstein's theory of gravitational fields holds that a mass affects a field, and the field interacts with another mass. On this analogy, the OOP paradigm can be thought of as the classic theory of gravity, while the paradigm centering on advanced shared data spaces fits nicely with the gravitational fields theory.(*Fig. 7*) In this case a "field" is a data space, which has the semantic of itself interacting with something else.

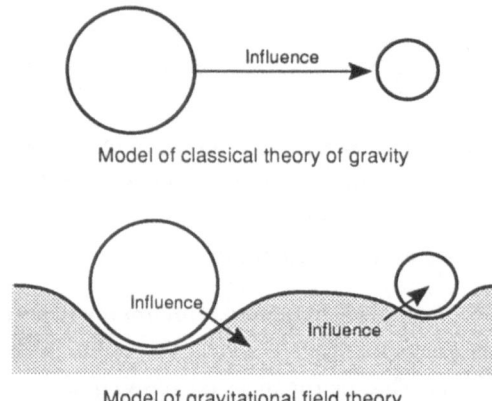

Fig. 7 Field model in theory of gravity

That is, a program constructed on this paradigm takes the form of more than one shared data space. The program is distributed among these shared space addresses or address areas. A read access to one of those addresses, accompanied by an argument, is evaluated in that space as an event having the meaning of data input or control. The content of that data space is then altered, and a value is returned as the result of the initial read access.

4.2 Comparison with Other Paradigms

In comparing the field paradigm with other paradigms, the differences between the conventional procedure-based paradigm and a field-oriented paradigm can be seen in the same light as the differences between a simple shared memory communication model and the advanced shared memory model. The same can be said for comparisons between a procedure-based paradigm and an OOP paradigm; that is, the procedure paradigm is characterized by a low degree of abstractness, requiring side effects to be taken into account and therefore increasing the programmer's load. In contrast, with the advanced shared memory model, when memory access threatens to become a problem it can be made more abstract as needed, thus easing the burden on programmers.

Comparisons between the OOP paradigm and a field-oriented paradigm can also be made in the same way as for communication models. The field-oriented paradigm is less abstract than the OOP paradigm, but this is because it so faithfully models actual use patterns of actual computers. It therefore has the advantage of greater efficiency than is possible with the more abstract OOP paradigm.

In other words, the "field" paradigm is an abstract model sufficiently tuned to computer environments. By comparison, the OOP paradigm is too abstract, and is too lacking in the qualities of actual computer environments; moreover, in attempting to fill in this gap in the process of implementing this paradigm, there is the danger of ending up with virtual environments that are quite different in nature from actual environments, giving rise to efficiency problems. For similar reasons, when programming is performed on the OOP paradigm, there is the practical problem that many applications are difficult to reflect adequately in objects. This is because the model is too far removed from reality.

A specific example of the advantage of the field paradigm is that it permits interaction to take place not only through messages but also through "fields," thereby making it possible to represent interference in the same space, which is not directly possible by means of messages in the OOP model. Information exchange, and influence on others, are thus possible without knowing the other party and without introducing an object called "environment," which requires special handling.

Suppose a model of nature insisted that flowers could not bloom unless the wind were instructed to blow with specific flowers in mind. Such a model would never be able to simulate a meadowland. There are some applications for which a broadcasting model is more appropriate; it would be highly inefficient to realize these by placing telephone calls.

In actuality, however, most so-called OOP languages today permit procedure-oriented programming; and although the nuances differ from the shared memory object model, they end up being hybrid languages incorporating the advantages of both paradigms. It therefore makes little sense to compare a pure OOP paradigm against a field-oriented paradigm. Here, unlike the case with communication models, introducing the qualities of procedures is not simply a matter of administration. Rather, it is a real blending of both approaches; and aspects are hidden in objects only in places where abstractness is required. Thus, even if a language is called OOP, optimization is performed in compiling so that efficiency problems are largely overcome.

What really needs to be looked at here in comparison with OOP languages is the interrelation among modules. Objects in an OOP paradigm are essentially all on an equal level. Another way of putting it is that they are not structured. By contrast, in the field-oriented paradigm, dynamic structuring is possible during execution, by making use of locations (addresses) in dynamically created fields.(*Fig. 8*)

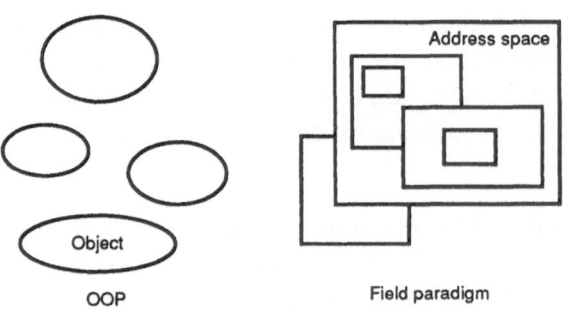

Fig. 8 Interrelation between models

As an example, consider a window system implemented on a field-oriented paradigm.

Suppose panels are to be displayed on the screen. In the OOP paradigm the panels would naturally be considered as objects. In reality, however, these objects are displayed only as the result of a panel instance making a draw request to the instance handling display primitives. In other words, the panel graphic displayed on the screen is no more than a side effect, and is not the object itself.

For this reason, the decision as to whether the panel should react in response to a clicking action by a pointing device — a so-called picking operation — requires explicit programming in the panel object class (or higher class). And if there is more than one object in the same position, the question as to which object a click operation should be processed in must be decided by message exchange on the object's responsibility.

Actual implementations generally handle this by creating an object in charge of controlling the screen as a whole, in batch processing. This is really a matter of introducing a kind of shared memory object. Functions that should normally have been given to more basic primitives, considering the needs of applications, are instead performed in an object that is on the same level as a user-defined object. This is an unnatural approach, as a result of which it becomes impossible to take advantage of the OOP paradigm merits. Instead, window system functions require procedural programming inside a giant object.

The field-oriented paradigm, by contrast, can be specialized in such a way that the structure of the two-dimensional area on the display screen is reflected directly in the program structuring. Thus, a panel displayed on the screen can be instructed so that the panel itself is a specific "reacting field." Making use of this capability, it is a simple matter to implement a window system. This approach also has the benefit of efficiency in that more basic processing can be directly implemented from the start as primitives.

The same is true for all applications in which the computer environment is presented as a "reacting field," including spreadsheet programs, CAD software, and even artificial intelligence applications such as neural networks and blackboard models. Applications such as databases, which indicate some sort of relational information like position in space or mutual distance, are possible. Moreover, the HFDS aimed at in TRON is itself a "reacting field" with a physical backing.

5. FIELD SPECIALIZATION

Next, the mechanism for specialization of fields will be discussed, to the extent that studies have proceeded to date.

The specialization mechanism involves setting three elements, namely, the shared data space semantics, the addressing mechanism, and structural restrictions. The settings of these three elements are made public to other systems, and can be found out by making inquiry. These tell the other systems how access is to be made, without their needing to know the internal specifications.(*Fig. 9*)

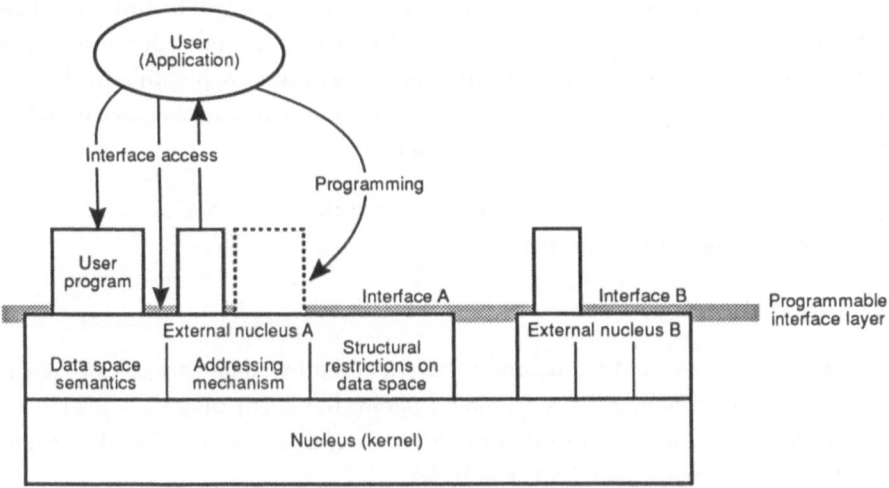

Fig. 9   Field specialization mechanism and use of programmable interface

5.1 Semantics of Data Space

A data space in a field-oriented paradigm is itself a "reacting field," in the sense that programs are executed by triggering of processing when access is made to that data space. In this paradigm there is no distinction, as seen from the user end, between reactions based on the language specifications when used as intended and general programmed reactions. This is a quality shared with Smalltalk and other programming languages and environments. It means that the language specifications themselves can be expanded as programs predefined using the programming mechanism of the language itself. This quality is useful for realizing dynamic programmable interfaces.

A specialization capability for adding functions to the language specifications is thus provided in the form of a data space with predefined functions. This provision of data space semantics is described in TULS in terms of dictionaries and predefined system macros.[4] A dictionary consists of a macro entry part and macro body. Data spaces are expressed as sets of dictionaries arranged in a tree configuration.

Macros, which are symbols, are stored in the macro entry part, while data are stored in the macro body. This enables data in the body to be represented by the macro. The macro body contains not only character strings and numerical values but also multimedia data such as graphics, and can even contain a lambda equation for the macro. By grouping dictionaries which are sets of these kinds of items, a program can be expressed in accord with TULS. It can also become TAD data, if considered as a means of confirming data of some kind.

Program execution takes place in the form of macro evaluation by expansion. This expansion consists of rewriting a macro in the macro body. If the macro body contains a lambda expression, evaluation/expansion proceeds in accord with the rewriting rules in that expression. Here a macro whose macro body contains a binary program will be called a predefined macro. When this is evaluated, the binary program is executed. A macro definition by means of data either finds its way to an embedded program or continues expanding in the dictionary until the macro search fails, in which case it continues the search in the parent dictionary, tracing its way along the tree structure toward the root.

In this way a data space, which is a set of dictionaries, can function as an evaluation environment for both data and programs.

5.2 Addressing Mechanism

The start of this evaluative expansion is triggered by some sort of external event. If, for example, the environment is a window system, the event may be a user input event or a display request from an application program. In file servers and the like, it may be the arrival of a data access request via the network.

This external event is evaluated as a macro, but other than in cases where the data space is configured as a single dictionary only, first of all the initial dictionary must be decided as the starting point of evaluation, from among the tree of dictionaries in the data space. The mechanism for this purpose is the addressing mechanism in the shared data space. There are many possibilities for this mechanism, so it is possible to specialize it for different applications. It is also possible to support a distributed shared data space through this mechanism. And if the shared data space has more than one port, different addressing mechanisms can be used for each. Service requests between different shared data spaces can be sent as external events specifying ports. The function for sending events to specified ports is provided in the operating system nucleus, or kernel, and is realized at a level close to the physical level.(*Fig. 10*)

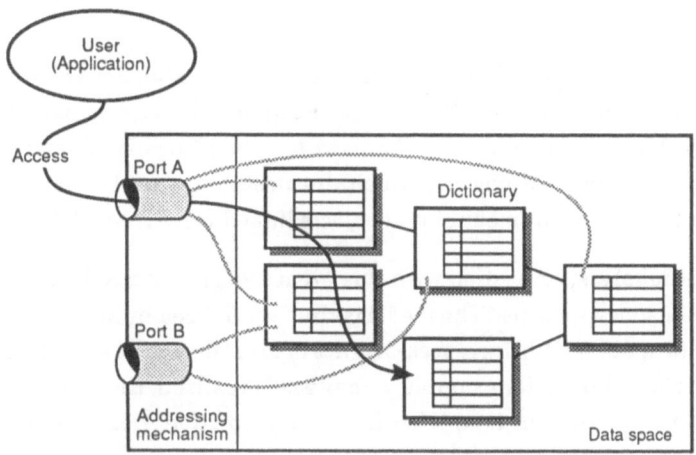

Fig. 10   Relation of addressing mechanism and data spaces

As a specific addressing mechanism, a framework is provided in which a mechanism can be realized corresponding to the data segment supported in TAD. Among the possibilities are addresses that are pointers corresponding to fusen, addresses that are names corresponding to character strings, addresses that are random areas on a plane, corresponding to unit drawings, and addresses that are unit sounds.

An address consisting of an expanse, such as a random area, can be accessed by means of points or areas within it. Overlapping of areas is possible, but all defined addresses are assigned a unique order of priority, and on this basis the address is determined. Cases where the same name is registered more than once are handled similarly. When access is made, an upper limit on the degree of priority can be assigned so that access is made only to dictionaries below a specific priority; in this way starvation can be prevented. A function is provided also for fetching dictionaries in the order of priority. The priority is determined by the order in which dictionaries are registered, but there is also a primitive for shifting the priorities of specific addresses. These priority management functions are realized making use of the real-time processing functions in the operating system nucleus.

When an event occurs during macro evaluation, it is possible to have this re-evaluated by the addressing mechanism, in which case addressing is possible not only by means of the above addresses but also by designating relative position from the dictionary from which the event occurred in the tree structure. As an example, in a pointing event by means of a pointing device in the graphical user interface (GUI), the position of the pointing is taken as the address, and the event is seen as access to the window's shared data space. In this way a program defined in that plane area (address) is executed. Thus a basic event loop in GUI realization is implemented as an addressing mechanism.

5.3 Structural Restrictions on Data Space

The shared data space configuration, or tree-structured set of dictionaries explained above as the semantics of data spaces, is the largest specification of data space structure. Another way of putting it is that this structure can be used to expand nearly all structured data in its original form, including real objects, which are nestable, variable-length record streams. (Network data consist of a number of real objects linked via virtual objects.)

In most applications, a specification with this great a degree of freedom is in many cases not necessary for efficiency reasons. The model is thus specialized by applying structural restrictions on the data spaces. This increases the rate of error detection as well as making possible improved efficiency. When, for example, a mailbox is realized, the dictionaries form a queue structure, and the restriction is applied that parent dictionaries may have only one child dictionary.

6. CONCLUSION

A communication model and programming model/paradigm, proposed as design guidelines for realize a programmable interface in TRON, have been described above. When considering a programmable interface in a loosely coupled distributed environment, this model and paradigm express the same qualities from different standpoints, and thus can all be discussed in terms of the concept of "fields," which are advanced shared memory spaces.

The working out of a specific programming model, TULS, is now proceeding in our laboratory based on these design guidelines. A window system for BTRON is also being devised as a realistic specialization example of this model. These developments will be reported in subsequent papers after they have been completed.

As a final word of caution, it should be noted that the programming languages and environments discussed here are interpreter languages, which are executed using the system external nucleus as interpreter. For this reason it is guaranteed at the system level that programs based on these can be evaluated independently of the application program. This is an important point, since even though computer architecture is adhered to closely for the sake of execution efficiency, if a complex addressing mechanism is adopted this will not amount to a program written in native code.

The fact is that actual programs of various kinds, including operating systems and application programs, are largely provided as predefined macros. The actual use of programming languages and environments based on the field paradigm, with the exception of TACL and other end-user programming, will be for programmable interfaces with other systems.

In the future, compilers could be provided at the system level for compiling dictionaries consisting of macro bodies only of macros that predefine specialized shared data spaces. This will make it possible to use these programming languages and environments not only for interfaces and small-scale user programs but for application program development as well.

As one more approach, the addressing mechanism can undergo thoroughgoing simplification, the structural restrictions on data spaces can be made more rigid, and instruction pointer values can be applied cyclically as macro calls. Studies are now proceeding in order to determine whether in this way it will be possible to provide a programmable interface for the system as a whole, and a highly consistent macro assembler.

Among the topics to be researched in the future, it will be necessary to consider network security in order to block up any security holes that may arise from the capability of sending programs as data. Here a mechanism is assumed for performing the necessary control of accessibility to ports. In this connection, when multiple macro evaluation takes place at the same time, one possibility is to impose access restrictions per each dictionary for the sake of exclusion/synchronization. The mechanism for this restriction is now under study.

In addition, an expansion of the TAD specification is being made, taking into account coming advances in user interfaces, including cooperative control of human living environments aimed for in HFDS, and artificial reality. Here too, the concept of "fields" is likely to be incorporated, allowing generalized TAD data such as random areas in space, and physical environmental variables such as temperature, to be used as addresses.

In all of these research efforts the main goal will be to make it possible to expand libraries and adjust interfaces readily, independently of application programs. If this concept is realized, it will bring about an unprecedented degree of freedom, merging functions in application programs developed independently of each other, and achieving the heretofore almost inconceivable goal of combining system unity with extensibility.

REFERENCE

[1] Ken Sakamura, *"The Objectives of the TRON Project,"* TRON Project 1987 (Proc. of the Third TRON Project Symposium), Springer Verlag, pp. 3-16 (1987).

[2] Ken Sakamura, *"Multi-language character Sets Handling in TAD,"* TRON Project 1987 (Proc. of the Third TRON Project Symposium), Springer Verlag, pp. 97-111 (1987).

[3] Ken Sakamura, *"TULS: TRON Universal Language System,"* TRON Project 1988 (Proc. of the Fifth TRON Project Symposium), Springer Verlag, pp. 3-18 (1988).

[4] Ken Sakamura, *"TACL: TRON Application Control-flow Language,"* TRON Project 1988 (Proc. of the Fifth TRON Project Symposium), Springer Verlag, pp. 79-92 (1988).

[5] Michael Stumm and Songnian Zhou, *"Algorithms Implementing Distributed Shared Memory,"* IEEE COMPUTER, Vol.23, No.5, pp. 54-63 (May 1990).

Ken Sakamura is currently an associate professor at the Department of Information Science, University of Tokyo. His main interests lies in computer architecture, the basic design of computer systems. Since 1984, he has been the leader of the TRON project and has made efforts to build new computer systems based on the TRON architecture.

His interest in the TRON computer systems now extends beyond ordinary computers. He is now interested how the society will change by the use of computers in 1990's and beyond and now his design activities include those for electronic appliances, furniture, houses, buildings, and urban planning.

He is a member of the Japan Information Processing Society; the Institute of Electronics, Information and Communication Engineers; ACM; and a senior member of IEEE. He servers on the editorial board of IEEE MICRO magazine. His papers won awards from IEEE, IEICE, and JIPS.

Dr. Sakamura may be contacted at the Department of Information Science, Faculty of Science, University of Tokyo, 7-3-1 Hongo, Bunkyo-ku, Tokyo, Japan.

Chapter 1: ITRON

Considerations of the Performance of a Real-Time OS

Akira Yokozawa, Katsuhito Fukuoka, Kiichiro Tamaru
Toshiba Corporation

ABSTRACT

In discussing performance of a real-time OS, we usually talk about the interrupt latency and the task switching time. But if you want to calculate the real-time performance of an application that uses the real-time OS as a kernel, these two parameters are not enough. Furthermore, the definition of the "task switching time" varies among available materials on real-time OS products, so that it is sometimes meaningless just to compare the values found in them.

In the former half of this paper, we summarize several parameters of real-time OS performance. Then we discuss the relation of these parameters to the performance of real applications and see the importance of other parameters.

In the latter half of this paper, regarding the parameters above, we discuss some topics specific to the ITRON2 specification. Since ITRON2 specification is fairly large for a kernel, there are a few points OS implementors should consider when they want to make their products have good real-time performances.

Keywords: real-time OS, performance, ITRON2 specification, TRON specification processor, TX1

1. INTRODUCTION

A quick response to external events is the most important characteristic of real-time processing. In many cases there are several sources of external events, and the events happens asynchronously with each other. A real-time OS provides a quick response to interrupts and multitasking synchronization facilities as a programming environment for programmers of such applications.

In this paper, we introduce five parameters listed below as parameters of real-time OS performance.

1) Interrupt penalty

2) Interrupt latency

3) Task switching penalty

4) Task switching latency

5) System call cost

Then we see how the parameters above affect the response performance of actual real-time applications listed below.

1) Handler response to an interrupt

2) Task response to an interrupt

3) Task response to a task

The definitions of items listed above appears in the next two sections. The discussion here can be appled to any real-time OS as long as it is for a single processor system and it uses interrupts of several priority level and its task scheduling is priority based.

Then, the latter half of this paper discusses a few topics regarding the performance of an OS which conforms to the ITRON2 specification. The basis of the discussion is our experience in implementing an OS kernel which supports the full set of the ITRON2 specification version 2.02.00.00. This kernel was implemented on the TX1 microprocessor, which is one of the TRON specification processors. It has 103 system calls and code size of 20KB.

2. PERFORMANCE PARAMETERS OF A REAL-TIME OS

In this section, we define five parameters of a real-time OS performance. Here, we use the words "penalty", "latency" and "cost" in the following manner. A "penalty" is a time elapsed by the OS or the hardware in processing an event. A "latency" is a time elapsed by the OS before processing an event. The processor is doing some other activity during the time. A "cost" is a time elapsed by the OS in processing a function requested by a programmer.

2.1 INTERRUPT PENALTY

The *interrupt penalty* is the time a processor needs to detect an interrupt and to invoke the handler corresponding to the interrupt. In cases where the interrupt is accepted first by the OS and the OS invokes a handler connected to the interrupt, the interrupt penalty includes the software penalty of the invocation. This penalty depends on both the hardware and the software of the system. Figure 1 shows the definition. Please refer to Figure 2 for the meaning of the bar patterns used in the figures from now on.

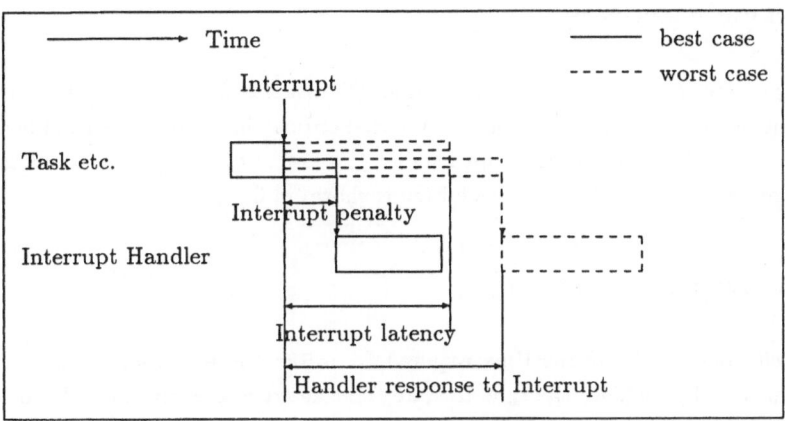

Fig. 1: *Interrupt penalty and latency*

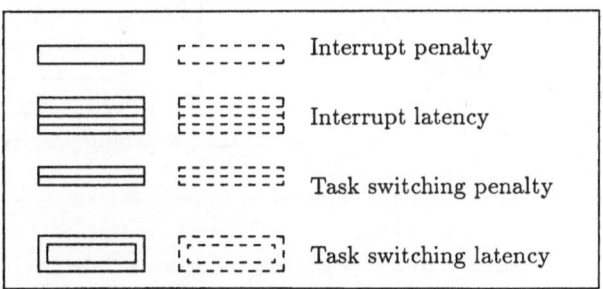

Fig. 2: *Meaning of bar patterns*

2.2   INTERRUPT LATENCY

The *interrupt latency* is the time during which an OS disables the services to the external interrupts. This is necessary for an OS to protect internal critical data structures from being modified by a system call called from an interrupt handler. To lower this latency has been an important goal in designing real-time OS's. The definition is shown in figure 1.

2.3   TASK SWITCHING PENALTY

The *task switching penalty* is the time required to switch the execution right from a task to another. This usually includes the time to store the context of the current task, to select a task to be executed next, to restore the context of the next task, and to start its execution. In other words, the task switching penalty is the difference of the time spent in the system between the cases when a system call causes task switching and when it doesn't. The definition is shown in figure 3.

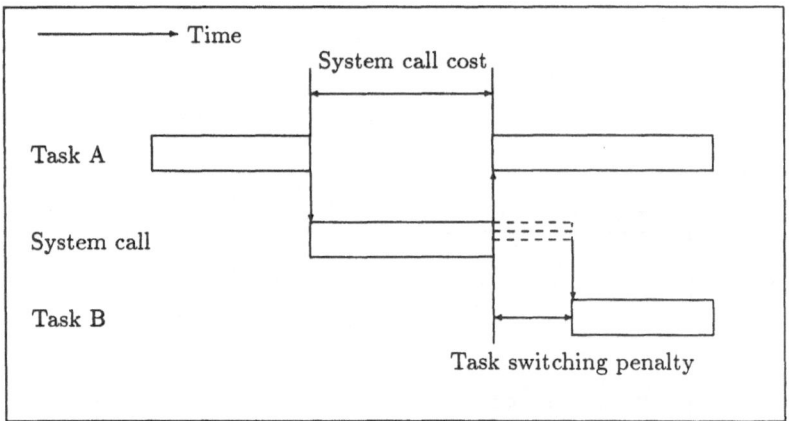

Fig. 3: Task switching penalty and System call cost

There is a similar term, "task switching time." It has been used in two ways. One is as the same as the definition of the "task switching penalty" mentioned above. The other includes the execution time of system call that causes the task switch besides the "task switching penalty" time. When you think of the time required to transfer control from a task to another, the value of the second meaning is straightforward. But, since it is not primitive, we will use the "task switching penalty" as a parameter of performance in this paper. We will discuss the second meaning of the "task switching time" as the "task response to a task" in the later section where we discuss the response performance of applications.

2.4 TASK SWITCHING LATENCY

The *task switching latency* is the time during which an OS can *not* dispatch a new task even if an interrupt occurs and a higher priority task is readied by a system call called from the interrupt handler. A real-time OS should schedule tasks in a pre-emptive way, and should not have such a latency. But depending on the design of the OS, there may be such a latency.

Note that the interrupt latency is included in the task switching latency. Unless an interrupt is detected, the request of task switching can't happen. Thus the task switching is regarded as disabled while interrupts are disabled. The definition is given in figure 4.

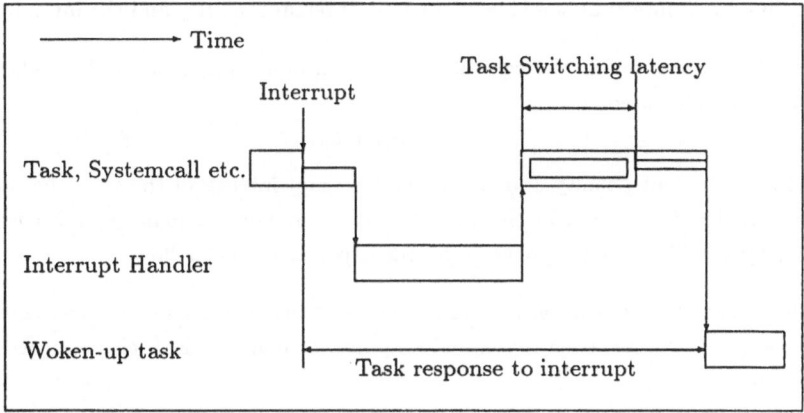

Fig. 4: Task switching latency

2.5 SYSTEM CALL COST

The *system call cost* is the time spent by the OS to execute a system call. This is also called the "system call execution time." The definition is shown in Figure 3. In our definition, the system call cost does not contain the task switching penalty.

In some implementations, for the purpose of reducing the interrupt latency, the execution of part of a system call called from an interrupt handler is delayed until the interrupt handler ends. In this case, there are two kinds of system call cost. One includes the time of the delayed execution and the other doesn't. The former one should be used in calculating the task response to an interrupt. On the other hand, the latter should be used for the handler response. We will discuss this issue in the later section.

3. RESPONSE PERFORMANCE OF APPLICATIONS

In designing application systems using a real-time OS, one need estimate how quickly each external event can be responded. There are two kinds of program to respond to an external event. One is an interrupt handler and the other is a task. If you want to transfer control among tasks, the response of a task to another need be concerned.

3.1 HANDLER RESPONSE TO AN INTERRUPT

An interrupt handler is a program invoked by an external interrupt to the processor. Therefore, its response time to an interrupt is a sum of the OS's interrupt latency and the interrupt penalty.

The relationship is displayed in the equations below. Handler response to the highest priority interrupt $R_{\mathrm{hdr;int}}$ is calculated as

$$R_{\mathrm{hdr;int}} = T_{\mathrm{int}} + L_{\mathrm{int}}, \tag{1}$$

where T_{int} is the interrupt penalty and L_{int} is the interrupt latency of the OS. The name of the term in the right hand is chosen in the way that T_{xxx} represents a penalty or a cost and L_{xxx} represents a latency. This rule is applied to all the expressions that follow.

In real applications, there are usually several sources of interrupt; and each source is assigned a priority concerning the response required. Response of handlers in such applications can be calculated as follows.

We assume two conditions in the discussion below. One is that the interrupts occur randomly with each other. And the other is that the execution time of each interrupt handler is much shorter than the interval of the corresponding interrupt. The latter should rather be considered as a requirement when you build a system having good real-time performance.

Figure 5 shows the worst response of second priority handler. As you see, the response to a low priority interrupt depends on the execution time of handlers of higher priority interrupts. The worst case is when higher priority interrupts occur just after the low priority interrupt occurs. If you require fairly quick responses to the low priority interrupt, you have to make handler(s) of higher priority interrupt as short as possible.

Thus the response to the nth interrupt $R_{\mathrm{hdr;int}}(n)$ is expressed as below.

$$R_{\mathrm{hdr;int}}(n) = L_{\mathrm{int}} + \sum_{P_i \geq P_n} \left(T_{\mathrm{int}} + T_{\mathrm{hdr}}(i) \right) + T_{\mathrm{int}}, \tag{2}$$

where P_i is the priority of the i th interrupt and $T_{\mathrm{hdr}}(i)$ is the execution time of the handler of the i th interrupt. T_{int} and L_{int} are the same as those in the above expression.

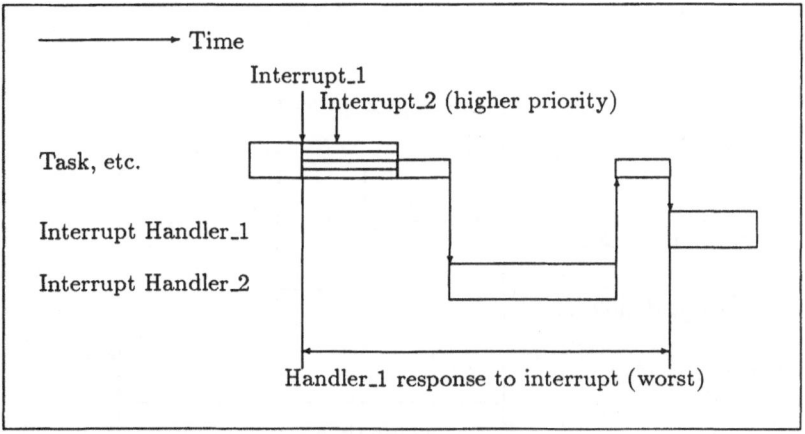

Fig. 5: Worst case handler response of 2nd priority

3.2 TASK RESPONSE TO AN INTERRUPT

If you wake up a task in response to an interrupt, you need an interrupt handler to receive the interrupt and to wake up the task. The response time in this case can not be calculated from the interrupt latency. You need the execution time of all the interrupt handlers, the task switching latency and the task switching penalty.

Interrupt handlers have higher execution priorities than any task, so that the task woken up by an interrupt can be blocked if other interrupts happen.

Furthermore, if the interrupt occurs while dispatching is disabled, the woken-up task won't start execution until dispatching is enabled. And the task switching penalty time is required to start execution of the woken up task.

We assume the same conditions as in the previous section. We also assume that the woken-up task has the highest execution priority. If they are accepted, the worst case is when all the interrupts occur in a very short time. Figure 6 shows such a case in a system with two interrupts. The task response to an interrupt $R_{\text{tsk;int}}$ is calculated with the equation

$$R_{\text{tsk;int}} = \sum_i \left(T_{\text{int}} + T_{\text{hdr}}(i)\right) + L_{\text{swt}} + T_{\text{swt}}, \tag{3}$$

where L_{swt} is the task switching latency and T_{swt} is the task switching penalty defined in the previous section. Please note that the interrupt latency does not appear here. As stated earlier, the interrupt latency is included in the task switching latency. When you talk about the task response to an interrupt, it does not matter how quickly the interrupt is accepted. If dispatching is disabled for some time after the interrupt handler exited, the woken up task can't start execution for the period. This is the reason the interrupt latency is included in the task switching latency.

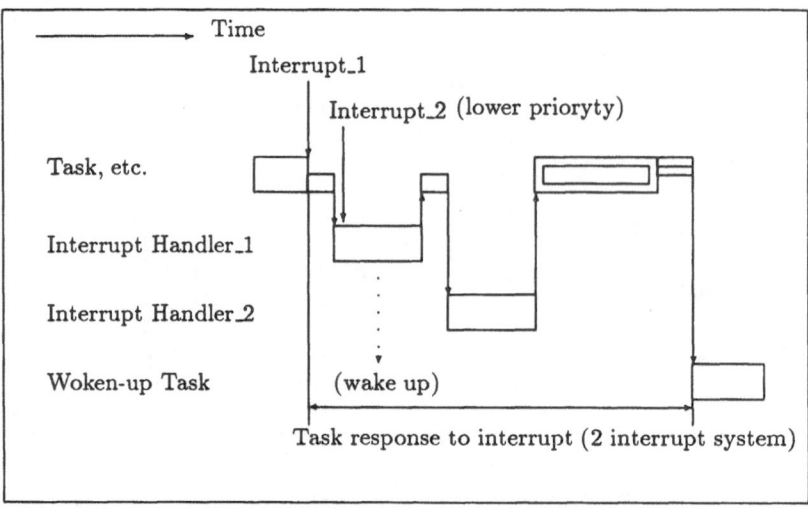

Fig. 6: Worst case task response in a system with two interrupts

3.3   TASK RESPONSE TO A TASK

The task response to a task is the time during which a task calls a system call and wakes up another higher priority task and the woken up task actually starts execution. As stated earlier, some material of real-time OS products use the "task switching time" in this meaning.

This response $R_{\text{tsk;tsk}}$ can be simply calculated in the following way,

$$R_{\text{tsk;tsk}} = T_{\text{sys}} + T_{\text{swt}} \tag{4}$$

where T_{sys} is the execution time of the waking-up system call. But in real applications, there is a possibility that an interrupt happens during this action. If you must consider the influence of external interrupt, the response time is given by

$$R_{\text{tsk;tsk}} = T_{\text{sys}} + T_{\text{swt}} + \sum_i \left(T_{\text{int}} + T_{\text{hdr}}(i) \right). \tag{5}$$

The symbols used here are the same as above and our assumptions here are the same as those described in the previous section. If the woken up task is not of the highest priority, you have to add the execution time of higher priority tasks that can be woken up by external events.

4.   RELATION OF OS PARAMETERS TO APPLICATION RESPONSES

The relationship between the parameters and the responses discussed in the previous two sections are summarized in the table below. A circle mark indicates that an OS parameter has a contribution to the response of an application. Please note that the system call cost has indirect contributions to responses via the execution time of interrupt handlers.

Table. 1: Relation of Parameters to Responses

parameter response	Interrupt penalty	Interrupt latency	Task Switching penalty	Task Switching latency	System Call cost
Handler to Interrupt (highest priority)	O	O			
Handler to Interrupt (low priority)	O	O			O
Task to Interrupt	O		O	O	O
Task to Task			O		O

From table 1, we can tell the following.

- The handler response to the highest priority interrupt can be told from only the interrupt latency. So for systems having only one urgent interrupt source, an OS with low interrupt latency is suitable.

- If you need a fairly good response to plurality of interrupts, a low system call cost is also desired. This is because the system call cost would occupy most of the execution time of higher priority interrupt handlers.

- If you need a quick task response to an interrupt, the task switching latency becomes significant. The system call and task switching penalties are also important because you have to consider execution time of all the interrupt handlers. OS's with long task switching latency are not suitable for such heavy applications.

5. COMPARISON OF TYPICAL EXAMPLES

In this section, to help understanding of the relations of parameters and responses, we will calculate some response time using some typical parameter examples. Here we emphasize the effect of three parameters, L_{int}, L_{tsk}, and T_{sys}. In order to simplify the discussion, we assume that the other parameters T_{int} and T_{swt} are 0 and that the execution time of interrupt handlers are same as T_{sys}. We know these assumptions are unrealistic, but they make the discussion clearer.

Table 2 gives the parameters of typical examples of real-time OS. The values are in arbitrary unit and they are chosen to characterize the effect of each parameter.

Example A features the shortness of both the interrupt latency and the task switching latency. Example B has a higher system call cost than Example A. Example C has a higher task switching latency than Example A. Example D has both a higher interrupt latency and a higher task switching latency than Example A.

Table. 2: Parameters of Examples

Example	Interrupt latency L_{int}	Task Switching latency L_{swt}	System Call cost T_{sys}
A	1	1	5
B	1	1	7
C	1	5	5
D	5	5	5

Now, we calculate the responses discussed in section 3.

First, the handler responses to interrupts are calculated as in figure 7. Here we show the responses of several priority interrupt handler.

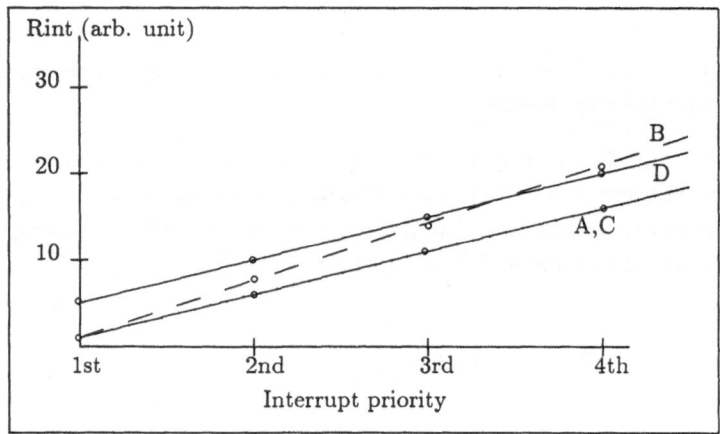

Fig. 7: Responses of Handlers

Second, the task responses to interrupts are calculated as in figure 8. We calculate the responses of the systems having several different number of interrupts.

We rephrase the result of section 4 again.

- The lower the interrupt latency is, the quicker is the handler response to the highest priority interrupt (Examples A, B and C).

- When you use multiple interrupt, the handler responses to the lower priority interrupts are strongly affected by the system call cost (Example B).

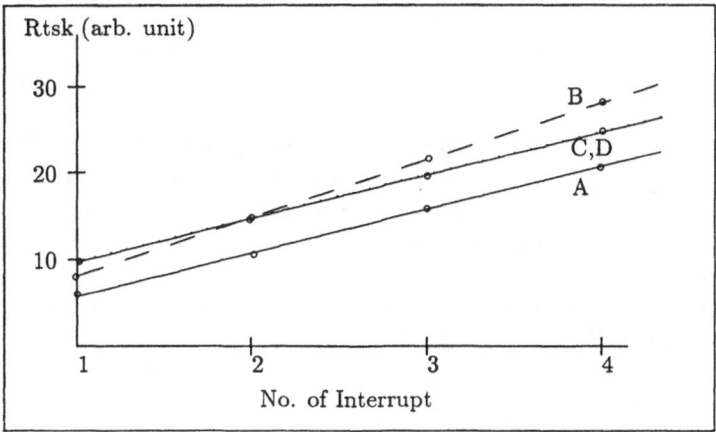

Fig. 8: Responses of a Task

- If you consider the task response to an interrupt seriously, both the system call cost and the task switching latency must be low. The interrupt latency does not matter as long as the task switching latency (including the interrupt latency) is same (Examples C and D).

If an OS implementer concentrates too much on lowering the interrupt latency or the task switching latency and adds some overhead in the system call cost, the resulting OS may show a degraded performance in an actual application.

6. SUGGESTIONS ABOUT THE IMPLEMENTATION OF THE ITRON2 SPECIFICATION

In our implementation of an OS kernel conforming to the ITRON2 specification, we could not guarantee a finite task switching latency and the exception handling mechanism in the kernel caused a overhead in the system call cost.

In this section, we will give a few solutions to these problems. Some of them are specific to the TRON specification processor.

We are sorry to note that this section assumes a good understanding of both the ITRON2 specification and the TRON specification processer. Those who would like to fully understand the discussion are recommended to refer to the references available from the TRON association[1][2].

6.1 VARIABLE SYSTEM CALL COST

The ITRON2 specification has several system calls with variable execution time. For example, set_flg to an event flag with the TA_WMUL attribute and sig_sem to a semaphore with the TA_VAR attribute are some of those system calls. In these system calls, there is no limit to the number of tasks released from the wait state in a single call. The execution time of these system calls are dependent on the number of tasks released. There is no way to guarantee a fixed cost for such system calls.

Although it depends on the implementation whether these system calls are callable from interrupt handlers, if you use these system calls in an interrupt handler, the execution time of the handler becomes also variable. So venders should reveal the behavior of such system calls especially when they are callable from interrupt handlers.

In our implementation, the variableness of the system call cost introduced a difficulty to achieve a finite task switching latency.

6.2   TASK SWITCHING LATENCY

It has been said that in implementing an OS which conforms to the ITRON2 specification on a TRON specification processor, the use of the delayed interrupt mechanism (DI) greatly eases the implementation of the delayed dispatching principle of ITRON. But a simple use of DI caused the task switching latency to be the same as the longest system call cost. As mentioned above, there are several system calls with variable execution time, we could not guarantee a finite value for the task switching latency.

We will show the reason briefly. First, we explain some basic term used here.

The delayed dispatching principle states that even if a new task is readied within an interrupt handler, the dispatching to the new task is delayed until the interrupt handler exits. When multiple interrupts are nested, the dispatching occurs after the top level interrupt handler exits.

The delayed interrupt mechanism of the TRON specification works in the following way. There is a register called DIR (Delayed Interrupt Request) in the processor. When interrupt mask level becomes larger than the value stored in the DIR, a DI exception corresponding to the DIR level occurs with clearing the DIR to its maximum value 15. (Note that in the TRON specification processor, a higher interrupt priority level has a lower value in the numerical expression.)

We implemented the principle in the following way.

Tasks are executed at the interrupt mask level 15 (nothing masked), the mask level during execution of an interrupt handler is less than 7, and the mask level during execution of a system call is less than or equal to 14. If you use the DI level 14 to invoke an dispatcher, the dispatcher is automatically invoked at the end of a system call called from a task or at the end of an interrupt handler which has called a system call to change the top-priority task.

In this method, if an interrupt occurs during a system call, the dispatcher won't be invoked at the end of the interrupt handler. It will be invoked at the end of the system call. Thus the task switching latency becomes the same as the longest system call execution time.

When there is a system call with variable execution time, it is impossible to guarantee a finite task switching latency time. There are two ways around this problem. One is to make some restrictions on the use of system calls. If an application doesn't use the system calls with variable execution time, a finite task switching latency time can be guaranteed. But this is not a smart way. The other way is to permit dispatching during system call execution.

Even if you use the DI mechanism, you can permit dispatching during system call execution. If you use the DI level 13 instead of 14, the dispatcher can be invoked inside the system call.

Please note that besides permitting dispatching within a system call, the primitiveness of the system call required in the ITRON specification should also be kept. These two requirements seem to be inconsistent, but there are some ways to compromise. One of them is to permit execution of the woken-up task as long as it does not invoke a system call. If it invokes a system call, the rest of the interrupted system call is processed. This is enough for most cases because the urgent code appears in a task is to shoten an interrupt handler. Such code rarely require system call invocation.

6.3   Cost of Checking Exception

The ITRON2 specification is fairly rich in the functions of exception handling. They are useful when your application needs a special treatment of CPU exception, asynchronous communication between tasks, and so on. But any function requires some cost to implement. The exception check is included in the system call cost. As discussed in sections 4 and 5, the system call cost has a large contribution to the real-time performance of applications. So reducing the overhead in checking exceptions has a vital significance.

In our implementation, the cost in checking exceptions caused a bad response of task. When a system call wakes up a task, exception checks are done at the end of it and also at the start of the woken up task as a post checking of the system call that had been called just before the task lost execution right. These costs are paid even if no exception condition is being pended. Each of the check costs about 10 μs and it takes 20 μs longer to transfer a control to the woken up task than without exception checking. See figure 9.

What was wrong in the implementation? The problem was that although exceptions happen very rarely, the exception conditions were checked every time a system call exited. It would be acceptable that when you request an exception to occur, or an exception really occurs, there might be some costs required. But it should be avoided that when exceptions are out of concerns, there still is some cost.

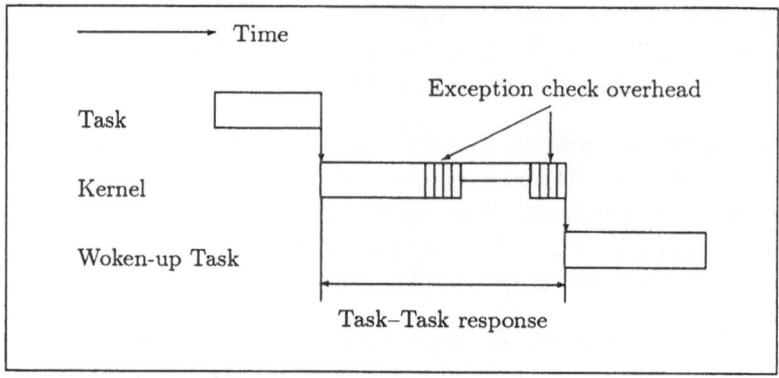

Fig. 9: Exception check overhead in waking up a task

With utilizing the delayed context trap function (DCT) and the delayed interrupt function (DI) of the TRON specification processor, it is possible to make the processor to detect the exception conditions and to reduce the system call cost required to the check. DI is described in the previous section. DCT is described later in this section. In our implementation, a task runs at the protection ring level 3 or 1 and an extended SVC and a system call run at the ring level 0. An interrupt handler also runs at the ring level 0 but uses different stack. On the other hand, there are four types of exceptions in the ITRON2 specification. They are a termination request, a system call exception, a CPU exception and a forced exception.

Among these, the CPU exception is detected by the processor, and no code is needed to detect it. In tables 3, 4 and 5 we summarize the detection conditions of the other exceptions and the changes of internal state of the processor. In these tables, SMRNG and IMASK are the bit fields in the PSW register of the TRON specification processor. SMRNG shows the ring level of the processor and IMASK shows the interrupt mask level. SMRNG is shown in a binary expression and IMASK is shown in a decimal expression.

From these tables, we can see first that exceptions that can happen in a task can be detected at the change of SMRNG to larger or equal to 101. This change can be trapped by the DCT function. DCT (Delayed Context Trap) is very much like the DI function, but it uses the protection ring level instead of the interrupt mask level. It uses a bit field in the CSW (Context Status Word) register called DCT and if the SMRNG field becomes larger than the DCT field, a trap occurs with clearing the DCT field to its maximum value 111 (in binary). So if you set the DCT field to 100 in requesting an exception, it is automaticly detected by the hardware. Note that the DCT field is included in the task context.

Secondly, exceptions that can happen in a non-nested extended SVC can not always be detected by the value of SMRNG, but can be detected by the change of IMASK to 15. This can be trapped by the DI function.

Table. 3: System Call Exception Detection Timing and Processor Status Changes

system call	$\Longrightarrow$ extended SVC	100	$\Longrightarrow$	100	(SMRNG)
		< 15	$\Longrightarrow$	15	(IMASK)
system call	$\Longrightarrow$ task	100	$\Longrightarrow$	101 or 111	(SMRNG)
		< 15	$\Longrightarrow$	15	(IMASK)
system call	$\Longrightarrow$ interrupt handler	000	$\Longrightarrow$	000	(SMRNG)
		< 7	$\Longrightarrow$	< 7	(IMASK)
extended SVC	$\Longrightarrow$ extended SVC	100	$\Longrightarrow$	100	(SMRNG)
		15	$\Longrightarrow$	15	(IMASK)
extended SVC	$\Longrightarrow$ task	100	$\Longrightarrow$	101 or 111	(SMRNG)
		15	$\Longrightarrow$	15	(IMASK)
extended SVC	$\Longrightarrow$ interrupt handler	000	$\Longrightarrow$	000	(SMRNG)
		< 7	$\Longrightarrow$	< 7	(IMASK)

Table. 4: Termination Request Detection Timing and Processor Status Changes

interrupt handler	$\Longrightarrow$ extended SVC	000	$\Longrightarrow$	100	(SMRNG)
		< 7	$\Longrightarrow$	15	(IMASK)
system call	$\Longrightarrow$ extended SVC	100	$\Longrightarrow$	101 or 111	(SMRNG)
		< 15	$\Longrightarrow$	15	(IMASK)
extended SVC	$\Longrightarrow$ extended SVC	100	$\Longrightarrow$	101 or 111	(SMRNG)
		15	$\Longrightarrow$	15	(IMASK)
interrupt handler	$\Longrightarrow$ task	000	$\Longrightarrow$	101 or 111	(SMRNG)
		< 7	$\Longrightarrow$	15	(IMASK)
system call	$\Longrightarrow$ task	100	$\Longrightarrow$	101 or 111	(SMRNG)
		< 15	$\Longrightarrow$	15	(IMASK)
extended SVC	$\Longrightarrow$ task	100	$\Longrightarrow$	101 or 111	(SMRNG)
		15	$\Longrightarrow$	15	(IMASK)

Table. 5: Forced Exception Detection Timing and Processor Status Changes

interrupt handler	$\Longrightarrow$ task	000	$\Longrightarrow$	101 or 111	(SMRNG)
		< 7	$\Longrightarrow$	15	(IMASK)
system call	$\Longrightarrow$ task	100	$\Longrightarrow$	101 or 111	(SMRNG)
		< 15	$\Longrightarrow$	15	(IMASK)
extended SVC	$\Longrightarrow$ task	100	$\Longrightarrow$	101 or 111	(SMRNG)
		15	$\Longrightarrow$	15	(IMASK)

Thirdly, exceptions that happen at the return from an nested extended SVC does not accompany any status change in the processor. But a special system call ret_svc is used in these circumstances. Our aim is to reduce the cost in the normal system call execution, so it is acceptable to add some code in the ret_svc system call to detect these conditions.

Fourthly, a system call exception within an interrupt handler doesn't accompany any state change within the processor, either, and that some code is necessary to detect it. Whether to implement this feature or not is an implementation-dependent specification, so if you want to reduce the cost of this feature, you can omit it.

Fifthly, (this is not included in the tables) if an extended SVC is called from a task while the task is masking interrupt, the IMASK in the extended SVC is less than 15. Therefore, the above discussion can't be applied to this case. But it should be avoided to call such a heavy function as an extended SVC while interrupt is masked. So our suggestion here is to neglect this case and to describe the behavior as a limitation of the implementation.

Finally, (this in not included in the tables either) exceptions can happen when a exception handler exits. A special system call ret_exc is used at the end of exception handlers and some cost in it is acceptable.

Exceptions are context-dependent and the DCT function is also context-dependent. But the DI function is not context-dependent and is already used to invoke a dispatcher. So the utilization of the DI function needs some more considerations to avoid conflictions between different usages. These considerations accompanies some overhead, but we think the cost-reduction of normal system call execution is more significant.

Employing this method makes it possible to remove the cost in checking the exception conditions from normal system calls. Thus you can improve the parameter of system call cost and the task responses.

7. CONCLUSIONS

We have discussed the relation of the five kinds of parameters to the three kinds of application response performance. Then with considering the performance, we have seen some aspects specific to the ITRON2 specification and the TRON specification processor.

In the applications that uses multiple external interrupts, in order to maintain fairly good responses of handlers to lower priority interrupts, you should make the interrupt handlers as short as possible. If you make them short enough, some part of rather urgent code will appear in a task. In this case the responses of tasks to interrupts should be in an acceptable range. Then the shortness of the task switching latency time becomes significant. The system call cost should also be low because it is included in the execution time of the interrupt handlers.

This discussion shows that a performance of a real-time OS can not be measured only by the interrupt latency and the task switching penalty. The system call cost and the task switching latency should also be considered.

In the ITRON2 specification, there are some system calls with variable length execution time, so dispatching should be permitted within system call execution. Otherwise, the task switching latency can not be guaranteed to have a finite value. The primitiveness of the system call should be kept at the same time.

The utilization of the DI and the DCT functions of the TRON specification processor can reduce costs required in checking the exception conditions. Thus, the cost of the normal system calls can be lowered.

We would like to emphasize the importance of the parameters such as the task switching latency and the system call cost. We would also like to recommend both users and implementors of real-time OS's to pay attention to them.

8. ACKNOWLEDGEMENT

The authors would like to thank Dr. Ken Sakamura of University of Tokyo for his many helpful suggestions and the members of the TRON Association for their cooperation in standardizing the ITRON2 specification.

REFERENCES

[1] K. Sakamura, "ITRON Specification: ITRON2 Ver.2.02.01.00," TRON Association, 1990 (in Japanese).

[2] K. Sakamura, "SPECIFICATION OF THE CHIP BASED ON THE TRON ARCHITEC-TURE, Ver.1.00.00.00," TRON Association, 1990.

[3] J. Iwamura, et al. "Implementation and Evaluation of the TRONCHIP Specification for the TX1", TRON Project 1988, Springer-Verlag, pp. 285–300, 1988.

Akira Yokozawa is a researcher of real-time OS design in the department of Advanced Microprocessor Development at the Semiconductor Device Engineering Laboratory(SDEL) of Toshiba. He received his BS and MS degrees in physics from Tohoku University, Sendai, Japan, in 1984 and 1986. Since joining the department in 1986, he has been engaged in research and development of software development tools and real-time OS.

Katsuhito Fukuoka is a researcher of real-time OS design in the same laboratory. He received his BS and MS degrees in electronic engineering from University of Tokyo, Tokyo, Japan, in 1985 and 1987. Since joining the department in 1987, he has been engaged in research and development of real-time OS.

Kiichiro Tamaru is a specialist at the same laboratory. He received the BS, MS, and PhD degrees in electrical engineering from Keio University, Tokyo, Japan in 1976, 1978, and 1981, respectively. After joining Toshiba Corporation in 1981, he has been engaged in research and development of the VLSI processor and the software systems for microprocessors.

Above authors may be reached at: Advanced Microprocessor Technology, Semiconductor Device Engineering Laboratory, 580-1, Horikawa-cho, Saiwai-ku, Kawasaki, 210 Japan.

Dynamic Stepwise Task Scheduling Algorithm for a Tightly-Coupled Multiprocessor ITRON

Nobuhiko Nishio, Hiroaki Takada, Ken Sakamura

Department of Information Science, Faculty of Science, University of Tokyo

ABSTRACT

Recent real-time systems increasing complexity need high computation power, high dynamic adaptability, and high reliability. We adopts the multiprocessor system for computation power with tight coupling for dynamic adaptability, and aims at the reliable scheduling of real-time tasks. This paper proposes a real-time kernel equipped with a *stepwise scheduler*, which improves dynamic adaptability.

Conventional studies for single-processor or loosely-coupled multiprocessor through static scheduling are not enough for tightly-coupled multiprocessor. Existing dynamic algorithms, however, only care for the computation order of algorithms and not their real-time properties. This paper proposes a stepwise scheduling algorithm, in which some algorithms are stepwisely applied according to their processing time. The behavior is investigated through simulation for various parameter settings. The simulation gives us guidelines for the limit of an algorithm's effectiveness.

We also present the way to include the stepwise scheduler into the ITRON kernel keeping the specification continuity from the single processor version.

Keywords: ITRON, real-time programming, scheduling algorithm, tightly-coupled multiprocessor

1. INTRODUCTION

Of late years, the importance of real-time processing is rapidly increasing in the various areas than ever applied. It ranges from embedded systems in home electronics, plant control, and robot arm control in the factory to neucleus reactor control in the power plant and navigation control of aero avionics. As for space shuttles, they could not even go straight up into the sky without their controlling systems. This reveals us an apparent trend of huge system application, and the hugeness of the application requires the system some new features. Although the improvement of the *predictability* on the system's behavior has ever been and will be the most essential feature of real-time systems, recent huge application in various areas has made the conventional simple or *ad-hoc* approaches intolerable, and requires much more advanced features. Among the important requirements are:

1) High processing power,

2) Dynamic adaptability, and

3) High reliability and safety.

The requirement 1, high processing power, is emerging from the increase of the processing load with the system's hugeness. In spite of the improvement of micro processors speed through the advanced hardware technology, the recent huge applications have required much more processing power. Studies on tightly/loosely-coupled multiprocessor system are flourishing through the idea that multiplication of processors is more promising than the speed-up of single processor itself. Furthermore, multiprocessor systems would be efficient for the requirement 3, high reliability, especially in fault tolerance, and the investigations on it are also popular. The requirement 2, dynamic adaptability, aims at the optimal controlling of the large-scale system in harmony with the ever changing environment without halting the system. Conventional small-scale systems have been designed in the static way, however, the environments we have to control nowadays could not be described statically. Furthermore, the large-scale applications could not be halted so easily. For example, halting the big power plant system may bring us the undesirable situation. The requirement 3, high reliability and safety, means the guarantee of the system's behavior which warrants the timing and resource constraints as the real-time system, and the fault tolerance in the case of accidents. The larger the system is, the more terrible situation a failure in the system brings us. Neucleus power plants controlling, for instance, embeds a social problem in itself. Although it is true that constructing the system which never breaks their constraints is the best way, it is also desirable the technology which limits the penalty to the minimum even in the case of system's failure.

Considering the history of real-time systems more precisely, real-time systems mean a single microprocessor controlling system equipped into home electronic products in the early stage. Basically, they have both sensors and actuators and they periodically loop the I/O controlling routine. Of late years, constructing the systems with harder timing constraints, a specific microprocessor is assigned for the device (or the task which drives it) that has much harder timing constraints and high-speed network is established among the loosely-coupled multiprocessors. Although some tightly-coupled multiprocessor systems appear equipped with shared memory, which enables tasks to communicate fast and easily, all the tasks are statically fixed to run on their specific processors without any dynamic load-balancing facility. Our target systems such as large-scale applications has more timing critical devices and loosely-coupled multiprocessor burdens the central processor site with the central controlling load, and that site tends to become a tightly-coupled multiprocessor, namely processor-pool. As a result, they evolve to a hybrid system that consists of tightly/loosely-coupled multiprocessor systems. In such a system the requirements described before are capital issues.

Regarding these situations, this paper investigates the real-time task scheduling aiming to enhance the conventional single-processor-based ITRON as may be improved in:

1) dynamic adaptability
2) in a tightly-coupled multiprocessor environment.

The multiplication of processors can be done in two environments; tightly-coupled multiprocessor environment and loosely-coupled one. This paper stresses on the tightly-coupled environment. In the loosely-coupled environment, the real-time constraints could hardly be properly guaranteed by means of dynamic load-balancing. Besides, considering the implementation issue, the real-time services in the loosely-coupled environment could only be done in the task-level, outside the real-time kernel. Therefore, the circumstances warrants starting investigation from the tightly-coupled environment.

The requirement 1, dynamic adaptability, is among the dynamic task scheduling with task migration, dynamic reconfiguration of the real-time kernel to the optimum and realization of fault tolerance. This paper explains the necessity of dynamic real-time task scheduling, investigate the method, propose the stepwise scheduling method, and evaluate the effectiveness of the method through simulating experiments.

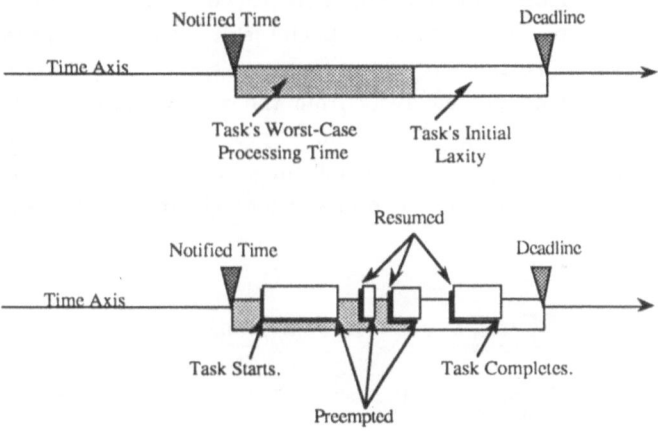

Fig.1 Timing constraint of a task

In the next section, we survey the studies on real-time task scheduling, and explain that dynamic scheduling is inevitable in a tightly-coupled multiprocessor environment. A brief survey of dynamic scheduling is also provided. The third section considers the effectiveness of applying dynamic scheduling stepwise in order to improve the dynamic adaptability. We evaluate scheduling success ratio using this stepwise manner through simulations. In the fourth section, we explain the current scheduling mechanisms of the ITRON and propose the way to include the stepwise scheduler into the ITRON. The last section concludes the evaluation of our dynamic scheduling algorithm and gives the future research issues.

2. REAL-TIME TASK SCHEDULING

Real-time systems features as follows:

1) comprises multiple tasks which tightly communicate one another,

2) has timing constraints as well as resource constraints, and

3) dispatches tasks by means of interruptions raised by the changes of the environment.

These features determines a multitasking system, task scheduling is one of the major issues to satisfy these constraints, and study on scheduling has been done for long years. The timing constraints of tasks are cited below:

1) the time the task is requested to run,

2) the worst case processing time of the task,

3) the time the task has to complete,

4) the time the task is permitted to start, (release time) and so forth.

Here we consider a problem of real-time task scheduling for instance. Three resources (maybe including processors) and five tasks are given with the timing/resource constraints shown in Figure 2 (a), and the table shown in Figure 2 (b) is created. These two figures have the time axis in common. Each task's deadline is expressed by the point on the time axis marked by the arrow from each task's line. The notify time and release time of each task already passed away from the zero point of the time axis. This calculation is called scheduling. This kind of processing is generally regarded as a "packing" problem which belongs to the NP-complete problem. The investigations on scheduling have been competing the effectiveness of creating the schedule table in various ways.

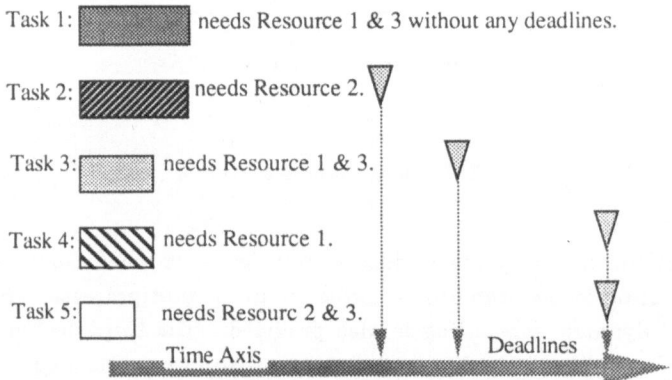

Fig. 2 (a) Requirement of real-time tasks with timing / resource constraints

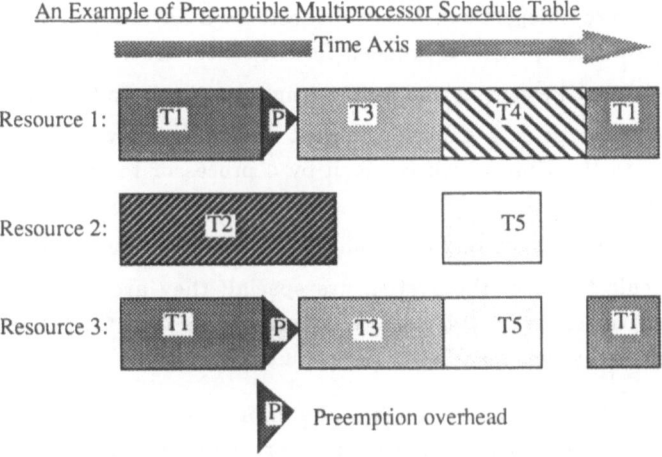

Fig 2 (b) Creating a schedule table for the requirement

2.1 Classification of Studies on Real-time Task Scheduling

Studies on real-time task scheduling can be classified according to their processing principle or environment. The primary classification is:

1) static scheduling and
2) dynamic scheduling.

Static scheduling means the scheduling process for every task is done before the system runs, and this scheduling burdens little run-time overhead. However, it is impossible to create scheduling table statically unless the behavior of all tasks are known beforehand. Hence, static scheduling can naturally not support dynamic task generation nor correspond with the changes of the environment dynamically either. Basically the system adopting static scheduling is considered to process the controlling by means of polling (periodic task wake-up) pattern. Dynamic scheduling, on the contrary, creating schedule table run-time, must be accompanied with pretty heavy run-time overhead in comparison with static scheduling. However, dynamic scheduling enables to correspond with the environment changes.

Some famous theorems from the old studies on static scheduling has become the today's basement, especially the rate monotonic scheduling algorithm presented in Liu and Layland's [1] is the most fruitful. This algorithm holds under the assumptions below:

1) The requests for all tasks for which hard deadlines exist are periodic, with constant interval between requests.
2) Deadlines consists of run-ability constraints only; i.e. each task must be completed before the next request for it occurs.

3) All the tasks are independent in that requests for a certain task do not depend on the initiation or the completion of requests for the other tasks.

4) The system must be constructed on the single-processor environment.

5) Processing time for each task is constant and does not vary with time. Run-time here refers to the time which is taken by a processor to execute the task without interruption.

6) Any new task with hard real-time constraints doesn't generate dynamically.

7) Any aperiodic tasks in the system are special; they are initialization or failure-recovery routines; they displace periodic tasks while they themselves are being run, and do not themselves have hard, critical deadlines.

The algorithm is scheduling on the basis of the priority providing with the higher priority for the task with the shorter period. The paper proved that under these assumptions this method schedules tasks to the optimum. As for a static scheduling for the periodic tasks the rate monotonic algorithm is the optimum. This ensures that in the worst case the least upper bound to achievable processor utilization ratio would amounts at $m\,(2^{1/m}-1)$ where m is the number of tasks.

Therefore making the number of tasks to the infinity the least upper bound achievable processor utilization ratio, about 69%. Furthermore, we got the theorem that for a set of independent periodic tasks, if each task meets its first deadline when all tasks are started at the same time, then the deadlines will always be met for any combination of start times. Another feature that supports safety of the system is provided: If a certain task should miss its deadline, it is the task with the least priority. The other investigation [10] reports that the worst case processor usage ratio 69% is a pretty pessimistic value. The investigation also presents that statistically the average processor usage ratio outrages 80%.

The recent studies propose various facilities in order to integrate the aperiodic task scheduling on the basis of the rate monotonic algorithm. Among them:

1) back-ground processing,

2) polling processing,

3) aperiodic task server, and

4) sporadic task server

are proposed and evaluated their effectiveness through simulations. The rate monotonic algorithm deals only with task set without synchronization dependency. R. Rajkumar, L. Sha, and J.P. Lehoczky proposed protocols which warrant not to happen the unbounded priority inversion through resource control using binary semaphore [2, 3]. They are:

1) Priority inheritance and

2) Priority ceiling protocol.

The problem happens when low-priority task and high-priority task share the same resource. Once the low task acquires the resource, the high task issues the P call and is blocked. Meanwhile, such a task as is with the priority between them can run unboundedly blocking the low task with the resource occupied by the blocked low task. This situation causes the unbounded priority inversion for the high task; that is, the high task could be blocked for the unpredictable period with the lower tasks running. The protocols proposed guarantee not to happen the priority inversion more than one stage stage at most by increasing the priority of the low task sharing the resource while it occupies the resource. The priority ceiling protocol also guarantees not to happen dead locks. These protocols are effective only in a single-processor environment, and no effective protocols in a multiprocessor environment are proposed. Sorry to say, these protocols are designed for binary semaphores and can not be applied to the resource control that must be managed by counting semaphore as memory blocks.

Considering a situation where dynamic scheduling is applied, when and what kind of task will arrive in the future is hard to predict. In particular, Mok and Dertouzos [4] showed that, for multiprocessor systems, there can be no optimal algorithm for scheduling preemptable tasks if the arrival time of tasks are not known *a priori*. Dynamic scheduling, therefore, adopts some heuristic rules. After an evaluation of task's criticalness in the light of some heuristics, the more critical task is scheduled with the higher priority. Among the heuristic rules are:

1) the least laxity task first, where laxity of a task is an extra time from the current time to the deadline subtracting the remaining processing time,

2) the task with the earliest deadline should be scheduled first, and

3) a task requiring the busiest resource first.

To improve the performance of scheduling, these heuristics are linearly combined or backtrack technique is applied in [5].

Dynamic scheduling is promising in a situation where it is unable to predict the arrivals of tasks in the future. The role of dynamic scheduling can be regarded as that of a recent aperiodic task server [6, 7, 8] which supports the aperiodic task scheduling in the rate monotonic algorithm on the side of static scheduling. Hence, the selection of dynamic and static scheduling might cause a dispute. However, as the rate monotonic algorithm itself bases on a single-processor environment, that is, most theorems that the algorithm relies on hold only in a single-processor one, dynamic scheduling becomes important for a dynamic load-balancing in a multiprocessor one. Applying dynamic scheduling algorithm brings a defect which doesn't appear in static scheduling, that is, runtime overhead is inevitable. The more sophisticated algorithm needs the more runtime scheduling overhead, even though the order of the algorithm may be relatively low. Especially in real-time systems this causes a crucial issue. No studies on a real-time property of real-time task scheduling can be found. This paper investigates especially on this topic.

A classification of studies on real-time task scheduling like:

1) Single-processor scheduling
2) Multiprocessor scheduling
   (a) Tightly-coupled multiprocessor scheduling
   (b) Loosely-coupled multiprocessor scheduling

is in terms of the running environment. We choose a multiprocessor environment for high computation power and a tight coupling for an improvement of dynamic adaptability. A single-processor environment is a usual and conventional one for embedded systems and is easy to adopt the rate monotonic algorithm. The difference between a tight coupling and a loose one means mostly an existence of task migration overhead. The investigation can be classified in other ways; with or without preemption and resume of task, with or without consideration of resource constraints.

2.2 Real-Time Systems in a Tightly-Coupled Multiprocessor Environment

Here, we start to present some properties of a tightly-coupled multiprocessor environment. Even though a tightly-coupled multiprocessor environment is promising to offer high computation power and high safety, the conventional systems are constructed almost in a static approach. The word 'static' means that the number of tasks and each processor for each task to run are specified off-line. Some encouraging features for this are as follows:

1) Fixing all tasks to specific processors makes the environment that of single-processor, where the rate monotonic algorithm is effectively applicable.
2) Real-time tasks' access to specific peripheral device limit a set of processors to run.
3) A tightly-coupling enables to communicate at high speed through shared memory.
4) Static scheduling brings little runtime overhead.
5) As static approach turns a multiprocessor environment into several single-processor environments, the priority ceiling protocol is applicable and this limits the priority inversion period boundedly.

On the contrary, unsatisfactory features are as follows:

1) Only applicable for an environment where static analysis of system's behavior is possible.
2) Change of the environment to be controlled burdens a

programmer with re-designing of the system.

3) A multiprocessor environment would encourage neither fault tolerance nor dynamic load balancing.

Our aim to improve the system's dynamic adaptability and safety requires a real-time kernel on a dynamic approach. The next section explains dynamic scheduling algorithm which considers the crucial issue on dynamic scheduling, real-time property of scheduling.

3. IMPROVEMENT OF DYNAMIC ADAPTABILITY OF A TIGHTLY-COUPLED MULTIPROCESSOR REAL-TIME KERNEL

3.1 Dynamic Adaptability of Real-Time Systems

Dynamic adaptability of real-time systems relies upon performance of its task scheduling. Hence dynamic scheduling requires processing time on the fly, a trade-off exists as follows:

1) High performance scheduling algorithm tends to have heavy runtime overhead.

2) It is difficult to warrant the constraints using a light runtime overhead algorithm.

In order to solve this trade-off such a scheduling service as behaves in proportion to system's overhead is ideal.

3.2 Stepwise Scheduling Algorithm

In order to improve system's dynamic adaptability we consider preparing some scheduling algorithms and selecting one of them according to the load of the system.

Here we prepare two scheduling algorithms; a *quick* scheduling algorithm and a *regular* one.

The number of stages, two, is meaningful in that a quick service is performed inside the kernel through system calls and a real-time task is assigned to serve the regular algorithm.

The exact difference between two services we propose is the way of handling the already-scheduled tasks. When a new task is arrived and a quick schedule is called, it schedules only the new task and the other already-scheduled tasks are not modified. A quick scheduling tries to find out the spare space in the existing scheduling table. On the other hand, regular one re-schedules all the ready-state tasks as well as the newly arriving task. This deserves to re-creating a new scheduling table for all the existing tasks.

3.3 Simulations for System's Dynamic Adaptability

Considering the real-time property of dynamic scheduling algorithm, we can't neglect the period the scheduling takes. The period of an algorithm which requires high processing power for its performance is sometimes comparable with that of a normal real-time task. Little conventional studies care this real-time property in their simulations, and they were statically simulated.

In [5] Zhao, Ramamritham, and Stankovic says:

1) Preparing a set of tasks with time/resource constraints.

2) Applying their proposing algorithm on the set and creating the schedule table.

3) Creating the schedule table satisfying all the constraints means a success of scheduling.

4) Through a number of preparing a set and creating a table calculate the scheduling success ratio.

The method above doesn't evaluate the real-time property of the scheduling algorithm.

The procedure we propose to evaluate the real-time property of dynamic scheduling algorithm is to prepare a sequence of task arrivals not a task set and to schedule the sequence during the simulation. The evaluation is to calculate the scheduling success ratio when changing the proportion of scheduling time to the average processing time of real-time tasks. Our major interest is to find out the permitted processing time for a given dynamic scheduling algorithm. That can be expressed in terms of the proportion to the average processing time of real-time tasks to be scheduled.

Our simulation procedure is carefully on this topic as follows:
1) Creating a task arrival sequence with time/resource constraints.
2) Preparing a quick scheduling algorithm and a regular one.
   (a) A quick one uses a simple heuristic rule and isn't preemptive.
   (b) A regular one serves preemptive scheduling and task migration.
3) Varying properties of the simulator, correcting the statistics.
   (a) Scheduling only by a quick one, varying the average period of task arrivals.
   (b) Scheduling only by a regular one, varying the scheduling time and the average period of task arrivals.
   (c) Repairing an algorithm which stepwisely applies the two scheduling services, varying the regular scheduling time and the average period of task arrivals.

Our stepwise scheduling algorithm is as follows:
1) A task arrives. (A task changes its status to ready.)
2) If a regular scheduling is proceeding, the new task is pending till the regular scheduling completes. (The new task could be appended to the pending task list[1].)

If a regular scheduler is not proceeding, a quick scheduling starts.
3) If a quick scheduler succeeds, scheduling for the new task completes.
4) If a quick scheduler does not succeed,

And if a regular scheduler is set to run[2],

   (a) If the next regular scheduler can be in time for the timing constraints of the new task, it leaves a regular one and does nothing.

---

[1] A data structure which lists a set of ready-status tasks that is under processing but not scheduled yet by the scheduler.

[2] This state means a regular scheduler task is not running but appears on the scheduling table.

Otherwise, it re-schedules a regular scheduler so that it might be in time for the constraints.

(b) If a regular scheduling task is not set to run,

It sets a regular scheduler to run so as to be in time for the constraints.

The setting of a regular scheduler should be done in the steps below lest the most critical task should fail:

i) Insert a regular scheduler in a spare slot of the scheduling table, if any.

ii) Exchange any task on any processor to be scheduled to run after a running task on the processor completes

iii) Preempt the task that is running and with the most value of heuristic function, that is, the least critical one.

The simulation experiments are performed with the parameters as follows:

1) Statistical distribution of task arrivals

This is the Poisson distribution with the average period 20, 25, 30, and 40 (unit time) between task arrivals. This condition is pretty severe, as is explained afterward.

2) Processing time spent for a regular scheduling task

This varies from 5 to 50 (unit time)[1]. Since the distribution of the processing time of the normal scheduled tasks is the Poisson distribution with the average 50, spending 50 units for a regular scheduling means it is comparable with the normal task processing.

3) Simulation continuation time

This is 10000 units, which includes the first 1000 units for an initial warm-up time. In that period no statistical data are logged.

4) Number of resources

We call processors active resources which each task must acquire, and other resources passive resources[2] . Our setting is four active resources and six passive resources.

5) Preemption overhead

Preemption of a running task requires 1 unit as an overhead.

6) Parameters on each task

(a) Processing time of a task

---

[1] The experiments afterward adopt the values 100 and 200.

[2] The reason this simulation cares the resource constraints is that multiprocessor scheduling could not adopt the priority ceiling protocol as limits the unbounded priority inversion.

This distributes according to the Poisson distribution with the average time 50 (units). The processing time means the worst case time for the task to complete, and this simulator always requires the worst case time.

(b) Deadline of a task

This is also the Poisson distribution with the average period between task's arrival and the deadline, five times of each task's processing time. Only for the task with processing time less than 20 units the processing time is regarded as 20 units and the deadline is calculated.

(c) Processor set a task can run

The simulator assigns a set for each task from the four active resources in the OR condition. The simulator specifies one of the four active resources randomly, and this is repeated four times. The result is that the probability for a task to run only on the one specified processor amounts to 1/64, on the two 15/32, on the tree 27/64, and on all the processors 3/32.

(d) Passive resources a task requires

Each task randomly requires passive resources at the average two resources from six. The passive resources can be used in the two disjoint mode; the one is the exclusive mode and the other is the shared mode[1]. The exclusive mode does not permit any task to share the resource, and the shared mode does. Task selects the mode at the probability 1/2.

7) A quick scheduling algorithm

8) A regular scheduling algorithm

9) A stepwise scheduling algorithm

These three algorithms are adaptable. The quick scheduling algorithm set the task into the spare slot found in the schedule table in the order of the least laxity first heuristic. A regular scheduling algorithm cancels or preempts all the tasks which are scheduled after the time the regular scheduling completes, and creates the table according to the least laxity first heuristic. This scheduling is the repetition of creating a portion of the table by an appropriate time slice[2] through preemptions. The stepwise scheduling algorithm is provided in the previous.

The algorithms in this experiments remove the tasks which are turned out to fail their timing constraints even before their completion from the set of ready-status tasks to be

---

[1] The priority ceiling protocol could not accept the counting semaphore resource controlling, it is desirable to be capable of requiring a number of the same passive resource. e.g. a memory block is like this kind of resource.

[2] The timing of slices is the earlier of any task's completion and the time when any not-running task's laxity becomes 0.

scheduled. In our initial experiment the algorithms consumed all the worst case processing time even if it completes with satisfying the constraint or not. However, this approach decreases the scheduling success ratio to a great degree. This is because to process the tasks that have already failed its constraint prevents the newly arrived tasks from successfully processing. That is the reason we changed the algorithms.

The result is depicted in Fig. 3. The horizontal-axis measures the average period of task arrivals. The vertical-axis measures the scheduling success ratio. The success ratio means the proportion of the number of completed tasks satisfying their constraints to the number of tasks that arrive during the simulation[1]. The upper the line is located, the better the algorithm's performance is. The plots on the right side are the results of scheduling the easier task sequences. Naturally, the left side means the severe sequences.

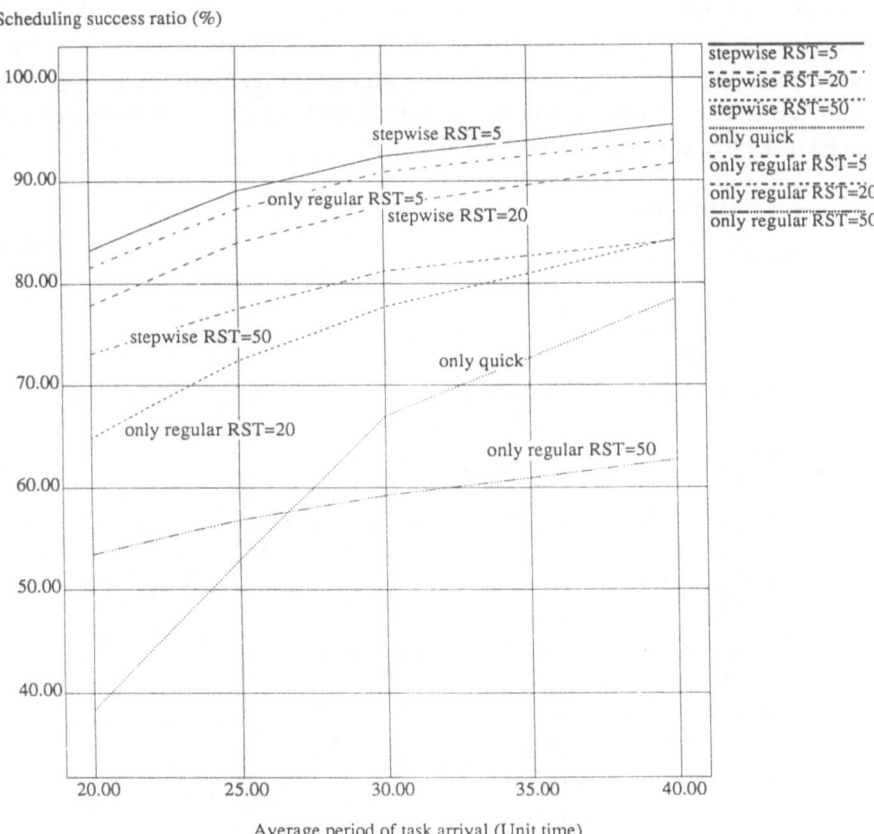

Fig. 3 *Only quick/only regular/stepwise scheduling success ratio*

[1] The result is calculated excluding the initial 1000 units, and the number of total arrived tasks excludes the tasks which don't complete at the end of simulation and can't be proved to succeed or fail their constraints.

Fig. 3 tells us that the stepwise scheduling is the best of the three even if varying the processing time of a regular scheduling. We also get the result a regular scheduling is not always superior to a quick scheduling in the case a regular scheduling takes considerable processing time. Meanwhile, varying range of a regular scheduling time to 200 units (this deserves to 4 times of the average processing time of the scheduled tasks), we investigate the behavior of a regular and stepwise scheduling. This experiment is done varying the regular scheduling time from 5, 20, 50, 100, to 200 units and the average task arrival period 25, 30, and 40 units. This experiment's result is shown in Fig. 4, 5, and 6. Fig. 4, which is the case of the average task arrival period 30, gives the result that the stepwise scheduling endures the task sequence as the best one of the three even if a regular scheduling takes twice as long as the normal task's processing time. As for an only regular scheduling, it becomes inferior to an only quick scheduling if the regular scheduling time is comparable with the normal tasks'. As a whole, the success ratio is absolutely bad for real-time systems. This badness comes from the task arrival distribution is so peaky that makes scheduling too difficult, and the passive resource requirements prevent multiprocessor's computation power from increasing more than a certain limit. The former could be solved by making the task sequence mixing the periodic tasks to a certain degree.

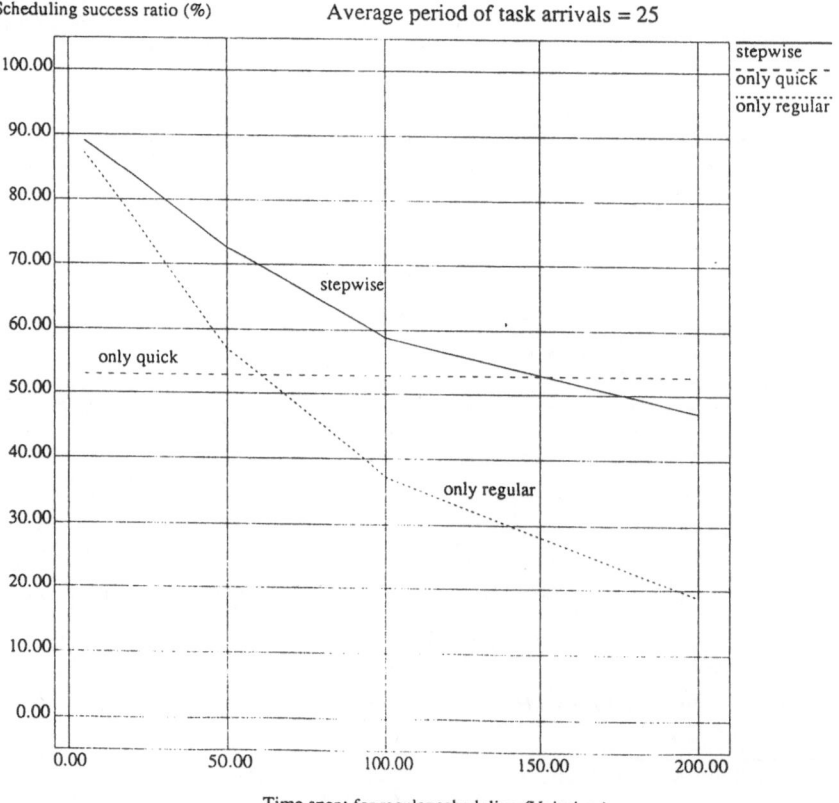

Fig. 4 *Limit of time spent for regular scheduling (a)*

4. APPLYING THE STEPWISE SCHEDULER TO THE ITRON SYSTEM

The current ITRON specification targets for the single-processor environment. This means it is theoretically incapable of continuously extending the system to the multiprocessor environment. One of the *ad hoc* approaches of this kind is to regard the multiprocessor environment as the group of static-based single-processor environments. This approach means that in each processor each ITRON kernel manages only their own tasks statically assigned. In a sense, this approach will guarantee the continuity from the conventional system and give the high processing power, however, also give the system designer much more load and not give the high dynamic adaptability even in the tightly-coupled multiprocessor environment.

Since each of the applications of the real-time systems like the ITRON systems will have functions so peculiar to itself and would be quite different from one another, the continuity of the system won't be necessarily efficient in almost all the cases. However, the dynamic adaptability is one of the most capital issues of the recent real-time systems. Furthermore, education of the programmers matters much on this continuity.

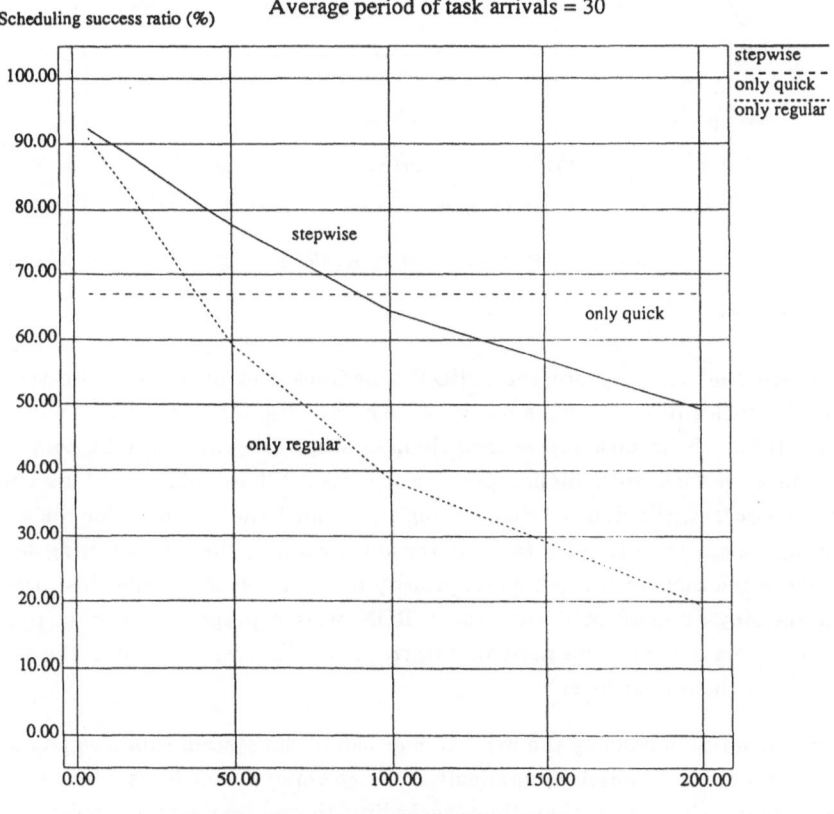

Fig. 5 Limit of time spent for regular scheduling (b)

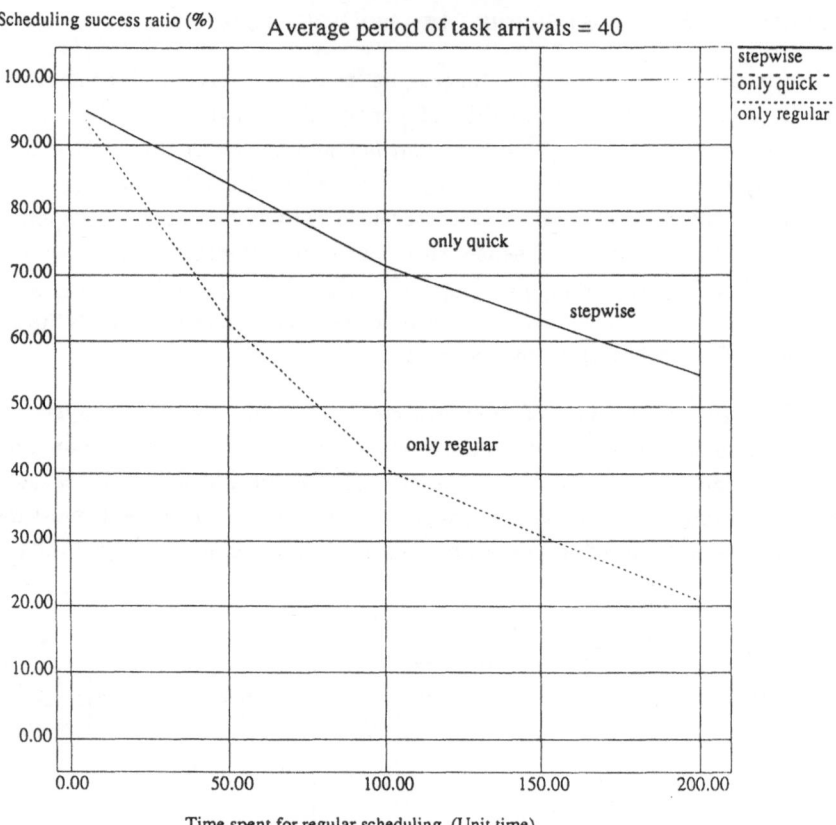

Fig. 6 *Limit of time spent for regular scheduling (c)*

The conventional single-processor ITRON schedules and dispatches the tasks on the basis of the task's priority. This means a task with the highest priority will obtain the running status. This task precedence changes when the running task completes their processing or a task with higher priority arrives. When some event as causes task dispatching occurs, the delayed dispatching interrupt handler works for the appropriate scheduling before the ordinary task processing resumes; that is, selecting and context switching to the task with the highest priority at the time. Although this priority-based scheduling may seem so primitive, the ITRON system prepares the chg_pri (change priority) system call and the periodic interrupt handler, which enable the round-robin scheduling at the higher level.

The task's priority is fixed by the programmer before the system runs and changed by the tasks or interrupt handler dynamically. Programmer schedules all the tasks only through their priorities rather than according to the worst-case processing time or deadlines. This may seem indirect fashion of a system designing. Matters are worse, when it comes to the multiprocessor environment; i.e. programmers must specify the appropriate processors for all the tasks. Therefore, we introduce the stepwise scheduler as the filter from the more direct attributes description of the real-time tasks into the priority-based description. These more direct task attributes description like the worst-case processing time, the resource constraints and timing constraints like their deadlines are given through the External Kernel Call in NISHIO and Sakamura's [9]. This EKC should be implemented as a set of the Extended SVC's.

Our stepwise scheduler consists of two schedulers; e.g. a quick scheduler and a regular scheduler. A regular scheduler functions as one of the ordinary real-time tasks. This doesn't bother the continuity from the conventional ITRON systems, and regular schedulers are maintainable independent of the real-time kernel. Regular schedulers could be appropriately developed and selected according to the system's requirements.

The problem would be the way to include a quick scheduler into the ITRON. A quick scheduler must be processed quickly and included into the kernel. However, this scheduler must refer to the same schedule table that the regular scheduler depends. Hence, we propose the way to include it into the kernel by implementing it as a delayed interrupt handler like the ITRON's delayed dispatcher, but should be assigned at the one higher[1] IMASK level than the delayed dispatcher. Fig. 7 shows the conceptional mechanism of a quick scheduler.

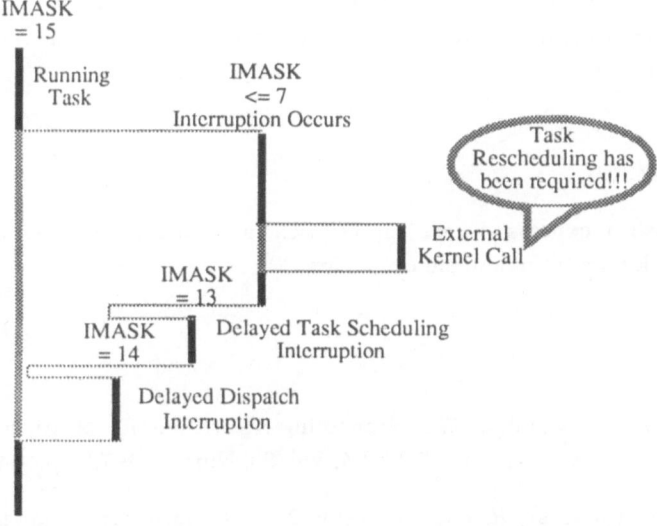

Fig. 7 Installing a quick scheduler into the ITRON system as a delayed interrupt handler

---

[1] The value of the IMASK amounts lower number than that of the delayed dispatching interruption.

This method enables a quick scheduler to be removal and exchangeable. We only prepare the EKC to register a code as a quick scheduler. If a programmer does not want to use the stepwise scheduling method, he does not have to register a quick scheduler; this leaves him a well-continuous but primitive multiprocessor-based ITRON system from the conventional single-processor based one, although he must assign the appropriate processor for each of tasks.

5. CONCLUSION

This paper proposes the significance of the real-time property of dynamic scheduling in the real-time system, and this property is important for the improvement of dynamic adaptability of the systems in a tightly-coupled multiprocessor environment where dynamic scheduling is much more promising than static one. This paper investigates the real-time property of dynamic scheduling through the simulation experiments, and evaluates a stepwise scheduling we propose, which is superior to a single algorithm scheduling in the view of the success ratio. This paper also presents the way to include the stepwise scheduler into the ITRON.

In the future research plan we are engaged in the integration of dynamic and static scheduling for a tightly-coupled multiprocessor environment, as well as the dynamic safety scheduling algorithms. We expect that this would absolutely increases the success ratio to a great degree.

ACKNOWLEDGEMENT

The authors wish to express sincere appreciation to the members of the Sakamura laboratory for their kind and invaluable comments.

REFERENCES

[1]   Liu, C. L. and Layland, J. W., "Scheduling Algorithms for Multiprogramming in a Hard Real Time Environment," JACM, Vol. 20, Num. 1, 1973, pp.46-61.

[2]   Sha, L. and Rjkumar, R. and Lehoczky, J. P., "Priority Inheritance Protocols: An Approach to Real-Time Synchronization," Tech. Report CMU-CS-87-181, Dept. of Computer Science, Carnegie Mellon Univ., 1987.

[3]   Rajkumar, R. and Sha, L. and Lehoczky, J. P., "Real-Time Synchronization Protocols for Multiprocessors", Proceeding of IEEE Real-Time Systems Symposium, IEEE CS Press, Los Alamitos, Calif., 1988, pp.259-269.

[4] Mok, A. K. and Dertouzos, M. L., "Multiprocessor scheduling in a hard real-time environment," Proceeding of the Seventh Texas Conference on Computing Systems, November, 1978.

[5] Zhao, W. and Ramamritham, K. and Stankovic, J. A., "Preemptive Scheduling Under Time and Resource Constraints", IEEE Transactions on Computers, Vol. 36, No. 8, 1987, pp.949-960.

[6] Sha, L. and Lehoczky, J. P. and Stronsnider, J., J. P., "Enhancing Aperiodic Responsiveness in a Hard Real-Time Environment", Proceeding of IEEE Real-Time Systems Symposium, IEEE CS Press, Los Alamitos, Calif., 1987, pp.261-270.

[7] Sprunt, B. and Lehoczky, J. P. and Sha, L., "Exploiting Unused Periodic Time For Aperiodic Service Using The Extended Priority Exchange Algorithm", Proceeding of IEEE Real-Time Systems Symposium, IEEE CS Press, Los Alamitos, Calif., 1988, pp.251-258.

[8] Sprunt, B. and Sha, L. and Lehoczky, J. P., "Aperiodic Task Scheduling for Hard-Real-Time Systems", The Journal of Real-Time Systems, Vol. 1, No. 2, 1989, pp.27-60.

[9] NISHIO, N. and Sakamura, Ken, "Considerations on Designing the ITRON Specification for a Tightly-Coupled Multiprocessor Environment – Real-Time Scheduling of the ITRON External Kernel –", TRON Technical Research Meeting, Vol. 2, No. 3, October, 1989, pp.53-62 (In Japanese).

[10] Lehoczky, J. P. and Sha, L. and Ding, Y., "The Rate Monotonic Scheduling Algorithm – Exact Characterization and Average Case Behavior," Proceeding of IEEE Real-Time Systems Symposium, IEEE CS Press, Los Alamitos, Calif., 1989, pp.166-171.

Nobuhiko NISHIO is a D.S. course student of Department of Information Science at the University of Tokyo. He is now, under the supervision of Dr. Sakamura, engaged in research on Multiprocessor ITRON, real-time software development environment and human-machine interface in BTRON and MTRON for the TRON project. He received B.E. degree in mathematical engineering and M.S. in information science from University of Tokyo. He is a member of ACM, IEEE, and Information Processing Society of Japan.

E-Mail: vino@spica.is.s.u-tokyo.ac.jp

Hiroaki Takada is an educational staff of Department of Information Science at the University of Tokyo. He is now, under the supervision of Dr. Sakamura, engaged in research on software development environment and programming language for the TRON project. Takada is also interested in hypertext systems. He received B.S. and M.S. degrees in information science from University of Tokyo. He is a member of ACM, IEEE, Information Processing Society of Japan, and Japan Society for Software Science and Technology.

E-Mail: hiro@spica.is.s.u-tokyo.ac.jp

Ken Sakamura is currently an associate professor at the Department of Information Science, University of Tokyo. He holds Ph.D. in EE. Being a computer architect, he has been the leader of the TRON project which he started to build a new computer system architecture for 1990's since 1984. His promotion of the TRON architecture now extends to architecture of buildings and furniture. He servers on the editorial board of Institute of Electrical and Electronics Engineers (IEEE) MICRO magazine and is a chair of the project promotion committee of the TRON Association. He is a member of Japan Information Processing Society, Institute of Electronics, Information and Communication Engineers, ACM, and is a senior member of IEEE. He has received best paper awards of IEICE twice, of JIPS once, IEEE best annual article awards, and other awards from Japanese and over seas organizations.

Above authors may be reached at: Department of Information Science, Faculty of Science, University of Tokyo, 7-3-1 Hongo, Bunkyo-ku, Tokyo, Japan.

A Graphical Debugger for HI8

David Wallace
Hitachi Europe Limited

Abstract

The European Design and Engineering Support Centre (EuroDESC) of the Electronic Components Division of Hitachi Europe Limited, based in Maidenhead, England; together with Cambridge Beacon Limited of Cambridge, England; have been active in the support of the design-in within Europe of HI8 (Hitachi's implementation of the µITRON Specification). In order to facilitate this, they have designed and developed the Hitachi Integrated Development Environment (HIDE) to assist the HI8 System Designer with system configuration, integration and testing.

The next phase of the development of HI8 support tools has been the design and implementation of the Integrated System Debugging Tool (ISDT) for HI8. ISDT is an extension of the functions offered by the combination of the HI8 Debugger and the H8 Executive Monitor System (EMS) which runs on the EuroDESC H8 Evaluation Board.

The ISDT represents a major enhancement in the support for HI8 which moves beyond the comprehensive facilities offered by HIDE to allow for easier HI8 system design, integration and debug.

Keywords: µITRON Specification, ISDT, HIDE, HI8

INTRODUCTION

In its role as the European Design and Engineering Support Centre, EuroDESC is at the centre of European electronic components design activity (from Hitachi Europe's point of view) in the area of Real Time Operating Systems. As such, it is uniquely placed to assess and implement support requirements for the European customer. In 1989, EuroDESC introduced the concept of HIDE - the Hitachi Integrated Development Environment - to the European market. This, together with HIDE's powerful Configurator and Make Utilities allowed the system designer an easier path to the integration of system designs based on Hitachi's implementation of the µITRON Specification - known as HI8.

It became clear however that, while the introduction of HIDE offered a significant aid to design, there was still room for enhancements to the HI8 support. Discussions with the customer base and research by and on behalf of

EuroDESC have resulted in the specification and implementation of the Integrated System Debugging Tool (ISDT) which has been designed and developed jointly by EuroDESC and Cambridge Beacon Limited, an independent design consultancy of Cambridge, England.

Support for a Real Time Operating System is not a simple task and is certainly much more complex than support for a microcontroller. It is important that the support tools are made available ahead of user requirements, that a common environment is offered and that a clear upgrade path is made available. The details of what is currently on offer and what the future holds is described during the course of this paper but it is clear that the ISDT represents a major piece of the HI8 support jigsaw.

It is worth noting that while this paper has been prepared using the experience gained in design and research work carried out for and by Hitachi Europe, it is felt that there are basic principles involved which can be applied to any of a number of implementations of the ITRON specification. Specifically, the development work being carried out by Hitachi in relation to HI8-3X will be monitored closely with a view to delivering the ISDT when HI8-3X is fully released.

In addition it should be noted that the development work has been based exclusively, for all the HI8 support tools, on the IBM-PC® and its compatibles. The reason for this is that this host is common within the engineering departments of Europe and so offers the HI8 support tools to the widest possible audience. It is however recognised that the developments being carried out under the auspices of the TRON Project and specifically those concerning the BTRON Specification cannot be ignored. The nature of the ISDT, HIDE and the Configurator is that they are graphically orientated. As such they offer the strong possibility of migration into the area of presentation covered by the BTRON Specification and this migration is something that should be investigated in the near future.

The purpose of this paper is to present ISDT for the first time, to examine its importance, to see how it fits in with the HIDE concept and finally to look at the future for ISDT.

In order then to understand the place of the ISDT in supporting the design in of HI8 it is worthwhile first of all to review briefly the functionality of HIDE.

HITACHI INTEGRATED DEVELOPMENT ENVIRONMENT (HIDE)

HIDE was implemented to meet a specific market need within Europe for an easier design and debug route for the users of HI8 (Hitachi's implementation of the μ ITRON Specification).

EuroDESC was given the task of porting HI8 from VAX/VMS® to the IBM-PC® environment which is commonly available within Europe. While this work was being carried out, our research indicated that the possibility existed of enhancing the HI8 package by using the facilities of the IBM-PC® to the full.

This led to the creation of HIDE - a whole environment specifically dedicated to the design and development of HI8 systems.

What HIDE offers the user is a windowed environment with pull-down menus allowing fast and easy access to support tools such as C Compilers and Linkers together with a powerful Make utility for building the final system. The start up configuration for HIDE is shown in Figure 1.

The Command Window offers access to a subset of DOS commands as well as command line alternatives to the menu options. The Console Window in the HIDE front end provides the user with an interface to the EuroDESC H8 Evaluation Board which plugs in to the IBM-PC® bus and acts as the target hardware for the HI8 system. The Printer Window is available to act as the target for the output from the HI8 Printer Drivers.

In addition, HIDE has a Configurator which, through a series of menus and windows, prompts the user for the information necessary to implement a full HI8 system, modifies the appropriate configuration files and then creates the Make and Linker Subcommand files needed for the generation of an HI8 System. Various error checks are included in the Configurator to ensure that, for

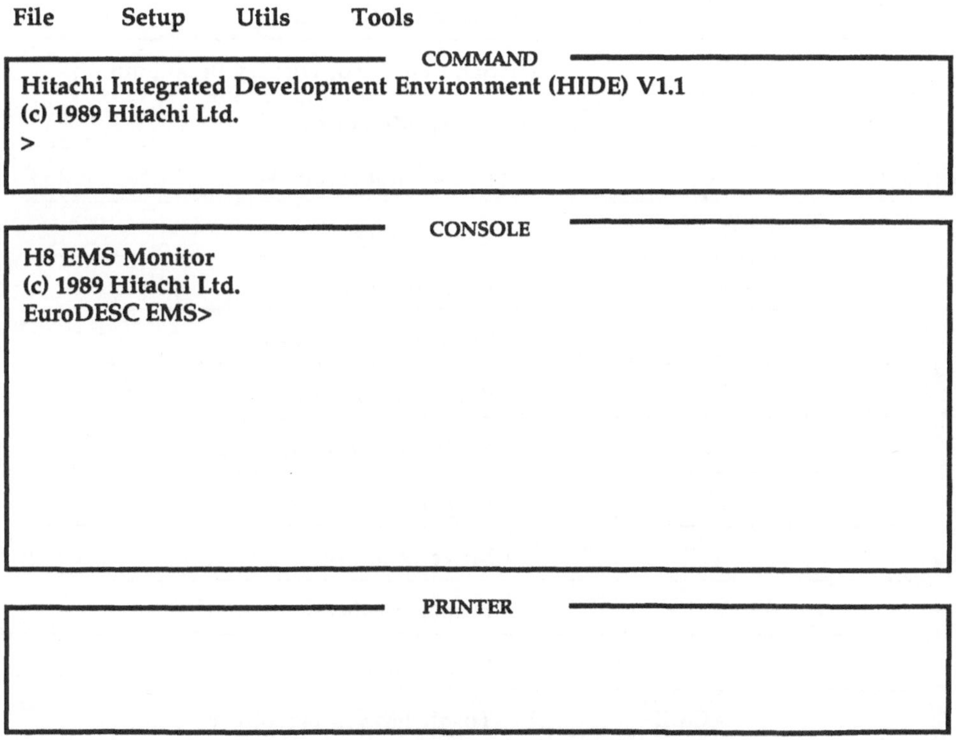

File   Setup   Utils   Tools

```
──────────────────────── COMMAND ────────────────────────
Hitachi Integrated Development Environment (HIDE) V1.1
(c) 1989 Hitachi Ltd.
>
```

```
──────────────────────── CONSOLE ────────────────────────
H8 EMS Monitor
(c) 1989 Hitachi Ltd.
EuroDESC EMS>
```

```
──────────────────────── PRINTER ────────────────────────
```

Figure 1 - HIDE User Interface

example, it is not possible to build a system with no tasks in it, nor to create tasks with an invalid start address.

To summarise, the benefits to the designer of using a proven Real Time Operating System - reliability, flexibility, shorter design cycle, etc. - are supported by a comprehensive development environment.

When the HI8 system has been created using HIDE, the next logical step is that of debugging the code. The H8 Evaluation Board offers an on board monitor which includes the standard memory and register manipulation instructions (see Table 1) which are perfectly adequate for "normal" program debugging. However, the inclusion of HI8 in the application means that the debugging task ceases to be "normal" because HI8 is a Real Time Operating System and as such requires a Real Time Operating System Debugger which has the "intelligence" to understand the multi-tasking nature of the system.

Table 1 - H8 EMS Instruction Set

Instruction	Description
?	Display Help Information
A	Assemble Instruction
B	Set, Remove or Display Breakpoint
D	Dump Memory
DA	Disassemble Memory
F	Fill Memory
G	Execute Program
IL	Load Data from Host
IS	Save Data to Host
IV	Verify Memory against File
M	Display or Modify Memory
MV	Move Memory
R	Display Registers
S	Single Step
XCMD	Toggle EMS Debug Mode
.(register)	Modify Register Value

HI8 has such a Debugger which can optionally be included as part of the HI8 system when it is built and it is this which we will consider next on our way to understanding the nature of and the necessity for the ISDT.

THE HI8 DEBUGGER

The Debugger which is supplied with HI8 is designed to offer the HI8 system designer a tool which will aid with the debugging of a Real Time Operating System-based application. It allows the user interactive input and output by using a console display connected to the target hardware.

The Debugger runs as a task within the HI8 system with the highest possible priority in the Operating System. User input and output is handled by a Console Driver which can be tailored to the particular requirements of the target hardware while printer output is handled by a customised Printer Driver. The user gains access to the Debugger by entering an interrupt (CNTL+D) through the console keyboard.

The Debugger, like the rest of HI8, is modular in nature and the user has the option of including the following modules if required in addition to the basic Debugger module:-

1. System Call Function
2. Memory Management Function
3. Break Function
4. Print Function
5. SVC Function

Selection of these different functions can be carried out using the HIDE/Configurator combination which was described in the previous section.

When the user has initiated the Debugger, the prompt **DBG>** appears on the Console. When this prompt appears, a range of Debug commands, as listed in Table 2 is available to the user for the purpose of debugging the application. When command entry is completed, the Debugger can be terminated by typing **EXIT** at the **DBG>** prompt.

The HI8 Debugger is a tool specifically designed for the purpose of debugging HI8 system designs. However, as part of the porting of the HI8 System and associated support tools to the IBM-PC® environment, it has been considered appropriate to look at how the debugging of a real time operating system can be enhanced by accessing the full capabilities of the IBM-PC® and its compatibles.

Given that this is the case, the question must be asked, why undertake the design and development of a tool like the ISDT? There are two answers to this question. One is that there are certain functions which would be desirable from the point of view of system debugging that are not implemented in the existing HI8 Debugger - these will be discussed in more detail in the next section. The second point is that the existing Debugger would benefit from its integration into the HIDE environment - pull-down menus and multiple windows can make the debugging function much more comfortable.

Table 2 - HI8 Debugger Command Options

Command	Description
STA_TSK	Initiate Task
SUS_TSK	Suspend Task Execution
RSM_TSK	Resume Task
TER_TSK	Terminate Task
FB	Initialise Memory
DB	Display Memory
MB	Modify Memory
BS	Breakpoint Set
B	Display Breakpoints
BC	Cancel Breakpoint
GO	Execute Task
RM	Modify Task Registers
TSK	Display Task Status
LST ON	Allocate Printer
LST OFF	Deallocate Printer
EXIT	Terminate Debugger
SVC	Issue System Call

In the next section we will discuss the top level functionality of the ISDT and describe some details of the specific benefits that it offers over and above the HI8 Debugger and H8 EMS.

INTEGRATED SYSTEM DEBUGGING TOOL (ISDT) OVERVIEW

The ISDT is a real time, interactive, IBM-PC® based graphical debugger with facilities that are a superset of those provided by the Executive Monitor System (EMS) and the HI8 Debugger. ISDT is needed because the existing debugging facilities provided with the H8 EMS and the HI8 Debugger have certain limits. As was noted in the previous section, basic debugging facilities are available but are not presented in a way which provides the maximum efficiency from the point of view of the design engineer. Given that the debugging stage is often the most arduous and lengthy stage in the software development cycle, it should be a high priority for this stage to be made more efficient. As has been noted already, the introduction of the HIDE/Configurator combination was the first step along this path. The ISDT is the second step.

The additional facilities which the ISDT was required to provide can be broken down as described in the following paragraphs.

Symbolic Debugging

The HI8 Debugger allows access to address and data values only through the use of hexadecimal numbers.

Flexible Breakpoints

The HI8 Debugger only offers breakpoint setting on address values.

Trace Buffering

This is only available in the HI8 Debugger on system calls. When active, it traces on all system calls.

User-friendly Interface

The HI8 Debugger works through a command line interface, based on the serial port of the target hardware. There are no graphical displays of the system state as a whole, nor can system objects be watched.

These then are perceived to be the basic limitations of the existing debugging environment and it was to get round these problems that the ISDT was created. We will look in detail at the facilities offered by the ISDT but it is first of all necessary to understand the hardware and low level software environment in which the ISDT runs.

ISDT FUNCTIONALITY

The ISDT uses the same target hardware as that used by HIDE - specifically, an IBM-PC® or compatible as the host computer with an H8 Evaluation Board plugged into the PC bus acting as the H8 target hardware. This ensures a reliable and familiar hardware platform for the ISDT.

The ISDT software breaks down into two basic modules - ISDT-HI8 and ISDT-PC - with various sub-functions. This arrangement is shown diagrammatically in Figure 2.

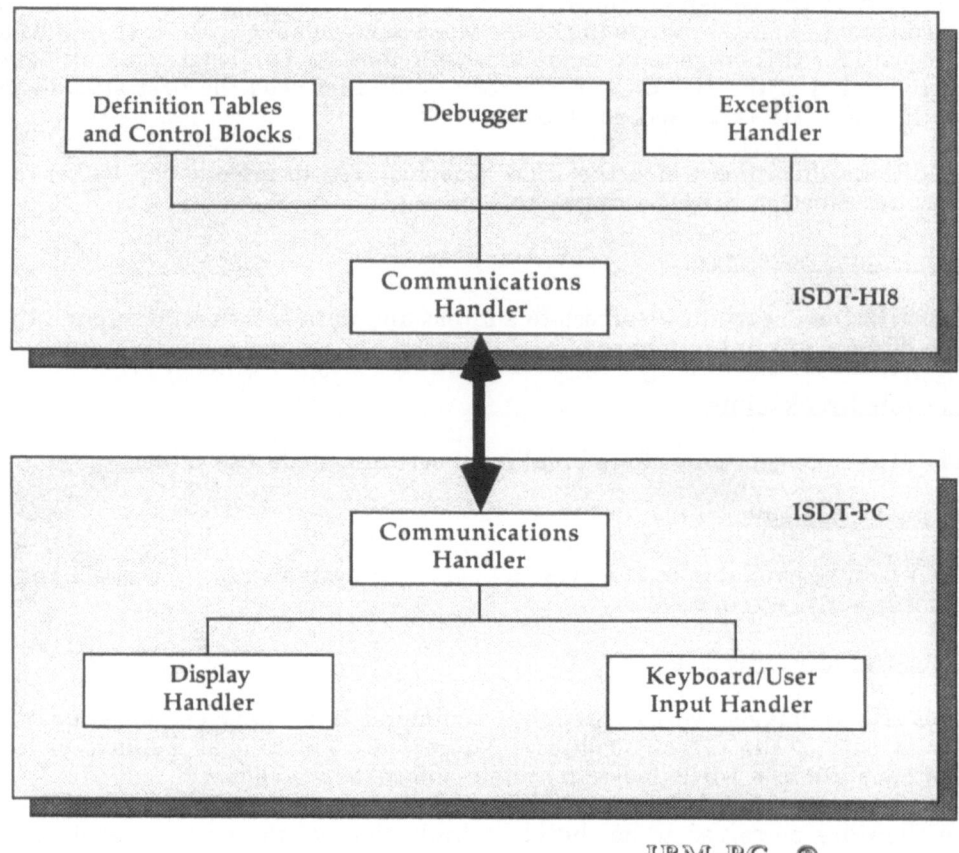

Figure 2 - ISDT Modules Overview

ISDT-HI8

This module runs as part of the HI8 system - on the H8 Evaluation Board with the highest priority of any task in the system (compare this with the HI8 Debugger) and with full system accessibility. The main function of this module is to regularly monitor the current state of the HI8 system in real time and to update the module ISDT-PC with this information. At power on, this module will set all system tasks to the Dormant state. The effect of this is to allow the user to debug only selected tasks.

Breakpoints on Program Counter values will be set by inserting an illegal instruction at the appropriate point. When the illegal instruction is executed, the exception handler will return control to the Debugger.

Requests for breakpoints on HI8 objects such as signalling to semaphore or sending a message to a mailbox are stored within this module. The relevant

C Interface Library routines are modified so that they check whether or not a breakpoint has been set on the object. If it has, control is returned to the Debugger, if not, the object is processed as normal.

For Trace Buffering, as for Breakpoints, the ISDT-HI8 module maintains an internal table of traceable events according to user requests. Requests for traces on objects - such as signal a semaphore or send a message to mailbox for example - are stored internal (to ISDT-HI8). The relevant HI8 C Interface Library routines are modified to firstly check if logging has been enabled on the chosen object and then informs the Debugger which in turn logs the call to the object. If logging has not been enabled for that particular object, the object will be processed in the normal way.

Symbolic information as provided by the specific set of development tools used by the system designer (within limits) is used to cross-reference function names and variable names as required.

The final part of ISDT-HI8 is that part which handles communications over the IBM-PC® bus to the ISDT-PC module which runs on the PC itself. The existing parallel interface driver for the H8 EMS has been modified slightly to handle the slightly different communications protocol used by the ISDT. The use of the parallel interface has, of course, left the user with free access to the serial port for the use of the application software.

ISDT-PC

This module, which runs on the IBM-PC®, can be broken down into three basic functions - screen handler, keyboard handler and ISDT-HI8 interface handler.

The screen handler is concerned with the generation of the ISDT's multiple windows and menus. The user is able to open, size and position windows as required for the purpose of debugging the particular application. The use of the windows is left very much up to the user - the next section describes in more detail the actual functions available in the ISDT - but as a an example, a likely configuration might include a window containing details of a particular task, another window containing the CPU registers, another containing a listing of the assembler list file for the particular task being debugged and a finally a watch window showing symbol values relevant to the system being debugged. Probably the most significant window available is however the one which gives a full system queues overview - this includes information on the whole system in one window which can show all of the current task states and, if appropriate, which tasks, mailboxes, event flags or memory pools the tasks are waiting for. An additional facility allows the user to "zoom in" on a particular system object to gain more detailed information. These functions are described further in the next section.

The user communicates with the ISDT by means of pull down menus - the functions available through these menus are listed in detail in the next section but, as an example, they include options to control task states, display tasks and objects. In addition, there is an option for creation of an MS-DOS®

shell and a calculator facility. This activity is all processed by the keyboard handler.

Communications with the ISDT-HI8 module will, under normal circumstances, only consist of regular polling of ISDT-HI8 to determine the current HI8 system status - this being passed on to the relevant display modules. When the user requests specific information, such as more detail on the status of a particular task, the communications module will be responsible for communicating with the communications function within ISDT-HI8 and gathering the required information. It is also through the communications function that the executable files are transferred to the target H8 hardware.

To recap then, the ISDT is made up of two basic modules - ISDT-HI8 which runs as part of the target HI8 system and ISDT-PC which resides on the IBM-PC® and handles the user interface and communications with the target H8 hardware. In order that the system is not overloaded, communications between the two modules is kept to a minimum unless there is a specific user request or the response to that request is being transferred from ISDT-HI8 to ISDT-PC.

In the next section, the options available within the ISDT are listed in detail with an illustration of a potential screen configuration for debugging purposes.

ISDT MENU AND WINDOW OPTIONS

There are many different menu and window options available through the ISDT - so many that it is not within the scope of this paper to describe all of them here - the place for the that is the ISDT User Manual! It is possible however to look at the main groupings of menu options and also to examine one possible combination of windows which could be created by the user.

The basic menu headings are File, View, Data, Control, Break, Exec and Options and we will consider each of these in turn, discussing details as appropriate.

File Menu

The primary function of this menu is to allow the user to download a file to the target hardware. It also provides a means of changing directory and creating a DOS shell. Finally, it is the route through which the user exits the ISDT.

View Menu

This menu gives access to the multiple windows available in the ISDT. These windows can be used to view memory contents, assemble/disassemble code, access the ISDT calculator, view selected expressions and view text files. The user can also view system queues - an example of the information displayed is shown in Figure 3. The Tasks are displayed in their queues with the currently active task being highlighted. With this window, the user can get a snapshot overview of the entire HI8 System. If necessary, the option is

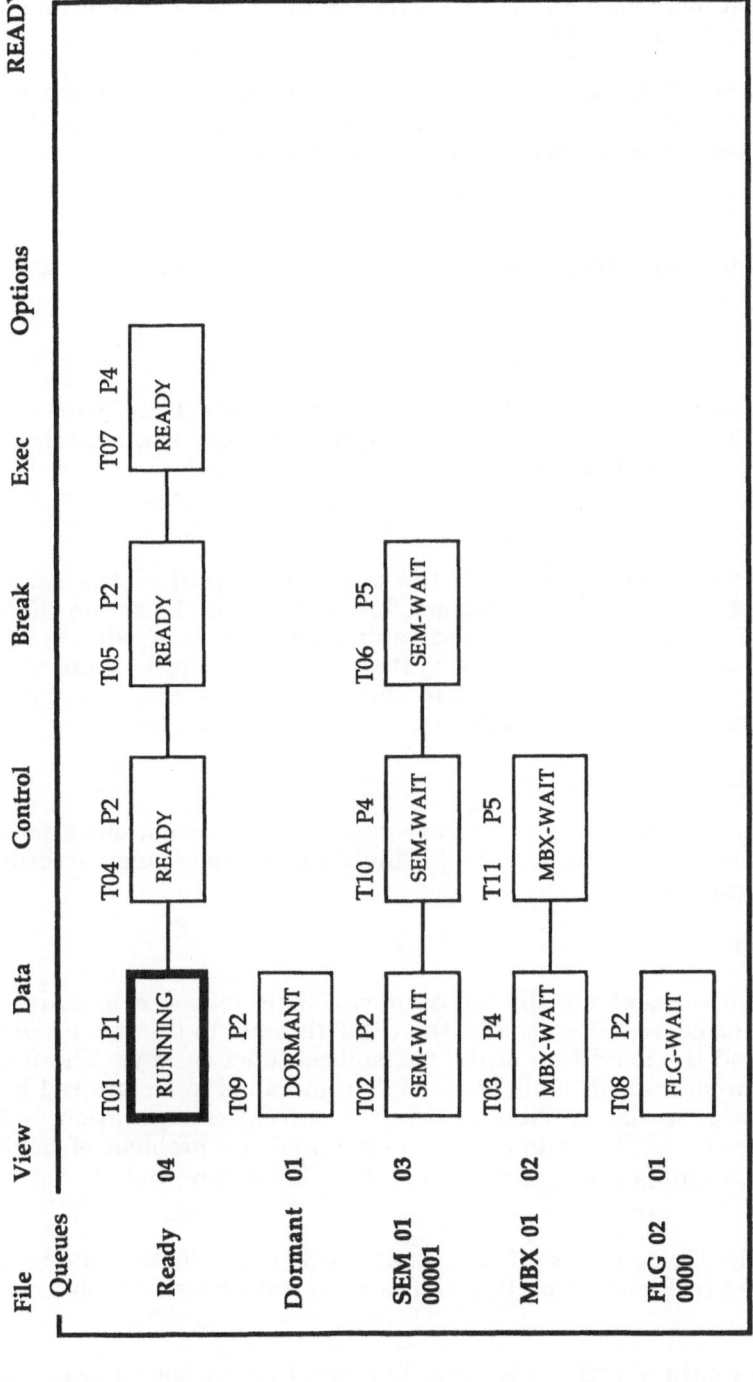

Figure 3 - System Queue Viewing Window

available to get more data on the currently running task or to select a specific task using the menu options.

Of course there will be instances where the information available is greater than that which can be shown on the screen at one time. If this is the case, the user has the option of resizing and moving the windows on the screen.

Data Menu

The data menu is used simply to add items to the watch window or to inspect variables.

Control Menu

This menu gives the user full task and object control facilities - as an example, options are available to terminate tasks, send mail, signal semaphores, set event flags and acquire memory pools.

Break Menu

The options within this menu are the ones which control the setting of breakpoints. As with the HI8 Debugger, breakpoints can be set on PC value. However the ISDT offers additional options to break on specific tasks, semaphores, mailboxes and other system objects. This is done through monitoring system calls to the system objects - as an example, for memory pools, it is possible to break on release and get memory blocks.

Exec (Execute) Menu

The execute menu controls program execution. The basic options offered are execute and trace. The trace can be for multiple or single steps according to the user's requirements.

Options Menu

The options menu controls the environment. This means everything from the path for the source files used by the ISDT through to the colours used for the display and the definition of the customised function keys. The function keys can be programmed to allow multiple commands to be entered for just one keystroke. It is also possible to save the current configuration and load previously saved configurations. This gets round the problem of having to reload complex configurations every time the ISDT is powered up.

This then is the ISDT. To round off this section, it is worth looking at the screen display illustrated in Figure 4 as this shows a typical debugging configuration for the ISDT.

The diagram shows three active windows. Window 1 shows the System Queues, Window 2 has the source listing for the HI8 Setup file and Window 3 contains the ISDT Calculator. Windows 1 and 2 are not full screen and therefore only show part of the information available. It is possible to make any window into full

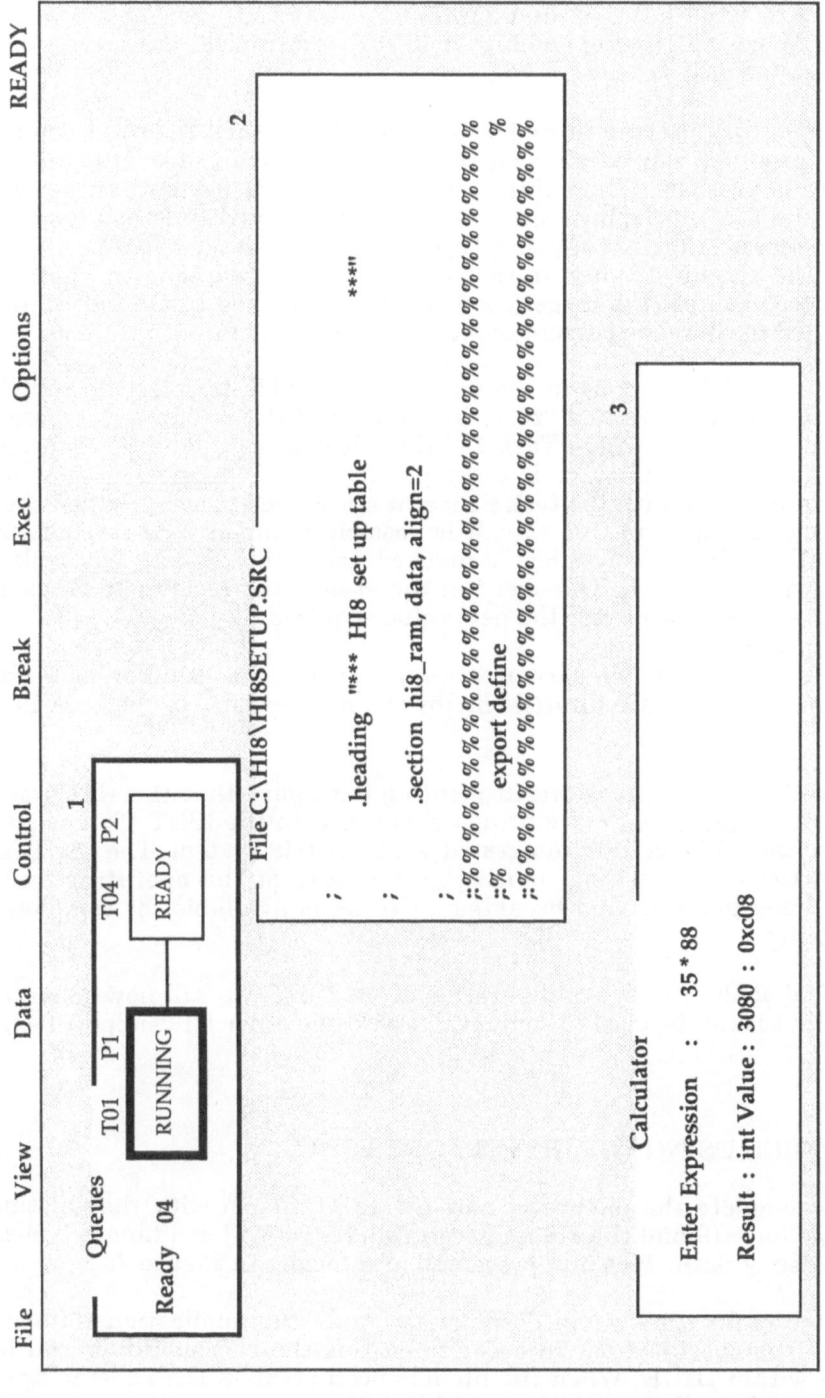

Figure 4 - Example ISDT Debugging Configuration

screen size or to scroll data, up and down or left and right within the windows. By selecting Window 1 and expanding it to full screen size, the screen display shown in Figure 3 will appear.

The HI8 System will execute in real time on the Evaluation Board in one of two modes. The program can be allowed to free run and will only stop when the CTRL-C key is pressed. When this occurs, the current system status will be reflected in the screen display. Alternatively, a trace facility is available which updates the screen after a number of cycles so that the user can see dynamic changes to the screen display as tasks move from one queue to another. In addition, if, for example the target code is being displayed in a window, that to will be updated to show the current execution location.

With the Queues displayed as in Figure 3, it is possible to select an individual task using the cursor keys and "zoom in" on that particular task. The effect of this is shown in Figure 5 where Task 1 is the selected task. Detailed information on the tasks registers and stack is displayed in a superimposed window in the format shown together with the task's current status and priority. When the task is selected and "zoomed" in this way, it is possible to modify the task's registers using the ISDT - the Edit Window is invoked using the Alt-F10 keystroke and looks as shown in Figure 6. The user can then select the register to be modified using the cursor keys and enter the new value required.

It should be noted that this is an example only - the number of different configurations available are limited only by the memory size of the IBM-PC® or compatible.

To conclude this section, it is worth pointing out again that the HI8 system is able to execute in real time while being debugged with the ISDT. This is possible only because the ISDT is fully integrated with the HI8 system. The ISDT is also sensitive to the multi-tasking, multi-object nature of the operating system - monitoring, manipulation and breaking on tasks is available for complete real time debugging.

Having looked at the current configuration of the ISDT, we will now go on to look at the way that it can be used in conjunction with the other HI8 support tools.

SYSTEM DEBUG USING THE HI8 SUPPORT TOOLS

In order to complete the picture of how the ISDT fits in with the existing support tools for HI8 and the H8 microcontrollers, we will examine a typical design and debug path. This is represented graphically in Figure 7.

The first step is for the system designer to create the application software according to the specification. In order to do this the chosen Editor can be called from within HIDE. When the file has been created, the Assembler or C Compiler can be called, again from within HIDE.

The second step is to integrate the HI8 kernel and selected Drivers. The Configurator is used to modify the HI8 Startup file and also to create the

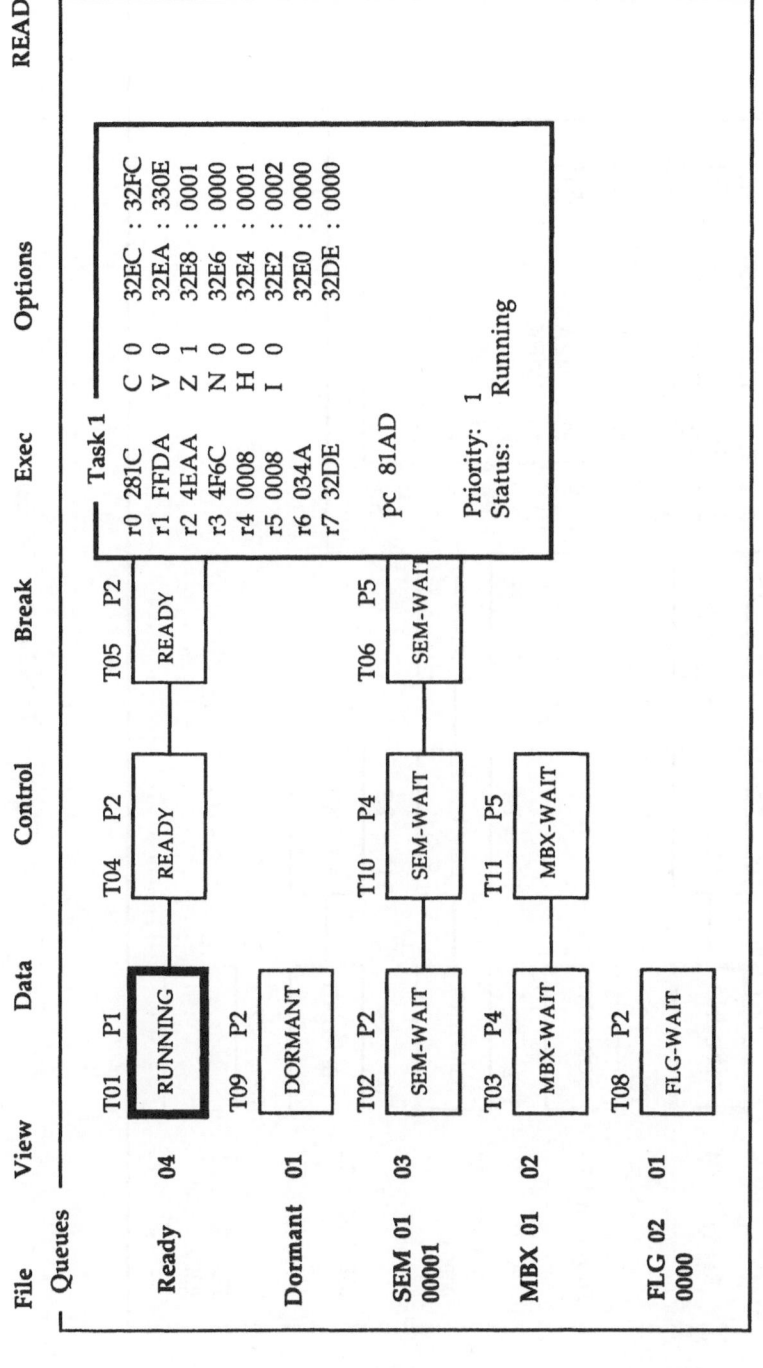

Figure 5 - Task Detail Viewing

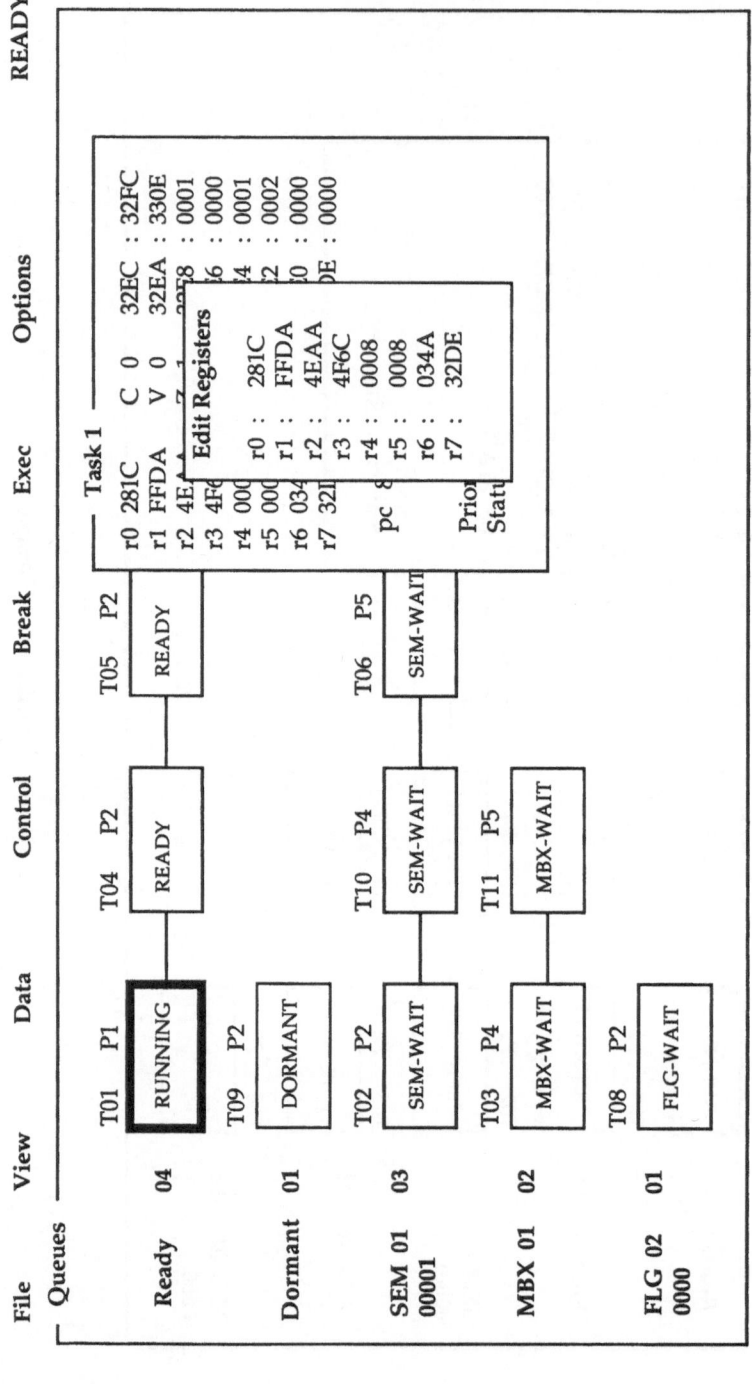

Figure 6 - Task Register Editing

Linker Subcommand and Make files necessary to build the system. This can all be done from within HIDE.

The third step is to debug the HI8 system that has been created. The ISDT is the tool to use for this task and it would be called from within HIDE to debug the HI8 system on the H8 target hardware. The designer can use the facilities of the ISDT that have already been described in order to achieve this.

The fourth step is either to celebrate a successful HI8 system design and debug or, more likely to go back to the first step and modify the source files which contain bugs! The cycle is then repeated as necessary.

The flow just described is obviously much simplified but should provide a clearer picture of how the ISDT fits in to the HI8 support tool structure within the common HIDE environment. As the development environment, HIDE provides a focus for all of the development and, with the introduction of the ISDT, and debugging of HI8 systems.

Having shown the current status of the support software, we will now go on to look at the way ahead for HI8 support in Europe.

FUTURE DEVELOPMENTS

In the same way that the HI8 Debugger offers a base for real time operating system debugging so the ISDT is at the stage of offering complete and stable HI8 system debugging support. There is, however always scope for improvement and enhancement, as there is for any particular piece of software.

The imminent introduction of HI8-3X provides an indication of the path which ISDT must follow in the future. In order to achieve the aim of the support tool being available at the same time that the software becomes available, EuroDESC and Hitachi are liasing closely so that the ISDT can be modified to provide full real time debugging for HI8-3X.

As part of this migration to HI8-3X, it seems appropriate to consider alternative target hardware. The EuroDESC Evaluation Boards are very capable pieces of hardware but they are still only an Evaluation Board. The next logical step from a hardware point of view will be up to an In Circuit Emulator (ICE). The benefit of this would be to introduce the possibility of debugging the HI8-3X system on the users own target hardware.

HI8-3X system debugging is possible using the Evaluation Board but there are limitations - for example, HI8-3X must usually co-exist in the same memory space on the board as the monitor software. The advantage of using the ISDT with an ICE is that the full HI8-3X system can be downloaded and run without any effective "hindrance" from the monitor software.

From the point of view of designing the software at the lowest level of the ISDT, the task is somewhat different. Communications between the IBM-PC® and the Evaluation Board differ significantly from communications with an ICE. The

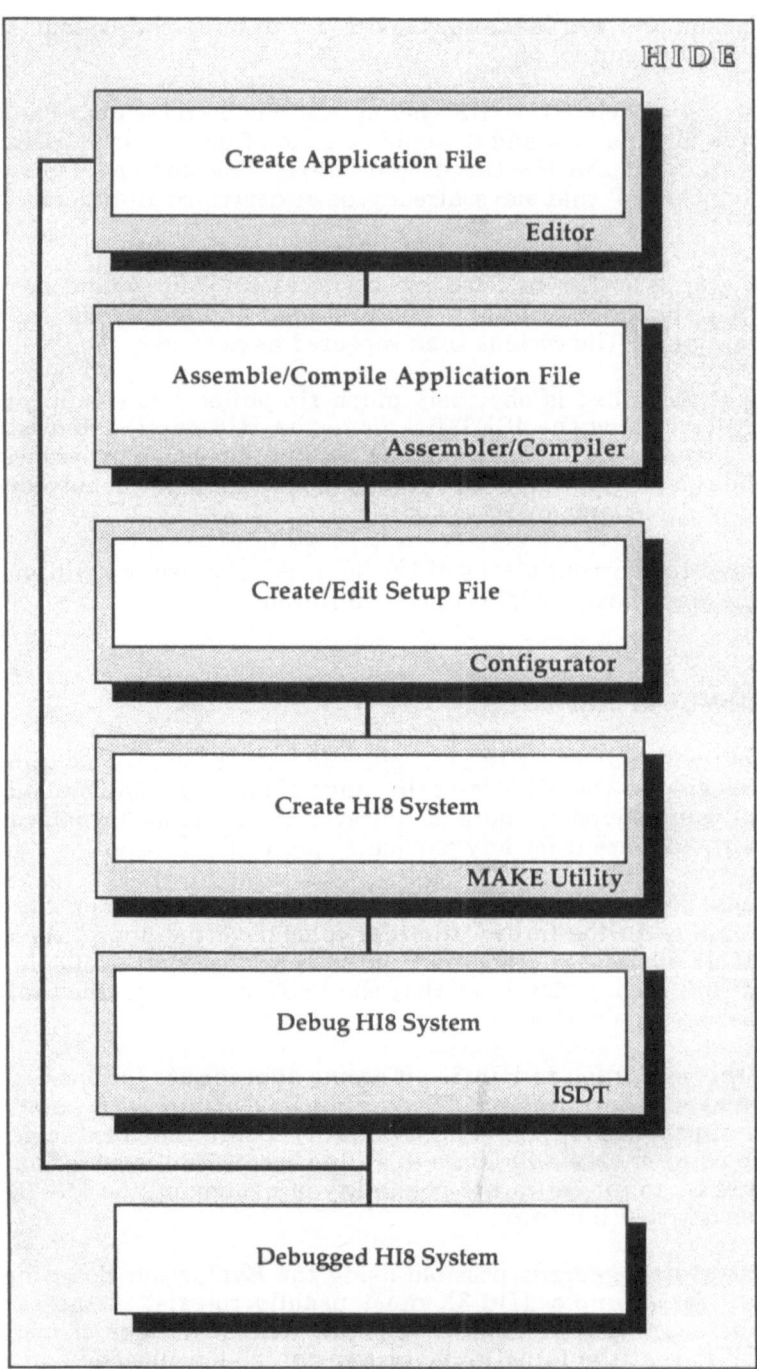

Figure 7 - HI8 System Development Flow

nature of the commands passing back and forth is different and the nature of the target hardware is radically different. The benefits are however enormous as has been indicated earlier.

CONCLUSION

That then is the ISDT - the Integrated System Debugging Tool. It is worthwhile to summarise in this conclusion some key points which have been described and discussed in the course of this paper.

EuroDESC have provided European customers with a development environment appropriate to the Hitachi implementations of the µITRON specification and based on a common development environment - the IBM-PC® and its compatibles.

The creation of the ISDT was triggered by the observation of the ways in which the HI8 Debugger could be improved and also by the necessity to provide a strong and consistent support strategy for HI8. Rather than simply add these functions to the Debugger however, it was decided to make the extra functions a part of an integrated debugging tool which visually fitted in with the existing EuroDESC HI8 support tools so that the existing user of HIDE can easily upgrade to the enhanced facilities offered by the ISDT.

It was important that this development was done with minimum disruption to the existing functions of HI8 and the HI8 Debugger and this has been achieved. The only modifications that were necessary were slight modifications to the existing C Interface Library for HI8 and minor changes to the existing communications software for the HIDE system.

It is worth emphasising the fact that, of necessity, this paper concentrates on HI8 but this does not exclude the use of the basic principles of HIDE and the ISDT on any operating system. As has been stated earlier in this paper, Hitachi are currently working on HI8-3X and this will be the next target for the enhancement of the exisiting version of the ISDT.

Setting aside the Hitachi-specific applications, most embedded controller oriented real time operating system would benefit from the implementation of an effective development environment (like HIDE) which gives easy access to the software support tools (C Compiler, Assembler, Linker, etc.), has a powerful Make utility and also a Configurator which fully automates the often laborious process of building a system.

The development environment should offer access to the target hardware. Arguably the most important part of the support software for a real time operating system is however the provision of a real time operating system Debugger. What has happened with the ISDT is that the features of the existing HI8 Debugger has been enhanced and integrated with the existing support software to offer full system debugging with the capability of gaining detailed information on the status of the operating system without actually disrupting it - obviously crucial in any real time system.

The IBM-PC® and its compatibles are, as has already been stated, widely used within Europe and so represent a good platform for the HI8 support tools. This is not however regarded as being the only potential platform. Work must be carried out to investigate migration of the HI8 support tools into the kind of environment described in the BTRON specification so that the kind of consistency of support tools offered already on the IBM-PC® can be expanded into the general sphere of the TRON Project.

Finally, the question will be asked - what is new about the ISDT, and how does it compare with the debugging facilities offered by other designers of Real Time Operating Systems? The debugging of a Real Time Operating System requires facilities which are likely to be similar irrespective of the Operating System. Visual presentation may vary but functionality will be along the same lines - users will wish to set breakpoints, access memory, manipulate tasks and system objects and so on. What is new about ISDT is that it is addressing the debugging requirements for the **European** user of the HI8 Real Time Operating System and as such opens up a whole new market area for the introduction of the TRON Project in general and Hitachi's implementation of the µITRON Specification in particular.

ACKNOWLEDGEMENTS

Thanks are due to the following:-

Dr.K.Sakamura of the Department of Information Science, Faculty of Science, The University of Tokyo for his work on the TRON Project

Mr.H.Takeyama, Mr.T.Shimizu and the HI8-3X design and development team at Hitachi Limited, Tokyo, Japan for their good support of EuroDESC in the development of the HI8 support tools

Cambridge Beacon Limited - developers of the Integrated System Debugging Tool for their design expertise and ideas

---

VAX/VMS is a trademark of the Digital Equipment Corporation
MS-DOS is a trademark of the Microsoft Corporation
IBM-PC is trademark of IBM

REFERENCES

1. EuroDESC - HIDE Users Manual

2. EuroDESC - ISDT Users Manual

3. Hitachi Limited - H8 Programming Manual

4. Hitachi Limited - HI8 User's Manual

5. Sakamura K - µITRON, Vol. 1 No. 1, TRON Study Group, Japan

6. Sakamura K - ITRON Real-Time Operating System, Vol. 3, No. 5, J.Robotics Soc.   Japan

7. Sakamura K - (April 8-14 1988) The TRON Project, IEEE Micro

8. Sakamura K - ITRON Real-Time Operating System, Operating System Study Group, Japan

9. Takeyama H, Shimizu T, Kobayakawa M (1988) - HI8: A Realtime Operating System with µITRON Specifications for the H8 (K.Sakamura Ed. TRON Project)

David Wallace is the Applications Engineering Manager of the European Design and Engineering Support Centre of Hitachi Europe Limited. He graduated from Bath University in 1977 with an Honours Degree (B.Sc.) in Physics with Physical Electronics.

His career since graduating has included 4 years with Marconi Avionics as a Design Engineer working on Airborne Radar, 2 years with Multitone PLC designing Radio Paging Systems and 1 year with Acorn Computers designing peripherals for Home Computers.

He has been with Hitachi since February 1985.

As Manager of Applications Engineering, he is responsible for the initiation and co-ordination with Hitachi Europe of applications projects which cover the whole of the Hitachi electronic components product range.

The above author may be reached at: Hitachi Europe Limited, Whitebrook Park, Lower Cookham Road, Maidenhead, Berkshire, SL6 8YA, United Kingdom.

HI8-3X: A μITRON-Specification Realtime Operating System for H8/300 Series Microcontrollers

Manabu Kobayakawa, Toshiaki Nagasawa, Tsuyoshi Shimizu, Hiroshi Takeyama

Microcomputer System Design Department
Semiconductor Development & Design Center, Hitachi, Ltd.

ABSTRACT

An embedded operating system conforming to the μITRON specification has been implemented for the Hitachi H8/300 Series of 8-bit microcontrollers. The operating system is compact enough to be widely applicable in small-scale control systems, such as those found in consumer products. The OS work area is minimized by stack sharing and by selection of task context registers.

KEYWORDS: ITRON specification, μITRON specification, microcontroller

INTRODUCTION

For its original series of microprocessors and microcontrollers, Hitachi is currently developing operating systems conforming to the ITRON specification[1, 2]. For the H32/200 and H32/100 chips, which conform to the TRON specification[3], Hitachi has already developed the HI32-200[4] and HI32-100 operating systems. For its H8/500 16-bit microcontroller series, Hitachi has developed two operating systems conforming to the μITRON specification[5, 6]: HI8[7, 8] and HI8-EX.

Two more operating systems are currently under development: HI32-300, an operating system conforming to the ITRON2 specification for the H32/300, which is the high-end device in the H32 family at present; and HI8-3X, an operating system for the H8/300 series of 8-bit microcontrollers.

1 H8/300 SERIES

The H8/300 series of microcontrollers has an original Hitachi architecture based on an 8-bit CPU core. These microcontrollers are designed for applications ranging from smart cards to control of consumer equipment.

1.1 H8/300 Series Features

The H8/300 Series can be briefly characterized as follows.

1) General-register architecture

The CPU has eight 16-bit general registers, which can also be used as sixteen 8-bit general registers.

2) High speed

The maximum system clock frequency is 10 MHz. The RISC-like instruction set is tailored for high-speed operation and includes 57 basic instructions, all of which are 2 or 4 bytes in length.

— 8- and 16-bit register-register operations: 0.2 µs

— 8 × 8-bit multiply: 1.4 µs

— 16 ÷ 8-bit divide: 1.4 µs

3) Variety of products

The H8/300 CPU core has been developed into a series of ASIC microcontrollers that can be easily designed into application systems. Table 1 lists the H8/300 line-up. Additional models are available with different amounts of on-chip ROM and RAM.

Table 1   H8/300 Series Lineup

On-Chip Features	H8/330	H8/350	H8/325	H8/310[Note]
ROM	16 kbytes	32 kbytes	32 kbytes	10 kbytes
RAM	512 bytes	512 bytes	1 kbyte	256 bytes
Timers	5 channels	11 channels	3 channels	—
Serial interface	1 channel	2 channels	2 channels	—
A/D converter	8 channels	16 channels	—	—
I/O ports	9 ports	9 ports	7 ports	1 port
External interrupt lines	9	9	4	—
On-chip interrupt sources	19	47	17	—
Other features	DPRAM			8-kbyte EEPROM ROM data security

Note: Designed for smart cards.

1.2 Overview of H8/300 Functions

(a) Register Configuration

Fig. 1 shows the H8/300 register configuration.

The CPU has sixteen 8-bit general registers (R0H and R0L to R7H and R7L). As control registers there is a 16-bit program counter (PC) and 8-bit condition code register (CCR).

The general registers can be used as data registers and address registers without distinction. They can also be used as eight 16-bit registers (R0 to R7).

The condition code register includes an interrupt mask (I) bit, H, N, Z, V, and C bits indicating instruction result status, and two user bits. HI8-3X employs the two user bits for system control, using one bit to distinguish between the task and task-independent portions, and the other bit to indicate task switching requests.

(b) Memory Map

The memory map differs for each chip in the series, depending on the size and location of the on-chip ROM and RAM. Fig. 2 shows the memory map of the H8/330. The modes are selected by hardware according to inputs at the mode pins (MD0 and MD1).

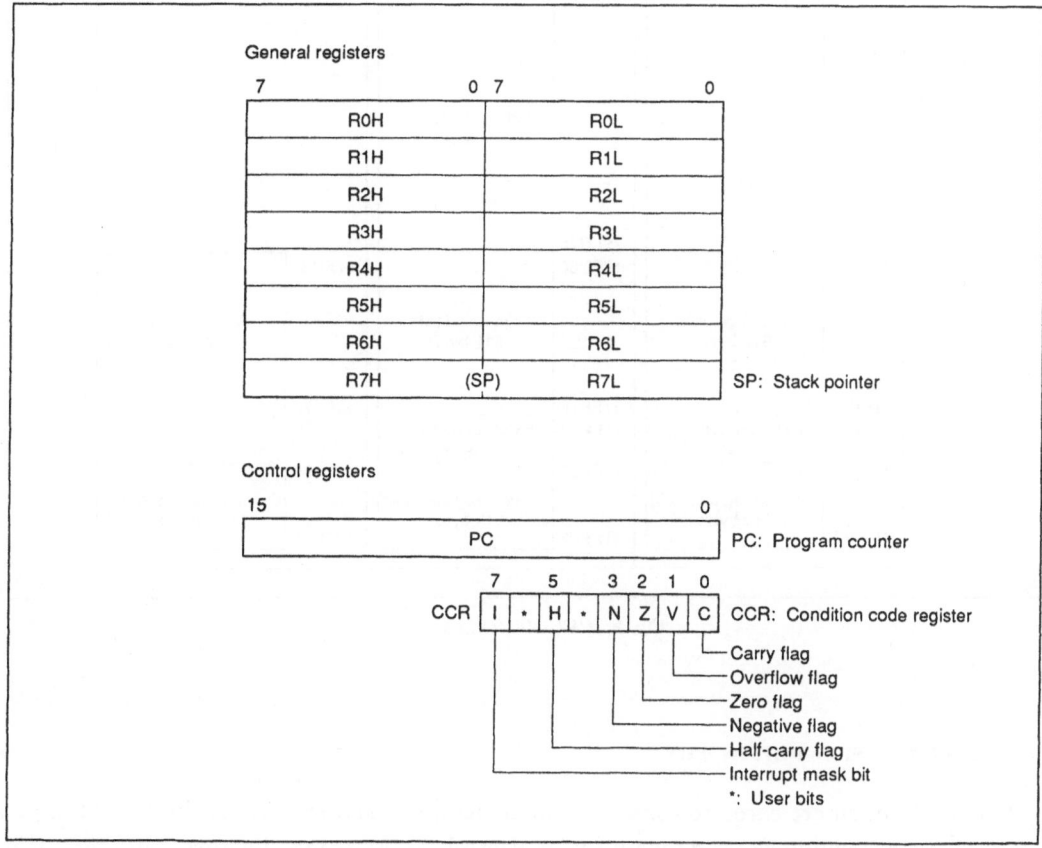

Fig. 1   H8/300 Series Register Configuration

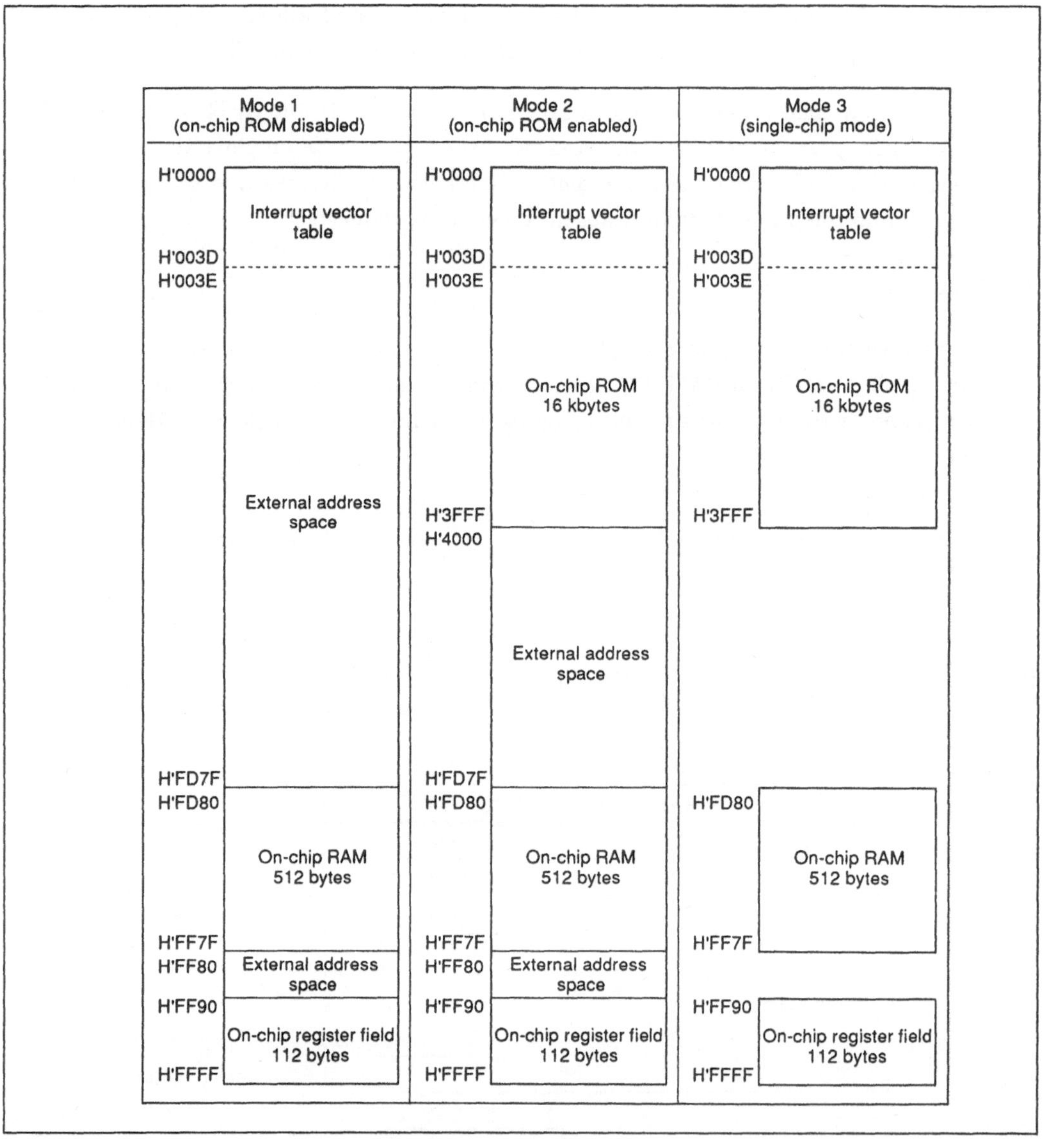

Mode 1 (on-chip ROM disabled)	Mode 2 (on-chip ROM enabled)	Mode 3 (single-chip mode)
H'0000 Interrupt vector table	H'0000 Interrupt vector table	H'0000 Interrupt vector table
H'003D H'003E	H'003D H'003E	H'003D H'003E
External address space	On-chip ROM 16 kbytes	On-chip ROM 16 kbytes
	H'3FFF H'4000	H'3FFF
	External address space	
H'FD7F H'FD80 On-chip RAM 512 bytes	H'FD7F H'FD80 On-chip RAM 512 bytes	H'FD80 On-chip RAM 512 bytes
H'FF7F H'FF80 External address space	H'FF7F H'FF80 External address space	H'FF7F
H'FF90 On-chip register field 112 bytes	H'FF90 On-chip register field 112 bytes	H'FF90 On-chip register field 112 bytes
H'FFFF	H'FFFF	H'FFFF

Fig. 2   H8/330 Memory Map

2   HI8-3X Design Philosophy

Ranging from smart cards to consumer appliances, the applications of the H8/300 Series include fields usually covered by 4-bit microcontrollers. Most manufacturers in these fields have been creating systems without using operating-system concepts, or have developed their own monitor programs. In these fields, accordingly, a standard operating system employing traditional concepts would not be readily accepted.

The design philosophy of HI8-3X is summarized below.

1) HI8-3X is designed to completely satisfy the standard µITRON specification. It should be noted that the µITRON specification is highly adaptable.

2) HI8-3X is designed for high-speed operation.

The traditional requirements of a realtime operating system are high processing speed and guaranteed processing time. Recently it has become common to seek guaranteed constant processing times that are unaffected by the system environment, or to guarantee a worst-case processing time. Hitachi operating systems that conform to the 16- and 32-bit ITRON specifications are designed to minimize the worst-case processing time.

In the fields at which the H8/300 Series is targeted, however, guaranteeing these values is less important than wringing extra speed out of a small-scale system while minimizing memory usage. HI8-3X is designed to attain high processing speeds in systems with about five to ten tasks.

3) Minimal memory usage

Most applications of the H8/300 Series are single-chip applications in which the operating system must share the on-chip ROM and RAM with application software. An attempt was therefore made to minimize the OS overhead: the size of the OS program code and its work areas. Among the work areas, a particular effort was made to minimize the size of the task stack areas.

3 HI8-3X FUNCTIONS

HI8-3X is aimed at level 2 of the µITRON specification and supports the system calls listed in table 2. These include level 2 of the µITRON specification completely. The functions of HI8-3X are summarized below.

3.1 TASK MANAGEMENT

Fig. 3 shows the task state transitions supported by HI8-3X. The minimum configurations support three states: run, ready, and wait; or dormant, ready, and run. The maximum configuration supports four states: run, ready, wait, and dormant. Either dormant or ready can be selected as the initial task state.

A maximum of 31 tasks can be managed. Task priorities of −1 and 1 to 31 can be assigned.

A task's priority is basically fixed, but a designated section of a task can be dynamically assigned the highest priority of −1 (by the chg_pri system call) in order to guarantee its execution time.

Table 2   HI8-3X System Calls

Name	Function
Task management	
sta_tsk	Start task
ista_tsk	Start task (for task-independent portion)
ext_tsk	Exit task
chg_pri	Change task priority
get_tid	Get task ID number
tsk_sts	Get task status
Task-dependent synchronization	
slp_tsk	Sleep task
wai_tsk	Wait for wakeup task
wup_tsk	Wakeup task
iwup_tsk	Wakeup task (for task-independent portion)
can-wup	Cancel wakeup task
Synchronization and communication	
set_flg	Set event flag (word)
iset_flg	Set event flag (word) (for task-independent portion)
clr_flg	Clear event flag (word)
wai_flg	Wait event flag (word)
pol_flg	Poll event flag (word)
flg_sts	Get event flag status (word)
sig_sem	Signal semaphore
isig_sem	Signal semaphore (for task-independent portion)
wai_sem	Wait on semaphore
preq_sem	Poll and request semaphore
sem_sts	Get semaphore status
snd_msg	Send message to mailbox
isnd_msg	Send message to mailbox (for task-independent portion)
rcv_msg	Receive message from mailbox
prcv_msg	Poll and receive message from mailbox
mbx_sts	Get mailbox status
Timer management	
set_tim	Set time
get_tim	Get time
Interrupt management	
chg_ims	Change interrupt imask
ret_int	Return from interrupt handler
ret_wup	Return and wakeup task
System management	
get_ver	Get version number

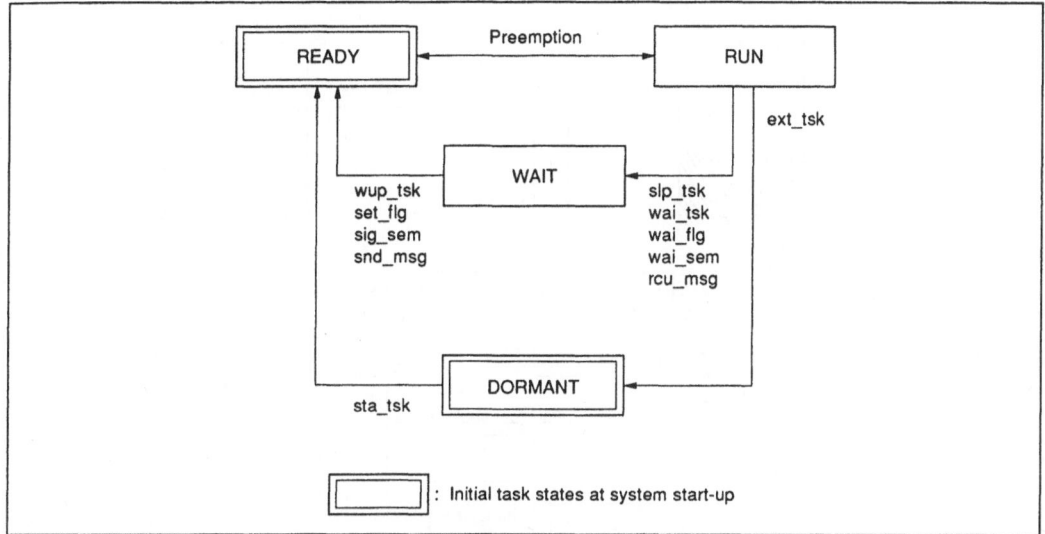

Fig. 3   HI8-3X Task State Transitions

3.2 SYNCHRONIZATION AND COMMUNICATION BETWEEN TASKS

Three functions are supported: eventflags, semaphores, and mailboxes. There can be a maximum of 31 objects of each type.

To take advantage of the performance of the H8/300, 8-bit eventflags are used, and AND or OR operations can be performed on the 8 bits. Semaphores and mailboxes support the functions described in the µITRON specification.

3.3 INTERRUPT HANDLING

One of the features of the H8/300 Series is its powerful interrupt-handling functions. The interrupt sources include both external signal lines (IRQ0 to IRQn) and sources in the on-chip supporting modules. The number of sources varies depending on the particular chip in the series. Fig. 4 shows the hardware response to an interrupt. The interrupts are individually vectored. In HI8-3X the addresses of the user-coded interrupt handlers are written directly in the interrupt vector table, so when an interrupt occurs it can be served quickly, without OS overhead, and without having to discriminate between interrupt sources.

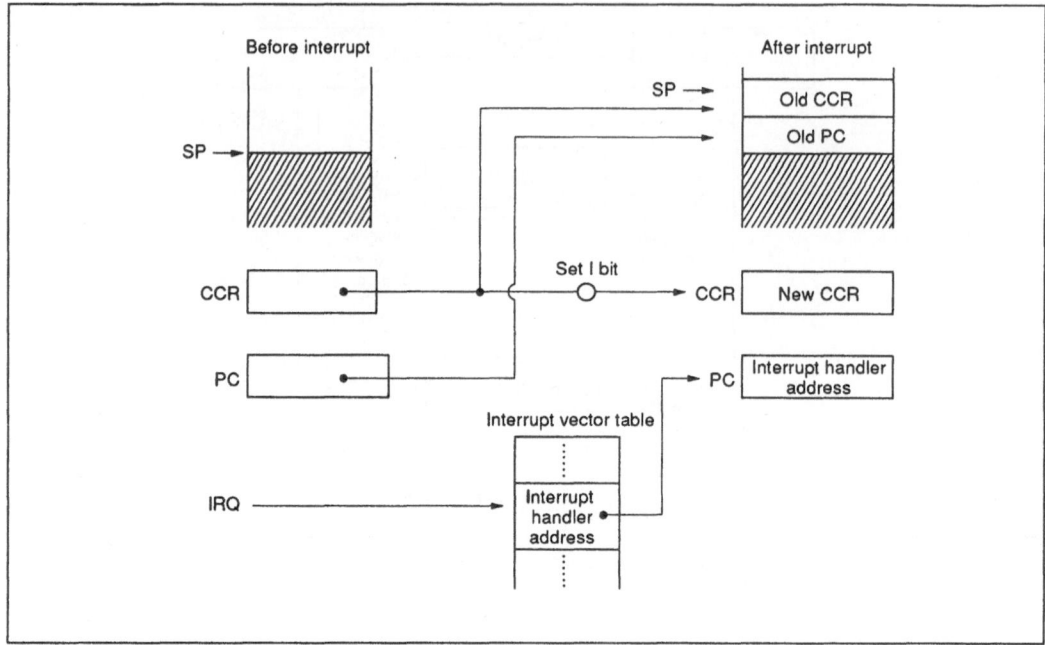

Fig. 4   H8/300 Interrupt Response

3.4 CONFIGURING THE OPERATING SYSTEM

The system calls are supplied in subroutine format. The operating system is configured automatically by using a linkage editor to link application programs with the OS subroutine library. Accordingly, only system calls actually used by the application programs are linked. Each system call is supplied in two forms: with and without parameter checking.

4   MINIMIZATION OF WORK AREAS

The greatest problem in using an operating system in a single-chip or other application with extremely limited RAM is to avoid running out of work space. Work areas used by the operating system include system-wide variables, control tables for managing objects, and stack areas for saving task contexts. In conventional embedded applications not employing an operating system, processes are carried out by subroutines. When an operating system is introduced these processes become tasks, requiring special areas for saving registers.

The H8/300 Series has sixteen 8-bit registers, one program counter, and one condition code register (CCR). The 20 bytes required to stack these registers become a major burden in systems with only 512 or 1024 bytes of on-chip RAM.

To lighten this burden, HI8-3X allows the selection of task context registers and sharing of stack areas.

4.1 SELECTION OF TASK CONTEXT REGISTERS

Conventional operating systems normally treat all CPU registers as part of a task's hardware context. This is a natural requirement when application programs are coded in high-level languages. When application programs are coded in assembly language, however, it is not necessary to include all the general registers in the hardware context.

In HI8-3X, whether the hardware context of a task includes all general registers or only designated registers can be specified when the system is configured. Registers not included in the task context are saved and restored as necessary during chip kernel processing. These registers can accordingly be shared with other tasks and interrupt handlers. (See fig. 5.) Registers not included in a task's context can be shared with other tasks and interrupt handlers. (See fig. 5.)

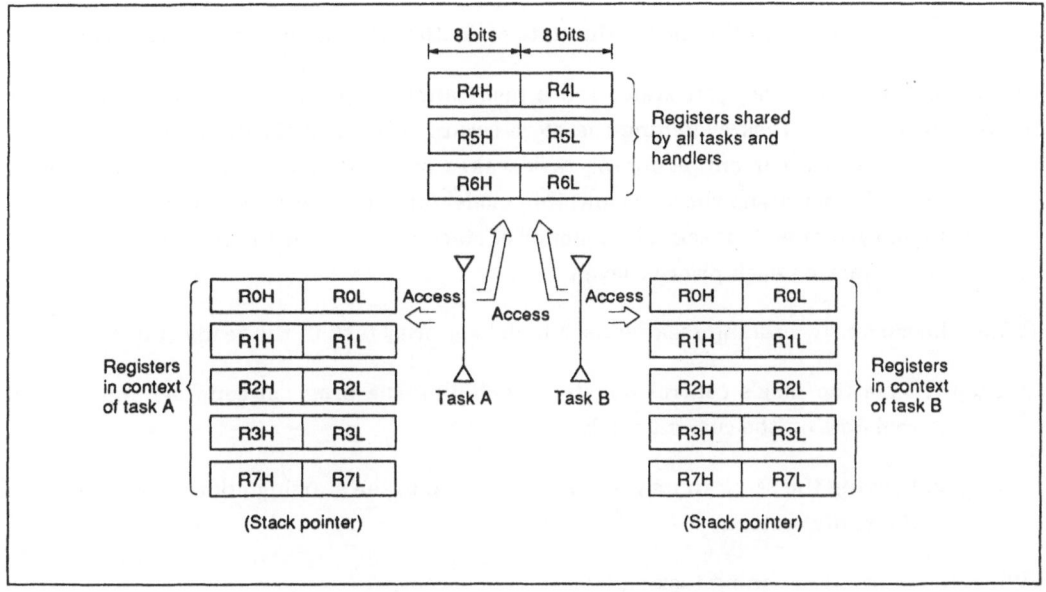

Fig. 5   Example of Selection of Registers in Task Context

4.2 SHARING OF STACK AREAS

Even small-scale 8-bit microcomputer systems consist of many elements. A system in a consumer appliance, for example, may receive sensor inputs, control a stepping motor, and switch output signal lines on and off. It is typical for tasks that must operate in real time to be implemented by small programs. Conversely, larger-scale tasks, such as controlling a display, do not generally have severe realtime requirements. The synchronization needs of small, high-priority tasks can usually be met by the slp_tsk and wup_tsk system calls of the μITRON specification. A study was made of several consumer applications of the type described above to derive a simplified multitasking OS model using minimal stack space. This model was then adapted to the μITRON specification.

(a) Simplified Multitasking OS Model

The following model shows one way to minimize stack space.

(Simplified Multitasking OS Model)

   − Three task states: dormant, run, ready

   − Task execution is scheduled according to static priorities. Tasks with the same priority are scheduled on a first-in-first-out basis.

   − The only system call that alters the state of another task is the wakeup-task call.

In this model there is no wait state, and a task cannot request priority changes or force another task to end. Task switching therefore occurs only when (1) the currently-running task ends, or (2) the currently-running task wakes up another task with higher priority. Using the stack operations shown below, this model operating system can be implemented with a single system-wide stack. The amount of stack space needed is the sum of the sizes of the largest stack on each priority level.

(When the currently-running task places a higher-priority task in the ready state)

Step 1. Save the task's control registers (including the program counter) and general registers on the current stack.

Step 2. Leaving the stack in its present state, jump to the starting address of the task in the ready state.

(When the currently-running task ends)

Step 1. Restore general registers and control registers (including the program counter) from the current stack.

(b)   Implementation of the model on the μITRON specification

We next considered how to implement this stack-efficient model within the bounds of the μITRON specification. HI8-3X was developed by adding the functions listed below.

−   The stack area for each task is specified in advance, when the system is configured. The same area can be specified for two or more tasks (stack sharing).

−   When a task is started, the task goes into a virtual wait state if its stack is shared and is currently in use by another task. When a task having a shared stack ends, the shared stack is assigned to a task that was waiting to use it. Assignment is on a first-in-first-out basis.

The wait state entered when a stack is unavailable is referred to as 'virtual' because it is reached without passing through the ready and run states. This is not strictly in accordance with the state transitions of the μITRON specification. No problems occur, however, if application programs regard this wait state as having been entered via the ready and run states.

HI8-3X does not allow a task to be forcibly released from a wait state (there is no rel_wai system call). Further functions would have to be added to support the rel_wai system call.

−   When a task using a shared stack ends, the stack is assigned to a task that was waiting to get it. The assignment is made on a first-in-first-out basis, like the semaphore and mailbox assignments of the μITRON specification.

−   The ista_tsk system call was introduced to enable an interrupt handler to request the start of a task with a shared stack.

In an operating system conforming to the μITRON specification with these additional functions, scheduling equivalent to the simplified model can be implemented by having tasks on the same priority level share the same stack, and using the sta_tsk and ext_tsk system calls to control these tasks. The amount of memory that must be reserved for stack usage is the sum of the maximum stack sizes of the tasks on each priority level, the same as the stack size in the simplified model.

The simplified model does not permit stack waiting, but if this feature\ is added, tasks that share the same stack can still avail themselves of the synchronization and communication functions of the μITRON specification.

The addition of this stack sharing function enables the task concept of the μITRON specification to be preserved while reducing the system stack to the size given by the simplified model. Stack sharing is especially effective in single-chip applications.

To minimize HI8-3X work space, task execution priorities are fixed and a task's ID number is used as its priority. This precludes assignment of the same priority to two or more tasks, but the same effect can be achieved by having the tasks share the same stack.

Fig. 6 shows an example of stack assignments to tasks in an HI8-3X application. Tasks tid1 to tid10 are small tasks, controlled only by the sta_tsk and ext_tsk system calls. Tasks tid1 to tid3 have identical priority and share stack S2. Similarly, tasks tid4 to tid6 have identical priority and share stack S3, while tasks tid7 to tid9 have identical priority and share stack S4. Tasks tid1 and tid11 use the task-dependent synchronization functions of the μITRON specification, and the synchronization and communication functions, so these tasks have their own stacks.

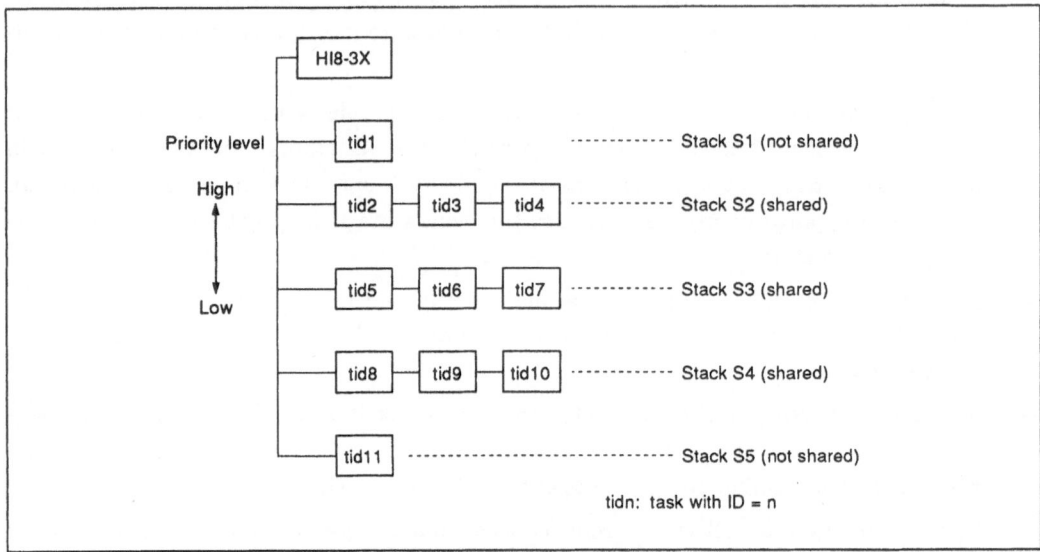

Fig. 6   Example of Task Configuration in HI8-3X Application

4.3 WORK AREA SIZE

Table 3 lists the size of the control tables.

Table 3   Size of Object Control Tables

Object	Table Size
Task	4 bytes
Event flag	2 bytes
Semaphore	2 bytes
Mailbox	4 bytes
Shared stack	2 bytes

In an environment in which tasks use registers R0 to R3 and R7 (the stack pointer), HI8-3X requires only 12 bytes to save the context of each task. The context consists of the program counter, condition code register (CCR), and registers R0 to R3.

The size of the OS stack and system-wide variable area is 16 bytes.

For the system with 11 tasks shown in fig. 6, if there are two event flags, the HI8-3X memory overhead (in RAM) is

$$(11 \times 4) + (5 \times 12) + (3 \times 2) + \quad (2 \times 2) + \quad 16 = 130 \text{ bytes}$$

| Tasks | Stacks | Shared stacks | Event flags | OS stack |

System-wide variables

which means that even a chip with only 512 bytes of RAM has ample room to use HI8-3X.

Concerning two critical parameters in realtime operation, it appears feasible to hold the interrupt mask time in the operating system to 10 µs in the worst case, and the total time for task switching by the wup_tsk system call to 20 to 30 µs, again in the worst case.

5 ON-LINE DEBUG FUNCTIONS

A conventional on-line debugger executes as a task under the operating system, using a console controlled by the operating system itself. This type of debugging on an in-circuit console is not relevant to most H8/300 applications, however, because of the limited RAM available and the need for a console port. HI8-3X therefore supports task execution control and other on-line debugging functions from the console of an in-circuit emulator, rather than from an in-circuit console.

6 CONCLUSION

An operating system conforming to the µITRON specification has been implemented for the H8/300 series of 8-bit single-chip microcomputers. The implementation is designed for small-scale H8/300 application systems. Minimization of OS work areas makes HI8-3X fully usable in single-chip systems with 512 bytes or 1 kbyte of on-chip RAM. Concerning two critical parameters in realtime operation, it appears feasible to hold the interrupt mask time in the operating system to 10 µs or less in the worst case, and the total time for task switching by the wup_tsk system call to 20 to 30 µs in the worst case (in a system with 10 tasks).

HI8-3X will soon be made commercially available.

The authors would like to express their gratitude to Dr. Ken Sakamura of the Department of Information Science, Faculty of Science, The University of Tokyo for his guidance in the development of HI8-3X, and to TRON Association members for their cooperation in standardizing the external specifications.

REFERENCES

1) Ken Sakamura, TRON Project 1987, Springer-Verlag, 1987

2) Ken Sakamura (Ed.), Introduction to ITRON, Iwanami Shoten, 1988

3) ITRON2 Specification, TRON Association, 1990

4) Yamada et al., "HI32: An ITRON-Specification Operating System for the H32/200," TRON Project 1989, Springer-Verlag, pp. 77 – 97

5) μITRON Specification, TRON Association, 1990

6) Ken Sakamura, "μITRON Design Directions," TRON Study Group, TRON Assoc., Vol. 1, No. 1, June 1988, pp. 1 - 17 (in Japanese)

7) Takeyama et al., "HI8: A Realtime Operating System with μITRON Specification for the H8/500 Series," TRON Project 1988, Springer-Verlag, pp. 35-54

8) Takeyama et al., "Design Concept and Implementation of μITRON Specification for the H8/500 Series," Compcon Spring '89, IEEE Computer Society Press, February 1989, pp. 48 – 53

M. Kobayakawa joined Hitachi, Ltd. in 1985 and is now an engineer in the Microcomputer System Engineering Dept. at the Semiconductor Design & Development Center of Hitachi's Semiconductor Division. He is currently engaged in research and development of realtime operation systems for microcomputers. He was graduated from Hitachi Keihin Technical college in 1988.

T. Nagasawa joined Hitachi, Ltd. in 1989 and is now an engineer in the Microcomputer System Engineering Dept. at the Semiconductor Design & Development Center of Hitachi's Semiconductor Division. He is currently engaged in research and development of realtime operating systems for microcomputers. He received his BA in mathematics from Tokyo Denki University in 1989.

T. Shimizu joined Hitachi, Ltd. in 1978 and now an engineer in the Microcomputer System Engineering Dept. at the Semiconductor Design & Development Center of Hitachi's Semiconductor Division. He is currently engaged in research and development of realtime operating systems for microcomputers. He received his BA in informatics from the University of Osaka in 1976 and his master's degree from the same school in 1978.

H. Takeyama joined Hitachi, Ltd. in 1969 and is now a senior engineer in the Microcomputer System Engineering Dept. at the semiconductor Design & Development Center of Hitachi's Semiconductor Division. Since 1988 he has participated in research and development of realtime operating systems for microcomputers and in-circuit emulation software, and in product planning for microcomputer support tools. He received his BA electronic engineering from Fukuoka Institute of Technology in 1969.

Above authors may be reached at: Semiconductor Design & Development Center, Hitachi, Ltd., 5-20-1, Jousuihon-cho Kodaira, Tokyo 187 Japan.

Chapter 2: BTRON

Design Policy of the Operating System Based on the BTRON2 Specification

Ken Sakamura

Department of Information Science, Faculty of Science, University of Tokyo

ABSTRACT

BTRON2 specification for operating systems for workstations is a logical successor to an earlier BTRON1 specification. The BTRON2 specification has clarified some internal structures of the OS and has added functions assuming the existence of ample hardware resources on personal computers in the immediate future. BTRON2 specification calls for a layered modular structure to enhance the maintainability, support for distributed architecture, and extensibility. Design philosophy and characteristics of BTRON2 specifications are detailed in this paper.

Keywords: Uniformity, Transparency, Extensibility, Distributed Environment, Real/Virtual object model, BTRON2 Specification.

1. INTRODUCTION

The original objective of the BTRON subproject was to provide a uniform human-machine interface and the data compatibility using portable interchange format. However, for supporting application program portability, we need to offer standards for programming interface to OS services. The BTRON1 specification was proposed as such a standard.

BTRON1 specification was designed with a very limited hardware in mind. For example, it didn't assume the existence of large capacity hard disk storage and 16-bit CPU machine can run the OS based on BTRON1. However, this also mean that BTRON1-based OS can't really take advantage of the hardware resources on a powerful computer system based on TRON-specification VLSI CPU, large main memory, and large hard disk drives. Of course, the decreasing price and the increasing performance of hardware devices make it possible to use advanced hardware devices which were too expensive when the BTRON1 specification was designed.

BTRON2 specification is a new specification which is a successor to BTRON1. Assuming the availability of more hardware resources, BTRON2 use higher level of abstraction. Internal structure of the operating systems have a hierarchical structure and the internal structure now consist of a number of modules.

In the following, the design policy of the BTRON2 specification for operating systems is discussed.

2. DESIGN OBJECTIVES.

Design objectives of the BTRON2 specification are described.

2.1 Uniformity

BTRON2 specification must offer a uniform programming model which is the basis for the uniform human-machine interface. Although BTRON1 specification did offer such a model, it is important to offer such a uniform programming model even in the presence of more advanced and richer hardware resources; the higher level of virtualization and the support of distributed environment is important in BTRON2. BTRON2 offers resource management using real/virtual object data model, the classification of operations on resources, system calls to support such operations, and uniform handling of event-related operations.

(a) Real/Virtual Data Model.

In BTRON2, the resources within the operating systems are now handled from the viewpoint of real/virtual data model. This has made it possible to offer cleaner view of resources and has made it easier to understand the system operation. The abstract programming model of the system resources is now viewed as real object. The pointer to the real object is a virtual object. Virtual object can have structure and/or attribute.

(b) Uniform classification of operations

In BTRON2, we have standardized on the access method of the resources and thus obtained higher uniformity. Programs open a resource and then obtain a temporary name called access key. Access key speeds up the subsequent access. This access key identifies the original resource in every operation. When the access is finished access key is closed. This applies to all types of resources and the training should be now easy. If programmers need a complex operation where a series of operations must be handled efficiently, the specification does NOT prohibit the offering of such complex operations.

(c) System calls for operations

Generally speaking, system calls were usually designed in ad-hoc manner based the resources and the operations they perform. In the BTRON2, the system calls have been classified according the type of operations they perform in order to bring uniformity.

In the case of ITRON, there was not much problem since the hardware resources in ITRON-based systems were limited. However, in BTRON2 environment, we should expect the addition of new resources in the years ahead. For example, who expected addition of window systems as standard part of computer systems 10 years ago?

We have decided to offer generic system calls by classifying the operations and support such operations by system calls. Hence, there are nos special system calls applicable to only a limited set of hardware resources.

(d) Uniform handling of event-related operation.

It has now become possible to handle generation of events, or notification of events about all resources in an uniform manner.

In conventional systems, a limited number of special events such as the termination of a process, and window events existed and the computer system can generate and notify such events to programs. However, they lacked the uniform handling of all event from the view point of BTRON2 designers. So we have decided to incorporate event-handling capability to real-objects.

Now it is possible to generate notification upon the status change of a real object, or we can request a real object to generate an event.

2.2 Transparency

BTRON2 designers had to address the problem of distributed environment head on. Distributed environment here means an environment in which multiple number of physically distributed processing nodes can be viewed and handled as one integrated computer system. Distributed environment is more sophisticated than the environment which forces the users to recognize the physical distribution of nodes.

Among the different and varied meanings to attached the word "transparency" in the distributed environment, BTRON2 uses two important ones; one is the access transparency and the other is location transparency.

(a) Access Transparency

In order to run a program without knowing where it runs, namely on local node or on remote node, we need access transparency. This is the most fundamental requirement for a distributed system. Without access transparency, we can't build a distributed environment.

(b) Location Transparency

It is desirable that the users don't have to know the physical location of shared resources; location transparency.

However, if we need to know the position or to express the position explicitly, we need a method to do so. For example, we need to be able to tell where a removable diskette drive is.

Or, we don't want a remote printer in an next building suddenly printing our print job just because the remote printer is idle at the moment while the local printer is busy at the moment. Forcing location transparency is a bad idea.

Anyway, we classy the names used in BTRON2-based systems and incorporated the features to support location transparency for them. We discuss more about "name" later.

2.3 Extensibility

We must have functional extensibility and system extensibility. Functional extensibility here means the addition of new functionalities into internal of systems such as kernel enhancement. System extensibility here means the addition of new hardware and other devices to a distributed environment.

(a) Functional extensibility.

It is desirable to be able to incorporate new functions to support applications of the future although BTRON already has functions to support important applications of today and the immediate future. The importance of the functional extensibility is easily seen if you consider the new addition of window system and pointing device support into computer systems in the last several years.

In order to make it easy to add functions into systems, we have divided the kernel into three layers and defined the interface between them. The three layers are; inner kernel, outer kernel and shell. Also, the resources are now managed by independent managers.

The newly introduced hierarchy has made it possible to isolate the changes in one layer from others. The independent resource managers now make it possible to localize the management of resources and will make it easy to incorporate new functions.

(b) System Extensibility.

In conventional system, it is a time consuming job to introduce a new processing node into existing computing networks. Usually the configuration management necessitated by such an introduction is a tedious and error-prone. It is important to make it easy to introduce new machines into computer networks in the future because the number of nodes will become very large.

In BTRON2, We specify that resources are automatically recognized by the network management software and the addition/deletion of machines shall cause no problem. These features are available irrespective of the size of the network.

2.4 Security, Protection

It is important to offer security in a distributed environment. We have to prevent illegal data access by errors, but we must be ready for malicious tampering of data. We incorporate more access management in BTRON2 to add to the protection.

(a) More Powerful access control list

We offer a general access control list which is more powerful than access control based on owner, group, access level and password. This should be useful in distributed environment.

(b) Duplication of access key

It is possible to duplicate an access key and transfer it. The idea is similar to capability accessing. Usually inaccessible real object can let a program access it by giving out an access key to itself.

This function makes easy to offer access control at a detailed level and will be useful for system security management.

2.5 Reliability

One important issue in distributed environment is reliability. Reliability usually mean many things, but here we restrict our discussion to consistency and availability.

(a) Consistency

It is more difficult to keep consistency of the operation of a distributed environment as a whole than it is to manage a single independent machine. We need to update the view each node has about the operation of the distributed environment. Just running the nodes independently in the distributed environment is not enough to keep consistency correct. We need to offer a method to keep consistent operation even in part of the nodes break down.

(b) Availability

We must make the distributed environment fault tolerant so that the network node can function even if one the nodes break down.

2.6 Maintainability

It is important to make it easy to maintain the system. We have modularized the system to achieve high maintainability. Modularization was achieved by hierarchical kernel modules and system resource managers. Each resource manager is also easy to maintain since it can be coded and debugged alone.

2.7 Performance

We discus the performance issues in general and the use of multiprocessor system.

(a) Simplification.

It is very important to give a crisp operation to users on BTRON-based machines. From the viewpoint of marketing, features which are not functional enough or fast enough never get used. So we should offer functions which can be implemented to offer high performance. If it can't, maybe we should do away with such features.

We would like to remind the readers that the deletion of certain features doesn't necessarily mean that we can increase the performance of remaining functions. It is often the case that well considered uniform set of operations available in a simply structured program outperforms sluggish programs laden with features which are hardly users by average users.

We adopted the policy to avoid the performance bottleneck due to complexity by choosing simpler structures if we have a choice. Adopting simple overall structure will make it possible to gain insight to the bottleneck easily so that we can tune the system easily in the future. Also, tricks known today such as the use of cache will be easily applied to the resulting system since the simple structure of the system make it easy to incorporate such features.

(b) Multiprocessor

We have adopted a design so that multiprocessor configuration can be used to achieve high throughput.

In BTRON2, multiple tasks can reside in one process. Tasks don't manage resources directly and task switching should be a "light" operation. We hope that multiprocessor based on shared-memory can be used effectively with the current specification.

3. BASIC CONCEPTS IN BTRON2 SPECIFICATION.

3.1 Real Object

3.1.1 Real Object

Real object is an abstraction of system resources.

Most popular of the real objects is real object used for storage (file in conventional systems). This is offered as a collection (or sometimes called a stream) of variable-length records.

3.1.2 Name of Real Object

There are two ways to identify a name; real object name which is represented in TAD data (maybe a character string), and a unique identifier, real object ID, used internally by programs.

Real object name is given to real object when it is created by a user. It can be empty; process real object can have empty real object names.

Real object ID uniquely identifies a real object in the system as a whole. The length and representation of real object ID depends on the type of real object.

3.1.3 Expiration of real object

Real object will not disappear as long as the reference to it, which requires the real object to exist, continues to exist. When such references cease to exist, the real object can be deleted.

Upon generation of events that call for the deletion of the real object, some types of real objects can be deleted regardless of if the reference to them exist or not. In this case, the reference to the deleted real object becomes invalid.

Some real objects will continue to exist and don't get deleted even if the reference to them are no longer in existence; eg. device and storage type real object (file).

3.1.4 structure of real object

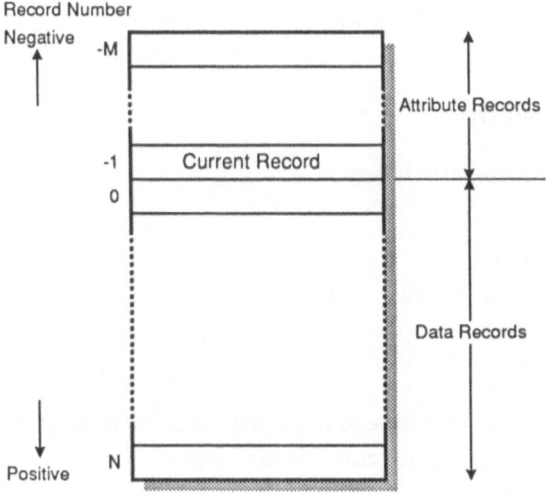

Fig. 1 Structure of Real Object in BTRON2

Real object is a collection of variable-length records. There are two types of records; attribute records, and data records. Each record in a real object has record number (an integer value). Record number is not necessarily contiguous. Attribute records have negative record number. Data records have non-negative record number. Usually, the record with the record number, -1, is used as the "current" record for processing.

3.1.5 Structure of Record

Record has a contiguous area which are divided into control fields and data fields.

Control fields can be accessed with negative offsets. Data length, record type, or extended control fields are contained there. Data field stores the ordinary "user data".

Record type has record main type and record subtype. Each data record carries a record type which is specified in TAD specification. Data length holds the length of only the data field.

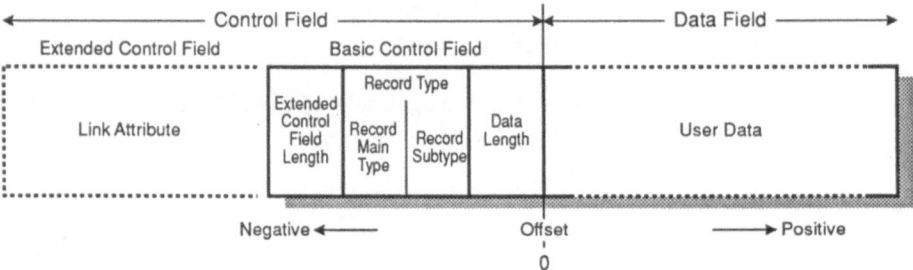

Fig. 2   Record structure in BTRON2

3.1.6 Attributes of Real Object

Real object has the following attributes.

(a) Name and ID.

Real object name and ID are handled as attributes.

(b) Access Information

Access control tree (similar to access control list) is used to restrict access to real object. Access control tree is a tree that has the following leaves.

- User name
- Group name

- Access level
- Password

The node of the tree have operators for logical OR and logical AND.

(c) Time stamp

Date and time of creation, expiration date, date and time of the latest access and modification are stored.

(d) Member Domain

Information of domain to which the real object belongs. Domain is discussed later.

(e) Basic Real Object Properties

These properties are attributes applicable to every real object and are presented by binary on/off value. (The reader should distinguish the usage of "property" and "attribute". Property is an attribute that can be represented by on/off value.)

- Application operations

  This shows what operations are applicable to the real object.
- Contiguous Data Record number.

  This shows whether the record number of the data record is always contiguous or not. For storage type real object, contiguous record number is standard.

(f) Reference Independence

This shows if we should preserve the object even if there is no (linked) reference to it. Object that is not reference independent is deleted when there is no (linked) reference to it. Object that is reference independent remains to exist.

Real objects that correspond to physical existence such as hardware devices are reference independent. One type of storage type real object called domain leader is reference independent. Domain leader is discussed later.

3.1.7 Fundamental type of real object

(a) Storage

This is an abstraction of file and memory. It is possible to map the record into address space. The mapped part can be accessed as part of memory. In real-memory version of BTRON2, there are restrictions to the mapping operation.

(b) IPC: Inter-Process Communication

These are used as semaphore and message queue and used for process to process communication.

(c) Device

This is an abstraction of physical devices. We have virtual (logical) devices and physical devices that correspond directly to physical devices.

(d) Process

This is an abstraction of address space. Process real objects don't have execution capability. Tasks are the entity that execute programs.

We should not assume that the code and data of processes are laid out in a contiguous area. Generally speaking, are area for data, heap, stack may have multiple region assigned to them.

(e) Task

This is an abstraction of CPU. This can start execute only after it belongs to a process.

(f) Transaction

This is an abstraction of series of operations. The specification for this is still to be designed.

3.2. Virtual Object

3.2.1 Virtual Object

A virtual object is a pointer to real object and has structure/attributes. We can pass virtual object to pass the access to the real object.

There are two types of virtual object that have different implementation; link record and access key.

(a) Link Record

Link record consists of real object pointer that identifies a real object and link attributes. There are different types of link records. Depending on the type of the record the reference via link record is considered linked reference or ordinary reference.

Link record expires when the real object that has the link record expires. Even when a computer system is restarted by power-on, the real object can be accessed by the link record. However, in this case the link record may point at a non-existing real object.

(b) Access Key

Access key is a generalization of BTRON1 file descriptor and device descriptor. The access key structure is unique and doesn't change according to the type and the position of real object it references. Reference by access-key is linked reference.

There is one and only one owner process of an access key. Only the owner process can access real object using the access key. When the owner process ceases to exist, all the access keys owned by the process become invalid. We can duplicate access key, and transfer the owner-ship of the access key to a different process.

Access key can identify a real object uniquely, and is an efficient and uniform way to access real objects during the operation of a computer system. Access key can't survive a system halt. When the system is restarted, we can't guarantee the validity of an access key.

(c) Basic Access Key Properties

- Operation Modes

  This shows what type of operations are possible via access key.
- Availability of Current record.

  This shows if we have the current record as attribute record or not.
- Prohibited Duplication

  This shows if we can duplicate access key or not. This prohibits the re-distribution of access key after this is transferred to another process. Also, this can be used to deter the proliferation of access keys that refers to a particular real object.
- Transferability of the ownership.

  This shows whether we can transfer the ownership of the transferability. If the transfer is prohibited, we can't change the owner process of the access key.
- Allowed Waiting

  This shows if the system should put a calling process into waiting queue if accessing a real object accessed via access key can result in a indefinite wait where system can't distinguish any error condition that forces waiting.

3.3 Domain

3.3.1 Domain

(a) Group

Explicit grouping of virtual objects inside a real object is considered to give a meaning to the association of the real objects and the real objects referenced by the virtual objects.

In BTRON2, we base the handling of real objects with the following rule. When a real object, A, is referenced from a data record of a real object, B, we view that A belongs to a certain "group" represented by B. This is like a directory. A parent real object refers to its sibling by a reference from the parent's data record and the child real object is considered as belonging to the directory represented by the parent object.

When a real object, A, is referenced from an attribute record of a real object, B, we view that B belongs to the group represented by A. This rule is used to build the concept of "domain" which is explained in more detail later. Each real object has an attribute record that shows to which domain the real object belongs.

However, there may be exceptions to this general rule, and we don't rule out such usage.

(b) Domain

Domain is a type of group which is supported by BTRON2-based systems. There is one and only one real object called domain leader (or root) in this group. The real object with domain property becomes the domain leader. Domain leader identifies the domain under consideration, so we use the two terms interchangeablly.

Ordinary real objects that are NOT domain leaders belong to one and only one domain. Domain leader belongs to the domain which it represents. Domain leader can belong to other domains also. When the domain leader doesn't belong to domains other than itself, then the domain is called independent. The relationship between domains can be represented as set of trees.

Deleting domain leader from a domain causes the whole domain to disappear. Every real object in the domain is deleted as well.

An independent domain can be made to belong to another domain temporarily during system operation. A removable media is handled using this feature. When a domain to which the real object should belong to doesn't exist at the time of the creation of the real object, the real object can be made to belong to another domain temporarily.

We can maintain the correspondence of domains and physical positions (domains) and thus can let users be aware of the locations.

3.3.3 Type of Domain

Not all types of real objects can become domain leader. Storage-type real object can become domain leader. Process real object is always domain leader.

(a) Storage-type Real Object.

Domain of a storage-type real object groups storage real-type real objects.

We can maintain the correspondence of the domain to locations/devices and can let users be aware of the locations even in the distributed environment.

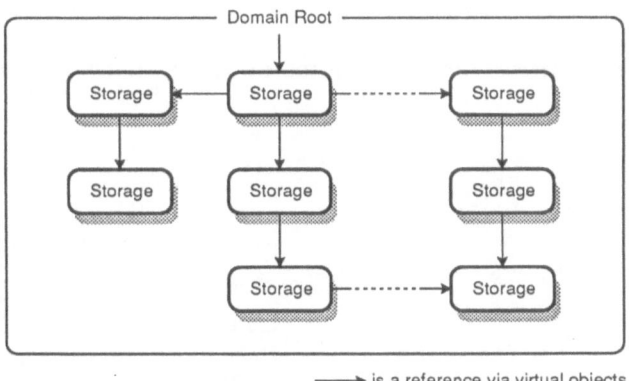

Fig. 3 Storage-type domain

A storage-type domain leader is called root. Within the domain, the reference relationship between real objects is a general network.

The root of a storage-type domain can keep account of the storage area held within the domain. Thus, quota function can be implemented easily.

(b) Process domain

We often calls the domain of which leader is a process real object as process. There should be no confusion. Only task real objects can belong to a process real object. Task can begin execution only when it belongs a process (domain).

When a task belongs to a process, a reference from process to task is considered to be generated.

Process domain holds many types of resources. There are resources and attributes which only a process can hold; address space and access right information. We can map storage-type record to address space. Access right information shows the access right with which tasks that belongs to the process can access other resources.

Process has current real object as attribute record. In UNIX parlance, current real object is current directory.

Process is deleted when the linked references to it no longer exist. This means all child processes get deleted when a parent process terminates. The termination of child processes can be avoided if the parent process transfer the ownership of access key to the child process to another process.

(c) Process, Tasks, and Resources

Each task belongs to the process (domain), but there is also a linked process from the process to the task.

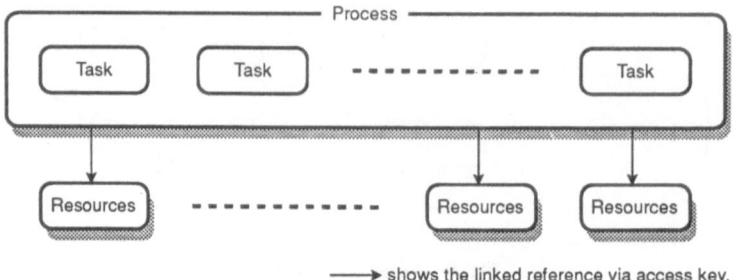

→ shows the linked reference via access key.

Fig. 4 Process, tasks, and resources

4. STRUCTURE OF BTRON2-BASED OPERATING SYSTEM

An OS based on BTRON2 specification has three layers. The three layers are; inner kernel, outer kernel and shell. The inner kernel and outer kernel are often called simply as kernel. The interface to inner kernel is called inner kernel interface, and the interfaces of outer layers are called BTRON2 kernel program interface.

4.1 Inner kernel

This offers fundamental resources management and inter-task communication facility. The following ITRON2 features are provided; task management, memory management, exception and interrupt handling, and semaphore and rendezvous.

Ordinary application programmers can't access this interface. Only the outer kernel can use this interface.

4.2 Outer Kernel

Outer kernel manages the BTRON resources visible to programmers. The BTRON2 kernel program interface is built on top of the functions available in inner kernel.

Outer kernel has independent resource managers. Each type of resources has one manager. (Although the specification explains the function of outer kernel manager as if they are processes, a manager doesn't have to be a process if the performance issues require other implementation methods.)

4.3 Shell

Shell offers a very high level functions. Shell has higher security status than those of other applications.

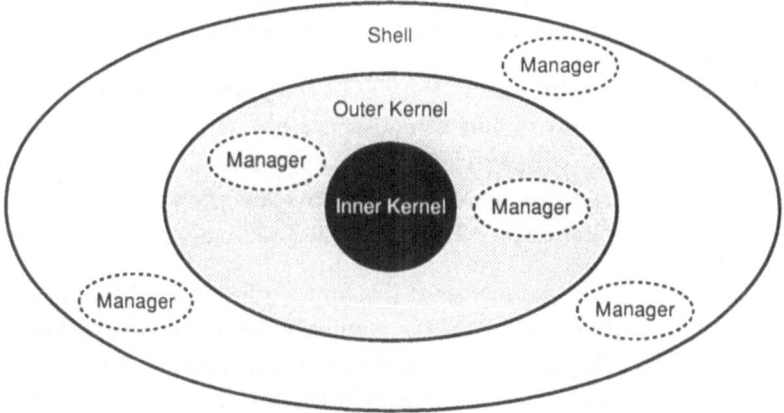

Fig. 5 Structure of BTRON2-based OS

5. CONCLUDING REMARKS

This paper briefly discusses the internal of BTRON2 specification. BTRON2 is a new OS specification for computer systems based on TRON-specification VLSI CPU and ample hardware resources and is a logical successor to BTRON1 specification.

BTRON2 calls for a layered structure and modular architecture so that extensibility, maintainability and support for distributed environment and multiprocessing can be easily achieved. However, the basic data model real/virtual object model, which was the basis of the BTRON1 specification, and the TAD data structure for implementing these real objects have not changed a bit.

Ken Sakamura is currently an associate professor at the Department of Information Science, University of Tokyo. His main interests lies in computer architecture, the basic design of computer systems. Since 1984, he has been the leader of the TRON project and has made efforts to build new computer systems based on the TRON architecture.

His interest in the TRON computer systems now extends beyond ordinary computers. He is now interested how the society will change by the use of computers in 1990's and beyond and now his design activities include those for electronic appliances, furniture, houses, buildings, and urban planning.

He is a member of the Japan Information Processing Society; the Institute of Electronics, Information and Communication Engineers; ACM; and a senior member of IEEE. He servers on the editorial board of IEEE MICRO magazine. His papers won awards from IEEE, IEICE, and JIPS.

Dr. Sakamura may be contacted at the Department of Information Science, Faculty of Science, University of Tokyo, 7-3-1 Hongo, Bunkyo-ku, Tokyo, Japan.

A Study on a Hypermedia Editor on BTRON1 Specification Operating System

Kazuo Kajimoto, Tomoyuki Nonomura
Kansai Information and Communications Research Laboratories,
Matsushita Electric Industrial Co., Ltd.

ABSTRACT

Hypermedia becomes popular bacause it gives us a method of assosiative information retrieval and information representative ability. So, hypermedia itself is very easy to use it, but it is very difficult to generate it for most of users.

In this paper, some concepts that are important for hypermedia editing are discussed.

At first, the concept named "reflective viewing" is described. Reflective viewing is such a concept that when an user do something, then he/she can immediately get the result of that operation. So reflective viewing concept enables users to edit hypermedia with trial and error way. And we designed human machine interface of a hypermedia editor according to this concept. The interface can edit not only text and graphic objects, but clip video objects which comes from optical video disks.

Next, the concept named "interactive synchronization" is described. This interactive synchronization has three features as follows;
(a) Dynamic buttons
(b) Objects an user focuses are interactively set front in the hypermedia.
(c) Relationship of synchronization is independent from clip video's play speed.
We developped this interactive synchronization by introducing event network graph representation. And we designed human machine interface to built this event network graph on screen.

After that, we implemented a hypermedia editor which can treat text, graphics, clip video and buttons as objects and set interactive synchronization between them.
As a result, it achieves programless and "trial and error" hypermedia editing.

KEYWORDS:

hypermedia, reflective viewing, interactive synchronization, human machine interface, event network graph

1. INTRODUCTION

Recently, personal computers have grown up so powerful that they have the ability to handle hypermedia.

The hypermedia enables us to represent information with proper media as text, graphics, video and so on[1]. Moreover it offers us the retrieval method according to our association process[1].

Hypermedia is useful as above description. But it is still difficult for most of users to built up hypermedia. In this paper, an aproach to resolve that problem is described.

2. REFLECTIVE VIEWING

WYSIWYG (What you see is what you get) is a famous concept of desk top publishing (DTP). We want to analyze why WYSIWYG becomes important.

At first, we decompose the process of making DTP documents into sub-processes as follows;
(1) Planning
(2) Making objects (typing text and drawing graphics)
(3) Composing a document with the objects
(4) Printing the document

Non-WYSIWYG systems often treat these sub-processes as water-fall from top sub-process to bottom one, that is, after finishing preceding sub-process completely, next sub-process begins to be processed.

But, it seems to be so difficult to decide all of a document completely before making objects. While making objects, we often imagine to modify the document plan. The more times repeating making objects and modifing document plan, the better the document becomes. This fact leads that our producing activities often prefer "trial and error" processing to water-fall processing.

On DTP, "trial and error" editing is implemented with WYSIWYG concept.

The key of "trial and error" processing is that the result of human's trial is reflected immediately on screen, and human can confirm it at the same time. I call this concept "reflective viewing".

Reflective viewing is important not only on DTP, but on hypermedia editing. On hypermedia editing, our making hypermedia process is decomposed into sub-processes as follows;
(1) Planning
(2) Making objects (typing text, drawing graphics, clipping video time range and so on)
(3) Composing a hypermedia with the objects
(4) Making links between hypermedia
Implementing reflective viewing concept, we can retry at every sub-process to go back or go forward other sub-processes until hypermedia editing is completed.

Our hypermedia editor is designed to support this reflective viewing concept.

3. DIRECT VIDEO MANIPULATION

Our hypermedia editor is designed to treat text, graphics, clip video which comes from optical video disk and buttons as objects. To handle video, we've already developped video interpolation hardware[2], and video manager which is a set of system calles in operating system layer[3].

We implement a hypermedia editor on BTRON1 specification operating system[4] that provides multi task and multi window environment. BTRON1 specification[5] reccomends application software which treats text and graphics to observe a manner of human machine interface to guarantee compatibility of operations[6]. The manner is called "TRON manner", and it consists of "direct manipulation" and "noun-verb model", that means, after objects selection, an user can do something on it.

We adopt this TRON manner for text and graphics, and apply it for clip video. So if an user has already used some application software on BTRON1 specification operating system, he/she can treat clip video by analogy.

For example, at the case that an user wants to move a clip video from a window to the other window, he/she does as follows;
(a) moving a pointer at the clip video on screen
(b) pressing the button of the pointing device, then he/she can grasps the clip video on screen.
(c) moving it to target window on screen with the pointing device
(d) releasing it
Fig.1 shows this sequence.

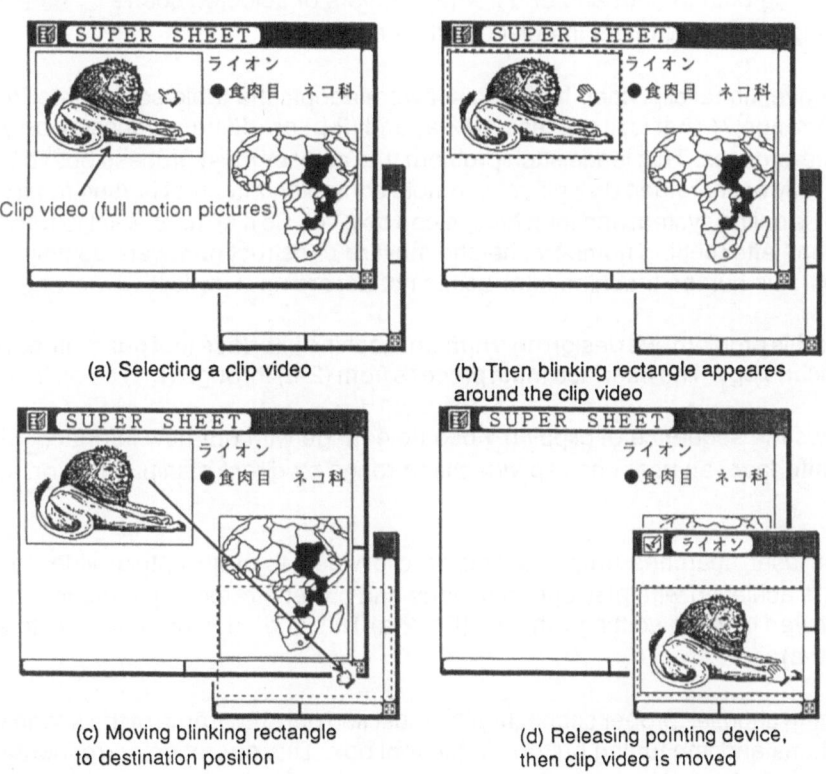

(a) Selecting a clip video

(b) Then blinking rectangle appeares around the clip video

(c) Moving blinking rectangle to destination position

(d) Releasing pointing device, then clip video is moved

Fig.1 An example of moving clip video operation

We call this human machine interface as "direct video manipulation". Direct video manipulation provides the methods of selecting, moving, coping, deleting, and resizing clip video only with the pointing device. And the manner is extended for clip video, that is, the methods of cutting focused area from clip video and changing play speed with the pointing device are added. All of these operations are according to reflective viewing concept.

4. CLIPPING VIDEO TIME RANGE

The human machine interface on clip video handling in space axis is described in preceding section. In this section, the human machine interface in time axis, that is, how to clip video time range is described.

Now, we describe sub-processes to make hypermedia, again.
(1) Planning
(2) Making objects (typing text, drawing graphics, clipping video time range and so on)
(3) Composing a hypermedia with objects
(4) Making links between hypermedia

Then, we want to focus second sub-process "making objects" on clip video. On clip video, second sub-process is devided into three sub-sub-processes as follows;
(2-a) Selecting proper scene in video disk as a clip video
(2-b) Checking both of start and end frame numbers of selected scene
(2-c) Setting both of numbers in editing software

Most of conventional clip video handling software adopts the table setting interface to clip video time range[7], that is, it processes (2-a) and (2-b) as offline-processes, only after (2-c) as online-process. This leads such problem that an user must process both of (2-a) and (2-b) with only optical video disk player's remote controller, after that he/she must construct hardware as online system and then he/she can do (2-c). So if an user want to retry to select proper scene after setting numbers, he/she must re-construct hardware as offline system. As a result, this human machine interface is not according to reflective viewing concept.

To resolve this problem, we design new human machine interface that guarantees reflective viewing technology. The interface must process from (2-a) through (2-c) as online-process.

Fig.2 shows the sequence of clipping video time range with our new interface.
With this interface, an user can clip video time range by direct manipulation on screen as follows;

At first, an user searches proper scene as clip video through optical video disk. This operation is achieved with play speed buttons and current frame bar in the tool box, while video is played in video editting window. (Fig.2-a) This operation corresponds to sub-sub-process (2-a)

When he/she chooses proper scene, he/she must find out start frame of the scene with play speed buttons and fine tuning buttons in the tool box. This operation corresponds to sub-sub-process (2-b)

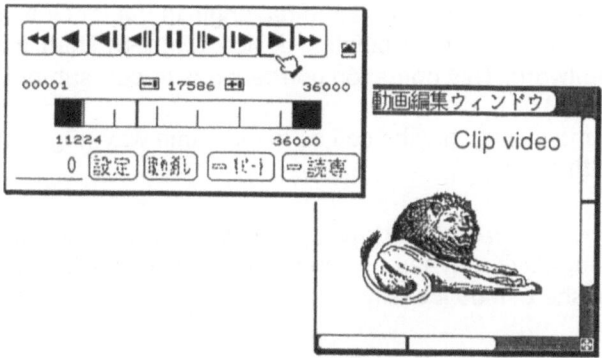

(a) Playing video and serching proper scene

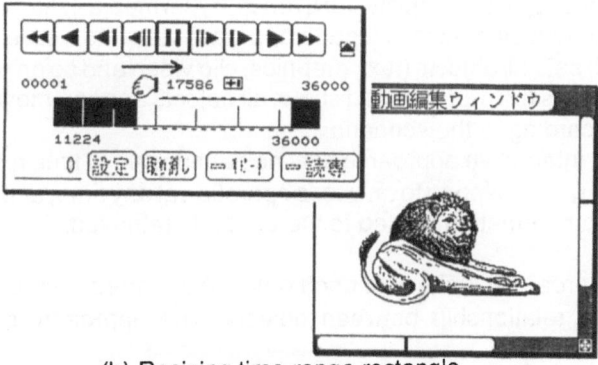

(b) Resizing time range rectangle

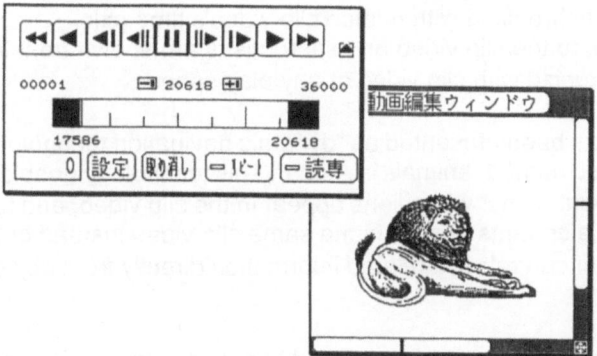

(c) Final result (clip video's time range is set between 17586 to 20618 frame)

Fig.2 The sequence of clipping video time range with our new interface

After that, he/she selects video time range rectangle in the tool box and resize it from left to right until the start frame with the pointing device. (Fig.2-b) Then, the start frame number is set in editing software. This operation corresponds to sub-sub-process (2-c)

About the end frame setting, he/she can do in the same way.(Fig.2-c) Clipping video time range is done as this.

Using this interface, an user does not have to write down any frame number, and he/she can do only with pointing device. When he/she wants to retry to select proper scene after set frame number, he/she can do it easily.

5. INTERACTIVE SYNCHRONIZATION

Hypermedia includes clip video objects. As a result, hypermedia itself must handle time axis. There are two approaches, that is, scenario approach and interactive approach.
Scenario approach sets all objects (text, graphics, clip video and so on) along one time axis, and after an user starts the programmed show, all objects appear, move, disappear and so on sequentially according to the scenario.
On the other hand, interactive approarch sets no relationship in time axis between objects. All objects, however, can respond to an user's operation at any time, and when an user clicks a button object, the information related to the button is retrieved.

Now, these two approaches unite with each other. We started from interactive approach, and introduce time relationship between objects. The approach is called "Interactive synchronization".

Interactive synchronization has three features as follows;
(a) Buttons are synchronized with related clip video's time axis.
(b) Objects related to the clip video an user focuses are shown front in the hypermedia.
(c) Objects synchronize with clip video at any play speed.

The first feature has been presented as "dynamic navigation technology"[1]. For example, there is an clip video named "animals in Africa". This technology enables an user to retrieve the information about "lions" when lions appear in the clip video, and to retrieve that about "elephants" when elephants appear in tha same clip video instead of lions. So, using this technology, an user can retrieve related information directly from objects appearing in clip video.

The second feature represents the concept that objects, an user is interested in, should be shown prior to the others. It can be determined what clip video an user is interested in, that is the one played as moving pictures. Because, in our system, there is only one clip video which can be played as moving picture at the same time.

The third feature means that an user can change play speed of clip video, interactively. The time relationship between clip video and the other objects depends not on the play speed, but on the scene of clip video.

Supporting the interactive synchronization concept which has above three features, an user can understand the information represented with the hypermedia as he/she likes.

6. EVENT NETWORK GRAPH

Implementing interactive syncronization concept, we introduce "event network graph" which represents the relationship of synchronization.

Window's open/close, object's apperance/disappearance and so on are regarded as events, then a scenario is defined as the relationship between these events. When events are represented as nodes and the relationship between them is represented as directed arc, a scenario is represented as a directed graph. This graph is called "event network graph".

Fig.3 shows an example of an event network graph. Fig.3 represents the relationship among 3 objects, that is, clip video, text and graphics. The appearance/disappearance events of text and graphics are set to synchronize with frames of clip video.

In event network graph, there are two kinds of arc. One is "invoking arc", the other is "succesive arc". In fig.3 (a) is invoking arc and (b) is succesive arc".

An event network graph has two special nodes. One is "entrance node", the other is "exit node". In fig.3 (c) is entrance node and (d) is exit node.

When scenario starts, the entrance node invoked at first. Next, the events related to the entrance node are invoked. As this sequence, the events which related to invoked events with invoking arc are invoked succesively. On the other hand, succesive arc makes the condition whether an event can be invoked, that is, when an event is invoked, the events related to it with succesive arc get the chance to be invoked. So even if an event is invoked, the event related to it with invoking arc cannot be invoked when preceding event with succesive arc has not been invoked. Finally, the final event, that is, exit event is invoked and the scenario finishes completely.

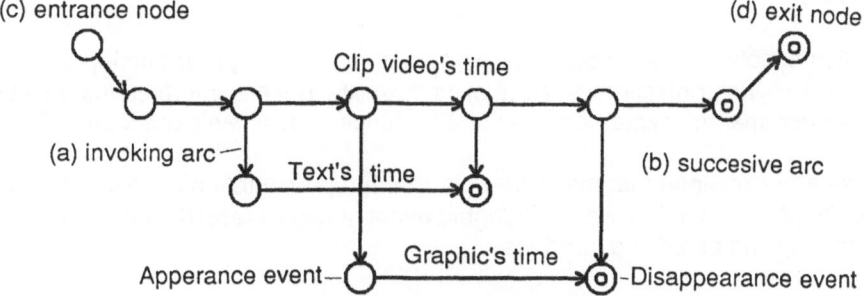

Fig.3 An example of event network graph

To implement interactive synchronization concept, we make a subset of the event network graph. In the subset, text, graphic and button objects are represented by two nodes and one succesive arc between these nodes. Two nodes represent appearance event and disappearance one. On the other hand, clip video is represented by appearance/disappearance nodes, multiple frame event nodes and multiple succesive arcs between these nodes. And invoking arcs can be drawn only from the node of clip video to appearance or disappearance node of other media. This subset of the event network graph can represent the synchronization relationship between clip video objects and other ones. This derives three features of interactive synchronization concept.

(a) The definition of the subset proves that the synchronization between button objects and clip video object can be represented by it.

(b) The second feature depends on the interpretation of the graph. Our hardware cannot play multiple clip video object at the same time, so we regard one clip video object in the hypermedia as active video. Of cource, this active video can be changed by an user interactively at any time. Then event network graph is interpreted as successive arcs of clip video are effective only when the clip video is active video. When successive arcs of a clip video are not effective, any appearance events are not invoked by the clip video.

(c) When the system adopts frame numbers as successive events of clip video, the relationship depends not on its play speed, but on the scene of it.

This event network graph is implemented in our hypermedia editor. The logical file format of editted hypermedia is defined to be interpreted as event network graph. And our hypermedia editor interpretes it, and construct event network graph in memory.

When an user selects a clip video in hypermedia as active video, the active video's succesive arc becomes effective, and hypermedia editor displays objects according to the event network graph.

7. MAKING EVENT NETWORK GRAPH

The last problem about our hypermedia editor is how to make an event network graph as an user likes.

Conventional software for desk top presentation adopts programming interface as description of synchronization because of its flexibility. But this interface forces an user to remember commands, syntax and so on, as a result, only a few users can user it.

We've already explained that event network graph representation is useful for interactive synchronization description. So, we adopted event network graph directly drawing instead of language typing as editing interface.

Fig.4 shows the tool box of implemented interface.

At first, our hypermedia editor draws skeleton of event network graph, that has no invoking arc. (Fig.4-a)

127

Secondaly, an user plays clip video with buttons in the tool box. When an user finds the scene he/she wants to adopt as invoking other object's appearance event, then he/she draws invoking arc in the tool box with pointing device directly. (Fig.4-b)
These sequence will be continued until all invoking arcs are set. (Fig.4-c)
Of cource, an user can retry to set arcs at any time, that is, reflective viewing technology is also available in this interface.

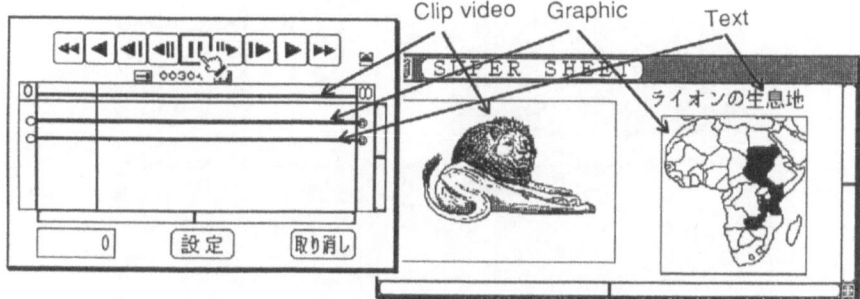

(a) In the tool box, skelton of event network graph is drawn.

(b) Making evnt node, and drawing invoking arc from it to destination node.

(c) Final result

Fig.4 Implemented tool box

Both fig.5 and fig.6 are hypermedia exmples played according to fig.4's event network graph.

Fig.5 shows the living area of lions, when a lion appears in the clip video. On the other hand, fig.6 shows that of elephants, when elephants appear in the same clip video instead of a lion.

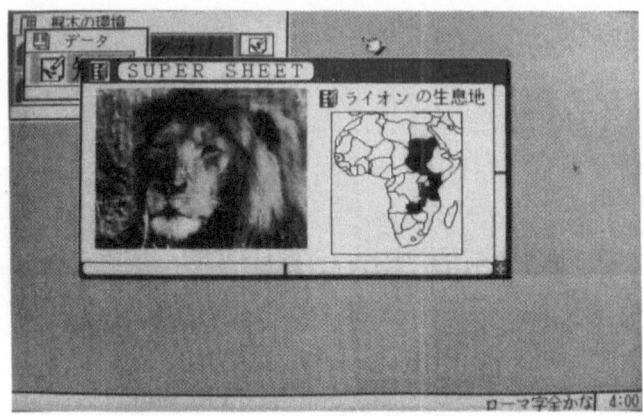

Fig.5 An example of hypermedia playing

Fig.6 Another example of hypermedia playing

8. CONCLUSION

In this pape, two concepts are discussed, that is, reflective viewing and interactive synchronization. These concepts are important for hypermedia editing.

After that, a hypermedia editor which can treat text, graphics, clip video and buttons is implemented on BTRON1 specification operating system. This editor is named "AV Super-sheet".
Our "AV Super-sheet" provides programless and "trial and error" hypermedia editting.

Our next interest is designing human machine interface to built complete scenarios without any programming, or water-fall approach.

REFERENCES

[1] Kajimoto, K et.al.: "New-media Document (NewDoc) and Dynamic Navigation on the BTRON Specification", Proc. of 34th IEEE COMPCON, 1989

[2] Tatsumi, T et. al.: "The Video Processor for a Personal Computer", Proc. of ICCE (International Conference on Consumer Electronics), 1989

[3] Kajimoto, K et. al.: "A Study on Video Manager of the BTRON Specification", Proc. of 5th TRON International Symposium, 1988

[4] Imai, Y et. al.: "An Implementation based on the BTRON specification", Proc. of 33rd IEEE COMPCON, 1988

[5] TRON Association: "HMI External Specification", Vol. 6 of "BTRON1 Specification, Software Specification", TRON Association, Tokyo, 1989

[6] Sakamura, K: "New Concepts from the TRON project", Iwanami-Syoten, Tokyo, 1987 (In Japanese)

[7] Inaba, N et. al.: "Multimedia starts to the 21st century", No.471, Nikkei BP- Sya, Tokyo, 1989 (in Japanese)

Kazuo Kajimoto is an engineer in Kansai Information and Communications Research laboratories of Matsushita Electric Industrial Co., Ltd. (MEI), Osaka, Japan. He received B.E. and M.E. degrees in information science from Kyoto University, Kyoto, Japan, in 1984 and 1986, respectively. He has been engaged in the research and development of human machine interface, especially hypermedia. He is a member of the IPSJ, IEICEJ and the ASJ.

Tomoyuki Nonomura is an engineer in Kansai Information and Communications Research laboratories of Matsushita Electric Industrial Co., Ltd. (MEI), Osaka, Japan. He received B.E. and M.E. degrees in information science from Osaka City University, Osaka, Japan, in 1986 and 1988, respectively. He has been engaged in the research and development of human machine interface, especially intelligent communication. He is a member of the IPSJ and the IEICEJ.

Above authors may be reached at Kansai Information and Communications Research Laboratories, Matsushita Electric Industrial Co., Ltd., 1006, Kadoma, Kadoma-shi, Osaka, 571, Japan.

Chapter 3: CTRON

CTRON Software Portability Evaluation

Tadashi Ohta, Takashi Terasaki
NTT Network Systems Development Center

Toshikazu Ohkubo, Mitsuru Hanazawa
NTT Electrical Communications Laboratories

Masayuki Ohtaka
NEC Corporation

ABSTRACT

The growing importance of information technology in society has increased the demand for improved software productivity. The CTRON Technical Committee in the TRON Association has produced a series of OS interface specifications (CTRON) designed to raise software productivity in communication and information processing fields. In order to confirm the extent to which Extended OS programs implementing these specifications achieve portability, the Committee is now conducting a portability trial. This paper outlines the experiment including its objectives and background, and discusses impediments to portability.

Keywords : CTRON, software portability, software reuse

1. INTRODUCTION

The sheer quantity of software required is increasing dramatically as the advanced information society begins to take shape, raising the demand for improved software productivity. Of all the many approaches tried, those that allow software to be reused (ported from one environment to another) are seen as the most effective; yet very little reuse actually takes place. Especially the porting of real-time applications is difficult. The reasons for this are various, but one is incompatibility among OS interfaces.

Standardization of OS interfaces in communications and information processing fields is seen as a way of raising software productivity. With this aim in mind, the CTRON Technical Committee in the TRON Association has drawn up the CTRON interface specifications. There are parts of these specifications, however, that depend to a great extent on system service conditions, operation conditions, configuration and other system-specific factors. Since these aspects are hard to standardize, only the bare outlines are specified, with the details treated as architecture-dependent and left up to the implementor. Moreover, even after the specifications have been drawn up it is still necessary to verify experimentally how effective the specifications are at achieving portability. The CTRON Technical Committee therefore decided to carry out an extensive trial in order to confirm whether it is possible to realize portable software on operating systems implementing the CTRON specifications.

The portability experiment is being conducted jointly with the Sakamura Laboratories in the Information Sciences Department, the Faculty of Science, the University of Tokyo. The preliminary phase of the experiment began June 1, 1990, at a test center installed at the University of Tokyo. Prior to the start of the experiment, theoretical studies of the specifications were made in order to draw up and classify a list of themes.

This paper first discusses the significance of software portability in section 2. Section 3 deals with the impediments to achieving software portability in the porting real-time applications, and classifies these into five main causes. Section 4 looks at the present state of the CTRON specification series from the standpoint of software portability, and notes the problems that can and cannot be solved by use of CTRON. The portability experiment is then discussed in the remaining sections. Sections 5 to 7 present the aims of the experiment, note the portability impediments that have been uncovered in theoretical studies, along with measures being taken to overcome them, and outline the nature of the experiment and the procedures involved. Finally, section 8 points out the benefits to be derived from the experiment and shows how the results are being reflected in CTRON Technical Committee activities.

2. SIGNIFICANCE OF SOFTWARE PORTABILITY

The significance of software portability includes improved software productivity, the possibility of multi-vendor product supply, and better software reliability.

As society turns increasingly to information technologies, the volume of software required is swelling to the point where supply can hardly keep up with demand. The cries for greater software productivity have been heard for a long time, but no better solution has been found than to stretch available software by re-using it in other than its originally intended environment. In order for software to be reused, however, software portability must first be achieved.

Another way in which software portability can be beneficial is when large-scale systems are being developed, and it is desired to procure system components from multiple vendors. The multivendor approach, however, is effective only if the products are all developed according to uniform standards; otherwise it turns out to be disadvantageous in terms of software development and maintenance. Thus when this solution is adopted the software specifications of products to be procured must be standardized, and the specifications must be designed to guarantee software portability.

One more benefit when software portability is achieved is that, after software is originally developed, it is used in many different applications, allowing problems to be discovered and corrected and resulting in a more reliable software system.

3. THE DIFFICULTY OF ACHIEVING PORTABILITY

3.1 Present status

In spite of the clear benefits to be gained from software portability, pointed out in section 2, the reality is that portability is very difficult to achieve. True, there is available today some portable package software for certain routine processing; but in fields demanding realtime processing, such as communications and information processing, portability attempts to date have shown minimal success. Realtime characteristics are considered the most important requirement of conventional systems in communication and information processing fields. As a result of this emphasis on performance, there is a lack of uniformity in software configuration models (division of interfaces among software modules), nor is there a clear division between applications and OS. Moreover, differences in hardware architecture and in OS processing methods tend to manifest themselves in the OS interfaces. When software developed for one system is used on another system, in nearly every case it must undergo extensive revision. In fact, in most cases the software must be recoded practically from scratch, even if the interfaces are essentially unchanged.

In non-realtime OSs such as UNIX*, on the other hand, ease of software development is a prime consideration. For this reason, the OS interfaces are sufficiently logicalized and a development environment is provided with the OS. Software developed on one UNIX system can thus be ported readily to another UNIX system. This portability, however, comes at the expense of realtime performance.

An aim of CTRON is to standardize OS interfaces while still maintaining realtime performance. Because of this need to guarantee realtime performance, however, some interfaces cannot fully hide differences in hardware architecture or in processing methods. (Details will be given in section 4 below.) Furthermore, CTRON specifies OS interfaces only, not the software development environment.

3.2 Classification of difficulties

In the domain of realtime systems, while there are many reasons for the difficulty in achieving software portability, the main ones include lack of conformity in modular division, in interfaces between modules, in hardware, in development environments, and in performance parameters.

---

*: UNIX is a registered trademark of AT&T.

(a) Differences in software module division

In conventional realtime systems, division of software into modules is determined optimally for each system, from the standpoint of performance. Since module units are not uniform from one system to another, modules cannot be ported readily. A module can be ported to another system only if the division of interfaces is the same in both the original and target systems; otherwise extensive revisions are required. (See Fig.1.)

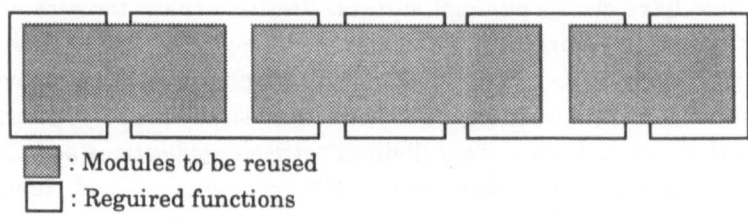

■ : Modules to be reused
☐ : Reguired functions

Fig.1 Inconsistency of module unit

(b) Differences in interfaces between modules

When each system has its own specific interface specifications, then even if the module units are the same, there will be differences in software processing methods, activation conditions, parameters that are passed, and other aspects, requiring extensive revisions before the software can be ported. In the worst cases, reuse is not possible. (See Fig.2.)

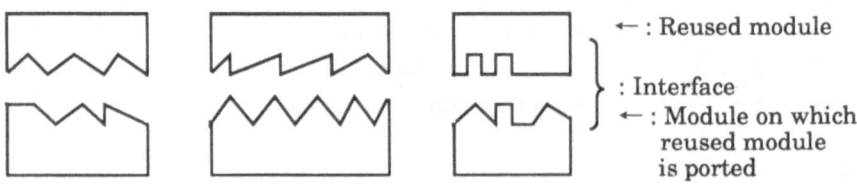

← : Reused module

} : Interface
← : Module on which
   reused module
   is ported

Fig.2 Inconsistency of interfaces

(c) Differences in hardware architecture

If the original and target systems use different processors or I/O devices, differences in hardware control requirements will manifest themselves directly in the software processing methods and interfaces. Even if there are parts that are functionally independent of hardware, in actuality the hardware differences will be reflected in the internal design of the software, making reuse difficult.

(d) Differences in development environments

Differences in compilers, debuggers, and development support hardware can affect portability. Compiler differences that may necessitate recoding include register conventions, provided libraries, and upper limits imposed by the compiler. Debuggers and various testers are essential for debugging software; if these cannot be used, then re-use of a module is effectively blocked.

(e) Performance differences

Realtime systems have especially stringent performance requirements. Even if the differences noted in (a) through (d) above are overcome, software that does not meet these performance requirements cannot be used in a realtime environment.

4. CTRON AND PORTABILITY

4.1 Aims and present status

CTRON is an attempt to improve software portability by standardizing operating system (OS) interfaces, and for this purpose the TRON Association has drawn up several volumes of CTRON specifications. The objects of these specifications are OS interfaces; the internal details of the OS are not specified, nor is the method of application program (AP) implementation, that is, the method of creating programs themselves. These are left up to individual OS and AP implementors.

Moreover, while the CTRON specifications fully define interfaces that are common to all application fields, there are some aspects that are unspecified or only partially specified. These are matters that are dependent on service conditions, operation modes, system configuration and the like, or that involve technologies still in the process of development. There is very little specification, for example, regarding operation administration and maintenance (OAM) management; and in the case of system generation (SG) and development support environments, only guidelines are given. The extent of CTRON specification can thus be classified as follows.

  Class 1: Fully specified
  Class 2: Partially specified
  Class 3: Not specified

Class 2 is further divided into three levels depending on the degree of specification.

  CO: Only the object part of system call names is specified.
  CS: System call names (object and operation) are specified, along with some parameter names.
  CP: System call names, parameter names, and some parameter content are specified.

The above classes and levels are shown in Fig.3. As indicated there, CTRON specifications cover only classes 1 and 2. Accordingly, the validation system is likewise limited to classes 1 and 2. An OS implementing interfaces other than those in the CTRON interface specifications cannot be certified. Namely, the software which provide class 3 interfaces should be separate from the software which is tested by the validation system. The relation between specification classes and CTRON validation is shown in Fig.4.

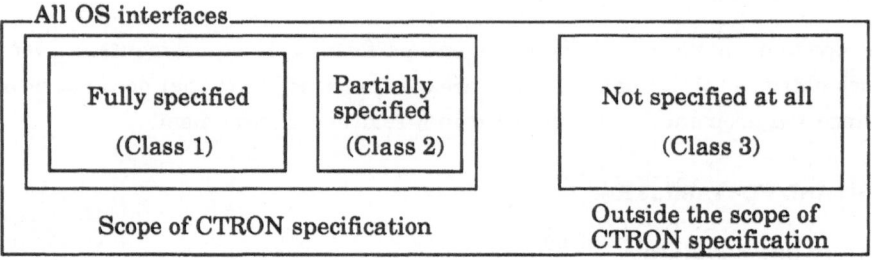

Fig.3 Scope of CTRON specification

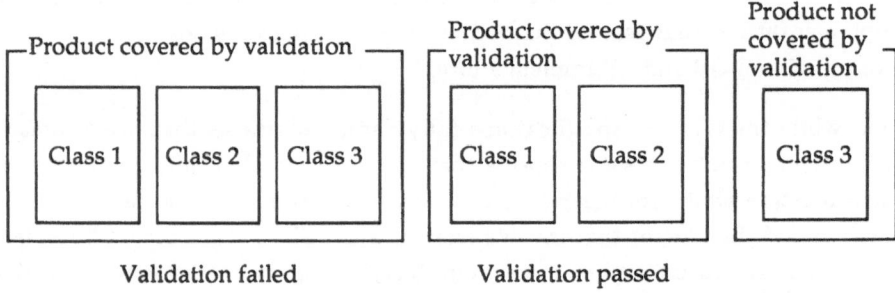

Fig.4 Relation between specification scope and validation

4.2 What CTRON can and cannot solve

Of the impediments to portability noted in section 3 above, use of CTRON specifications can solve many but not all of the difficulties.

As for differences in software module division, the CTRON interface reference model defines uniform module divisions, while the interfaces between those modules are standardized in CTRON interface specifications. These essentially deal with the problems of module division differences and non-standard interfaces. But these definitions are only for OS. So software module division for AP is left to users.

As for differences in hardware architecture, the CTRON Basic OS interfaces provide logical interfaces based on an abstraction of hardware features. Most interfaces are therefore independent of hardware conditions, solving to a large extent the portability impediments that relate to hardware architecture. As noted, however, in 4.1 above, there are certain aspects of some of the specifications that have had to be left to the implementors. These aspects need to be brought into conformity when software is ported.

Development environments are outside the scope of the interface specifications, but are important in achieving portability. Standard solutions are therefore laid out in books of portability guidelines.

CTRON specifications do not stipulate performance parameters. Inasmuch, however, as CTRON specifications apply only to interfaces and leave implementation up to different vendors in free market competition, it is natural to expect that modules meeting performance requirements will appear on the market. The above points are summarized in Table 1.

Table 1. Solutions in CTRON

Impediments	Evaluation	Notes
Inconsistency of module unit	P	
Inconsistency of interfaces	S	
Inconsistency of hardware	S	Devise in AP are needed concerning fault recovery processing
Inconsistency of developing environment	P	Portability guide book
Disagreement of efficiency	P	To be solved by increase of reusable software

S: Can be solved

P: Partially solution

5. AIMS OF THE EXPERIMENT

As noted in the previous section, in drawing up CTRON specifications there were certain matters that could not be standardized and had to be made implementation-dependent, since they are strongly influenced by service conditions and system configuration. There are also some matters that are not included within the scope of CTRON specifications but are in fact a necessary part of OS design, such as system startup and fault processing. In addition, there is always the possibility that interpretations of the specifications will differ from one implementor to another. For these and other reasons it is impossible to guarantee software portability on the basis of specifications alone. The portability experiment is therefore being run in order to verify the degree to which software developed based on the specifications is able to be ported. It is being carried out as part of the ongoing joint research with Tokyo University's Information Sciences Department in the Faculty of Science. The results gained through this experiment are to be reflected back in further refinements of the CTRON specifications and validation system, and will also be used in drawing up guidelines for designing highly portable software.

6. PORTABILITY IMPEDIMENTS AND SOLUTIONS

In preparing for this experiment, certain problems have had to be overcome in order to allow porting to take place smoothly. Originating points of impediments are shown in Fig.5. As noted in section 4, CTRON does not specify every interface completely. There are a number of implementation-dependent aspects for which each firm may have a different solution, and adjustments have to be made in these cases (B and C in Fig.5). Moreover, even where interfaces are specified in detail, there are instances where implementations differ due to ambiguities in the specification or differences in interpretation (A in Fig.5).

The places where such adjustment between interfaces is necessary are shown in Fig.5. Some representative examples of the areas where problems need to be worked out are noted below.

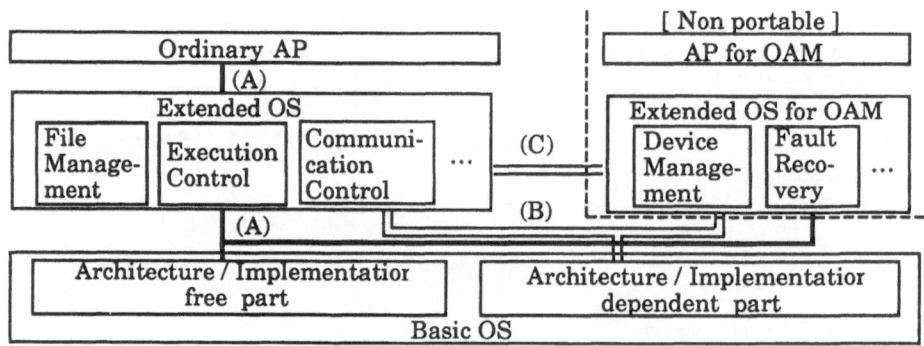

Fig.5 Where impediments originate

(a) Kernel architecture-dependent part

The Kernel interfaces involving OAM are closely tied in with factors such as processor architecture and system configuration. They are specified only partially, in the architecture-dependent part, with details left to implementors to decide.

(b) I/O Control architecture-dependent part

In I/O Control, architecture-dependent details that are left up to the implementor include fault indication and asynchronous event indication.

(c) OAM and other Extended OS interfaces

Details regarding the division of interfaces among Basic OS, Extended OS, and OAM are not specified in the case of system startup and initialization, Extended OS initialization, fault processing, etc.

(d) Other portability issues

Besides matters that are left up to implementors, other possible impediments to portability include duplication of external names when programs are linked, differences between compilers, and varying interpretation of specifications.

The basic solutions being taken in overcoming the above portability impediments are discussed next. The ideal, of course, would be to add further specifications so as to get rid of all matters that are left to implementors; but this is not feasible. Instead, the solution has to be divided along the following three basic lines, with the first given priority as being the ideal.

Solution 1: Adding further specifications
Solution 2: Localizing the places where adjustments are required (separating off the non-portable parts from the rest)
Solution 3: Providing detailed portability guidelines

The portability impediments and how they are being solved are summarized in Table 2.

Part of the experiment will involve surveying the aspects that need adjustment, having each firm make the necessary revisions, and evaluating the amount of revision required as well as the man hours involved. The results gained from the experiment will then be fed back into upgraded specifications and the validation system, and also into design guidelines for achieving software portability.

7. OUTLINE AND SCHEDULE OF PORTABILITY EXPERIMENT

The portability experiment, besides confirming the solutions described in section 6, is being carried out in order to discover additional problems that may have been missed in the theoretical studies phase, and to come up with possible solutions to these as well. Fig.6 shows a schedule of the experiment and its phases.

In the portability trial, Extended OS programs and APs are to be ported to different Basic OS implementations conforming to CTRON specifications. In CTRON, the Basic OS is

Table 2. *Main portability impediments and solutions*

Problem		Solution			
		1	2	3	
	Specification error	○			
	Unclear specification	○			
Kernel:	SG interface	○			Experimental specification
	Implementation-dependent interface	○	○		Experimental specification
	Shared memory			○	
	Memory protection	○		○	Partial specification
	Interrupt management		○		
I/O Control:	SG interface		○		
	Architecture-dependent interface		○		
	Implementation-dependent interface		○		
OAM:	System initialization	○	○		
	Error handling system calls	○	○		
Other:	Compiler differences			○	
	Interface subsets			○	
	Duplicated names	○		○	Vendor specification
	Extended OS work area	○			Experimental specification
	Garbage processing	○			
	Implementation-dependent error		○	○	

○: solution adopted

implemented separately for each hardware architecture. An Extended OS, however, if developed according to CTRON specifications, should be able to run on any Basic OS and thus any hardware. This experiment will give developers of Extended OS programs a chance to have their products ported to Basic OS implementations made by other firms for different hardware than that for which the Extended OS was originally developed. It will evaluate how well the ported program runs in its new environment, and also how much effort is required in the porting process. The steps involved and the schedule are shown in Fig.6.

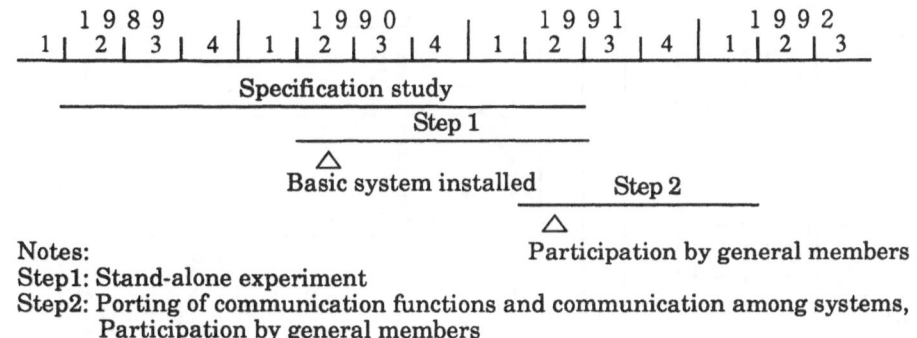

Fig.6 Schedule for portability experiment

In Step 1, porting will be made to each basic system individually. Then in Step 2, Extended OS programs including those with communication control interfaces will be ported, and the various basic systems will be interconnected to confirm their interoperability. The experiment is open to participation by all TRON Association members around the world. Participation by general members is scheduled to begin in April 1991. The TRON Association is now in the process of signing up participants for this later phase, and a number of firms have expressed interest.

The first phase will be carried out by eight firms represented on the CTRON Technical Committee, which is in charge of the experiment. Of these, five companies (Fujitsu, Matsushita Communication Industrial, Mitsubishi Electric, Oki Electric, and Toshiba) are providing the basic systems, consisting of hardware and Basic OS, to which programs will be ported. The processors for these systems are widely available Intel and Motorola chips as well as TRON-specification VLSI CPU implementations.

The plans for participation in the experiment by the eight CTRON Technical Committee member firms are outlined in Fig.7.

In the experiment, the source programs of Extended OS and application programs developed by each firm are being adjusted to conform with specifications set for the experiment. The adjusted source program is then compiled using the compiler for the basic system in the test center. Next it is merged with the basic system program files to form one load module. After loading to the basic system, operation is checked by means of test programs, commands, and the like. This procedure is shown in Fig.8.

A VAX computer is being employed as the host machine in the test center. Debuggers and other utilities are provided with the basic systems, for use in confirmation testing and in searching for causes of problems that arise. The configuration of the basic system is shown in Fig.9.

144

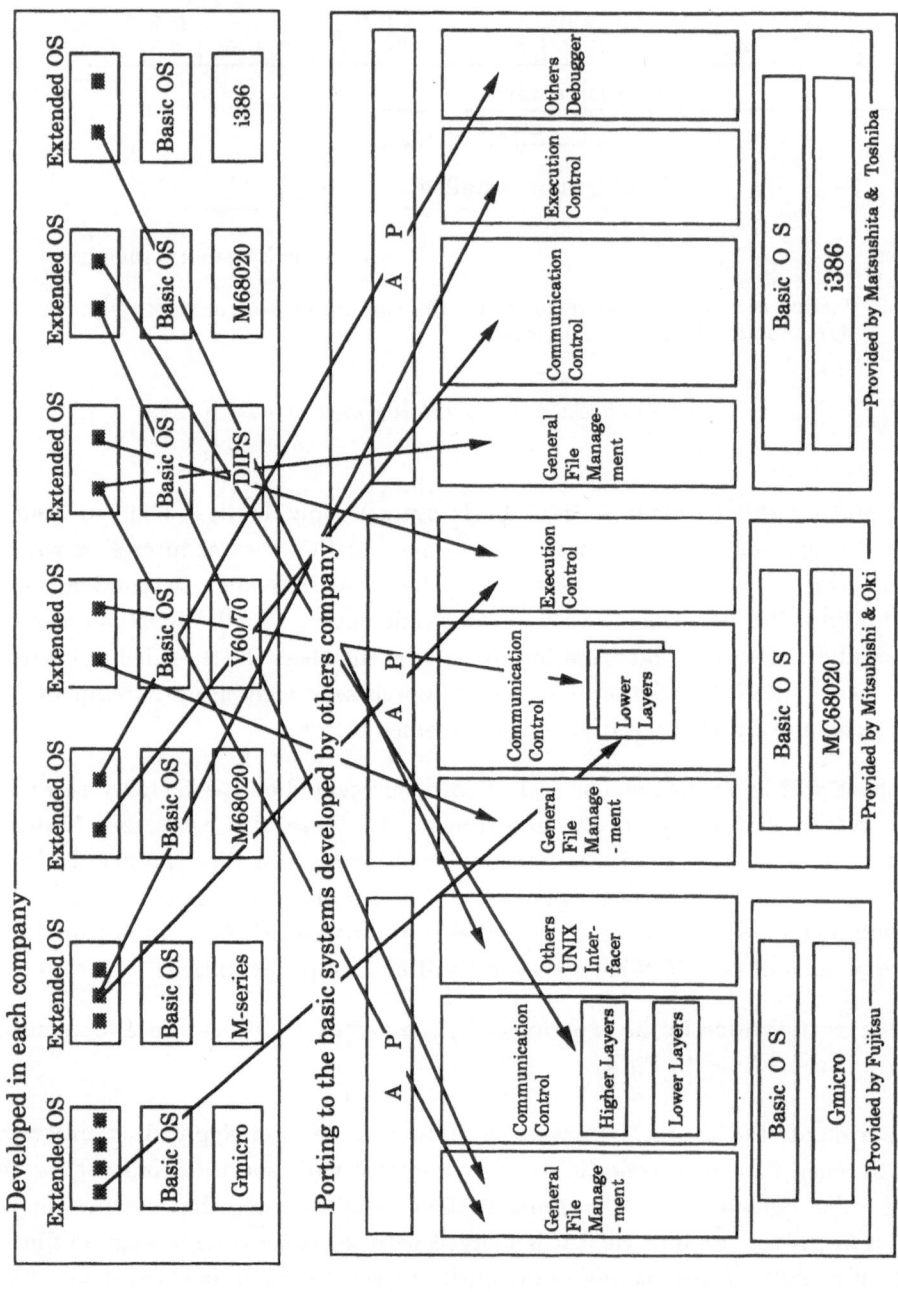

Fig. 7 Portability Experiment

MC68020 is a product of Motorola Inc.
i386/387 is a product of Intel Co.

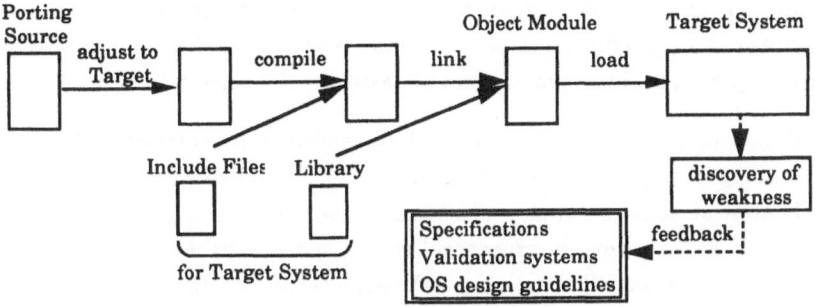

Fig.8 Porting Procedure

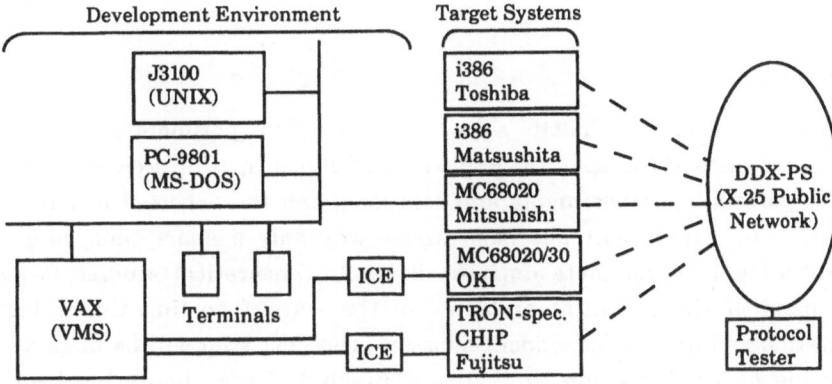

Fig.9 System Configuration

8. BENEFITS TO BE GAINED

Numerous benefits can be expected from this portability experiment. The first is that it will promote standardization of realtime OS interfaces. The experiment will allow the interface specifications to be confirmed, and to be upgraded as necessary to make them more effective. In addition to Extended OS programs, a variety of application programs are also to be ported in the course of the experiment, including a UNIX interfacer and a debugger. Since participation is expected not just by OS manufacturers but also by ordinary software houses and others, the experiment should go a long way toward promoting the spread of CTRON.

A second benefit is that the environment for Extended OS portability will be prepared. Problems encountered in porting will be overcome, and books of guidelines as well as support tools will appear, making porting much easier in the future.

A third benefit is the wide latitude that will be possible in selection of processors. Developers and users of application systems that use CTRON-specification OS products will enjoy the benefit of software that can be used on a wide range of systems, since the Basic OS will hide differences in processor architecture. System upgrades will be possible without having to sacrifice existing software resources. It will not be necessary, either, to use the same processor for prototype and commercial systems. The problem of processor obsolescence will be readily solved.

As Extended OS products and development tools become available, we can expect an increase in the number of software development firms creating products for CTRON-specification OSs. This will lead to the further spread of CTRON and also to increased software productivity.

9. CONCLUSION

The above overview of the CTRON software portability experiment has presented the background and aims of the trial, the approach to CTRON specification, the nature of the experiment, portability impediments and solutions, and the expected benefits from the experiment. The experiment has been under way only a short time, and the final evaluation will not be complete until April 1992. Theoretical studies to date have extracted most of the potential problems in the way of porting that relate to the implementation/architecture-dependent aspects. The next step will be to go ahead with actual porting of programs and evaluate the number of man hours involved. As the experiment proceeds, it is likely that other types of problems will be discovered, such as those noted in section 6.

As pointed out in section 8, carrying out this large-scale experiment is expected to promote OS interface standardization and establish an infrastructure for software portability, as well as leading to multi-vendor software procurement and the further spread of CTRON. It is also hoped that this will give a boost to greater software productivity.

Acknowledgments

The authors would like to express their deep thanks to Dr. Ken Sakamura of the University of Tokyo, to CTRON Technical Committee Chairman Dr. Fukuya Ishino, and to the corporations in charge of carrying out the experiment, namely, Fujitsu Limited, Hitachi, Ltd., Matsushita Communication Industrial Co., Ltd., Mitsubishi Electric Corporation, NEC Corporation, Oki Electric Industry Co., Ltd., and Toshiba Corporation.

147

References

[1] Outline of CTRON, Ohm-sha, 1989

[2] Kernel Interface, Ohm-sha, 1989

[3] I/O Control Interface, Ohm-sha, 1989

[4] Data Storage Control Interface, Ohm-sha, 1990

[5] Communication Control Interface, Ohm-sha, 1990

[6] Application Oriented Communication Control Interface, Ohm-sha, 1990

[7] ISDN User Control Interface, Ohm-sha, 1990

[8] Execution Control Interface / Operation Administration and Maintenance Management Interface, Ohm-sha, 1990

[9] T. Wasano, Y. Kobayashi, et al, "Design of General Rules in CTRON Interfaces", TRON Project 1989, Springer-Verlag, 1989

[10] M. Fukuyoshi, T.Ohta, et al, "Design of CTRON Fault Torelance Functions", TRON Project 1989, Springer-Verlag, 1989

[11] T. Ohta, T.Wasano "Realtime Operating System Interface and its Application to Distributed Processing", TINA '90,1990

Tadashi Ohta: A executive engineer at NTT Network Systems Development Center. Since joining the company in 1970, he has been engaged in the research and development of software systems for electronic switching systems. He received the B.S. degree, M.S. degree and Ph.D. degree from the Kyushu University in 1968, 1970, and 1987. He is a member of the Institute of Electronics, Information and Communication Engineers of Japan (IEICE) and of the Information Processing Society of Japan (IPS).

Takashi Terazaki: An engineer at NTT Network Systems Development Center. Since joining the company in 1979, he has been engaged in the development of DIPS computers and the system engineering on DIPS operating systems. He has played role in software portability and validation methodology for the CTRON interface. He graduated from Kurume Technical College in 1979.

Above authors may be reached at:2-1, Uchisaiwai-cho 1-chome, Chiyoda-ku, Tokyo, 100 JAPAN

Toshikazu Ohkubo: A senior research engineer, supervisor, group leader in the Second Project Team, NTT Communication Switching Laboratories. There, he conducts research into operating system architectures. Since joining the company in 1971, he has been engaged in developmental research on DIPS operating systems and communication control systems. He received the BE degree in 1969 and the ME degree in 1971 at Waseda University in Tokyo. He is a member of the IEICE, of the IPS, and of the IEEE.

Above authors may be reached at:9-11, Midori-cho 3-chome, Musashino, Tokyo, 180 JAPAN

Mitsuru Hanazawa: A senior research engineer at NTT Communications and Information Processing Laboratories, where he is presently engaged in development research on operating system architectures. Since joining the company in 1969, he has been engaged in developmental research on DIPS operating systems. He received the BE degree from University of Electro-Communications at Tokyo in 1969. He is a member of the IPS.

Above author may be reached at: 1-2356 Take, Yokosuka, 238 JAPAN

Masayuki Ohtaka: A Supervisor of 1st Switching Network Systems Division, NEC Corporation. He joined the company in 1980. He received the BE degree from Nagoya Institute of Technology in 1978 and the ME degree from Nagoya University in 1980. He is a member of the Information Processing Society of Japan.

Above author may be reached at: 1131, Hinode, Abiko, Chiba, 270-11 JAPAN

Portability Cosideration of i386™-Based Basic OS (OS/CT)

Kazuhiro Oda, Yuji Izumi, Harunori Ohta, Nobuo Shimizu, Nobuhiro Yoshida
Toshiba Corporation

Abstract

OS/CT is a CTRON-specification Basic OS designed for use on the i386 CPU ['88, Oda]. It implements the [C+I] subsets supporting virtual memory systems. It has been certified in both the document and function validations offered by the TRON Association.

In the upcoming portability trial, the Extended OS programs to be ported to this system are File Management and Execution Control.

This paper outlines the hardware and software configuration of the basic system, and discusses various matters to be considered in porting independently developed Extended OS and application programs onto the Basic OS. These have to do mainly with aspects related to system generation, which cannot be specified fully in the program interfaces alone, and with architecture-dependent aspects that are closely related to hardware design. The approach taken to overcoming these difficulties is described; then some future issues are taken up with regard to developing a Basic OS so as to achieve even greater portability.

Keywords: OS/CT, virtual memory system, program interface, system generation interface

1. Introduction

OS/CT was designed as an OS for workstation use. Today's workstations generally employ a multiwindow system, are able to have more than one program resident in memory (requiring logical space use to a certain extent), and make use of interactive human/machine interfaces. On-demand paging (ODP) is thus mandatory.

---

* i386 is a tradewark of Intel Corpration.

In supporting this virtual memory system, an interface designed for independence from hardware architecture was realized, and a UNIX interfacer was implemented on top of this interface. The system is discussed elsewhere in terms of functions and specifications ['89, Oda].

The present paper discusses considerations taken in designing the Basic OS, to allow for porting of Extended OS programs conforming to CTRON specifications but developed in total independence of this Basic OS.

2. Outline of Tested System

2.1 Hardware

OS/CT was designed for use with Toshiba's J-3100 and J-3300 series personal computers running the i386 processor. The system hardware consists of the following elements.

Processor: i80386   16 MHz to 25 MHz

Coprocessor: i80387   16 MHz to 25 MHz

Memory
    Main memory: 4 Mb to 14 Mb
    Cache memory: 64 Kb

I/O devices
    FDD: 3.5"   720 Kb to 1.2 Mb
    HDD: 3.5"   40 Mb to 200 Mb
    Display: 640 x 400/640 x 480 dots
    Keyboard: 84-key/103-key
    Printer: Centronics/Serial interface

Communications facility (advanced-function communications interface card)
    Interface: V.24/X.21
    Communications speed: 300 b/s to 64 kb/s

OS/CT uses a 32-bit address width in the i386 protected mode, and supports multiple virtual memory spaces of 4 GB each.

2.2 Software

OS/CT was designed as an OS for workstation use, and consists of the following software elements.

Kernel: implements [C+I] subset

I/O Control: implements logical DK, logical FD, GIO (printer, display)

3. Interfaces for porting an CTRON Extended OS to OS/CT

From the standpoint of allowing porting of independently developed Extended OS programs, the key in Basic OS design is to minimize the parts that are likely to interfere with this porting. The two points where there is contact between the Basic OS and ported Extended OS programs are the program interface and the system generation interface. Each of these is discussed below.

[1] Program Interface

The program interface is specified in CTRON as system call interfaces. However, when the OS is applied to workstations, there is no guarantee that the application programs running on the Extended OS will all be faultless; very likely there will be a number of latent bugs in these programs. In order to protect the OS itself from these bugs, normally passing of control from applications to the Extended OS is done as a hardware state transition. This process is strongly influenced by hardware architecture, and there are some cases where the Basic OS must perform state control. In implementing the Basic OS, sufficient consideration must be given to hiding the hardware architecture here so as to minimize any influence on the Extended OS programs.

Furthermore, from the standpoint of maintenance and portability, it would be best to employ hardware protection functions and assign the Basic OS and Extended OS to independent memory spaces, with their own protection levels. In terms of execution performance, however, it is better to use the same memory space for both and minimize the state transition cost to the extent possible.

[2] System Generation Interface

In this interface, when an Extended OS program is loaded on OS/CT, every effort must be made to minimize the influence on the Basic OS and on other Extended OS modules. Also, considering that the Extended OS programs and Basic OS may be developed independently, name spaces need to be kept independent of each other, and each OS module needs to be made an independent load module.

In CTRON specifications, File Management is an Extended OS. Thus the Basic OS, which is booted up before the Extended OS programs, cannot use ordinary file management functions. Moreover, File Management defines a program interface but does not specify the notational convention of the data structure to be used in external storage devices. Accordingly, the IPL (Initial Program Loader), which is strongly dependent not only on notational convention but also on physical structure, must have its own file system independent of the file system used by the File Management program; and the Basic OS must be inside this file system.

From the above consideration, we decided that:

1) The Basic OS and Extended OS must be logically separate and independent files; moreover, if there is more than one Extended OS program, these must also be independent files.

2) The file system space in which the Basic OS resides must be independent of the user file system space. Also, Extended OS loading cannot depend on use of File Management (in some configurations File Management may not even exist). For this reason, the Extended OS must also be in the same file system as the Basic OS.

The following sections consider Extended OS porting in more detail based on the principles derived above.

4. Portability Problems and Ways of Solving Them

4.1 Problems in Porting

There are a number of potential obstacles to porting of Extended OS programs and applications to a CTRON Basic OS. Some of these are common to all CTRON Basic OS implementations, such as differences in compiler specifications, or methods of naming kernel resources. Here the discussion will focus on problems arising from specific structural characteristics of Toshiba's OS/CT basic system.

Of the OS/CT characteristics, the following represent potential problems with respect to portability.

a. The processor for which it was designed is the Intel i386.

b. It supports a virtual memory system.

c. The Basic OS and Extended OS are assigned the same protection level (0) for the sake of improved performance.

d. The Basic OS, Extended OS programs, and application programs are each made separate load modules.

The main problems involved in the above characteristics are discussed below.

[1] Matters related to program interface

(1) Registration and activation method of Extended OS system call

The Extended OS system calls depend on which Extended OS programs are implemented, so that if a static system call mechanism were used, system calls would have to be changed in accord with the implemented Extended OS each time the system was generated.

In the OS/CT system, however, the Basic OS and each Extended OS are separate load modules, so in system generation it is not possible for the Basic OS to know in advance the entry address of Extended OS system calls. Instead it is necessary to create a system call transition mechanism dynamically in system initialization.

The CTRON kernel provides a mechanism for this as an architecture-dependent interface, namely, a function for defining system calls dynamically. This interface, however, is specified only at specification level CP (parameter names specified). The semantics of parameters are not specified, so in implementation, special care had to be taken to fit the specification to the i386 architecture.

(2) Extended OS access to application program space

If an application tried to access an illegal address, normally that would raise an exception and might lead to task abort. What happens when an Extended OS accesses an illegal address? Generally the Extended OS is also considered to be a system program, and it is assumed that there are no programming errors at this level, so this would normally be treated as a system error. In system call processing, however, where access is attempted to a user space address designated by a user, there is no guarantee that the address will not be illegal. In other words, when application space is accessed, even if there is no programming error in the Extended OS, it is still possible that an illegal address will be accessed.

There are two possible ways of getting around this problem:

a. Raise an exception when an illegal address is accessed.

b. Check the validity of all addresses before user space is accessed.

(3) Preserving and reproducing environments in general program control

When a user program is activated in general program control, it is necessary for control to be passed from a high protection level to a low one. This cannot be realized without some sort of hardware operation for switching over the stack area and changing the protection level. The processing involved is dependent on the processor and kernel control structure; thus, in order to maintain Extended OS portability, the Kernel Working Group in the CTRON Technical Committee has been requested to specify a system call for passing control from a high protection level to a low protection level (START_UPWARD_PROGRAM).

When the i386 processor is used, the following problem occurs in this regard. When control is passed from general program control to the user program, it is possible to return to general program control using the EXIT_PROGRAM system call for exiting from the user program; but in this case it is necessary to return control to the user program control passing point. Normally this can be done by using the provided "setjmp" and "longjmp" libraries to preserve and restore the environment.

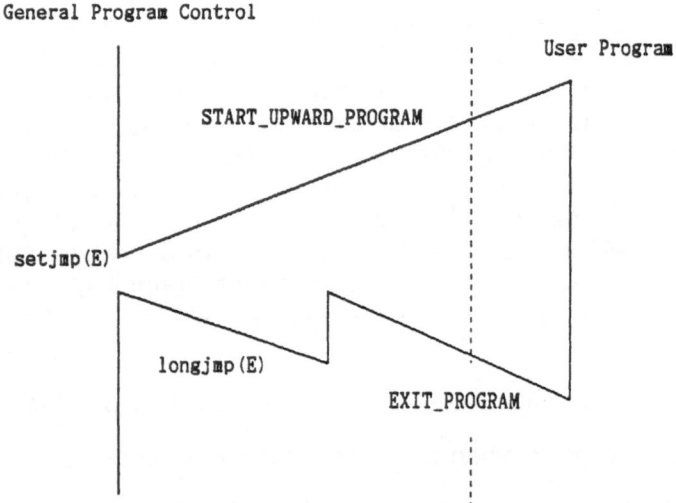

Figure 1. Passing of control to and exiting from user program

Naturally the stack pointer value is also included here in the environment. With the i386 processor, when control is passed from a low protection level to a high protection level, the assigned stack pointer value is stored in TSS (Task State Segment). The processor, however, does not change this value at all. That is, if the stack pointer value used when the protection level starts executing is the same as that used last time, then the above processing will take place correctly; but in the case of i386 it must be performed in software. Yet, only system programs can access TSS, so in this system the Basic OS must perform this access. On the other hand, setjmp and longjmp are libraries, so these cannot access TSS. This is a problem that must be dealt with when implementing the CTRON Basic OS on the i386 processor.

The architecture dependent part which is the special characteristics of intel hardware is hidden by way of "setjump/longjump" library and the partability.

[2] Matters related to system generation interface

(1) Position of device management

Device management is a system-dependent function, so the specific functions, their position, and their implementation method must be determined for each system. The process of connecting devices to the system, in particular, is closely tied in with system initialization processing.

(2) Loading of Extended OS modules

In this system the Basic OS and each Extended OS program are separate load modules, so the method of loading these modules has to be given special consideration.

One approach would be to have the system loader, which loads the Basic OS, also load the Extended OS modules; another would be to have Extended OS modules loaded by the Basic OS.

In the first approach, since the Basic OS and Extended OS have the same load module format, the procedures required for loading the Extended OS modules are simplified. The system loader, however, loads the load modules in real memory, so the Basic OS would have an added burden in managing available memory.

In the latter approach, it would be necessary to provide the Basic OS with new functions for system program loading, but the Extended OS programs could be loaded into virtual storage, reducing the memory management burden.

(3) Extended OS initialization

The way in which an Extended OS is initialized is likewise system dependent. The problem here is how the entry address of the Extended OS initialization routine is notified to the system. Some Extended OS interface classes specify system calls for use in initialization; but since, as noted earlier, Extended OS system calls are defined dynamically after the system is activated, it is hardly possible to start out by issuing a system call. Rather, the Extended OS initialization system calls are provided for restart processing after a fault occurs.

The following sections discuss how the above problems were dealt with in the OS/CT system.

4.2 Kernel

Of the above problems in achieving portability on the OS/CT basic system, those involving the kernel are discussed here first of all.

(1) Extended OS system call method

(a) Semantics of system call definition (SYC_DEF)

It would be possible to use SYC_DEF to define each of the Extended OS system calls, but this would not be efficient inasmuch as it would require issuing SYC_DEF numerous times in initialization processing, and would increase the number of Extended OS system calls managed in the kernel. If this approach were adopted, then when applications issued system calls for the Extended OS, the protection level would change, making it necessary to provide call gates in LDT or GDT (Local Descriptor Table/Global Descriptor Table). Let us assume that for each system call definition using SYC_DEF, one call gate descriptor has to be allocated in LDT. With the above approach, the same number of LDT descriptor slots would be used up as the number of system calls in the Extended OS. For file management alone, there are 78 system calls; if a large number of Extended OS programs were implemented, a considerable number of LDT descriptor slots would be used up. Moreover, the slot numbers allocated for descriptors in LDT would become necessary for issuing system calls between levels, and would have to be stored in the Extended OS system call runtime library; so these would have to be decided statically. As a result, the use of LDT slot resources would become prohibitively high.

For the above reasons, in this system one SYC_DEF is used to define system calls for one Extended OS, with the role of SYC_DEF being to define the Extended OS entry.

(b) Semantics of parameters

Based on its degree of architecture dependency, the specification level of the SYC_DEF system call is CP, meaning that it is specified only up to the names of parameters. These include systemcall_name and systemcall_entry.

The latter parameter, systemcall_entry, signifies the address of the system call entry. When an Extended OS system call is issued, control is passed to the entry part of that system call, at which point branching takes place to the individual system call that has been designated.

The systemcall_name parameter is used to identify the Extended OS. This corresponds to the call descriptor slot number in LDT.

(c) Transition method

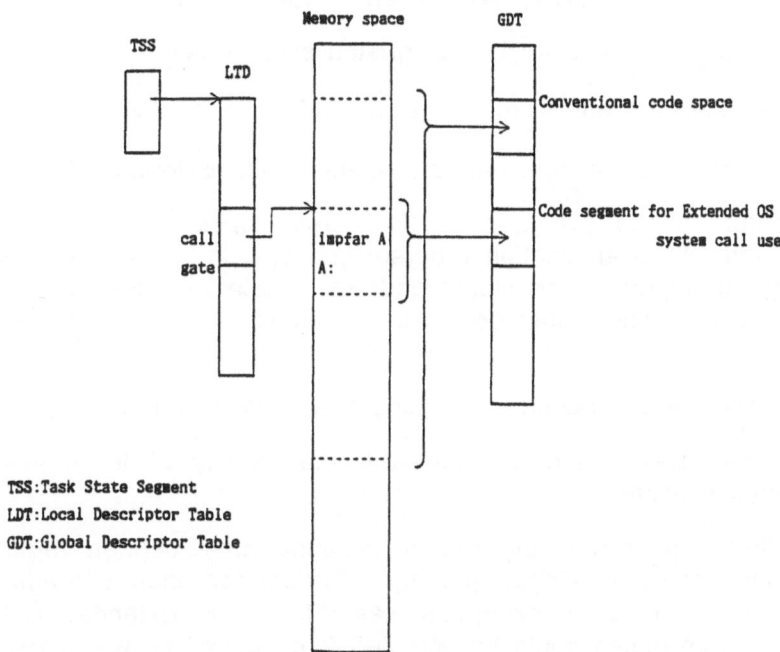

Figure 2. Extended OS system call transition

The specific method for Extended OS system call transition makes use of call descriptors in LDT. If, however, the address of the systemcall_entry defined using SYC_DEF were to be directly written to the call descriptor, since LDT exists for each task it would be necessary to update the LDT content of each task every time

SYC_DEF was issued. In the OS/CT system, therefore, the call descriptors in LDT are used to indicate the starting address of a fixed segment in GDT. The systemcall_entry defined by SYC_DEF is then the base address of this segment. In this way control is passed to the designated address. Since, however, this segment is different from the conventional code segment, a jump between segments is made (jmpfar), and the code segment is changed to its traditional form.

With this approach it is only necessary to use SYC_DEF to update the content of GDT; the content of LDT remains fixed.

(d) Extended OS system call entry part

The methodology outlined above requires that the following processing take place in the Extended OS system call entry part.

a. System call arguments are copied to user space.

b. Branching is made to the designated system call.

This reduces the efforts of porting extended OS to this basic OS.

(2) Access to application program space in the Extended OS

As noted in the previous section, when access is made in the Extended OS to application program space, it is possible that access will be attempted to an illegal address (space for which there is no page table). This could be dealt with in either of the following two ways.

a. An exception is raised when access is made to an illegal address.

b. Before user space is accessed, the validity of the address is always checked.

The first approach would require defining an exception routine for exception class 2 (illegal memory address) for each Extended OS. Then as soon as an exception was raised, the Extended OS from which it was raised could be detected (e.g., based on which Extended OS is currently running in the Extended OS work area), the exception routine of that Extended OS could be called, and in that exception routine an error could be returned for the currently executing system call. There are two problems, however, with this approach.

The first is that an exception routine is called asynchronously with the currently executing system call, making it difficult for the exception routine to return an error for the system call, which is the main routine.   The second problem is that exception routines are defined separately for each task.   It would be necessary every time a task was created to define an exception routine for this purpose, but it would be difficult to find the occasion for this definition.

As a result of the above considerations, the OS/CT system adopts the second approach (b).   In this method, checking of address validity each time access is made to user space inevitably involves a slight drop in performance; but it is also possible, as an option in system generation, to eliminate this check if desired.   The system can then be used in applications requiring a higher level of real-time performance.

In addition, in order to increase Extended OS portability, a runtime library for user space access is provided for use by those porting an Extended OS.   This library can be used to check the validity of addresses and return an error in case of an illegal address.   The check is performed making use of the memory protection reference function (MEMORY_PROTECTION_REFER) provided in the kernel architecture-dependent interface.

(3) Method of exiting from user programs

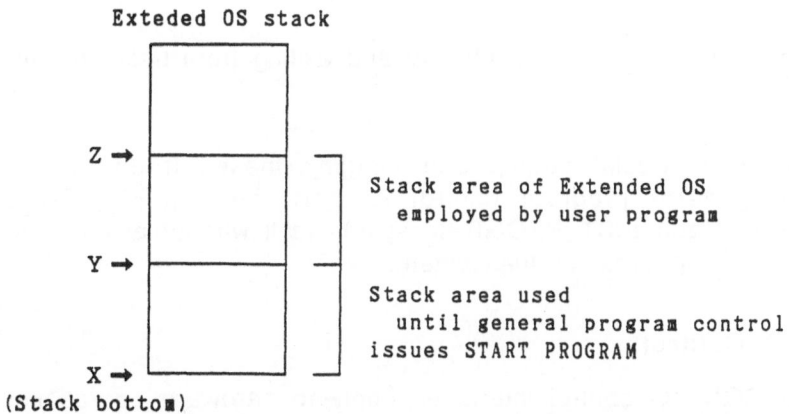

Figure 3.   Extended OS stack when user program is started

In order to implement the program exit system call of general program control, setjmp and longjmp runtime library functions have been added for processing the saving and restoring of the required environment.   A system call is provided in the kernel architecture-dependent part for referencing and changing the stack pointer (stored in TSS) that indicates the protection level at which the Extended OS is running.   This system call is used in setjmp and longjmp to adjust the stack pointer value stored in TSS.

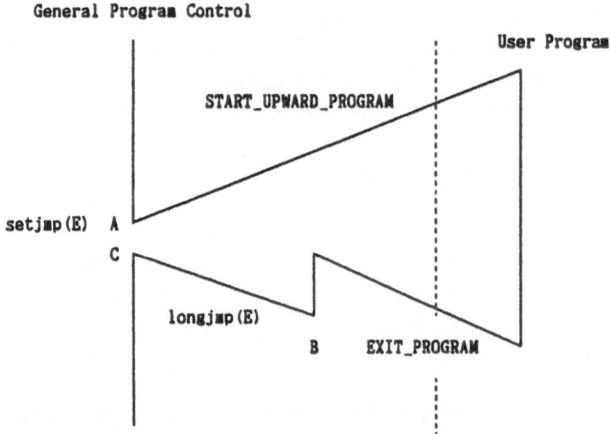

A: START_PROGRAM processing part in general program control
Saved value of Extended OS stack pointer is changed from X to current value Y.

B: EXIT_PROGRAM processing part in general program control
Current value of Extended OS stack pointer becomes Z.

C: START_PROGRAM exit part in general program control
Saved value of Extended OS stack pointer = X; current value = Y; environment at point A is restored.

Figure 4. Passing of control to and exiting from user program

Use of this special setjmp and longjmp makes it possible when porting general program control to port the START_PROGRAM system call and EXIT_PROGRAM system call without any adjustment whatever to the rest of the system.

4.3 I/O Control

The CTRON I/O control interfaces apply to hardware operations and control functions in I/O devices, and in many cases are closely tied in with system configuration control and operation mode. For these reasons, the number of architecture-dependent aspects is inevitably greater than those of the kernel interfaces. If, however, software portability is to be realized, which is the main aim of the CTRON interface specifications in the first place, then the architecture-dependent interfaces must be minimized to the extent possible. Thus every effort has been made to divide the Extended OS programs using I/O control into operation administration and maintenance (OAM) management and non-OAM, so as to increase portability.

Functions used only by OAM management take direct advantage of hardware architecture and other system characteristics, emphasizing functional expansion and performance over portability. For this reason the specifications here are relatively loose, allowing OAM design freedom. On the other hand, those functions used by general Extended OS programs other than OAM management have been specified in more detail and with a minimum of implementation-dependent aspects, giving priority to portability.

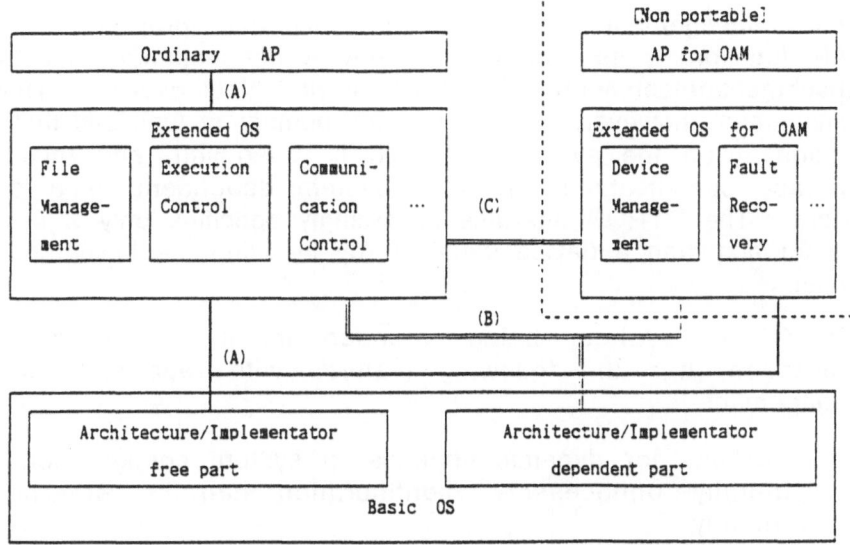

Figure 5. Where impediments originate

The OS/CT system, as well, has been designed in accord with a portable interface model based on the above I/O control interface design policies. The basic system consists of a separate OAM (device management) and Basic OS, so that Extended OS programs can be ported readily. That is, use of architecture-dependent I/O control interfaces is limited to device management, with the differences among architecture-dependent interfaces absorbed in device management in the basic system.

When device management is invoked, all devices in the system are created and initialized in accord with device configuration information set in advance for the system. The system-specific part of the device control block is used only at this time, and is hidden thereafter. Fault notification which includes architecture-dependent information is made to device management; other Extended OS programs need not be aware of it.

When an Extended OS is ported to this system, it acquires device identifiers. Thereafter it can issue read, write,and control requests without having to be aware of architecture-dependent information. Also, specifications that are indicated as being implementation dependent were avoided in this design wherever possible.

4.4 OAM Functions

(1) Device management

Device management is one of the interface units providing CTRON OAM functions. Its role includes device connection/disconnection (attachment/detachment), and allocation of logical devices. Device management, however, has a very large number of functions that are dependent on the system to which it is applied, and thus the interface specifications are also system dependent to a great extent. The CTRON interface accordingly specifies only a system call for acquiring a device identifier (by inputting the logical device name).

The OS/CT system, being intended mainly for workstation application, has the following features with regard to device management.

- Functions for dynamic changes to system configuration are generally unnecessary; configuration can be determined statically.
- In most cases the user and machine operator are the same.

Accordingly, device management in this system uses a system configuration description file (discussed below) in addition to the above system call for device identifier acquisition. This allows the following functions to be provided.

a. Device connection (attachment) function

Each device type (DK, FD, etc.) is assigned a logical device name and a unit number. Device management uses this information when issuing CREATE_DEVICE and INITIATE_DEVICE system calls for each device that is to be connected to the system.

b. Swap area designation function

Along with the logical device name, the starting block number of the area and the number of blocks are designated.

c. Defective/alternate block designation function

Logical device names are assigned a defective block number and alternate block number as a set.

(2) Function for loading Extended OS

The Extended OS load function reads the Extended OS load module into the memory area determined based on the hard disk driver. This function is mandatory with the OS/CT system because the Basic OS and Extended OS are divided into separate load modules. It is provided as part of the basic system because it would be highly inefficient for developers to have to provide this function with each Extended OS.

As noted earlier, file management is an Extended OS in CTRON. It is therefore not possible to use ordinary file management functions in activating the Basic OS and file management itself, before Extended OS activation. Moreover, file management interface definition includes a program interface, but does not specify the notational conventions for the data structure used in external storage devices. For these reasons, the IPL function and Extended OS load function, which are strongly dependent not only on notational conventions but on physical structure as well, must be given their own file system independent of that used by file management.

It is therefore necessary for the Basic OS and for file management and other Extended OS modules to be stored in this independent file system. Then in order for the Basic OS to avoid requiring awareness of this independent file system, the Extended OS load function must be included as an IPL function.

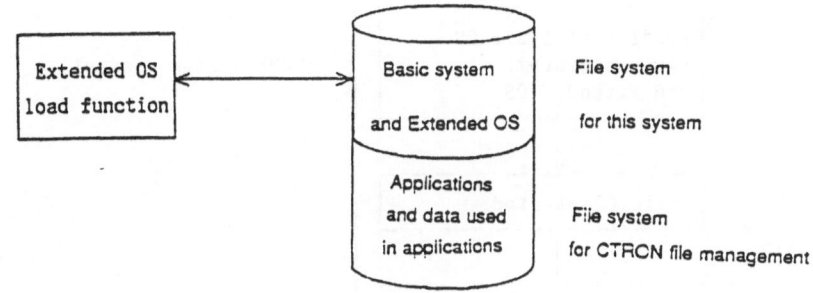

Figure 6. Extended OS load function

(3) Extended OS initialization

Initialization of this system, including the Extended OS load function, is described here.

(a) OS/CT system initialization takes place automatically when the power is turned on.

(b) The CTRON system loader (IPL), based on system configuration information stored in a disk file, loads the Basic OS, OAM management, and Extended OS modules. Information such as the entry address of each Extended OS initialization routine and that of OAM management is read into the system common area. Information set in the load module's program control information is used here as the load address of modules to be loaded and the entry address of each initialization routine. Finally, the CTRON system loader passes control to the Basic OS initialization routine.

(c) The Basic OS, after completion of its initialization processing, passes control to OAM management based on information set in the system common area.

(d) OAM management, likewise based on information set in the system common area, successively invokes the initialization routines of each of the Extended OS modules being loaded, and executes Extended OS initialization.

This system initialization process is outlined in Figure 7 below.

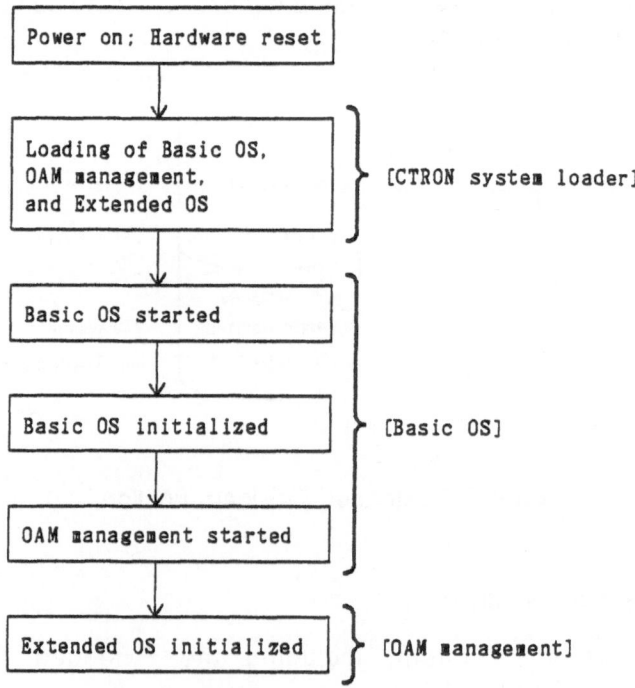

Figure 7. System initialization procedure

After completion of Extended OS loading, the memory configuration is as shown in Figure 8.

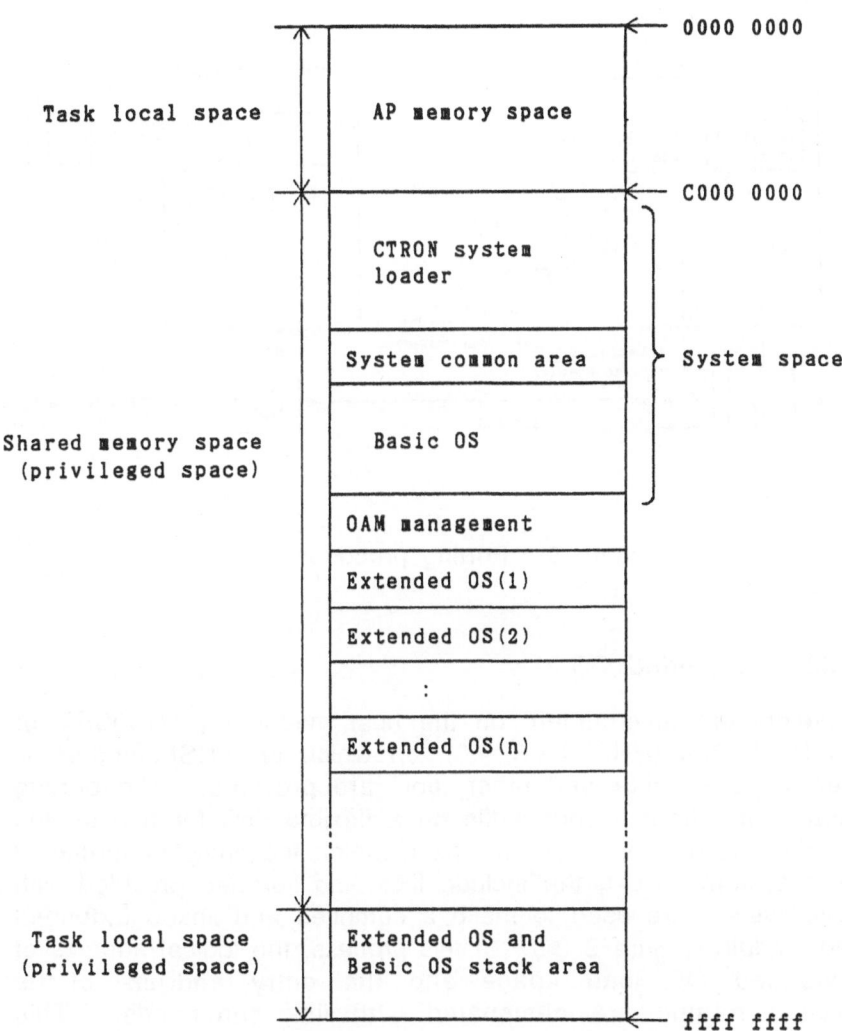

Figure 8. Memory configuration

5. Porting Procedure

The specific procedure used in porting an Extended OS to the OS/CT system is described here.

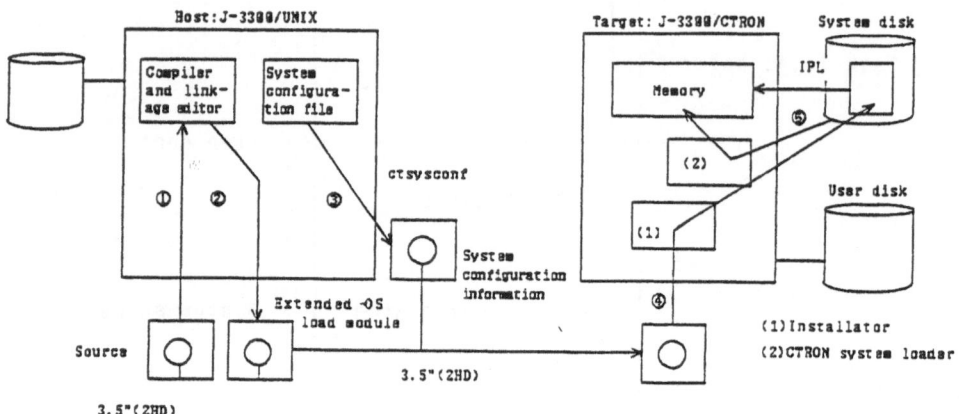

Figure 9. Porting procedure

5.1 Making Extended OS

The development environment on the host machine (J-3100SGT or J-3300) is UX/386 (UNIX SVR 3.0), on which an ANSI-standard C compiler, linkage editor and other tools are provided. The porting procedure starts from a source file on a flexible disk for use on the host machine (Figure 9 ①). This must match the compiler format of the basic system. Next, the include files and libraries provided with the basic system are used to make a compiled and linked Extended OS load module (Figure 9 ②). In this process, the logical address of the Extended OS load space and the entry address of its initialization routine are designated with link commands. This designation must be made in the load module.

The following files are provided in the basic system.

(1) Include files

common.h: Type definitions specified in the CTRON General Rules.
kernel.h: Type definitions, system constants, and symbol definitions specified in the CTRON Kernel Interface specification.

gioc.h: Type definitions and symbol definitions specified in the I/O Control Interface specification, and implementation-dependent type definitions and symbol definitions.

(2) Library files

syscall.o: Library routine for invoking the basic system.
Functions for use in debugging:
  printf(): Character string output formatted to display.
  getchar(): Character input from keyboard.
  panic(): Passing of control to debugger.
Functions for use by Extended OS:
  setjmp(), longjmp(), etc.

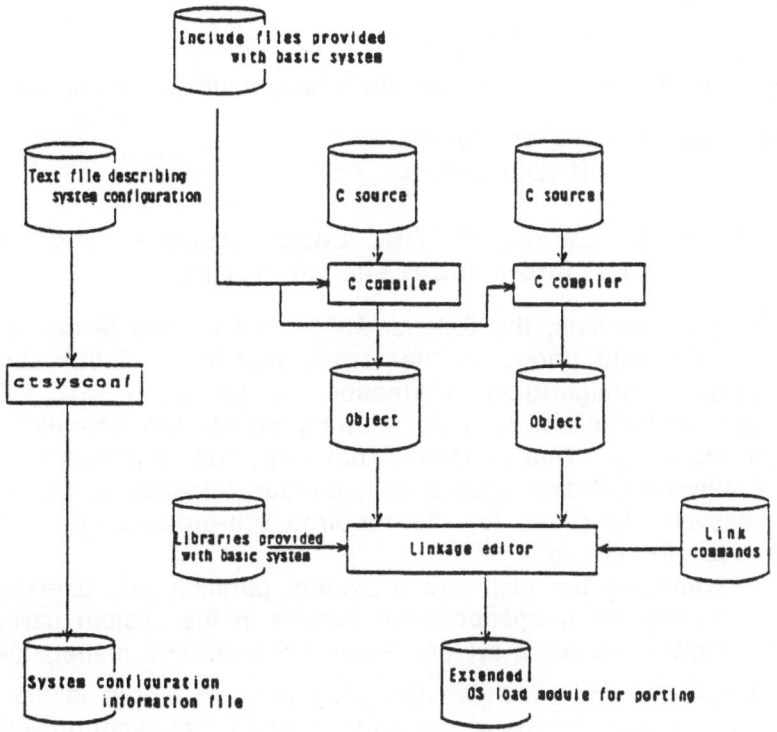

Figure 10. Development procedures on host machine

5.2 Making File Describing System Configuration

Using the notational convention below, a text file is created indicating the LM file type and device information. Then the tool ctsysconf is used to output to a flexible disk a system configuration information file.

(1) Notation in LM file

```
<LM file type> = <LM file name><carriage return character>
```

<LM file type>::= EOS (Extended OS)

<LM file name>::= Load module file name

<carriage return character>::= ¥n

(2) Format for designating device attachment information

```
<device type> = <logical device name>,<unit number> <carriage
return character>
```

<device type>::= DK (logical DK)
                |FD (logical FD)

<logical device name>::= Character string of up to 16 characters

<unit number>::= 0 (1st device)
                |1 (2nd device)

5.3 Porting Extended OS Load Module and System Configuration Information File to Target

In the host machine, the Extended OS load module is saved onto a flexible disk and ported to the target machine (J-3300) along with the system configuration information file (Figure 9 ④). For this purpose an installator is used allowing standalone operation on the target machine. This installator not only has functions for porting the Extended OS and system configuration information, but also has the following functions for the required pre-processing.
  a. Disk formatting
  b. Partitioning the disk into a system partition and user partition
  c. Creating an independent file system in the system partition
  d. Installing the basic system (Basic OS and OAM management)

The Basic OS and Extended OS programs are stored in the system partition, while the user partition contains application programs under control of file management (a CTRON Extended OS) and their data.

The system area must be on the system disk (the first of two disks); the second disk is used for the user partition.

Master boot area	
Area containing Basic system and Extended OS programs	System partition
Area containing application programs and their data	User partition

Figure 11. Disk partitions

5.4 Extended OS Loading and Debugging

(1) Extended OS loading

System initialization takes place when the power is turned on. The CTRON system loader is loaded and started by the 1st IPL (ROM), 2nd IPL (master boot record), and CTRON IPL (CTRON system partition boot record). The CTRON system loader contains built-in system debugging functions, and remains resident in memory.

The CTRON system loader, based on the LM type information in the system configuration information stored on the disk, first loads the Basic OS, OAM management, and Extended OS programs (Figure 9 ⑤), then passes control to the Basic OS initialization routine. After initialization processing is complete, control is passed to OAM management. OAM initializes devices based on the device information in the system configuration information, then calls in succession each of the initialization routines for the Extended OS modules that have been loaded, and executes this initialization.

(2) Debugging

The OS/CT system provides debugging functions at the following levels.

a. Using the libraries printf() and getchar() provided in the basic system

b. By means of system debugging

When control is passed to the debugger, a debugging mode is entered in which the current register content is displayed. A full range of functions are provided, with commands to the debugger for setting breakpoints, displaying the stack, deassembling the code part, etc.

6. Conclusion

In designing the OS/CT basic system, every effort was made to allow for ready porting of independently designed Extended OS programs. As the CTRON Portability Trial gets under way, this paper has noted the potential problems in the way of porting, and how these were overcome. The following points summarize the above discussion.

• Three problems involving the program interface were noted. These were approached using measures for hiding hardware architecture from the Extended OS, and designing the Basic OS in such a way as to minimize Extended OS dependence on Basic OS design.

• Three problems involving the system generation interface were likewise noted. The approach taken here eliminates interference between the Extended OS and Basic OS, and between Extended OS programs.

• For this experiment we were fortunate to be able to provide a Basic OS that has received certification in the CTRON validation process. It seems apparent to us that this validation testing is ample guarantee as to whether a product is able to achieve portability, which is the very large aim of the certification program.

There were some issues that could not be touched on within the scope of this paper. In the course of the actual portability trial about to begin, we hope to verify from many standpoints the correctness of the approaches taken to solving the problems in the way of portability. We also intend to continue every effort toward the widespread use of CTRON interfaces.

In conclusion, the authors would like to express their appreciation to TRON Project leader Dr. Ken Sakamura of the University of Tokyo, CTRON Technical Committee Chairman Dr. Fukuya Ishino, and Dr. Tadashi Ohta, head of the Portability Evaluation Working Group.

References

[1] K. Oda, N. Shimizu, et al. (Toshiba Corp.), An Implementation of CTRON Basic OS on a Lap-Top Workstation (Third TRON Project Symposium, Dec. 1988).

[2] K. Oda, N. Inoue, et al. (Toshiba Corp.), An Experimental Implementation for One Level Storage on CTRON Kernel (Fifth TRON Project Symposium, Dec. 1989)

[3] T.Wasano, Y.Kobayashi, et al. , Design of General Rules in CTRON Interfaces (TRON Project 1989, Springer-Verlag, 1989)

[4] T.Ohta, T.Terasaki, et al., CTRON Software Portability Experiment (The First Software Portability Symposium, Sep. 14, 1990. TRON Association)

Kazuhiro Oda is an assistant to group executive, technology Information & Control Systems Business Group of Toshiba Corporation. He is now a member of BTRON and CTRON technical committee of TRON Association. He received his B.E. from Kyuusyuu University at Fukuoka in 1964. He is a member of ACM and the Information Processing Society of Japan(IPSJ).

Yuji Izumi received his B.E. in information engineering from Kyoto University in 1975.   He is a manager of Personal Computer Software Design Dept. at the Ome Works of Toshiba Corporation. He has been engaged in Software design. He is a member of Information Processing Society of Japan(IPSJ).

172

Harunori Ohta received his B.E. and M.S. in information engineering from Nagoya University in 1978 and 1980 respectively. In 1980, he joined Toshiba Corporation. He has been engaged in developing data manage-ment of general purpose computer. He is a specialist of Personal Computer Software Design Dept. Currently he has interests in the field of data base management sys-tem. He is a member of Information processing Society of Japan(IPSJ).

Nobuo Shimizu is an engineer in Personal Computer Software Design Dept. at the Ome Works of Toshiba Corporation. He received his B.S. in mathematics from Waseda University in1983. He has been engaged in ope-rating systems design. He is a member of Information Processing Society of Japan(IPSJ)

Nobuhiro Yoshida received the B.A and M.S. degrees in electrical engineering from Waseda University in 1973 and 1975 respectively. In 1975,he joined Toshiba Corporation. He has been engaged in development of operating systems. Currently, he is a senior specialist of personal computer software design engineering depart-ment. His interests include fault-tolerant operating system, parallel processing and formal language system. He is a member of information processing Society of Japan(IPSJ).

Above authors may be reached at: Personal Computer Software Design Dept. in Ome Works, Toshiba Corporation 2-9, Suehiro-cho, Ome, Tokyo 198, Japan.

OS Subset Structure Achieving AP Portability

Hitoshi Shibagaki, Tetsuo Wasano
NTT Network Systems Development Center

ABSTRACT

General-purpose OSs provide abundant OS interfaces but include many interfaces that are unnecessary for individual applications. In order to get around this problem, it is necessary to structure OSs in such a way that interfaces can be selected as needed for different applications. On the other hand, from the standpoint of software portability, when the selection of OS interfaces varies, an AP for one system cannot run on another system, meaning a loss of portability. This paper reports on the OS structure and the subsetting method adopted in CTRON, which are aimed at achieving AP portability while also providing a wide choice of OS interfaces.

Keywords: Operating System Interface, Subset, Profile, Portability, Software

1. INTRODUCTION

General-purpose operating systems (OS) now in existence were originally developed for limited application programs (AP). Over the course of time, however, they have been expanded for use with a much wider variety of APs. The result is that they provide an extensive array of OS interfaces; but from the standpoint of individual applications they include many interfaces that are unnecessary, and leave much to be desired in terms of performance and ease of use. In order to get around this problem, it is necessary to divide the OS interfaces into subsets which can be selected as needed for different applications. This subsetting has to be based on a systematic organization of OS functions and interfaces.

The terminology used in this paper is defined as follows.

Interface: The structure presented by the OS to APs for use of OS functions.

Interface unit: A grouping of OS interfaces based on the resources controlled by the OS.

Interface primitive: The smallest unit of interfaces, equivalent to a system call.

Subset unit: A grouping of interface primitives based on their function.

Subset: A grouping of subset units required when an OS product is implemented.

Profile: A grouping of subsets that form the operating system as a whole.

At the same time, it is becoming increasingly essential to achieve software portability so that the same application software can be used in different environments. This is in order to meet the growing demand for software at a time when software is also becoming more complex and costly. Viewing OS interface subsetting from this standpoint of portability, when the selection of OS interfaces (AP execution environment) varies from one system to another, an AP for one system cannot run on another system, meaning a loss of portability. OS interface selection must therefore be made based on a fixed set of standards in order for portability to be maintained.

At the present time the concept of ISP (International Standardized Profiles)[1] is being considered, which would set certain combinations of necessary functions for making possible interconnectivity and interoperability among different systems. This concept has already been tried successfully in application to communication protocol profiles, for assuring interconnectivity among OSI systems, but has yet to be applied to OS functions and interfaces. As for OS subsetting, there has been a study of this,[2] but it has been limited to kernel interfaces and subsetting has not been applied to the interfaces of the OS as a whole.

This paper reports on the OS structure and the subsetting method adopted in CTRON[3][4][5][6] design, which is aimed at achieving AP portability while also providing a wide choice of OS interfaces.

2. SUBSETTING METHOD

Here subsetting refers to a selection of necessary interfaces from those specified for the OS as a whole, in order to allow each OS to be implemented with the minimum interfaces required for its purpose in the particular application field. CTRON adopts the three-stage subsetting method described below. This method allows the minimum necessary interfaces to be selected from among the various levels and kinds of CTRON-specified OS interfaces, but limits the choice to within the range that portability will not suffer.

1) OS interfaces are classified into a number of independent units based mainly on the resources that are controlled by the OS. These are called interface units.

2) In each interface unit, a classification is made into sets of related interface primitives (system calls), which are called subset units. These subset units are then organized into subsets, which are combinations of subset units required when an OS product is implemented.

3) Combinations of subsets are specified for each application field as profiles.

This subsetting approach is illustrated in Fig. 1 and explained in detail below.

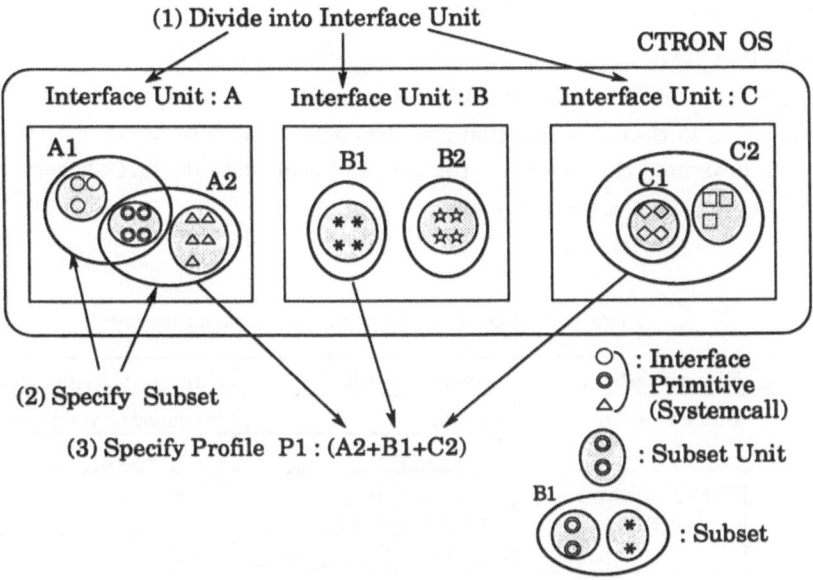

Fig.1 Subset and Profile

3. INTERFACE UNITS

The role of the OS is to manage the physical resources (hardware resources) and logical resources (software and database resources) making up a computer system. OS functions can be divided broadly along the following lines.

1) Functions that virtualize the distinctive characteristics of different resources and provide a means of access to them, so that users can make use of these resources efficiently and easily.

2) Functions that allow resources to be shared by multiple users.

3) In a broad sense, common functions that help users solve problems (library functions for mathematical operations, various utilities, etc.).

Examples of physical resources include central processing units, main storage devices, communication control equipment, and terminals, as well as I/O devices such as printers, and secondary storage devices such as magnetic disks and magnetic tape.

Logical resources include programs; data; jobs and sessions, which are units of work as seen by users; tasks, which are units of work inside the computer to which computer resources are allocated; and files, which are storage areas for programs and data inside secondary storage devices.

In CTRON, OS interfaces are classified and organized as follows.

1) Classification of OS

The resources controlled by the OS are classified by type. Groups of interfaces corresponding to that classification are then defined as interface units (see Table 1). OS or AP designers can delineate the range of required interfaces based on whether different resources are needed or not.

Table 1. CTRON interface units and resources managed

Classification		Interface Unit	Managed Resources
Basic OS		Kernel	Processor, memory
		I/O Control	I/O devices
Extended OS	Data Storage Control	General File Management	Files
		Database Management	Databases
	Communication Control	Layer Common	Buffers and timers for communication use
		Network Layer Control	Network-layer communication paths
		Transport Layer Control	Transport-layer communication paths
		Session Layer Control	Session-layer communication paths
		Etc.	
	Switching Control	ISDN User Control	Communication paths for switching
	Execution Control	General Program Control	Programs
		Process Control	Processes
	OAM Management	OAM Management	Management resources

2) Two-layer configuration

OS interfaces are given a two-layer configuration, consisting of an interface layer for virtualizing physical resources (called the Basic OS interfaces) and an interface layer corresponding to logical resources (called the Extended OS interfaces). The Basic OS interfaces provide the most fundamental OS interfaces as a platform for achieving software portability. Since the Basic OS interfaces themselves must be aware of the architecture of each physical resource, they are implemented separately for each specific architecture. Central processing units, for example, differ in architecture from one model to another, so that software must be

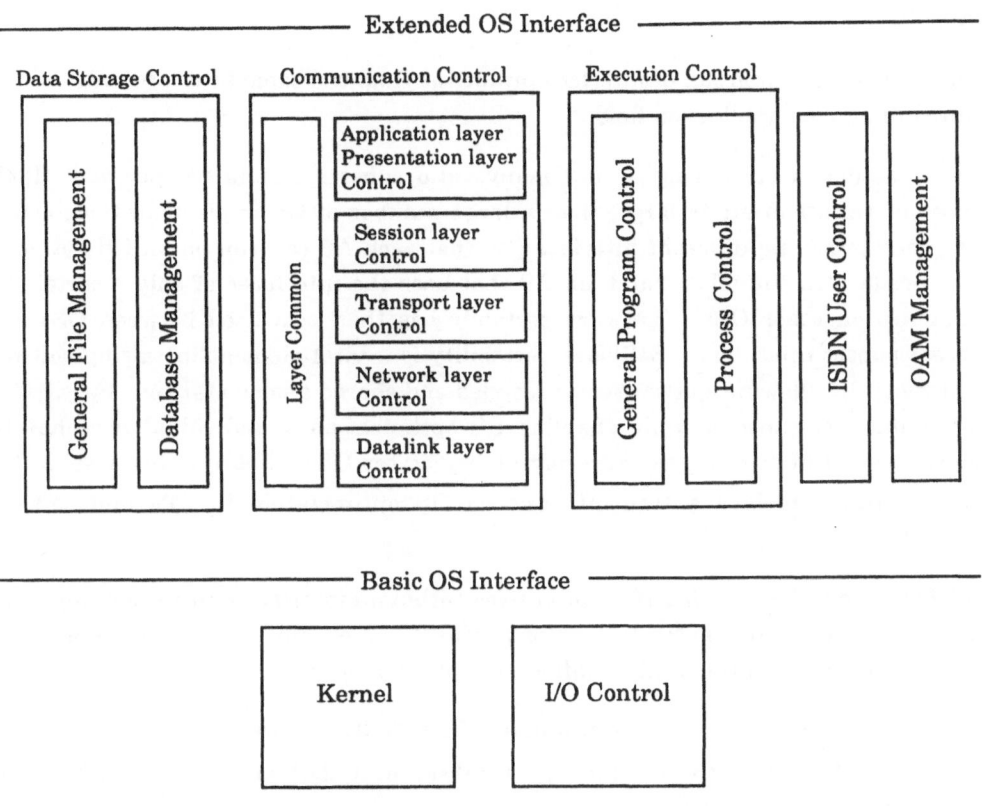

Fig. 2 CTRON Reference Model

implemented independently for each processor model. The Extended OS interfaces correspond to more logical resources such as files, processes, and jobs; these are located above the Basic OS interfaces. This two-layer configuration allows Extended OS and APs to be ported to different Basic OS implementations specific to each processor model or other physical resource.

CTRON defines the following interface units based on this approach.

The Basic OS interfaces are the Kernel, logicalizing processors and other processor resources such as memory, and I/O Control, providing standard access interfaces to different I/O devices. The Extended OS interfaces include File Management and Database Management, handling data storage resources required by APs, Communication Control (with an interface unit for each of the OSI layers) performing protocol processing to make possible communication with remote systems, and Operation Administration and Maintenance (OAM) Management, among others. A reference model of the CTRON interface units is shown in Fig. 2.

4. SUBSETS

A subset consists of a group of interface primitives from the same interface unit that are required in a given application field.

A key question in subsetting is how many valid subsets* should be specified. If the number of valid subsets is large, then a large number of OS implementations can be made, each providing different interfaces, so that each AP can run on an OS optimized for its needs. On the other hand, an AP that uses the interfaces of only a certain OS cannot run on other OSs. Software portability is then sacrificed between OSs with different subset conditions. Software portability is a vital element in raising software productivity, by allowing software to be recycled and shared among systems. Specifying a large number of subsets, while enabling OS optimization to individual APs, has the disadvantage of preventing software portability across OSs. Determining a subsetting approach thus involves a tradeoff between OS optimization to APs and software portability.

In CTRON, first of all the interface primitives within an interface unit were grouped into a number of subset units based on functions. These subset units were then combined into a few subsets based on the needs of different application areas.

The following principles were observed in deciding CTRON subsets.

1) All interface primitives belong to a subset unit, but only to one subset unit; overlapping is not allowed.

2) The scale of subset units is made as large as possible to the extent that there is likely to be no demand for further subdivision. This is to keep the number of different combinations from increasing unnecessarily.

3) Increasing the number of subsets will stand in the way of portability. The number is therefore kept to the necessary minimum that will allows optimization to APs.

4) In order to make clear whether an AP running on one interface subset will also run on other subsets, the relation between subsets is clarified in terms of the interfaces included and not included in each.

5) In each interface unit there are optional subset units, which are not closely related to other subset units and are highly independent. If subsets were designed based on the inclusion or not of these optional subset units, the number of subsets would swell. Accordingly, these subset units are not included in the CTRON-specification subsets.

---

* The term "subset" in this paper is not used in the same sense as in set theory, where all the subsets are considered valid. Hear only certain subsets are valid.

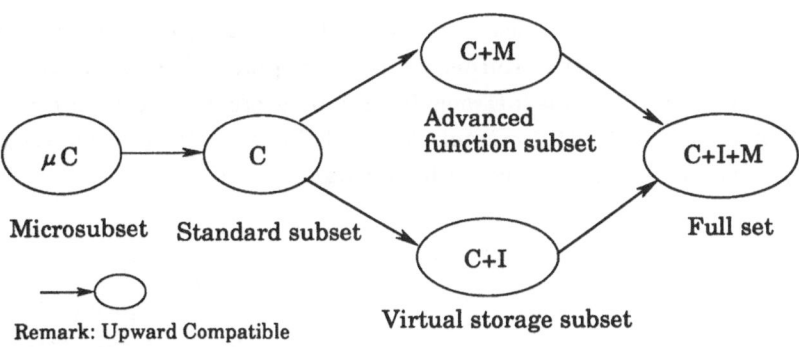

Microsubset   Standard subset

Remark: Upward Compatible

Virtual storage subset

Subset Unit	Function	Number of Interface Primitives
μC (Micro)	Task management Task synchronization and communication (event flag, message box) Interrupt management Timer management Memory management	44
C-μC	Task synchronization and communication (semaphore, serially reusable resources) Exception management Statistical Information management	40
M (Advanced function optional part)	Cyclic start procedure control Task cyclic start control Selective message receive control Rendezvous control Private timer control	19
I (Memory management optional part)	Virtual storage control Roll-in/roll-out control Basic program management	22

Fig.3 Subset Specifications (Kernel Example)

On the other hands, the existence of a large number of optional subset units would present an obstacle to AP portability because provision of optional subset units varies from one system to another. The optional subset units are therefore limited mainly to those that are strongly system-dependent, such as system management interfaces, where standardization is difficult. APs using these interfaces are inevitably less portable than others.

6) Subsets were arrived at based on the above principles, by surveying the OS interfaces of systems now in operation and those planned for the future and extracting the required interfaces. In this process the knowhow of OS implementors was drawn upon, but at the same time user needs were taken into account to the extent possible.

As an example of subsetting, the Kernel subsets[7] are shown in Fig. 3. The standard Kernel subset is [C]. An extension of this providing virtual storage interfaces for use in information communications processing is [C+I]. The [C+M] subset emphasizes processing speed. The full set of Kernel interfaces is provided in [C+M+I]. After these subsets were specified, there was a strong demand by users for a reduced-function subset for application to small embedded systems. To meet this need, the [μC] subset was added. AP porting is possible in the direction of the arrows.

5. PROFILES

5.1 PRINCIPLES OF PROFILE SETTING

In actual systems, each OS is provided in a combination of subsets. Normally an AP uses more than one interface unit; thus in order to increase AP portability, it is necessary further to decide the combinations of subsets to be offered. Such a combination is called a profile.

In CTRON, the following principles are employed in determining profiles.

1) Profiles are decided for each application field, so that the optimum subset combination can be applied to a given field. The number of profiles is kept to the necessary minimum.

2) The profile specification tells which subset is to be used when a given interface unit is implemented. The specification classifies subsets as mandatory (must always be provided), alternate (one or the other subset must be provided), or optional (does not have to be provided).

3) There are some other interface unit subsets that must be provided when a subset is provided. This dependency relation between subsets is taken into account when determining profiles.

4) Portability is improved to the extent that subsets are made mandatory; on the other hand, the need to implement compact OSs is best served by making subsets optional. This tradeoff has to be made based on a survey of needs of both users and OS implementors, as in section 4 above.

The notation used in specifying profiles is shown in Fig. 4.

5.2 APPLICABLE FIELDS

As noted above, subset profiles are specified for each application field. These application fields are defined within the range that APs are likely to share interfaces, so that the range of AP portability will be as broad as possible.

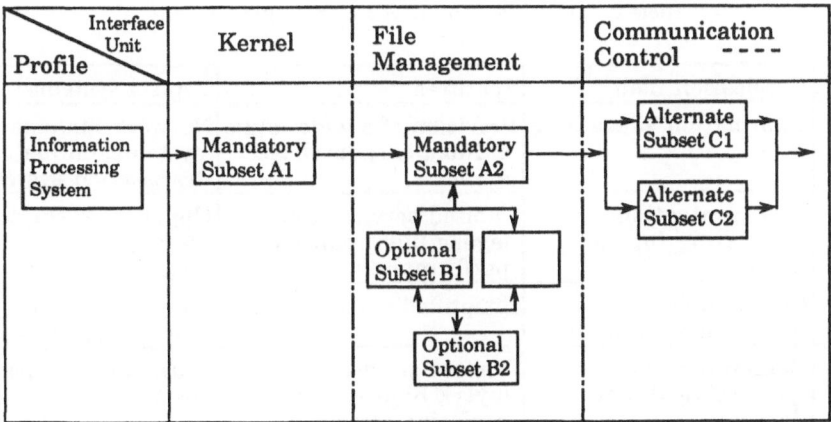

(Legend)

    Mandatory subset: A subset that must be provided as part of the specified profile.

    Alternate subsets: A pair of subsets of which one or the other must be provided.

    Optional subset: A subset that can be provided or not as desired.

(Remarks)

    Vertical groups of optional subsets mean upward compatibility. That is;

1) In this figure, optional subsets B1 and B2 include interfaces of mandatory subset A2. An AP running on a system that provides the minimum interfaces of this profile (i.e., that provides subset A2) can be ported to a system that provides optional subsets.

2) Optional subset B2 includes interfaces of optional subset B1. Subsets of lower boxes provide more interfaces, but AP portability is reduced because fewer systems provide the subset .

Fig.4 Description Method of Profile

The primary CTRON design objective is application to realtime processing fields. With this in mind, profiles have been determined for the eleven fields listed in Table 2. The main CTRON application fields of communication processing and switching processing have been subclassified into a number of areas, since the functional needs tend to vary quite widely.

5.3 PROFILE SETTING

Profiles were determined for each of the eleven application fields according to the following procedure.

1) The specification designers of each interface unit selected the optimum subsets for each application field.

Table 2. Classification of CTRON Application Fields

Profile	Application field	Features	Typical systems
P1	Information processing	Provision of a wide range of functions; database access	Network management systems; online transaction systems
P2	Communication processing (upper layers)	Limited services (upper layer); high realtime performance	Upper layer services (MHS, videotex, facsimile)
P3	Communication processing (simplified)	Simplified version of P2	Simplified version of upper layer services
P4	Communication processing (lower layers)	Limited services (lower layer); high realtime performance	PAD, gateway, packet switch
P5	Communication processing (network service nodes)	Additional services added on to switching system	network service nodes
P6	Office switching (local stage)	High multitask, realtime performance	ISDN switching system (local stage)
P7	Office switching (toll stage)	High multitask, realtime performance and support of high-speed circuits	ISDN switching system (toll stage)
P8	PBX (advanced models)	Realtime performance; wide array of functions	PBX (advanced models)
P9	PBX (simpler models)	Simpler, more compact version of P8	PBX (simpler models)
P10	Workstations	Interactive processing; outstanding HMI	Workstations
P11	Embedded systems	Reduced functional set; standalone operation	Embedded systems in robots, controllers, etc.

2) Groups of subsets were arranged into profiles, and the relation among subsets (the dependence of subsets on other subsets) was checked to make sure there were no problems in this regard.

3) The suggested profiles were further checked from the standpoint of OS implementors, AP developers, and system designers, to make sure all the necessary interfaces (and no more) were included.

4) The profile specifications were refined to reflect any problems pointed out in the checking process.

Examples of detailed profiles are shown in Fig. 5.

183

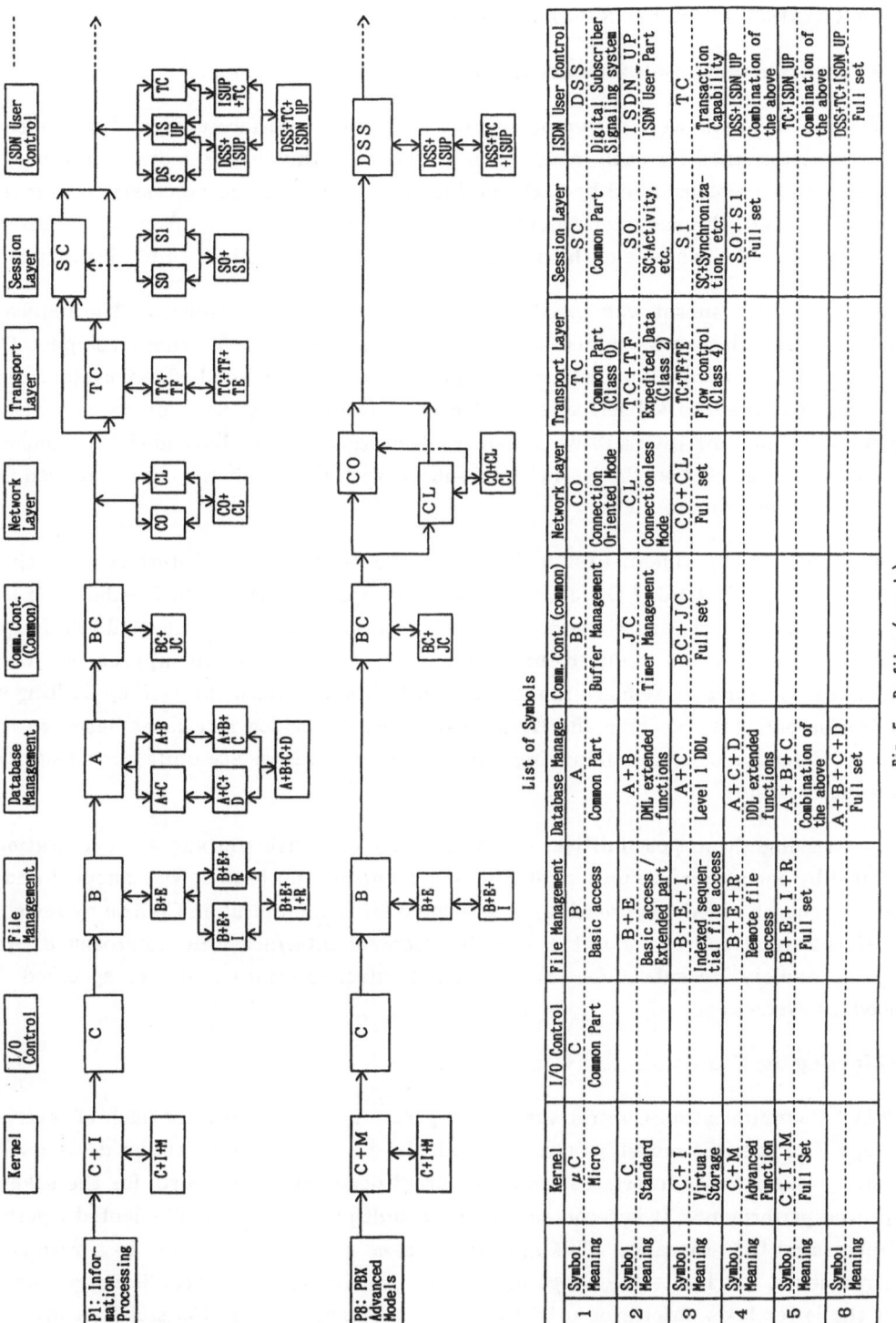

List of Symbols

Fig. 5 Profiles (example)

5.4 MAJOR CONSIDERATIONS IN PROFILE SETTING

(a) Reduced-function profile for embedded systems

CTRON specifications were drawn up separately for each interface unit, and the subsets were also determined for each interface unit. There is thus a slight divergence in the interfaces that are considered by each specification designer to be necessary for a given field. As a result, the range of required interfaces varies somewhat from one interface unit to another. An example of this is seen in the profile specified for embedded systems.

Originally the [C] subset was specified as the minimum Kernel subset. The reduced-function [μC] subset was added later to meet the demand for more compact OS implementations aimed at the limited application fields of embedded system use. However, the standard subsets of Extended OS interface units were designed without consideration for this [μC] subset. There were no cases where Extended OS standard subsets were premised on the Kernel [μC] subset, with the result that the Extended OS programs did not run on [μC].

To deal with this problem, first a list was made of the Kernel interface primitives required by each Extended OS, and these were compared with the [μC] subset. If the required interfaces of each Extended OS were incorporated in [μC], it would no longer meet user needs for a reduced-function subset. Three possible approaches were considered: 1) defining a reduced-function subset for the Extended OS itself by limiting its application range; 2) revising the Kernel [μC] subset-provided interfaces based on the needs of Extended OSs; and 3) making some Extended OS interface units unnecessary in embedded systems.

After studying these possibilities, it was decided to revise the subset specifications provided by each interface unit. For File Management, approach 1) was adopted and a new [μB] subset added. Approach 2) was adopted for Communication Control by revising the Kernel [μC] subset. For the Program Control interface unit, approach 3) was adopted, namely, no subset for the Program Control interface unit was specified for embedded system use.

(b) Limiting the Communication Control interface units

CTRON Communication Control specifies separate interface units for each of layers 2 through 7 in the OSI model, in order to meet the needs of communication devices with various protocol layer interfaces, and the varied needs of users. Also, for the sake of improved performance, it is recommended that multiple layers be implemented together as integrated OS programs. This approach makes possible application to a variety of environments, but limits the range of software portability since there is no guarantee that the lower layer interfaces used by APs or a Communication Control Extended OS will be included in the target system. This problem is dealt with by limiting the Communication Control interfaces units recommended for provision as profiles.

First a survey was made of commercial OSs and implementation plans by OS providers, with the aim of limiting the interface units recommended for provision to one if possible. In the course of these studies, however, the following points became clear.

1) There is a difference in the protocol layers as interfaces boundary points between information processing fields (P1 to P3 and P10 in Table 2) and the switching fields (P4 through P9).

2) In information processing fields, opinion is divided as to whether the transport layer interface unit or the session layer interface unit should be recommended. The transport layer is specified as the boundary layer in OSI and absorbing differences in communication media. The session layer is a higher layer and provides communication functions common to all application fields.

Regarding 1), it was decided to make a division in recommended interface units based on the application field. In the case of 2), for the time being a choice is to be offered between the transport layer interface unit and the session layer interface unit; these are to be narrowed down to one interface unit after more software appears and a weeding out process has taken place.

(c) Handling of optional subsets

As noted earlier, optional subsets are those which may be provided or not as needed. From the standpoint of AP portability, it is best to avoid these optional subsets to the extent possible, since systems having the same subset profile still might differ in terms of which optional subsets are implemented. If optional subsets are used, an AP configuration should be adopted that allows the parts using these optional subsets to be detached from the AP and ported along with the optional OS subsets. (See Fig. 6.) In any case, when portability is considered, mandatory subsets and alternate subsets have the greatest significance.

(d) Portability series between profiles

Portability series have been defined between profiles, to make clear whether or not an AP running on one profile will also run on another profile. These portability series are valid when APs use only mandatory subsets in the profiles. In Fig. 7, AP porting is possible in the direction of the arrows.

(e) Points to be observed in AP and OS implementation

When developing an AP with portability in mind, the developer should consider the application field within which the AP will operate, and use only the interfaces in the

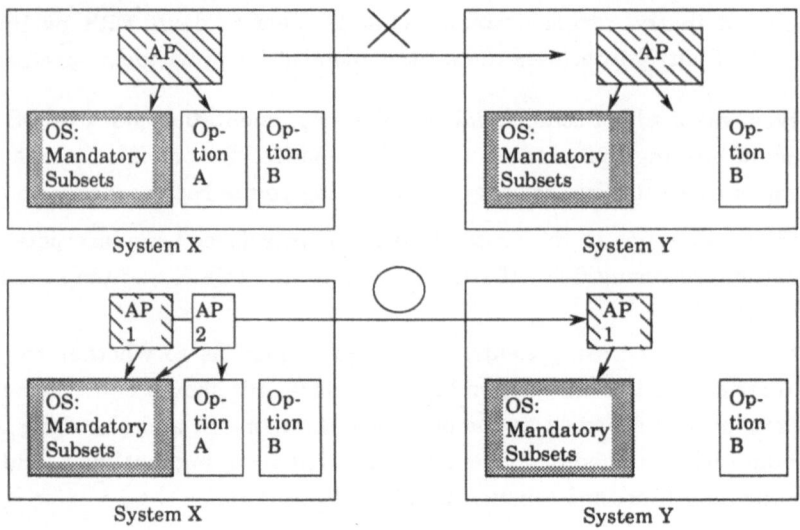

Fig. 6 Portable AP Configuration

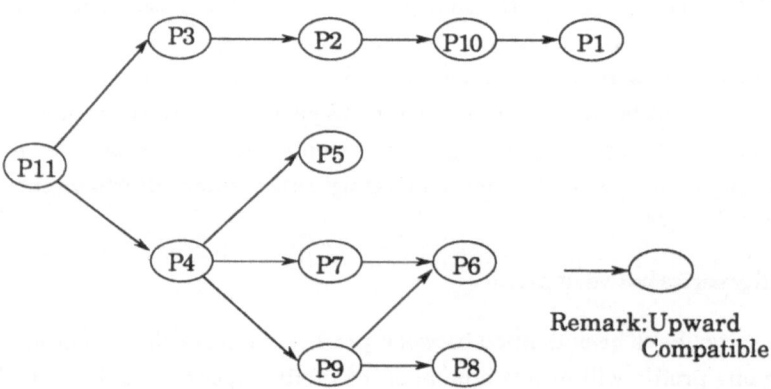

Fig.7 Portability series between profiles

profile for that application field if possible. Portability across different application fields is also possible, so long as the subsets used are limited to those common to different profiles (AND condition).

The OS implementor, likewise, should consider the range of application of an OS and provide OS interfaces in accord with the specified profile. If application to more than one field is to be allowed for, the profiles of each field (OR condition) need to be provided. The provision of optional subsets can be made based on individual performance requirements and the like.

A Portability Guide has been drawn up for CTRON detailing considerations like the above. Sticking to these guidelines will help assure a high level of AP portability.

(f) Validation

Validation of CTRON implementations is currently being offered separately for each interface unit, to check that the right interfaces are implemented for each subset. In addition to this, AP portability would be assured more fully if validation were made of profiles. Whereas subset validation is made of individual software products, profile validation would validate entire systems consisting of OS software units in combination. For the time being only subset validation will be offered, but profile validation is being considered for the future, after more software development has taken place.

6. EVALUATION

The validity of subsets and profiles talked about here needs to be evaluated ultimately by seeing the extent to which software can actually be ported. Specifically, an evaluation needs to be made of three main points, namely 1) porting across the same profile (since even if the profile is the same, there can be differences in interpretation or other aspects), 2) the effects of optional subsets or optional subset units on porting across the same profile, and 3) porting between different profiles.

In CTRON, the first point has been evaluated in the Software Portability Experiment [8]. The porting of a file management extended OS to different Basic OS implementations has been completed in the first phase of the experiment, and the validity of Kernel and I/O Control subset specifications has been confirmed. Other subset specifications and additional evaluation points will be examined in subsequent phases of the experiment.

7. CONCLUSION

This paper has focussed on the need for subsetting and the approach taken to CTRON subsetting, which are aimed at achieving AP portability while also providing a wide choice of OS interfaces. Subsets and profiles are something that should be decided based on the needs of OS users. Moreover, as computer technology advances, the required OS functions and interfaces will undergo change. The profiles noted in this paper are therefore not set in stone but will need to be upgraded as CTRON applications proceed. At the same time, however, the classification and systematization of OS interfaces described here, necessary in forming subsets and profiles, as well as the subsetting method, can be regarded as established techniques that will continue to be usable in the future as general methodology.

In addition to the matters that have been discussed above, other issues include how to select optional and alternate subsets, and dynamic adaptation by which a running AP can determine if a given subset is present and behave accordingly. Those will need to be studied further in the light of actual application.

REFERENCES

[1] ISO/IEC, "Information Technology — Framework and Taxonomy of International Standardized Profiles", ISO/IEC TR 10000-1 (1990).

[2] IEEE Computer Society, "Draft Standard for Microprocessor Operating System Interfaces", P855/Draft 7.1 (1988).

[3] TRON Association, "Outline of CTRON", Ohmsha (1988).

[4] TRON Association, "Kernel Interface", Ohmsha (1988).

[5] T. Wasano, et al., "CTRON Reference Model", Proc. of 5th TRON Project Symposium (1988).

[6] T. Wasano and Y. Kobayashi, "Application of CTRON to communication networks", Microprocessors and Microsystems, Vol. 13, No. 8, Butter worths (1989).

[7] T. Ohkubo, et al., "Configuration of the CTRON Kernel", IEEE Micro, Vol. 7, N0. 2 (1987).

[8] T. Ohta, et al., "CTRON Software Portability Evaluation", Proc. of 7th TRON Project Symposium (1990).

Hitoshi Shibagaki: a senior engineer at NTT Network Systems Development Center. Since joining NTT in 1980, he has been engaged in development of DIPS Operating systems. He is presently working in the area of computer architecture strategy planning. He received his BS and MS degrees from the University of Tokyo in 1978 and 1980, respectively. He was a research associate at West Virginia University in 1989. He is a member of the Institute of Electronics, Information and Communication Engineers of Japanese (IEICE), the Information Processing Society of Japan (IPS) and the IEEE Computer Society.

Tetsuo Wasano: an executive engineer at NTT Network Systems Development Center. He is presently engaged in computer architecture strategy planning. Since joining the laboratory in 1970, he has been engaged in development research on DIPS operating systems and in research into artificial intelligence. He graduated from the University of Tokyo in 1970 with the BS degree. He is a member of the Institute of Electronics, Information and Communication Engineers of Japanese (IEICE), the Information Processing Society of Japan (IPS) and the IEEE Computer Society.

The above authors may be reached at: NTT Network Systems Development Center, 2-1, Uchisaiwai-cho 1-Chome, Chiyoda-ku, Tokyo, 100 Japan

An Evaluation Method of Kernel Products Based on CTRON

Hisayoshi Kurosawa, Osamu Watanabe
Mitsubishi Electric Corporation

Yoshizumi Kobayashi
NTT Network Systems Development Center

Abstract

The performance is a key factor in real-time operating systems and its evaluations have been made by the vendors. However, their results are not compared because they have the following problems.

1) Measurement items vary for each evaluation.

2) Evaluation results are affected by the environment such as hardware and compilers.

3) Load effects such as the number of created tasks are not considered.

It is important for CTRON to solve these problems and define an evaluation method applicable to various products, because CTRON-based products may be implemented by many different vendors. This paper proposes an evaluation method for kernel products compliant with CTRON and shows some evaluation results and the effectiveness of this method.

Keywords: Real-time operating system, CTRON specification, CTRON performance evaluation

1. Introduction

High performance is much needed in real-time operating systems. Users of these systems want to compare the performance of each system to decide the most suitable system to their requirements. However, each vendor has evaluated the performance of its product by its own way, so users can't compare the performance of each product. The problems of each evaluation are summarized as follows:

1) Measurement items vary for each evaluation.

2) Evaluation results are affected by the environment such as hardware and compilers.

3) Load effects such as the number of created tasks are not considered.

It is important for CTRON to solve these problems and define an evaluation method applicable to various products, because CTRON-based products may be implemented by many different vendors. Moreover, when CTRON-based products are ported from one environment to another, it is important to examine whether or not ported products maintain the same performance as before.

This paper proposes an evaluation method for kernel products compliant with CTRON and shows some evaluation results and the effectiveness of this method. The problems noted above are solved as follows:

1)Measurement items applicable to each evaluation are defined.

2)Evaluation results are normalized by Dhrystone values and environment effects are deleted.

3)Performance is evaluated in proportion to load increase.

2. Items for Performance Evaluation

2.1. System Call Performance

In general, operating systems have a model structure as shown in Figure 1. The processing time of system call is the sum of each processing time of the following parts.

(1) Interface part : processing software interrupts for system calls.

(2) Processing part : main part of each system call processing.

(3) Task switching part : performing task switching.

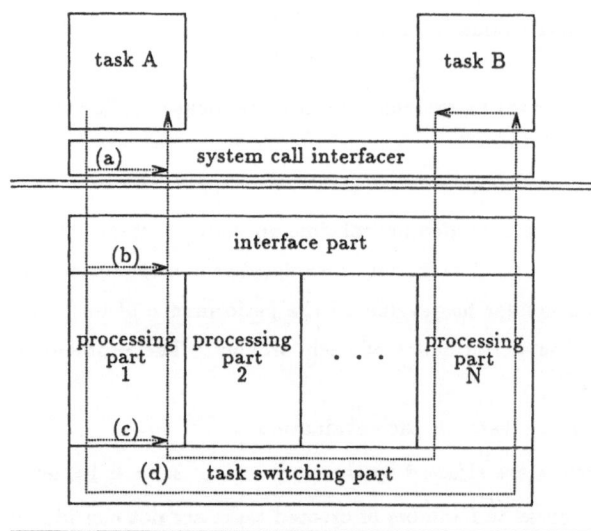

Base(Hardware, Compilers)

Fig.1 Base Model of Operating System Structure

In order to obtain the processing time of the parts above, the following items are measured.

(a) Function call/return processing

(b) System calls which hardly have internal processing (e.g. getting task information)

(c) System calls not raising task switching (e.g. sending messages when there are no tasks waiting)

(d) System calls with task switching (e.g. receiving and sending messages)

From these measurements, the performance of each part can be calculated as follows.

1) System call overhead: (b)-(a)

2) System call execution performance: (c)-(b)

3) Task switching performance: (d)-(c)

2.2. Load Performance

The deterioration in system call performance as the number of tasks running concurrently is increased is determined as follows.

1)Measuring the performance of a system call when one task is running (e.g. message receiving/sending)

2)Measuring the performance of the same system call when the number of tasks is m.

3)Measuring the performance of the same system call when the number of tasks is n. ($n>m$)

By comparing performance when there are 1, m and n tasks running, the type of the operating system can be determined according to Figure 2 and changes of a system call processing time with an increase of tasks can be evaluated.

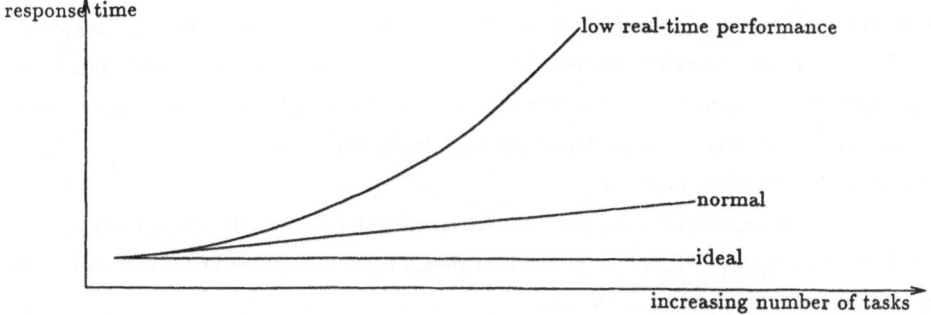

Fig.2 Dependence of System Call Processing Time on Number of Tasks

2.3. Interrupt Processing Performance

Interrupt processing performance is defined as the time taken to respond to an interrupt, which is time from the occurrence of the interrupt to the time that the interrupt handler goes into operation. This processing time includes the delay occurred from the disabled interrupt state to the enabled interrupt state, and the overhead to transfer control to the interrupt handler.

2.4. Performance of Operating System Execution Environment

Results of measurement obtained so far have depended upon the environment on that the target operating system is running. Therefore, the effects of the environment - in particular hardware and compiler effects - should be measured and deleted. The deletion of the effects means the normalization of the performance data obtained so far.

If the standard environment performance is H_0, the environment performance of the target operating system is H_1 and the measured performance of the operating system is P_1, then the normalized performance of the operating system P_r can be obtained from the following formula.

$$P_r = \frac{P_1 H_1}{H_0}$$

The greater the environment performance value, the higher the performance of the hardware and compiler; the smaller the measured value, the higher the performance.

3. Measurement Method

3.1. System Call Performance

Basic performance of an operating system was measured using methods listed below. A 32 bit processor was used for each measurement and the actual execution time ranged from several microsecond to several hundred microsecond. As available clocks in most systems measure time of the milliseconds, iterations of 100,000 times were used for each measurement. Depending on the target systems, the number of iteration can be changed. It may make possible to reduce the number of times somewhat, even for hardware with lower performance.

(1) Function Call/Return processing

This item is measured for compensation for overhead time resulting from the system call interface and loop execution. An evaluation program includes a function call and incremental statements are executed in the function.

(2) System Calls hardly including internal processing

System call overhead is measured. Actually, a system call for obtaining of kernel information is adopted.

(3)System calls without task switching

Execution time of message receiving and sending system calls are adopted, because they are expected to be frequently used among CTRON kernel system calls. Message box creation and message sending and receiving are performed in one task, without task switching. As the message box mode, the locate mode, which is included in all kernel subsets, is employed (refer to Figure 3).

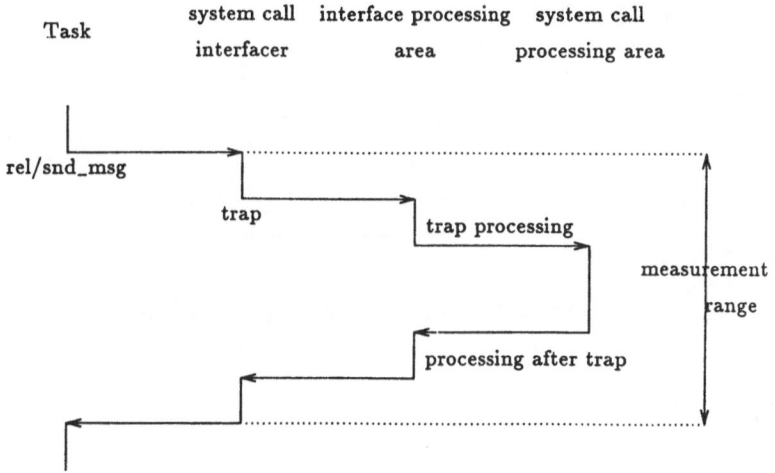

Fig.3 System Call Processing Time(with no task switching)

(4) System calls with task switching

Time needed to transmit message between tasks A and B is measured. Task A has a higher priority than task B. Task A is for receiving messages, and Task B for sending them. When task A issues a system call to receive a message from an empty message box, task A enters WAIT-state and task B immediately starts in execution. It sends a message to the empty message box and wake up task A. This method measures the time from just before task A issues a system call to receive a message to the time that it is waken up (when message has been received) (see Figure 4).

3.2. Interrupt Processing Performance

In order to measure interrupt processing performance accurately, events should be acquired from the hardware and operating system. The target operating system should be modified so that event can be acquired directly, and it is very difficult to do so. It is also difficult to get an event directly from the task level using an evaluation program. Therefore, the interrupt processing performance evaluation is left in the future.

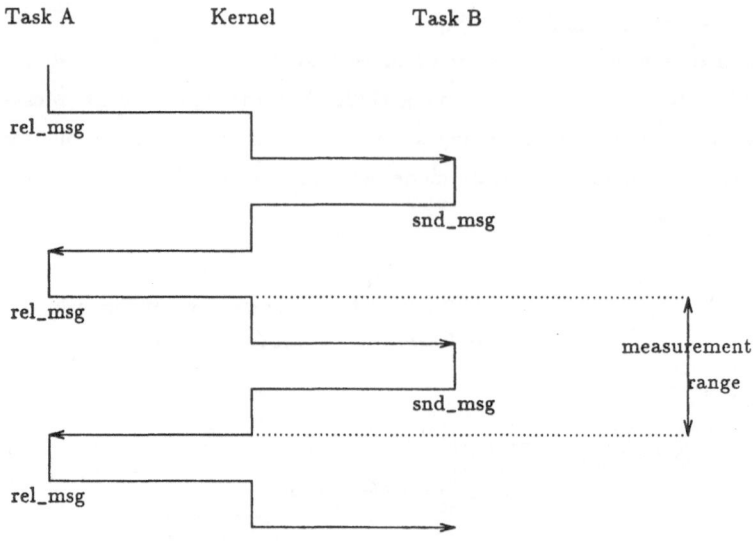

Fig.4 System Call Processing Time(with task switching)

3.3. Load Performance

The variance of system call processing time accompanying with an increase in the number of tasks is measured. The execution time of the same system call is measured for cases 1) to 3) listed below, where n is the maximum possible number of application tasks that the system can create.

1) One task is running

2) $\frac{n}{2}$ Tasks are running

3) n Tasks are running

The SUSPEND_TASK/RESUME_TASK system calls are adopted for measurements. A highest priority task issues SUSPEND_TASK/RESUME_TASK system call to control other tasks, each of which has different priority. The results obtained are the system call execution times for above cases 1) to 3).

3.4. Environment Performance

For environment performance it is necessary to consider (1) CPU performance, (2) CPU clock speed, (3) memory wait, (4) cache, (5) MMU function, (6) compiler performance. Dhrystone Benchmark program is used to evaluate all of above terms. This Benchmark program is widely used in UNIX's World. A few changes have been made to this program in order to execute it on CTRON-compliant kernels. Dhrystone Benchmark value is taken to be 83% of it on UNIX, because these kernels do not use floating point calculations.

4. Examples of Performance Measurement

4.1. Measurement Procedure

As CTRON kernel interface has no functions for input/output, this evaluation program writes its results on the memory. It is assumed that performance is measured according to the following steps.

1) Designate the results output address and other parameters in the evaluation program, and register it onto the tasks running on CTRON-compliant kernel to be measured.

2) Execute these tasks.

3) Copy results from the memory into a flexible disk or other media.

4) Display results on UNIX or other systems which accept these media.

In addition to results output address, the user also designates the maximum possible number of application tasks as a parameter.

4.2. Results

The values listed below are sequentially output onto the memory.

1) Function call execution time

2) System call overhead time

3) Time for sending message

4) Time for receiving message

5) Time for sending/receiving message

6) Task switching time

7) Time for suspend/resume task(when one task is running)

8) Time for suspend/resume tasks(when $\frac{n}{2}$ task is running)

9) Time for suspend/resume tasks(when n task is running)

10) Dhrystone Benchmark value

Each of the above results has the "long_t" form. The results 1) to 9) are normalized using the Dhrystone Benchmark value.

Table 1 denotes measurement environments. The results are shown in Table 2. In Table 2, the value in brackets means non-normalized one for reference.

Table 1 Measurement Environment

	system-A	system-B	system-C
OS	A	A	B
Kernel-subset	C	C	μ C
CPU	MC68030	MC68020	MC68020
clock	16MHz	16MHz	20MHz
memory-wait	non-wait	non-wait	2-wait
cache	disable	enable	enable

Table 2 Measured Results

	system-A	system-B	system-C
send-message	159(149)	156(116)	154(152)
receive-message	150(141)	149(111)	138(136)
send/receive-message	557(521)	544(404)	500(491)
task-switching	120(113)	115(86)	102(101)
one task	437(409)	434(322)	388(381)
$\frac{n}{2}$ tasks	436(408)	430(319)	398(391)
n tasks	436(408)	430(319)	398(391)
Dhrystone	3805/s	4794/s	3625/s

5. Discussion

The following discussions are induced from the evaluation results.

A: The evaluation program can be applied to different kernel products compliant with CTRON.

B: Items for comparison of each product performance are defined and the evaluation results can be obtained by the application program executed on tasks. Time for task switching, which is made within a kernel, can be measured

C: The effects of environments can be much diminished by using performance normalized by Dhrystone values. For example, the performance of OS-A on system-A is different from that on system-B. However, each normalized performance denotes almost the same value. So, each performance of various products on different environments can be compared if normalized performance values are used. Moreover, if performance values of a system and Dhrystone value of another system are given, performance of the another system can be estimated. For example, if OS-A runs on system-C, the performance of send-message system call of OS-A is estimated at ($\frac{116 \times 4794}{3625} =$) 153 micro-seconds.

D: The evaluation program is useful to evaluate load effects such as the number of created tasks.

6. Conclusion

This paper presents problems of real-time kernel evaluation so far and proposes a method to solve the problems. Moreover, this denotes the effectiveness of the method by making an evaluation program and applying it to kernel products compliant with CTRON. The remaining issue, the measurement method of interrupt processing performance, is under consideration.

References

[1] "Proposals for CTRON Control", "Data from Third TRON Study Group on Real Time Architecture" - Electronic Data Communications Study Association, October, 1987.

[2] "Special Feature - Real Time Operating Systems of the 32 Bit Generation" - Nikkei Electronics, No,458, October 17th, 1988.

[3] "On a Method of Performance Evaluation of CTRON Basic OS" - The First Software Pertability Symposium(international),Vol.3,No.2, TRON Association,September 14, 1990.

Hisayoshi Kurosawa: a engineer at Information Systems and Electronics Development Laboratory of Mitsubishi Electric Corporation. Since joining the company in 1986, he has been engaged in the research and development of operating system compliant with CTRON. He has played role in the design of kernel interface, process control interface and transaction control interface within CTRON. He received the BS degree at Tokyo Metropolitan University. He is a member of Information Processing Society of Japan.

Osamu Watanabe: received the BS degree at Osaka University in 1967. Since joining Mitsubishi Electric Corp. in 1973, he has been engaged in the research and development of computer terminals and computer system for engineering use at Information Systems and Electronics Development Laboratory. He is a member of the Information of Electronics, Information and Communication Engineers of Japan.

Above authors may be reached at: Information Systems & Electronics Development Laboratory, Mitsubishi Electric Corporation, 5-1-1 Ofuna, Kamakura, Kanagawa, 247, Japan.

Yoshizumi Kobayashi: a senior engineer at NTT Network Systems Development Center. Since joining the company in 1973, he has been engaged in the research and development of compilers and operating systems. He has played role in construction of principles required for the CTRON design and in the design of program control interface within CTRON. He received the BS degree in 1971 and the MS degree in 1973 at Osaka University. He is a member of the Institute of Electronics, Information and Information Processing Society of Japan, and of the Computer Society of the IEEE.

Above author may be reached at: Network Systems Development Center, Nippon Telegraph and Telephone Corporation, 1-2-1, Uchisaiwaicho, Chiyoda, Tokyo, 100, Japan.

Development of CTRON Operating System for Communication Processing

Masayuki Hatanaka, Yoshihiro Adachi, Nobuo Shigeta, Yuichi Ohmachi, Masato Ohminami
NTT Communications and Information Processing Laboratories

Abstract

POPS-100(R1) is a set of OS programs developed based on CTRON interface specifications. This OS features high-performance realtime processing, highly stable long-term online processing service, and improved portability both of application programs and OS program modules.

High performance was achieved by simplifying the software structure and devising original approaches to implementing CTRON-specification interfaces. The program structure enables modification of resources managed by the operating system (e.g., communication protocols and utilizable communication lines) to allow for ready expansion of communication processing services. Moreover, a flexible re-configuration function was developed.

POPS-100(R1) development establishes the basic technology for CTRON implementation and application to communication processing services requiring high throughput. Portability of OS programs is now being verified.

Keywords: CTRON, Communication Processing, System Generation, Portable operating system

1. Introduction

CTRON specifies OS interfaces based on the TRON architecture, and providing common functions for use in a broad range of information and communication network services.[1][2] POPS-100[1] is a CTRON-specification OS designed to run on the DIPS-V processor series in standard use at NTT for information processing. Development of release 1 was completed in June 1989 as POPS-100(R1).

This paper describes the characteristics and structure of POPS-100(R1). This OS is referred to throughout the rest of this paper simply as POPS.

---

[1] POPS: Portable OPerating System

2. Background and Aims

2.1. Relation to CTRON interface specifications

The work of producing CTRON interface specifications began in fiscal 1986. Development of POPS started around the same time and has been carried out in parallel with this specification work, since one reason for the development has been to confirm the feasibility of CTRON interface specifications as they are created.

For this reason, POPS development has been proceeding in gradual stages, based not only on already decided specifications but also on interface class specifications with a high likelihood of becoming adopted. Whenever problems with the specifications were noted in the course of development, improvements were proposed to the CTRON working groups. The CTRON interface classes are shown in Figure 2.1, while Table 2.1 lists the specifications implemented in POPS.

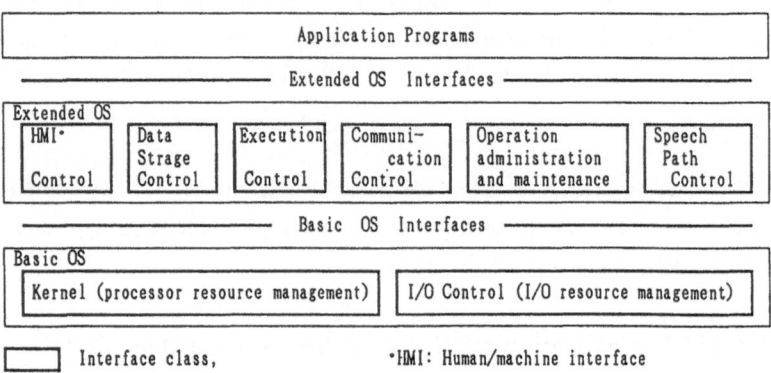

Fig. 2.1. CTRON interface classes

Table 2.1. *Interface specifications implemented in POPS-100(R1)*

Interface class	Interface specifications
Kernel	CTRON Kernel Interface Specification (Ver. 1 draft)[Oct. 1986]
I/O control	CTRON I/O Control Interface Specification (Ver. 1 draft) [Mar. 1987]
Data storage control	CTRON File Management Interface Specification (Ver. 1 draft) [Mar. 1987]
Execution control	CTRON General Program Management Interface Specification (Ver. 1)
Communication control	CTRON Communication Control Interface Specification, Basic Communication Control (Ver. 1 draft) [Oct. 1987]

In the case of interface classes for which CTRON specifications were not yet available, independent specification studies were first made by the POPS development team, and then proposed to the CTRON working groups. The process control interface specification adopted for this development, which belongs to the execution control interface class, was proposed in this manner.

2.2. Aims of POPS development

Of the CTRON application fields, POPS was designed for communication processing services. These services can be classified into the three modes shown in Table 2.2.

Table 2.2. *Classification of communication processing services*

Service mode	Outline Typical services	Examples
Immediate transfer services	Transfer processing in real time, with high throughput demanded	Protocol conversion
Data store and forward services	Data are stored temporarily in the system, then transferred while absorbing differences in access time	MHS, centralized-distribution mail service
Interactive services	Routine interactive processing	Database access service

POPS release 1 is aimed mainly at the first mode, immediate transfer, for which system components are of relatively wide availability.

In immediate transfer services, depending on the urgency of messages to be transferred, realtime performance must be guaranteed, and high throughput is required as well. To meet these needs, the following development policies were adopted.

1) For the sake of realtime performance, the task pre-emption scheduling and priority scheduling functions specified in CTRON are supported. The design also aims to reduce file access time.
2) In order to guarantee high throughput, emphasis was placed on speeding up protocol processing, which accounts for a significant portion of processing time in immediate transfer services. Specifically, measures were taken to reduce overhead between protocol layers and that in task communication. Also, special protocol processing tasks were devised in order to improve the MP coefficient.[2]

Functions for improving reliability and permitting long-term operation are being developed for separate releases, based on user demands. One such function in release 1 allows OS programs to be added or replaced on line.

---

[2] MP coefficient: Multiprocessor coefficient. This is a measure of software performance in a tightly coupled multiprocessor system, comparing it against single-processor processing capacity. When CPUs of the same model are implemented, MP coefficient $\leqq$ no. of CPUs.

3. POPS Implementation

3.1. Software configuration

The software configuration of POPS is shown in Figure 3.1. The functions and features of each program are outlined in Table 3.1. Each interface class consists of one or more program modules.

In the interface reference model adopted for CTRON communication control, interfaces are specified for each layer of the OSI reference model, with each interface belonging to the Extended OS.[3] (See Figure 3.2(A).) The extent of interface implementation, however, is left to the implementor to decide. Moreover, in selecting the Basic OS interfaces to be provided, the design allows mapping to appropriate layers based on the development trends in hardware implementation of lower protocols.[4]

Accordingly, since the DIPS-V series supports the data link layer by means of a communication control adapter (ICA), the data link layer is adopted also for the base communication controller (BCL) incorporated in the Basic OS for POPS communication control.

The communication controller (CCL) adopts the session layer (see Figure 3.2(B)), for the sake of convenience when used by applications, and because this allows greater latitude when upper layer protocols are implemented.

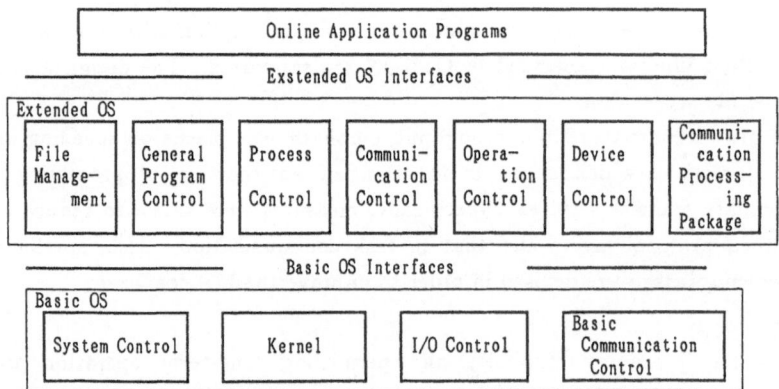

Fig. 3.1. Software configuration

Table 3.1. *POPS-100(R1) functions*

Layer	Interface class	Outline of functions	Features
Basic OS	Kernel	Task management, task communication, memory management, exception management, interrupt management, clock management, basic program control	i)Hides system hardware architecture ii)Conforms to CTRON
	System control	System initialization, system fault management	i)Processor system management specific to DIPS
	General I/O control	Peripheral device access, fault management functions	i)Hides peripheral system hardware architecture ii)Conforms to CTRON
	Basic communication control	ICA† access functions, line fault management	i)Hides hardware architecture of line system ii)Conforms to CTRON
Extended OS	Operation management	Console control and log management	Message control for improved HMI
	Device control	Peripheral device state control	State control of hardware-independent devices
	General program control	Application program loading, unloading, and execution	i)Loading in program modules ii)Conforms to CTRON
	File management	Disc management and file access functions	i)Provides basic access method files specified in CTRON ii)Conforms to CTRON
	Process control	Application program starting, termination, garbage processing of used resources	i)One process = one task ii)Independent POPS specification
	Communication control	Protocol processing and communication buffer management	i)Advanced communication control ii)Conforms to CTRON
	Communication processing package	Online process management, communication access functions, garbage processing functions, fault recovery functions	i)High-performance communication access functions ii)Detailed garbage processing chained to services
Support system	Integrated SG‡	Product-specific processing, common processing, data net processing	Presents uniform interface independent of implementations

† ICA: Integrated Communication Adapter
‡ SG: System Generation

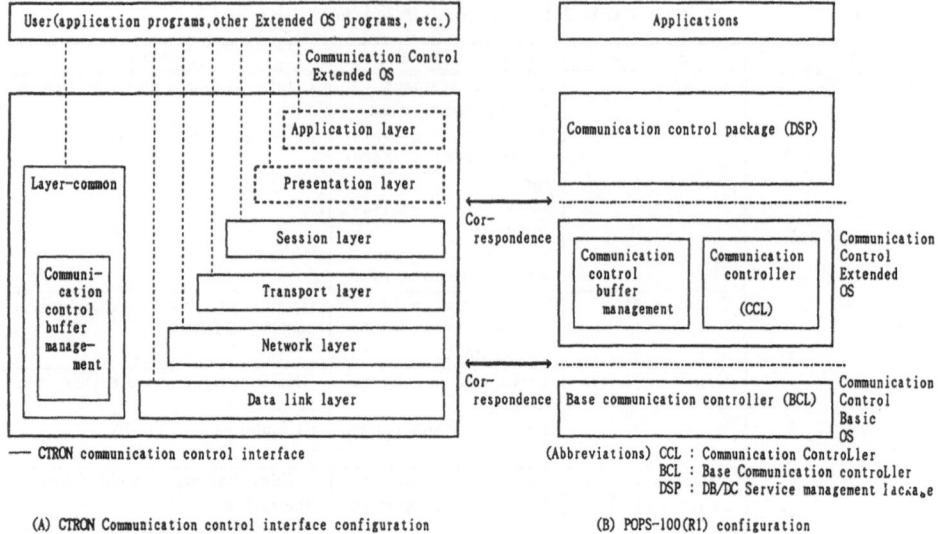

Fig. 3.2. Relation of POPS-100 to communication control interface model

3.2. Improving realtime performance

(a)Task scheduling

POPS makes use of two task attributes specified in CTRON, namely, execution level and, within the same execution level, priority. These are used to realize a two-stage task scheduling method employing pre-emption control along with priority control. Up to 5 task levels and 4 priority levels can be assigned, as required by the service to which the OS is applied.

(b)Disk storage area management

The performance requirements for file access functions are especially severe in a realtime processing system. This means that file physical storage area on disks should be allocated contiguously to the extent possible. To this end, POPS adopts the following method of disk storage area management.

1) The file control information area is smaller than the file physical storage area, so fragmentation tends to occur unless these are kept separate from each other. For this reason, the file control information area is made discrete from the physical storage area.

2) The discrete physical storage areas are managed as extents, allowing these areas to be allocated as contiguous areas.

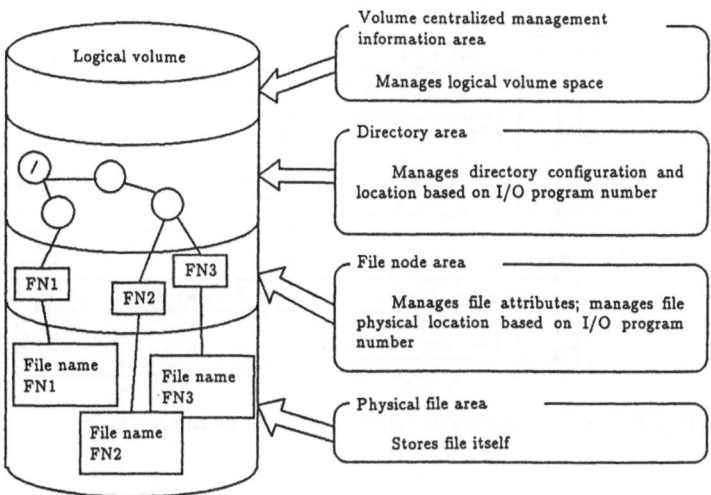

Fig. 3.3. Disk space management

3) In a tree-structured directory management system, if one directory is destroyed, access may become impossible to a large number of files under that directory. In POPS, the directory control area and file control area are physically localized, making it easier to restore files in case directory management information is lost.[5] As a result, the file restoration utility does not have to search the entire disk, so processing is faster.

The POPS disc space configuration is shown in Figure 3.3.

3.3. Realizing advanced communication control performance

(a)Communication control configuration

POPS communication control is configured as in Figure 3.4. The BCL consists of a device-specific part for processing corresponding to each communication control device, a line management part for keeping track of line states, and a common part.

The CCL consists of a protocol processing part and a common part. The protocol processing part is divided into separate parts for each protocol, all owing protocols to be implemented as needed and making future expansion easier. These protocol processing parts mainly run on separate tasks, a measure adopted in order to improve the MP coefficient.

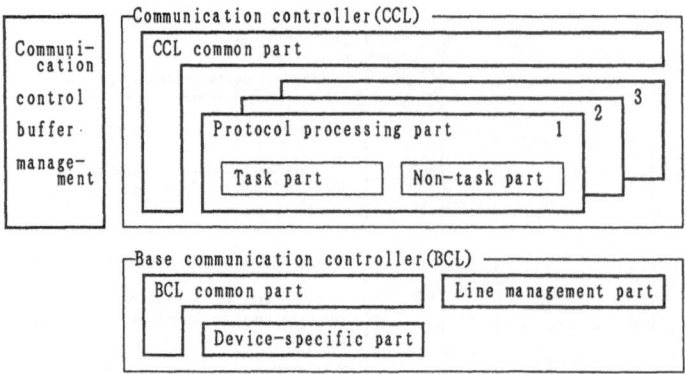

Fig. 3.4. Communication control software configuration

(b)Protocol processing method

1) Interfaces provided to upper layers

The POPS protocol processing part supports non-OSI protocols such as DCNA and basic mode procedures, for which there is likely to be continued strong demand. CTRON communication control specifications, on the other hand, assume use of OSI, so in implementation it was necessary to map these protocols to OSI session layer service primitives. In the case of basic mode procedures, implementation within the scope of CTRON specifications is possible. With DCNA, however, there are some functions that cannot be mapped, so these had to be dealt with by adding a new system call in the DIPS-specific part for sending protocol-specific information.

2) CCL common part

The CCL common part contains management functions and access functions for the protocol processing parts.

The management functions provided include those for activating and terminating each protocol processing part, reading system generation data, and collecting statistical information.

Access functions are provided for routing system call requests by upper layers to the appropriate protocol processing part. The mechanism for this distribution is outlined below and illustrated in Figure 3.5.

— At system initialization, the starting addresses of processing programs in the each protocol processing part corresponding to system calls are registered in the common part.

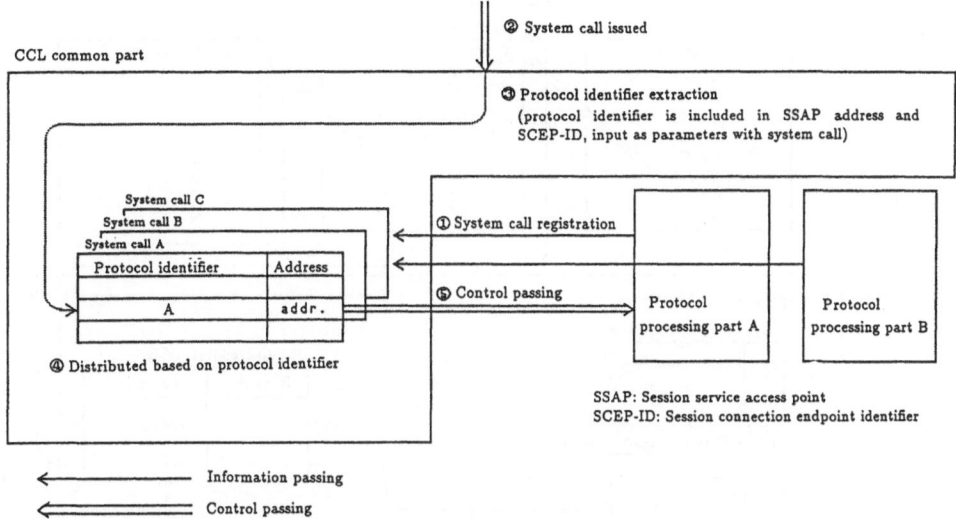

Fig. 3.5. Distribution scheme based on protocol identifier

— The common part keeps track of the correspondence between protocol identifiers and protocol processing parts. The protocol identifier is included in input information when a user issues a system call, and on this basis the protocol is selected. Then control is passed to the processing program for that system call.

— The protocol identifier is included in the SSAP address, and is passed on in the SCEP-ID issued by the CCL. Users therefore see differences in protocol only in terms of different SSAP addresses in OSI.

The above approach makes it possible for upper-layer users of the CCL to access different protocol processing parts by means of the same system calls.

3) Reducing overhead between layers

In order to reduce protocol overhead between layers, POPS adopts a method of inter-layer event passing that does not involve the usual queuing processing. That is, after an event is fetched from the queue and protocol processing is performed based on the state transition table of a given layer, a new event generated from this processing is not returned to the queue but is routed directly on to the state transition table of the next layer. This approach, illustrated in Figure 3.6, results in less queuing overhead between layers.

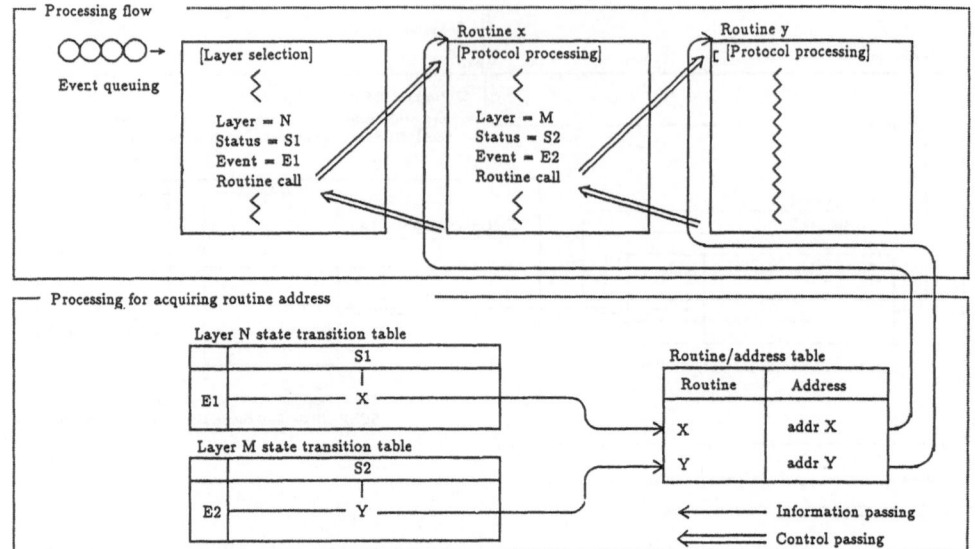

Fig. 3.6. Control passing between layers

4) High-speed message receive processing

The processing when messages are sent lends itself readily to a system call interface, since upper layers make use of lower layer functions. By contrast, message receipt starts out with a n interrupt by the communication control adapter, and control must be passed from lower to upper layers.

For this type of processing, CTRON specifies control passing by means of synchronous processing using a message box. In developing POPS, a new function known as an entry call was devised in addition to control passing via message boxes, as a way of improving the performance of this processing.[6] This function has been proposed to the CTRON communication control working group, where its specification is now under study.

The entry mechanism provided for this entry call method is shown in Figure 3.7. When the user (upper layer) registers a routine address with the entry mechanism, an entry identifier is assigned for that routine. This entry identifier is notified to lower layers, where it is used as a key for passing control to upper layer processing via the entry mechanism.

This approach makes it possible to reduce overhead for event waiting and task switching when control is passed. It is especially effective when processing tasks are to be selected depending on the message content. Figure 3.8 shows that the effect of entry call method on the task selecting process depends on the message contents. It realizes 45% reduction in the dynamic steps.

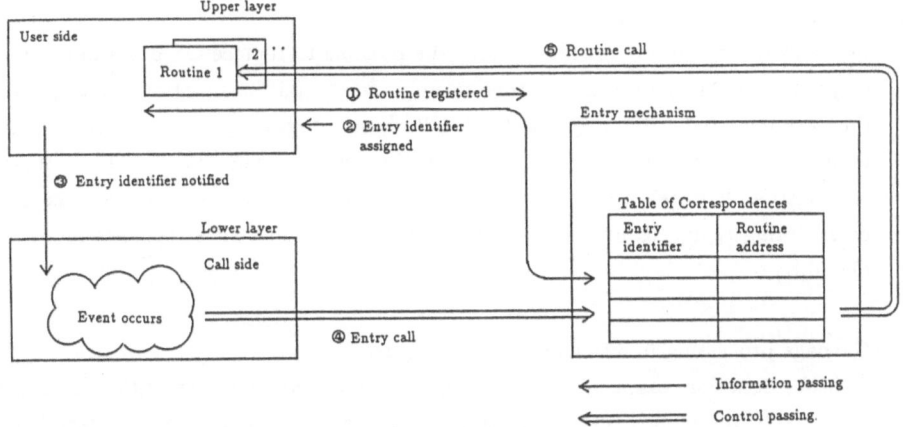

Fig. 3.7. Entry call scheme

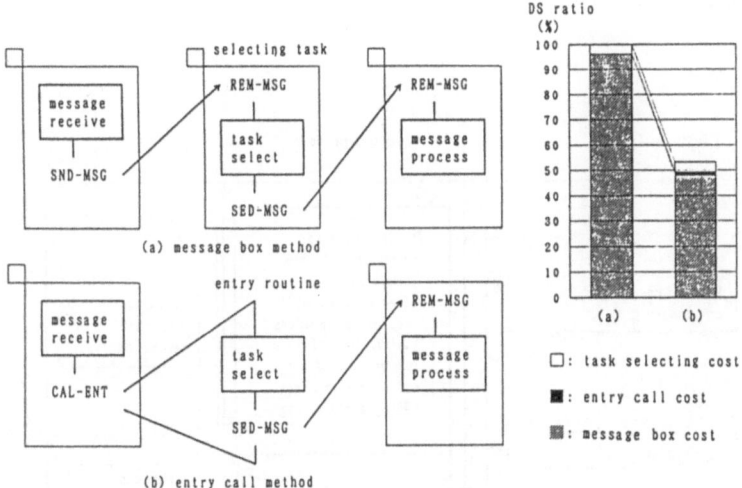

Fig. 3.8. Effect of entry call method

3.4. Functions for communication processing services

(a)Functions for realizing long-term operation

Communication processing services typically must be operated non-stop for long periods of time. POPS has introduced the following methods for meeting this demand.

1) OS program replacement method

   In realizing non-stop operation, it must be possible to replace OS programs without stopping system operation, in order to upgrade or add OS functions or to fix bugs that are detected. By supporting CTRON basic program control functions, POPS realizes an OS program replacement function in the Basic OS kernel. If there is competition between the replacement processing and user access, any access by users during replacement is held temporarily, and handled after replacement is completed.[7]

2) Garbage processing functions in process control

   Another function essential for realizing long-term non-stop operation is one for dependably releasing resources used by a process after that process is terminated. In POPS a method is adopted whereby process control keeps track of the correspondence between processes and the resources allocated by application programs. This method makes use of a process control function for returning resources whenever a process is deleted. An overview of process control functions is given in Figure 3.9.

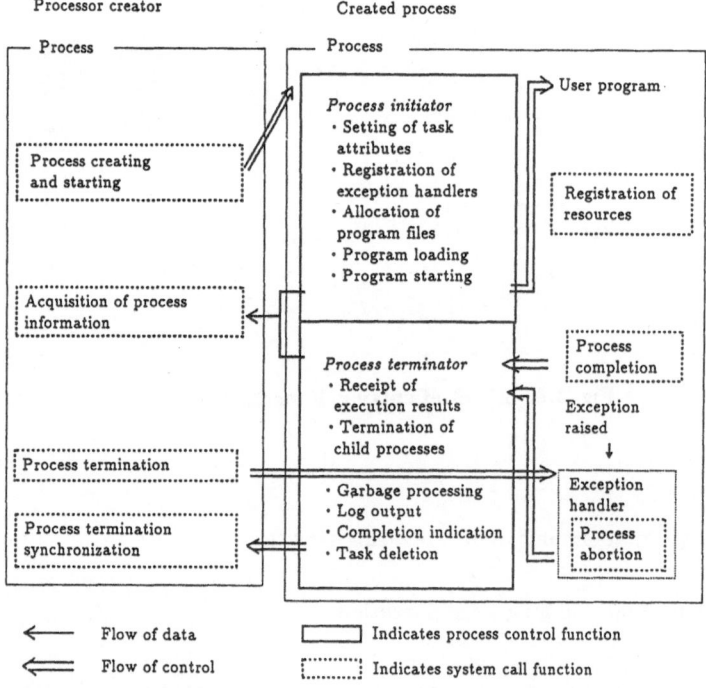

Fig. 3.9. Outline of process control

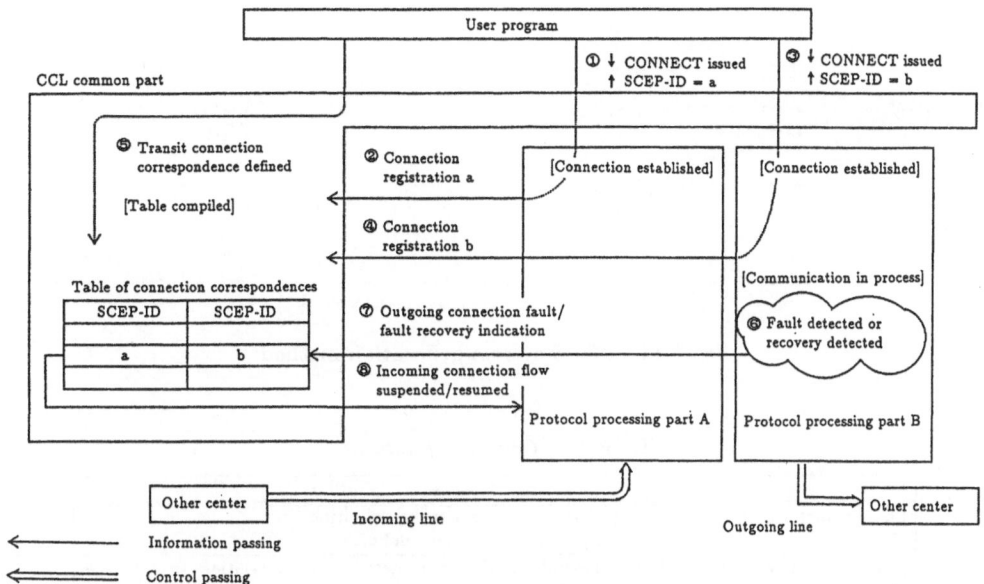

Fig. 3.10. Example of flow control by means of transit connection management

(b)Transit connection management function

A transit connection flow control function was realized for ease of building a transit system. This function keeps track of the correspondence between pairs of connections involved in a transfer. When the destination connection is faulty or recovers from a fault, or if the buffer pool on the outgoing end is overloaded or the overload is cleared, this function immediately reacts by suspending or resuming the flow incoming to the connection at the destination. An example of flow control when a fault is detected is shown in Figure 3.10. In this approach, flow control is carried out directly by communication control, which has a higher execution level than applications. Data congestion in high load conditions is minimized, making this method effective for transit systems. Ease of protocol conversion design is a further benefit of this approach, since correspondence is possible between any pair of connections even if the protocols differ.

3.4. System generation (SG) processing

If the programs for each interface class in a CTRON-specification OS used different methods of system generation, this would hardly present a good human/machine interface for the operator in charge of system generation. It is highly likely, however, that different CTRON interface units will be developed by different firms and that the SG interfaces will also differ. With POPS, however, a uniform SG method has been devised with an internal structure that takes into account the division into interface classes; the human/machine interface, on the other hand, does not require awareness of these divisions. (See Figure 3.11.) This method is outlined below.

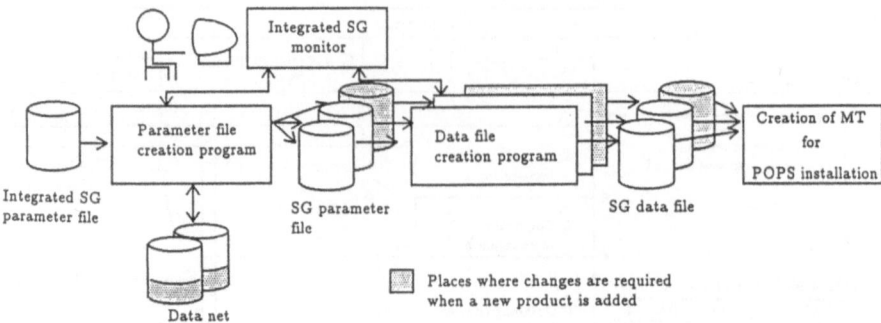

Fig. 3.11. POPS system generation method

Table 3.2. *Content of data net*

Function	Outline
SG parameter definition	i) Parameter existence definition ii) parameter format definition
Parameter expanded definition	Definition of a parameter and its relation to required products
Correlation check definition	Definition of correlation coefficient among parameter values
Definition of SG basic data	i) Definition of products to be activated ii) definition of usable logical space configuration

1) The SG program is divided into a common part and product-specific parts based on the interface classes. The common part hides this distinction among product-specific parts, providing a common interface to the operator in charge of system generation.

2) The common part passes necessary SG data for each product-specific part as files, based on data in a file called a data net, and executes these successively.

In this way the interface between the common part and product-specific parts is defined entirely as data. Thus, even when a new product is added it is only necessary to prepare an additional product-specific part and revise the data net accordingly.

The content of definition data in the data net is shown in Table 3.2.

4. Conclusion

The above has been a brief introduction to POPS, an OS developed based on CTRON interface specifications to run on NTT's standard information processing system. The aims in POPS development, the design policies, and main features have been outlined.

At present there are two main themes that are the basis of further POPS studies.

(1) Development of a POPS release fully conforming to CTRON specifications
POPS-100(R1) was developed before CTRON specifications were completed, and contains some functions that do not conform fully to the final specification. Release 2, now being developed, is aimed at full conformance to the specification.

(2) Verifying OS program portability
In the CTRON portability experiment currently under way, portability of file management and other Extended OS programs is being verified.

5. Acknowledgments

The authors wish to thank Dr. Fukuya Ishino, Executive Manager of the NTT Communications and Information Processing Laboratories, and Kouichi Matsuda of the Basic Architecture Research Department, as well as the rest of our colleagues, for their continued guidance throughout this development project.

References

[1] T. Wasano and Y. Kobayashi, "CTRON OS Interface for Information Communication Networks", Information Processing 30:5 (1989), pp. 553-564.

[2] TRON Association (K. Sakamura, Editorial Supervision), Outline of CTRON (Ohmsha: 1989).

[3] F. Ishino, "Multivendor-oriented Software Architectures", NTT R&D 39:3 (1990).

[4] TRON Association, Original Series of CTRON Interface Specifications: Communication Control Interface, Basic Communication Control, Ver. 1 (1988).

[5] Shinichi Nakahara, "A study on the reliability of the Tree-structure File System", Proc. 39th Information Processing Society Conference (1989).

[6] Shunsuke Miyata, "A High-speed Notifying Method of Asynchronous Events", Proc. 37th Information Processing Society Conference (1988).

[7] Junichi Gohara, "A control method of collision between OS module replacement and user access", Proc. Spring Meeting of the Institute of Electronics, Information and Communication Engineers of Japan (1989), pp. 6-76.

Masayuki Hatanaka: Senior research engineer, supervisor at NTT communications and Information Processing Laboratories, where he is presently engaged in research on operating system architectures. Since joining the company in 1978, he has been engaged in developmental research on DIPS communication control programs and operating systems. He received the BE and ME degrees from Nagoya Institute of Technology in 1976 and 1978, respectively. He is a member of the ISP.

Yoshihiko Adachi: Senior research engineer, Base Systems Architecture Laboratory at NTT Communication and Information Processing Laboratories, where he is presently engaged in development of operating system programs on DIPS. Since joining the company in 1983, he has been engaged in developmental research on DIPS-UNIX system and POPS. He received the BE and ME degrees from keio University in 1981 and 1983, respectively.

Nobuo Shigeta: Senior research engineer, Base Systems Architecture Laboratory at NTT Communication and Information Processing Laboratories, where he is presently engaged in development of communication control programs on operating systems. Since joining the company in 1981, he has been engaged in development on DIPS communication control programs. He received the BE and ME degrees from Kyoto University in 1979 and 1981, respectively. He is a member of IPS.

Yuichi Ohmachi:Senior research engineer, supervisor at NTT communications and Information Processing Laboratories, where he is engaged in research on operating system architecture. Since 1975, he has been engaged in development on DIPS operating system and research on operating system specification at NTT. He received the BE and ME degrees from Waseda University in 1973 and 1975. He is a member of IPS and EIC.

Masato Ohminami:Senior research engineer, supervisor at NTT communications and Information Processing Laboratories, where he conducts research into operating system architectures. Since joining the company in 1972, he has been engaged in developmental research on DIPS operating systems. He received the BE and ME degrees from Tohoku University at Sendai in 1970 and 1972, respectively. He is a member of the ISP.

Above authors may be reached at: Base Systems Architecture Laboratory at NTT Communication and Information Processing Laboratories, 1-2356, Take Yokosuka-city, Kanagawa, Japan

Chapter 4: CHIP (1)

Implementation and Evaluation of Oki 32-bit Microprocessor O32

Yoshikazu Mori, Yoshihito Haneda, Yoshihiko Arakawa,
Toshitaka Mori, Mutsumi Kumazawa
OKI Electric Industry Co., Ltd.

ABSTRACT

We have developed a 0.8μm CMOS technology-based 32-bit microprocessor, the O32, which, based on the TRON specifications, contains 700,000 transistors and features a processing speed of 10MIPS when operated at 33MHz. For use in communication systems, it has high reliability support capability and employs instruction/data caches, a six-stage pipeline and other high-speed processing techniques. The use of internal caches resulted in a 65% improvement in performance. The use of innovative LSI design environments and methodologies allowed us to develop a large system LSI, such as the O32, efficiently.

Keyword:microprocessor, cache memory, chip design, performance evaluation, O32

1. INTRODUCTION

The O32 is a 32-bit microprocessor based on the TRON specifications[1] and intended mainly for use in communication systems. It supports virtual memory and has processing power that is as high as 10MIPS (Million Instructions Per Second). It also supports a variety of unique functions, such as a bus comparator, to facilitate the building of systems with a high level of reliability, a must for communication systems.

To obtain improved processing power, the O32 uses built-in instruction/data caches, a six-stage pipeline, and other features. It also employs 0.8μm CMOS technology to permit the integration of as many as 700,000 transistors in a single chip.

This paper outlines the characteristics of the O32, evaluates the techniques used in it, and explains its device design/evaluation.

2. OUTLINE OF O32

Table 1 shows the specifications of the O32. It is a 32-bit microprocessor based on the TRON specifications (including Level 1 <<L1>> and part of Level 2 <<L2>>). The <<L1>> specifications call for the support of virtual memory. To meet this, the O32 has a 32-entry full-associative TLB (Translation Lookaside Buffer) to translate a logical address into a physical address. To provide more effective memory management, it uses a four-bit logical space identifier (LSID) to eliminate the wasteful invalidation of the TLB.

The O32 supports 102 different instructions, covering almost all instructions other than some <<L2>> instructions, such as co-processor instructions and extended decimal arithmetic instructions. It also supports backward option operations such as for the variable-length bit field manipulation instructions.

Table 1   Specifications of the O32

Performance	15 MIPS (max)
	10 MIPS (typ)
Spec.Level	L1+<L2>
Number of Instructions	102
Genaral Registers	16
TLB	32 Entries
	Full Associative
Memory Protection	4 Levels
Interrupt Level	7 Levels
Min.Bus Cycle	2 Clocks
	1 Clock (Burst)
Pipeline	6 Stages
Instruction Cache	1K Byte
	2-Way Set Associative
Data Cache	1K Byte
	2-Way Set Associative
Features	Fault Tolerant Support
	Stack Boundary Check
	Powerful Debug Support
	Process Timer

The O32 is intended chiefly to be used in communication systems such as switchboard systems and node processors. A processor used in a communication system is required to be powerful enough to handle a lot of communication transactions and at the same time have functions to ensure a high level of reliability, a must for any communication system.

The O32 focuses on the following two points to facilitate the building of a high reliability system. From the viewpoint of hardware, emphasis is placed on realizing a redundant configuration comprising multiple processors. This makes non-stop operation possible. From the viewpoint of software, it is possible to detect software faults easily by means of effective memory protection for stack areas. Specifically, the O32 is provided with a bus comparator and a stack boundary checker to ensure the high reliability of hardware and software respectively[2]. Other functions unique to the O32 include a process timer function, self-debugging functions, and a partial cache invalidation function.

Figure 1 shows the register set of the O32. It has a lot of registers with special functions as well as registers based on the TRON specifications. Of these, special function registers unique to the O32 are explained below. Stack boundary registers, SBI, SB0, SB1, SB2 and SB3, for individual protection levels as well as a control register, SBCW, are provided. To realize the stack boundary check function, each stack boundary register specifies the boundary of the stack area at each level.

The process timer function is used to measure the processor run time at a specified level. To this end, the O32 is provided with 32-bit counters PT0 and PT1, and a control register, PTCW. Self-debugging functions include a variety of trace functions, an instruction break, an operand break and a branch history function. There are two instruction break point registers, IBP0 and IBP1, and two operand break point registers, OBP0 and OBP1, to perform instruction and operand breaks, respectively. They are also provided with four 32-bit mask registers, IBM0, IBM1, OBM0 and OBM1, associated with the above four breakpoint registers respectively. The provision of the mask registers makes it possible to specify not only a specific address on a byte-by-byte basis but also a break for a certain area. Two registers, DCW and DSW, are provided to control and show the status of these self-debugging functions.

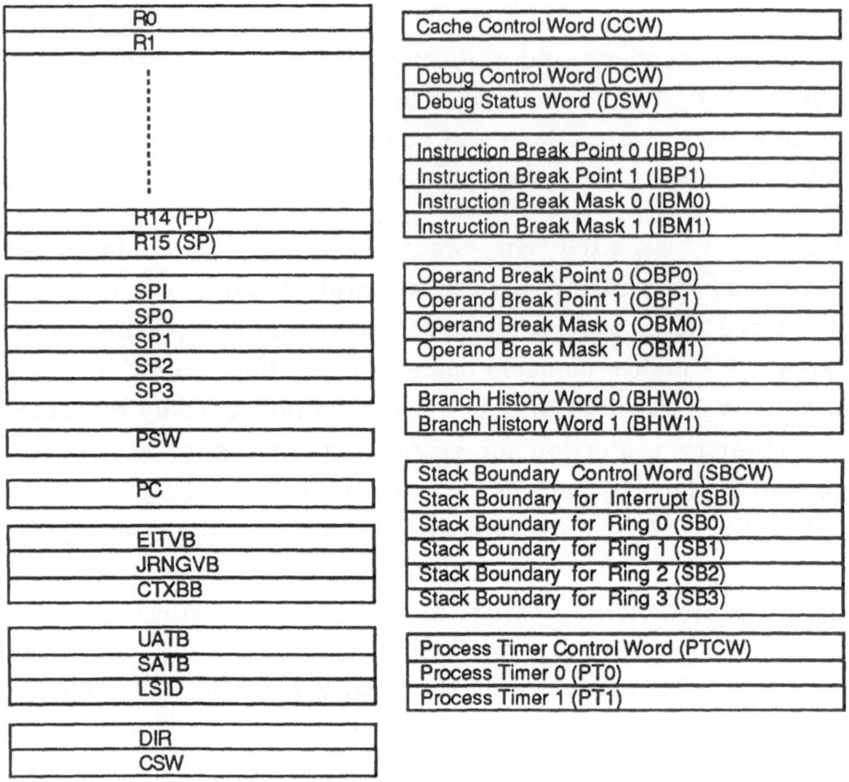

R0	Cache Control Word (CCW)
R1	
	Debug Control Word (DCW)
	Debug Status Word (DSW)
	Instruction Break Point 0 (IBP0)
	Instruction Break Point 1 (IBP1)
	Instruction Break Mask 0 (IBM0)
R14 (FP)	Instruction Break Mask 1 (IBM1)
R15 (SP)	
	Operand Break Point 0 (OBP0)
SPI	Operand Break Point 1 (OBP1)
SP0	Operand Break Mask 0 (OBM0)
SP1	Operand Break Mask 1 (OBM1)
SP2	
SP3	Branch History Word 0 (BHW0)
	Branch History Word 1 (BHW1)
PSW	
	Stack Boundary Control Word (SBCW)
PC	Stack Boundary for Interrupt (SBI)
	Stack Boundary for Ring 0 (SB0)
EITVB	Stack Boundary for Ring 1 (SB1)
JRNGVB	Stack Boundary for Ring 2 (SB2)
CTXBB	Stack Boundary for Ring 3 (SB3)
UATB	
SATB	Process Timer Control Word (PTCW)
LSID	Process Timer 0 (PT0)
	Process Timer 1 (PT1)
DIR	
CSW	

Fig. 1   O32 Register Set

In order to increase the system performance, it is often necessary to configure a multi-processor system, where each processor has its own local cache memory by sharing a global main memory. With this type of system, it is usually difficult to ensure the consistency among local cache memories. To solve this problem, the O32 is provided with a function, named the partial cache invalidation function, that eliminates the need for the useless invalidation of the internal cache memory by invalidating only the specified entry of the data cache from outside.

3. O32 INTERNAL STRUCTURE

Figure 2 shows a block diagram of the O32. The O32 consists of three subsystems: a memory subsystem, a decode subsystem, and an execution subsystem. Each subsystem comprises two to four functional units. The O32 chip consists of a total of ten units. The following is an outline explanation of each subsystem.

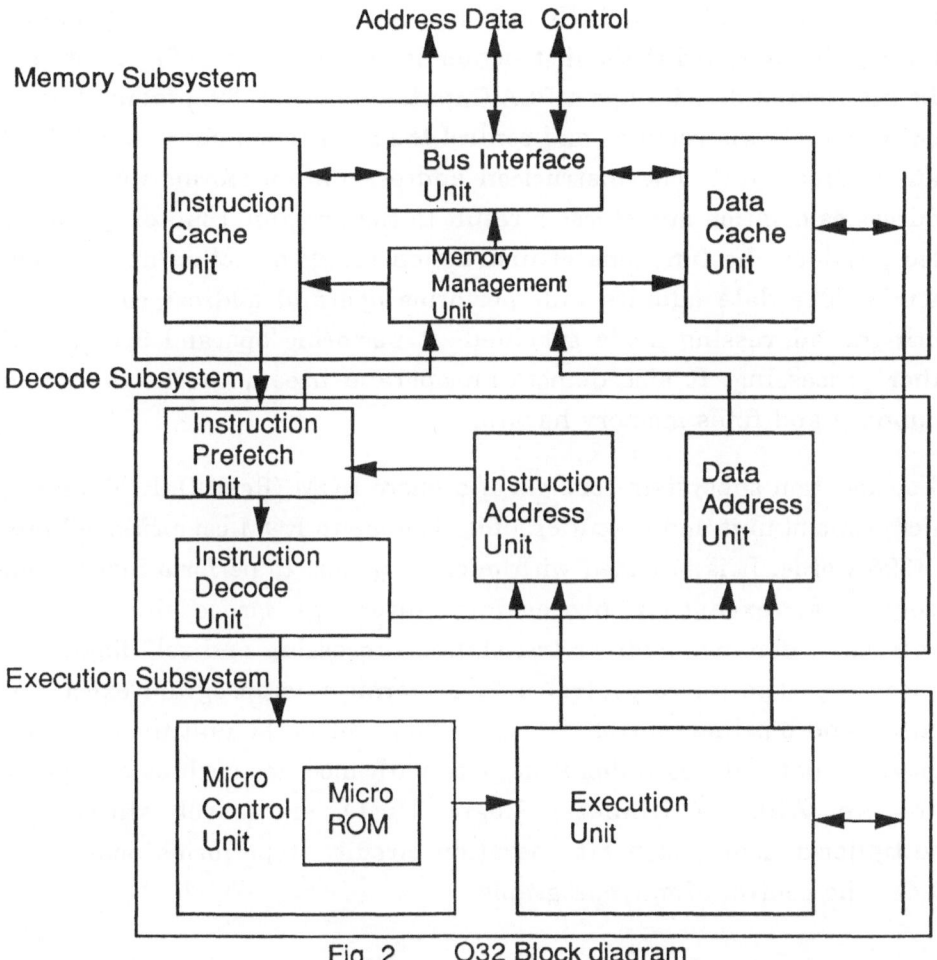

Fig. 2　　O32 Block diagram

The memory subsystem consists of an instruction cache memory, a data cache memory, a memory management unit, and a bus interface unit. The capacity of each cache memory is 1KB. The instruction and data caches each employ the 32-entry 2-way set associative organization. The memory management unit translates a logical address to a physical address. To do this, it is provided with a full-associative TLB, which uses the LRU (Least Recently Used) algorithm. The bus interface unit controls an interface with external systems. The minimum bus cycle is two clocks. The bus interface unit also supports the burst transfer mode. In this case, it transfers four-word data in five clocks.

The decode subsystem consists of four units: an instruction prefetch unit, instruction decode unit, instruction address unit, and data address unit. The instruction prefetch unit has a 16-byte instruction prefetch buffer. It is connected to the instruction decoder by means of a 32-bit bus. The instruction decoder has a PLA (input: 22; output: 39, product terms: 283) to decode instructions and control the instruction address unit and data address unit. The instruction address unit performs instruction address calculation and stores a result to the program counter queue. It also provides the functions of instruction break detection and branch history. The data address unit performs operand address calculation with the addressing mode specified. It performs operand access and other processing. It also detects an operand break, checks the stack boundary and finds memory hazards.

The execution subsystem consists of a micro ROM (Read Only Memory), micro control unit and execution unit. The micro ROM comprises 47 bits x 4096 words. It is provided with microprograms to perform instruction processing, exception processing, interrupt processing, TRAP processing, dynamic address translation processing and self-diagnostic processing. The micro control unit performs microprogram execution control and pipeline control. The execution unit is the unit that actually processes data. It has full-custom data-path modules such as a register file, an ALU (Arithmetic Logic Unit), a barrel shifter, a multiplier/divisor and a bit operation circuit. It performs operations under the control of microprograms.

4. EVALUATION OF HIGH-SPEED PROCESSING TECHNIQUES

This section discusses the effectiveness of the high-speed techniques explained above, namely, the cache memory and pipeline. We used the Dhrystone benchmark program[3] to evaluate the techniques.

4.1 CACHE MEMORY EFFECTIVENESS

The use of a cache memory is effective in increasing the access speed of instruction and operand fetching. Since the cache memory is divided into separate parts for instructions and data, it is possible to access an instruction and data independently. This prevents a penalty from arising even when these are accessed simultaneously.

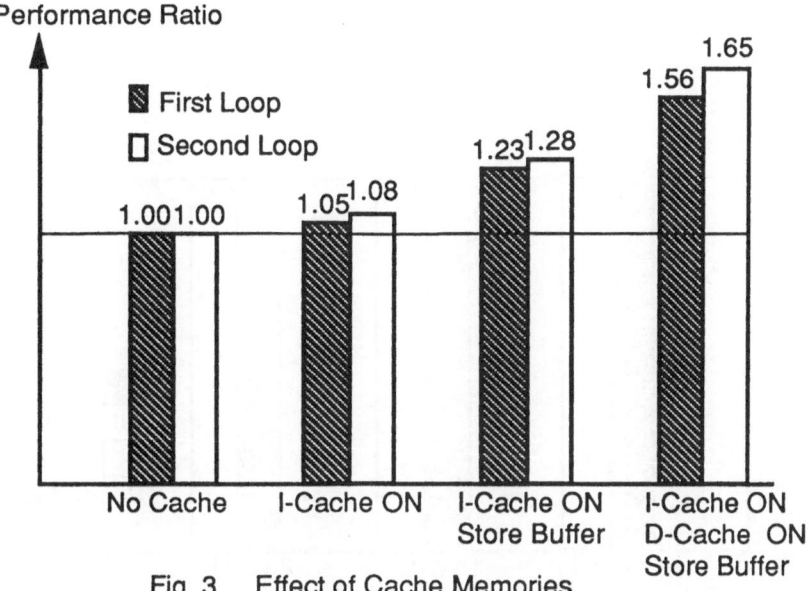

Fig. 3   Effect of Cache Memories

Figure 3 shows the result of the execution of the Dhrystone program in a variety of conditions. If the performance without cache is assumed to be one, this drawing shows relatively the performance in other cases. Because the same processing is repeated when the Dhrystone program is executed, the hit ratio of the cache is low in the first cycle. However, the hit ratio at the second cycle and thereafter goes up as shown in Table 2, i.e., performance improvement is realized.

The Dhrystone value with all of the cache used is found to be 1.65 times higher than the no cache system. The Dhrystone program used in this evaluation fetches operands and carries out write operations many times, i.e., it fetches operands 220 times and writes data 156 times. Figure 3 clearly shows that data cache and store buffer have contributed to the performance improvement.

Table 2   Cache Hit Ratio

	Instruction Cache Hit Ratio	Data Cache Hit Ratio
First Loop	84.6%	83.5%
Second Loop	100%	95.5%

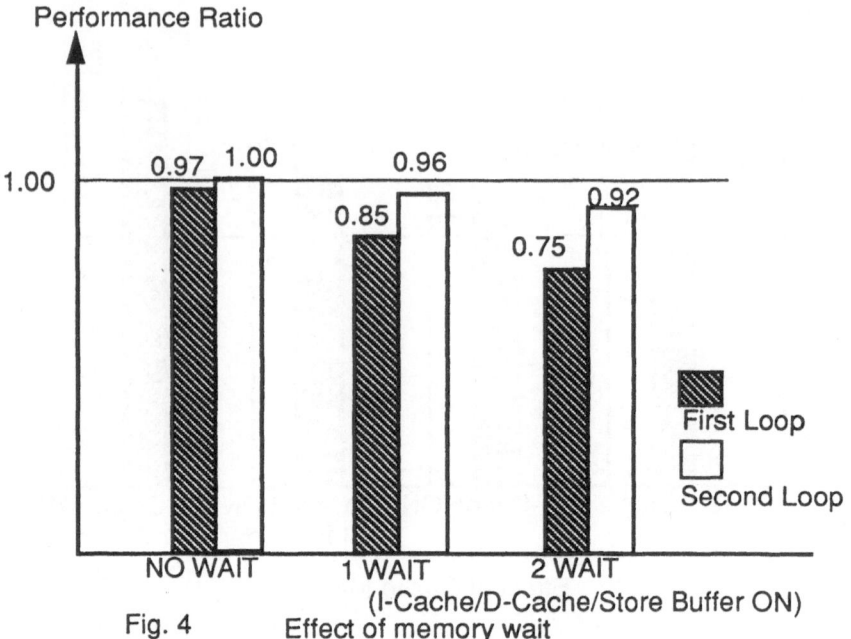

Fig. 4 Effect of memory wait

Figure 4 shows the relative performance when the number of memory wait times is changed. The drawing clearly indicates that the effect brought by use of cache memory prevents the second loop from being influenced by a performance decrease. In this case, performance decreases in number due to continuous operation of the store.

Because the number of simultanious accesses of cycles of an instruction and an operand amounts to 12% of the total number of cycles, separate instruction and data caches eliminate performance degradation caused by such conflicting accesses.

4.2 PIPELINE EFFECT

The O32 employs the pipeline processing to achive improved performance. Figure 5 shows the pipeline structure of the O32. The O32 performs six-stage pipeline processing - instruction fetching,instruction decoding, operand address calculation, operand fetching, execution and operand storing. Basically, one stage is processed in two clocks.

In order to absorb temporal mismatching of pipeline timing between these stages, several queues are inserted between these stages and EX stages. They include a decoded instruction queue(DIQ) which holds

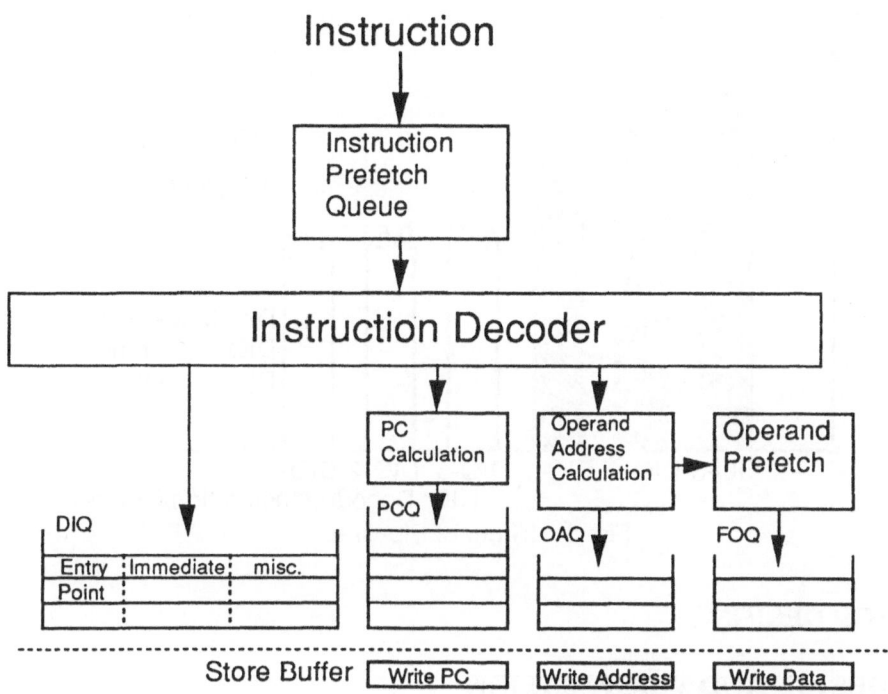

Fig. 5 O32 Pipeline

decoded instructions from the instruction decoding stage, an operand address queue(OAQ) whitch holds calculated operand addresses from the operand address calculation stage, a fetched operand queue(FOQ) which holds prefetched operands from the operand fetching stage, and a program counter queue(PCQ) which holds program counter values of the decoded instructions.

To evaluate the effect of the pipeline used, we compared its performance with that of fewer DIQ entry processors. Figure 6 gives the result of our simulation. It shows that the performance deteriorates gradually as the depth of the DIQ is reduced. Furthermore, the cache contained is found to heighten the effect brought by pipeline.

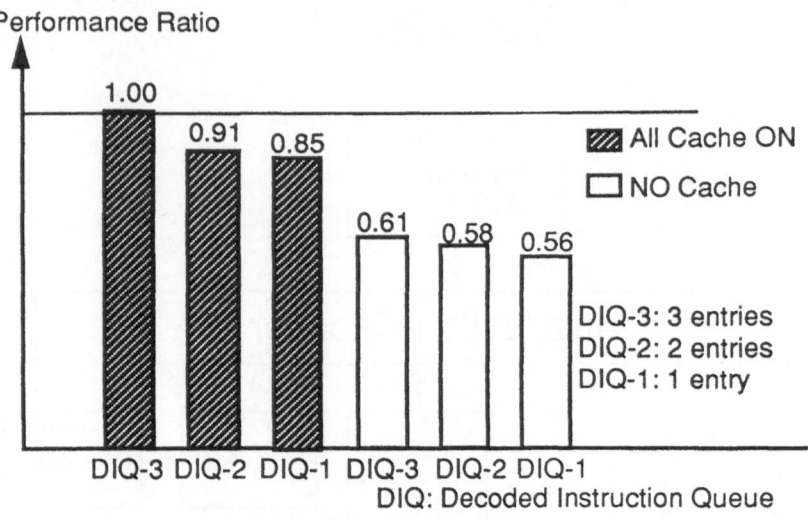

Fig. 6   Effect of Pipeline

5. CHIP DESIGN

5-1 DESIGN AND VERIFICATION

In developing the O32 it is necessary to incorporate the complex specifications into its logic design while achieving a high level of performance. We contrived an innovative LSI design environment and techniques to develop the chip that satisfy the two inconsistent requirements of complexity and high performance in a short period of time.

To develop the O32, we used a hardware description language entirely from abstract functional design to detailed logic design. In the functional design phase, we defined an outline of the internal architecture, divided the chip into three subsystems and further divided each subsystem into multiple units as explained in Section 2. By defining the functions and interfaces of these units, we started their abstract modeling using the hardware description language. In the process of modeling, we divided each unit into components such as control circuits, a data-path, memory and PLA and described them.

We verified each unit, each subsystem and finally the chip itself combining all units. A large system LSI like the O32 contains a large variety of functions. In some cases, it is inefficient to verify these units in a uniform manner. We therefore used different methods of verification for different subsystems. For example, we tested the memory subsystem using test patterns for each cycle. The decode subsystem and execution subsystem were tested by adding instruction streams and examining the results of their responses.

In the case of a microprogram-controlled microprocessor such as the O32, it is necessary to develop appropriate microprograms in parallel with the design of hardware. To this end, we made a microprogram development simulator[4] which consists of a simulation command interpreter, a break point monitor, microprogram storage model, and the above functional model to be verified. The simulation was started from the execution subsystem model. Later the simulator incorporated additional subsystems and eventually it was expanded as a system including the external circuits, the chip, and main memory. We also made an environment with interactive capability for microprogram/machine instruction debugging purposes. This substantially improved the efficiency of each level of the test processes.

After the testing of the function-level modeling, we expanded its description to the gate level. We checked the logic design for validity in the testing environment explained above using the same vector. In expanding the description to the gate level, we applied a logic synthesis system for some control circuits.

After completing the gate-level design of each unit, the net list was given to the floor planner. The floor planner made unit placement and routing plans. Then, the plans were examined in detail and the chip layout was finalized.

In the process of layout preparation, too, we tested the logic/delay designs for validity by incorporating into the testing environment the net list obtained after making the layout. We also developed a path analyzer for delay test purposes. We have performed pre-layout and post-layout path analysis, in order to achieve high-speed operations.

5-2 DEVICE DESIGN AND EVALUATION

Photo 1 shows a photograph of the O32 chip. Table 3 gives the specifications of the LSI.

The O32 uses a high-speed operating clock. When developing such a high-speed processor, there is the problem of a clock skew. The problem is particularly difficult to solve where automatic placement and routing techniques are used as with the O32. The O32 uses a non-overlapping two-phase clock. The insertion of clock drivers was all resolved at the layout design level, eliminating the need for extra load in logic/circuit design work. A driver is set for each column. At this time, the driving power is modified depending on the load status in the column. By providing this adjustment, it is possible to keep the clock skew less than 1ns.

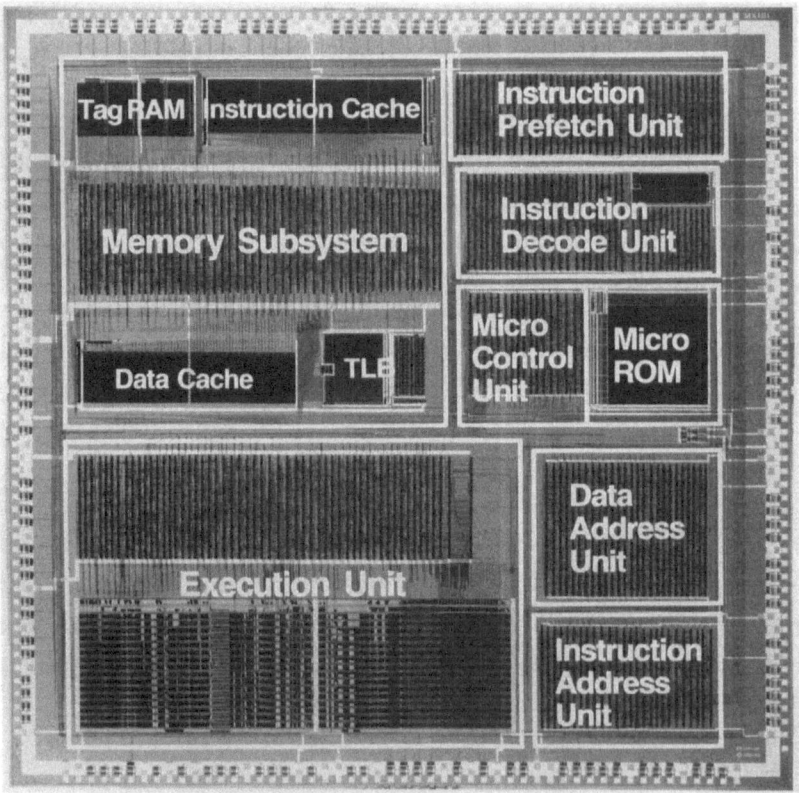

Photo 1 Photograph of the O32

Table 3   O32 Chip Characteristics

Process	Double-metal Layer CMOS
Design Rule	0.8 μm
Transistors	700,000
Chip Size	15.0mm X 15.0mm
Power Dissipation	4.0W
Power Supply	+5V
Package	208-pin PGA

6. CONCLUSION

The O32, a 32-bit microprocessor based on the TRON specifications, features a high level of reliability and the use of a variety of high-speed techniques such as a built-in cache memory. The O32 has an integration of 700,000 transistors and is operated with a high-speed clock. It is expected to be applied to switching systems and node processors for its high performance and reliability.

ACKNOWLEDGMENTS

The authors gratefully acknowledge the generous assistance they received from Mr. Uehara, chief of Microprocessor Development Center. They also thank all staff members of the Center who extended cooperation to them in developing the O32.

REFERENCES

[1]   K.Sakamura, "TRON VLSI CPU:Concepts and Architecture", TRON Project 1987, Springer-Verlag, pp.199-238, 1987.

[2]   N.Ito, H.Nojima,Y.Mori, "Architectural Feature of Oki 32-Bit Microprocessor", TRON Project 1988, Springer-Verlag, pp.247-262, 1988.

[3]   R.P.Weicker, "Dhrystone: A Synthetic System Programing Benchmark", Communications of the ACM, Vol.27, No.10, October 1984, pp.1013-1030.

[4]   Y.Haneda,T.Kobayashi Y.Mori, "A Microprogram Debug Environments for VLSI Processors", Proc.39th Annual Convention IPS Japan, pp.1696-1697, 1989 (in Japanese)

234

Yoshikazu Mori is a researcher of Microprocessor Development Center, Oki Electric Industry Co.,Ltd. He received the B.S. degree in electrical engineering from Housei University in 1981. He joined Oki Electric Industry Co.,Ltd. in 1981. He was engaged in research and development of the VLSI digital signal processors. Since 1987, he has been engaged in development of VLSI microprocessors.

Yoshihito Haneda is a researcher of Microprocessor Development Center, Oki Electric Industry Co.,Ltd. He received the B.S. degree in information engineering from Toyohashi University of Technology in 1982 and the M.S. degree in 1984. He joined Oki Electric Industry Co.,Ltd. in 1984. Since then, he was engaged in research and development of sequential inference machine at Systems Laboratory. He is currently engaged in development of VLSI microprocessors.

Yoshihiko Arakawa is an assistant manager of Microprocessor Development Center, Oki Electric Industry Co.,Ltd. He received the B.S. degree and M.S. degree in electrical engineering from Waseda University in 1980 and 1982. He joined Oki Electric Industry Co.,Ltd. in 1982. He was engaged in the design of electronic switching systems till 1987. He is currently engaged in the development of VLSI microprocessors.

Toshitaka Mori is a researcher of Microprocessor Development Center, Oki Electric Industry Co.,Ltd. He received the B.S. degree in photographic engineering from Chiba University in 1981. He joined Oki Electric Industry Co.,Ltd. in 1981. Since then, he was engaged in development of 16-bit microprocessors. He is currently engaged in development of VLSI microprocessors.

Mutsumi Kumazawa is a researcher of Microprocessor Development Center, Oki Electric Industry Co.,Ltd. He received the B.S. degree in electric engineering from Nagoya University in 1979. He joined Oki Electric Industry Co.,Ltd. in 1979. Since then, he was engaged in development of the VLSI computers. He is currently engaged in development of VLSI microprocessors.

The above authors may be reached at: Microprocessor Development Center, Oki Electric Industry Co.,Ltd., 10-3, Shibaura 4-chome, Minato-ku, Tokyo, 108, Japan.

Design Considerations of On-Chip-Type Floating-Point Units

Masato Suzuki, Tokuzo Kiyohara, Masashi Deguchi
Matsushita Electric Industrial Co., Ltd.

ABSTRACT

This paper is a report of the pipeline structure of a 32-bit microprocessor based on TRON specification with the on-chip floating-point unit (FPU). The FPU proposed here divides floating-point operations into two steps (each step performed during one clock cycle), and executes the second step in parallel with the succeeding instruction's operand fetch. In this way, memory-to-register and register-to-register floating-point instructions can be executed at the same speed. The paper also discusses high-speed methods of rounding operations to execute the floating-point operations in two steps. This microprocessor performs the Whetstone benchmark in 10.2MWIPS for single-precision and in 8.3MWIPS for double-precision (both at 20MHz).

Keywords: Floating-point, Floating-point unit (FPU), On-chip, Pipeline, Microprocessor.

1. INTRODUCTION

With the increasing levels of integration which accompany recent advances in semiconductor technology, there has been an increasing trend toward building floating-point units (hereafter abbreviated FPU) into the chip structure. By building FPUs into the chip, the FPU's operation execution stage can be built into the pipeline of the main microprocessor, thus allowing the floating-point operation instructions to be executed at high speeds and low cost. In order to realize these gains, attempts have been made to find an FPU which will conform to the pipeline structure of the main microprocessor.

It was from this perspective that we made our study of on-chip FPUs which make best use of the characteristics of the main microprocessor's pipeline structure. In this paper, we make proposals regarding the pipeline structure of a microprocessor with an on-chip FPU, one which executes memory-to-register and register-to-register floating-point instructions at a speed (two clock cycles) which is limited by the upper limit value of the main microprocessor's instruction-decoding speed.

In order to allow execution of memory-to-register operations with performance equivalent to register-to-register operations, the memory operand's pre-fetch mechanism is sometimes built into the pipeline. This technique, however, results in a complex system of access control for the memory operand, leading to higher hardware costs. Also, since the number of pipeline stages becomes higher, the overhead in case of branching becomes greater.

In contrast, the FPU proposed here makes use of the advantages found particularly in the pipeline structure of main microprocessors without any operand pre-fetch mechanisms. While making it possible to execute floating-point instructions in two clock cycles, the second clock operation is executed in parallel with the succeeding instruction's operand fetch, thus producing both higher-speed execution of memory-to-register floating-point instructions, and a reduction in the amount of hardware required.

In the following sections, we will discuss the basic specifications of the FPU implemented (section 2), the pipeline structure of the processor with the on-chip FPU (section 3), and evaluation models for expressing the effectiveness of this FPU (section 4). We will demonstrate an algorithm for the rounding operations required for executing floating-point instructions in two clock cycles, and a performance evaluation in terms of the Whetstone benchmark (section 5).

2. BASIC SPECIFICATIONS OF THE FPU

In this section, we will discuss the basic specifications of the FPU based on TRON specification.

(1) Data format

As shown in Fig. 1, this FPU supports the 32-bit single-precision and 64-bit double-precision data format specified by the IEEE Standard for Binary Floating-Point Arithmetic (ANSI/IEEE Standard 754-1985). The FPU does not support extended double-precision (normally 80-bit).

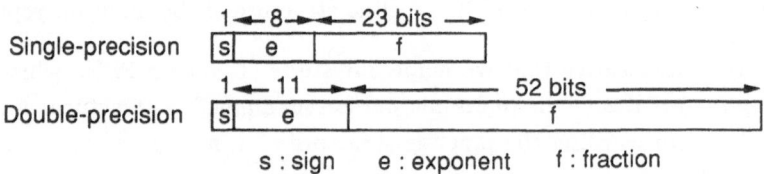

Fig. 1 Floating-Point Data Format

(2) Instruction format

According to TRON specifications, floating-point operation instructions use an instruction bit pattern allocated to co-processor instructions. The only floating-point operation instruction format is the 32-bit general format. Also, with the exception of the floating-point store instructions, destination operands are limited to floating-point registers. The instruction format is shown in Fig. 2.

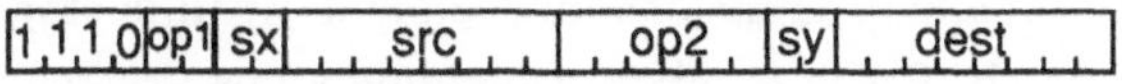

| 1,1,1,0 | op1 | sx | src | op2 | sy | dest |

op1,op2 : operation code
src,dest : operand addressing mode
sx : src-operand size
sy : dest-operand size (rounding precision)

Fig. 2 Format for Floating-Point Operation Instruction

(3) Instruction set

The instruction set supported by this FPU includes basic operations, load/store, and branching instructions. Trigonometric and other function operations are not supported in interests of reducing hardware. The instruction set is shown in Table 1.

Table 1 Implemented Instruction Set

Binomial operations	Addition, Subtraction, Multiplication, Division, Comparison
Mononomial operations	Absolute values, Sign changing, Square root
Transfers	Floating-point loading / storing, Integer loading / storing, Control register loading / storing,
Branching operations	Conditional branch, No operation

3. PIPELINE STRUCTURE

This section contains a description of the pipeline structure of the main microprocessor under consideration, followed by a discussion of the FPU which takes advantage of the merits of that pipeline structure.

3.1 MAIN MICROPROCESSOR PIPELINE STRUCTURE

Fig. 3 shows the pipeline structure of the main microprocessor. In that illustration, IF refers to the instruction fetch stage, DEC1 to the first instruction-decoding stage, DEC2 to the second instruction-decoding stage, OA to the operand-address-calculation stage, OF/EX to the operand-fetch and execution stages, and OS to the operand-store stage. The OA stage occurs in parallel with the DEC2 stage. After writing to the store buffer from OF/EX stage, the OS stage occurs independently of the OF/EX stage, thus performing writing of the operand to memory. Since no independent pipeline stage is provided for the memory operand's pre-fetch, fewer number of pipeline steps are required, thus allowing simpler control of the memory operand access. Since integer operations can be processed in a single clock cycle even without performing operand pre-fetch, execution can be performed in the same two clock cycles required for instruction decoding of general format integer operation instructions.

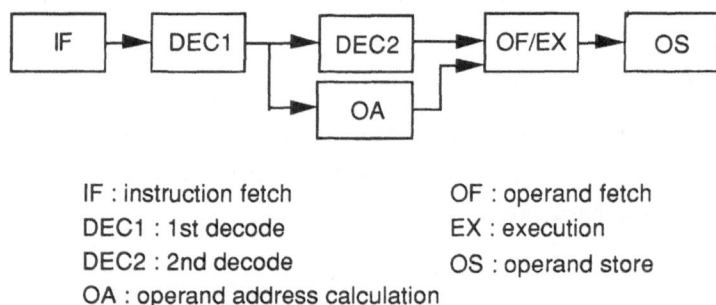

IF : instruction fetch   OF : operand fetch
DEC1 : 1st decode   EX : execution
DEC2 : 2nd decode   OS : operand store
OA : operand address calculation

Fig. 3 Pipeline Structure of Main Microprocessor

3.2 FPU PIPELINE STRUCTURE

However, floating-point operations cannot be processed in a single clock cycle due to the greater volume of processing required compared to integer operations. As a result, the number of clock cycles required for the execution of floating-point operation instructions is greater than the two clocks needed for instruction decoding. In other words, performing operand fetch sequentially with the operation execution in the execution stage results in a degradation of the speed of memory-to-register floating-point instructions.

In order to avoid this kind of performance degradation, two clock cycles are designated for the number of clock cycles for floating-point operation processing, with processing in the latter of the two being executed in parallel with the succeeding instruction's operand fetch.

As a result, the number of clock cycles required for execution of memory-to-register floating-point instructions is shortened to the same two cycles needed for instruction decoding. The minimum clock number of bus access for memory read is one. Also, destination operands are limited to floating-point registers with the exception of floating-point store instructions whose parallel execution is prohibited. In this way conflicts regarding the memory operands of the preceding and succeeding instructions are eliminated. With regard to the register operands as well, since floating-point operation processing for preceding and succeeding instructions is not performed simultaneously, no conflict is generated.

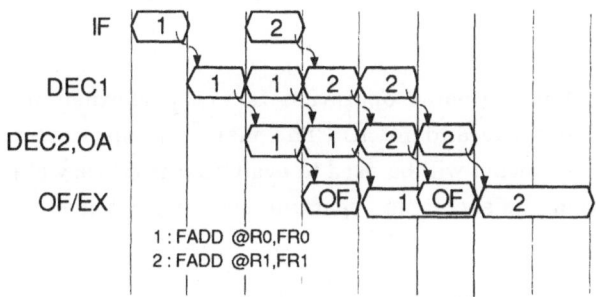

Fig. 4 Pipeline Flow

Fig. 4 indicates the pipeline flow in the case of continuous memory-to-register floating-point instructions. The pipeline operates smoothly without disruption. The floating-point operation instructions are decoded in two clock cycles, and based on the decoding results of the first clock, the source operand is fetched from memory in the OF/EX stage.

Based on the decoding results of the second clock, the floating-point operation is performed in the OF/EX stage. The OF/EX stage where the floating-point operation is performed, completes its processing in two clock cycles, but the latter cycle operates parallel to the OF/EX stage of the instruction which follows next.

This kind of control method is the same as for operand store, and the latter stage of the floating-point operation execution can be controlled by the mechanism of the operand store stage. When the instruction is for register-to-register operations, the floating-point register is read out in the OF/EX stage in place of the memory operand fetch; in other respects, however, the pipeline flow is the same as for memory-to-register operations.

4. EVALUATION OF PIPELINE STRUCTURE

In this section, we will demonstrate first that the parallel execution of floating-point operation and next-instruction operand fetch as performed by the test FPU under consideration is effective for performing both register-to-register and memory-to-register floating-point instructions in two clock cycles. Second, we will demonstrate that this structure delivers performance equivalent to those designs where the main microprocessor performs operand pre-fetch. To these ends, we will offer multiple pipeline models with structures differing from the pipeline structure noted in section 3, and construct programs to evaluate the pipeline structures.

4.1 COMPARATIVE PIPELINE MODELS

The following three models will be used for purposes of evaluation:

(1) Model A

In this model, the floating-point operation is not performed in parallel with the succeeding instruction's operand fetch. The main microprocessor does not perform operand pre-fetch. This model will be used to evaluate the efficacy of parallel execution of floating-point operation and succeeding operand fetch as performed by our test FPU.

(2) Model B

In order to demonstrate that the enhancement of performance resulting from parallel execution of floating-point operation and succeeding operand fetch in the test FPU is equivalent to the performance of operand pre-fetch, this model involves the provision of an independent memory operand pre-fetch stage within the main microprocessor's pipeline. The instruction decoding bandwidth is 16 bits within each clock cycle.

(3) Model C

In this model, the floating-point operation instruction is decoded and executed in a single clock cycle. As a result, the instruction decoding bandwidth is made 32 bits in each clock cycle, and an independent pipeline stage is provided for memory operand pre-fetch, with the floating-point operation execution stage being divided into two stages. This model is used to demonstrate the positioning of the test FPU relative to one performance limit.

4.2 EVALUATION PROGRAMS

Three evaluation programs were constructed, each with differing frequency of operand conflict. The programs are introduced below.

(1) Three-dimensional coordinates transformation:

Calculations were performed with the formula below. Of the three programs, this one demonstrates the lowest frequency of operand conflict.

$$\begin{bmatrix} a11 & a12 & a13 \\ a21 & a22 & a23 \\ a31 & a32 & a33 \end{bmatrix} \cdot \begin{bmatrix} x \\ y \\ z \end{bmatrix} + \begin{bmatrix} b1 \\ b2 \\ b3 \end{bmatrix} \rightarrow \begin{bmatrix} x' \\ y' \\ z' \end{bmatrix}$$

(2) Two-dimensional coordinates transformation:

Calculations were performed using the following formula:

$$\begin{bmatrix} a & b \\ c & d \end{bmatrix} \cdot \begin{bmatrix} x \\ y \end{bmatrix} + \begin{bmatrix} e \\ f \end{bmatrix} \rightarrow \begin{bmatrix} x' \\ y' \end{bmatrix}$$

(3) Polynomial calculations:

Calculations were performed using the formula below. Of the three programs, this one demonstrates the highest frequency of operand conflict. The degrees do not influence the frequency of operand conflict.

$$ax^5 + bx^4 + cx^3 + dx^2 + ex + f$$
$$= ((((ax+b)x+c)x+d)x+e)x+f \rightarrow x'$$

These evaluation programs were constructed in the following way:

- All variables were allocated in memory.

- For each model, assembler descriptions were made so as to minimize the frequency of pipeline interlock.

- The programs involved only floating-point operation processing routines, and included no call, return, register save or restore operations.

4.3 RESULTS OF MODEL EVALUATIONS

The aforementioned three evaluation programs were run using the microprocessor with the pipeline structure noted in section 3, and models A through C. When running the evaluation programs we assumed a sufficient capacity of on-chip instruction cache for each model, and all instruction fetches were considered to be achieved from the on-chip instruction cache. No data caching was implemented. Also, the bus access for memory read and write were completed in one clock cycle.

Fig. 5 shows the results of the program execution. The graph expresses performance (in terms of number of clock cycles) relative to the microprocessor with the test FPU, which is given a reference value of 1. The following is a consideration of the results, based on the graph:

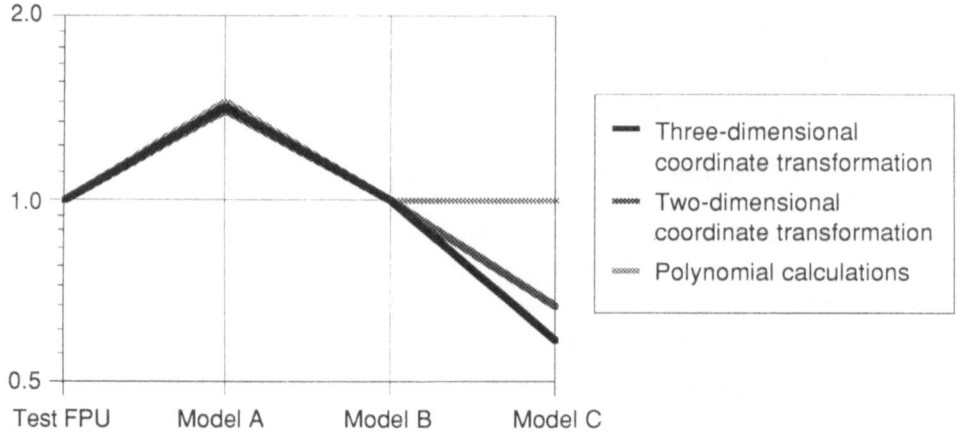

Fig. 5 Number of Execute Clock Cycles for Evaluation Programs

(with test FPU's execute clock cycles as 1)

In either of the evaluation programs, the test FPU decreased the number of clock cycles for execution by 30% or more compared to Model A, demonstrating the effect resulting from parallel execution of floating-point operation and succeeding operand fetch. A comparison of the test FPU with Model B illustrates that the number of clock cycles for execution are the same, and use of the test FPU's parallel execution makes unnecessary the operand pre-fetch mechanism, which tends to increase hardware expense. With Model C, even though the execution stage is divided into two, operand conflict makes it impossible to reduce the number of clock cycles required to 1/2 the number required with the test FPU. In applications with numerous conflicts, like the evaluation program for polynomial calculations, the number of executing clock cycle for is virtually the same as for the test FPU. With Model C, an operand pre-fetch mechanism and an instruction decoder with 32-bit per clock cycle decoding bandwidth are required, and the execution stage is divided into multiple stages, thus increasing the amount of hardware required. Further, in applications generating numerous operand conflicts, Model C also demonstrates the problem of reduced performance due to interlock.

5. IMPLEMENTATION

In this section, we will discuss implementation of an arithmetic unit which executes floating-point operations in two clock cycles and which we used for our test FPU, together with performance evaluation results based on the Whetstone benchmark program.

5.1 ROUNDING OPERATION ALGORITHM

As shown in the next add-subtract operation, processing necessary to floating-point operations is as follows:

a. Comparison of exponents

b. Fractional alignment

c. Fractional add-subtract

d. Normalization

e. Rounding

f. Normalization

In order to execute these steps in two clock cycles, if you consider a and b to be performed in the first clock with c through f performed in the second clock cycle, the amount of processing on the second cycle is too great. To bring the latter half processing amount into line with the amount on the first half, some modification of the rounding operation must be performed.

Conventional rounding operation is effected by performing the fractional add-subtract operation followed by adding 0 (rounding down) or 1 (rounding up) to the LSB. This processing is performed on the same adder at the same time as the fractional add-subtract operation. Here, we will explain the rounding operation algorithm used when the rounding mode is the "Round to Nearest even" mode specified by the IEEE Standard. Here, we will assume the operation to be adding (an add instruction with respect to operands of the same sign, or a subtract instruction for operands of the different sign).

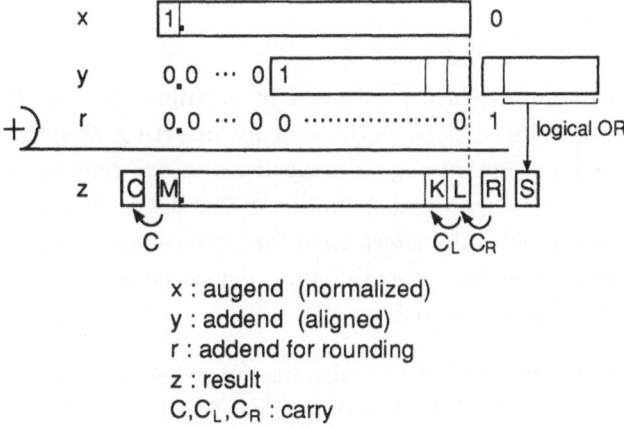

x : augend (normalized)
y : addend (aligned)
r : addend for rounding
z : result
C, C_L, C_R : carry

Fig. 6 Fraction Adding Performed Simultaneously with Rounding

Fig. 6 shows a fractional adding process which performs simultaneous rounding. Here, the normalized fraction x is added to the exponent-aligned fraction y, and the addend for rounding r (which has 1 set in the round bit position). Based on the following logical expression, the result z is either compensated or re-rounded in order to produce the correctly rounded value z':

```
if (C==0)
    if (LRS==100)        z'=z(L is made 0);                    ...Compensation (A)
    else                 z'=z;
    else if (KLRS==1110 || KLRS==1111)     z'=z>>1+r;     ...Re-rounding (B), (C)
        else if (KLRS==0111)     z'=z(K is made 1)>>1;     ...Compensation (D)
            else                 z'=z>>1;
```

Here, C is the carry in addition, K and L are the least significant two bits of result z, R is the round bit's position, and S is the sticky bit. Also, >>1 indicates the normalization of the right-shifted 1 bit. Details of this algorithm are shown in the accompanying appendix.

In the case of subtraction (a subtract instruction with respect to operands of the same sign, or an add instruction for operands of the different sign), the same kind of algorithm can be applied when adding the fraction complemented on 2. By performing rounding simultaneously with fractional processing in this way, the processing required of floating-point add-subtract operation can be shortened as follows:

a. Comparison of exponents

b. Fractional alignment

c. Fractional add-subtract and rounding

d. Normalization

The work load when c and d are performed in a single clock cycle is thus reduced substantially. Re-rounding can be performed by inserting additional cycles. When performing this additional operation, three clock cycles are required in all, however as the occurrence rate is low (when the distribution of 0 and 1 for bits C,K,L,R,S is uniform, the rate is approximately 6%), the effect upon the performance is negligible. Also, since fractional add-subtract operation and rounding operation are performed on the same adder, less FPU hardware is required.

This algorithm can also be applied to multiplication when adding the multiplier's sum output to the carry output. Modes other than "Round to Nearest even" mode can also be processed using these same principles.

5.2 BENCHMARK PERFORMANCE EVALUATION

The performance resulting from application of the aforementioned test FPU to the TRON-specified 32-bit microprocessor MN10400 [1],[2] was evaluated using the Whetstone benchmark program. This processor's pipeline has no independent stage for performing memory operand pre-fetch, and the instruction decoding bandwidth is 16 bits long in each clock cycle. Table 2 indicates the Whetstone performance. These numbers were calculated from the average instruction execute clock cycles, based on code generated by compiling the Whetstone benchmark program which was written in "C" language.

Table 2 Whetstone Benchmark Performance (at 20MHz)

Single-precision	Double-precision
10.2 MWIPS	8.3 MWIPS

With the Whetstone benchmark program, add-subtract and multiplication appear with high frequency. The absolute number of function operations performed is low, but the execute time is long, and this has a great part in determining Whetstone performance. This test FPU does not have instruction support for function operations, but since add-subtract and multiplying operations are performed at high speed, function operations can also be executed quickly, thus contributing to improvement of Whetstone performance.

6. CONCLUSION

This paper has made proposals regarding the pipeline structure of a microprocessor with on-chip FPU, which can execute both memory-to-register and register-to-register floating-point operation instructions in the same two clock cycles required for instruction decoding. With this FPU, the second of the two clock cycles is used for parallel processing of the floating-point operation and succeeding instruction's operand fetch. Features of the test FPU can be summarized as follows:

- The FPU can make optimum use of the structural advantages of main microprocessor's pipeline which has no operand pre-fetch mechanism and which has instruction decoding bandwidth of 16-bit per clock cycle.
- By limiting floating-point operation instruction destination operands to the floating-point registers, the problem of operand conflict which accompanies parallel processing can be avoided.
- The control mechanism of the operand store stage can be utilized in parallel execution of floating-point operation and succeeding operand fetch.

We have also demonstrated an arithmetic unit implementation for the purpose of executing floating-point add-subtract and multiplication in two clock cycles. One particular characteristic is the ability to use the same adder while performing fractional processing and rounding operations at the same time. The Whetstone benchmark performance of the test FPU was 10.2MWIPS (single-precision, at 20MHz).

REFERENCES

[1]   T. Kiyohara, et. al., "Design Considerations of the Matsushita 32-Bit Microprocessor for Real-Memory Systems," TRON Project 1988, 263-273.

[2]   M. Miyazaki, et. al., "The Pipeline Control System and Verification Method of a 32-Bit Microprocessor MN10400 Based on TRON Specifications," IEICE Technical Report ICD90-3, April 1990, 15-22.

APPENDIX

[Demonstration of the Simultaneous Rounding Algorithm]

In Fig. 6, the lower two bits of the sum of x and y (not including the addend for rounding r) is assumed to be $\underline{K},\underline{L}$, and the round bit is $\underline{R}$.

$$KLR=\underline{KLR} + 001$$

On the other hand, according to the IEEE standard, the "Round to Nearest even" mode is specified as follows:

When the round bit = 0, round down (add nothing to LSB)

When the round bit = 1,

if the sticky bit = 1, then round up (add 1 to LSB)

if the sticky bit = 0 (in case of a tie),

if LSB=0, round down (add nothing to LSB)

if LSB=1, round up (add 1 to LSB)

(1) When C=0 (namely, when 1 <= fraction of sum < 2),

The round bit is $\underline{R}$, LSB is $\underline{L}$, and the sticky bit is S.

(i) When $\underline{R}$=0, must be rounded down.

Since $\underline{R}$=0, even if the addend for rounding r is added, R merely becomes equal to 1, and C_R=0. Accordingly, nothing is added to LSB, and the result M...L is correctly rounded down.

(ii) When $\underline{R}$=1, after the addend for rounding r is added, it results in C_R=1.

(ii-A) When S=1, rounding up must occur.

Since C_R=1, 1 is added to LSB, and the result M...L is correctly rounded up.

(ii-B) When S=0 (in case of a tie),

    - When $\underline{L}$=0, rounding down must occur.

        Since C_R=1, rounding up occurs. But as a result of adding the addend for rounding r,

$$KLR=\underline{KLR} + 001 =\underline{K}10$$

and since C_L=0, the carry propagating from LSB upwards does not exist, L should be thus compensated from 1 to 0, and rounding down is effected   [Compensation (A)].

    - When $\underline{L}$=1, rounding up must occur.

        Since C_R=1, 1 is added to LSB, and the result M...L is correctly rounded up.

Based on the above, when LRS=100, correcting rounding results will be achieved if the L bit of the operation result z is compensated to 0.

(2) When C=1 (namely when 2 <= fraction of sum < 4),

The round bit is $\underline{L}$, LSB is $\underline{K}$, and the sticky bit is the logical-OR of $\underline{R}$ and S.

(i) When $\underline{L}$=0, rounding down must occur.

    Since $\underline{L}$=0, even if the addend for rounding r is added, carry from the lower bit does not propagate, and C_L=0. Accordingly, nothing is added to LSB, and the result C...K is correctly rounded down.

(ii) When $\underline{L}$=1,

(ii-A) When $\underline{R}$=1, the sticky bit is 1, so rounding up must occur.

        Since $\underline{R}$=1, after the addend for rounding r is added, it results in C_R=1. And since $\underline{L}$=1, the carry propagates upwards, with the result that C_L=1. Accordingly, 1 is added to LSB, and the result C...K is correctly rounded up.

(ii-B) When $\underline{R}$=0, even if the addend for rounding r is added, R merely becomes equal to 1, carry propagating from R upwards does not exist, and C_R=C_L=0.

(ii-B-a) When S=0, namely, when the sticky bit is 0 (in case of a tie),

    - When $\underline{K}$=0, rounding down must occur.

        Since C_L=0, nothing is added to LSB, and the result C...K is correctly rounded down.

    - When $\underline{K}$=1, rounding up must occur.

        Since C_L=0, the result is rounded down. As a result of adding the addend for rounding r,

$$KLR=\underline{KLR}+001=111$$

and the compensation of K, L, and R will not result in rounding up. In this case, rounding addition will be required once more [Re-rounding (B)].

(ii-B-b) When S=1, namely, when the sticky bit is 1, rounding up must occur.

    - When $\underline{K}$=1,

        Since C_L=0, so rounding down is performed. As a result of adding the addend for rounding r,

KLR=<u>KLR</u>+001=111

and the compensation of K, L, and R will not result in rounding up. In this case, rounding addition will be required once more [Re-rounding (C)].

- When <u>K</u>=0,

Since $C_L=0$, so rounding down is performed. But as a result of adding the addend for rounding r,

KLR=<u>KLR</u>+001=011

and K should be compensated from 0 to 1, thus resulting in rounding up [Compensation (D)].

From the above, re-rounding addition will be required when KLRS=1110 or 1111. Also, when KLRS=0111, if the K bit of the operation result z is compensated to 1, the correct rounding results can be obtained.

Masato Suzuki: He received B.E. and M.E. degrees from Osaka University in 1983 and 1985. After joining Matsushita Electric Industrial Co., Ltd. in 1985, he has been engaged in the development of the VLSI processor and application systems. He is a member of IPSJ.

Masashi Deguchi: He received B.E. and M.E. degrees from Nagoya Institute of Technology in 1974 and 1976. After joining Matsushita Electric Industrial Co., Ltd. in 1976, he has been engaged in the development of the VLSI processor and application systems. He is a member of IECEJ.

Tokuzo Kiyohara: He received B.E. and M.E. degrees from Kyoto University in 1980 and 1982. After joining Matsushita Electric Industrial Co., Ltd. in 1982, he has been engaged in the development of the VLSI processor and application systems. He is a member of IECEJ and IPSJ.

Above authors may be reached at: Kansai Information and Communications Research Laboratory, Matsushita Electric Industrial Co., Ltd., 3-15, Yagumonakamachi, Moriguchi, Osaka 570 Japan.

The Design Method of High Speed Cache Controller/Memory (CCM) for the Gmicro Family Microprocessors

Akira Yamada, Hiromasa Nakagawa, Masayuki Hata,
Mitsugu Satoh, Koichi Nishida
LSI Research and Development Laboratory, Mitsubishi Electric Corporation

Toshiyuki Hiraki
Kita-Itami Works, Mitsubishi Electric Corporation

ABSTRACT

We present Cache Controller/Memory (CCM) of 16K bytes. The CCM is used for the Gmicro family of microprocessors (Gmicro/100, Gmicro/200, and Gmicro/300) which are based on the TRON architecture specification. The CCM is fabricated with 1.0 micron CMOS design technology and is implemented in a 9.24 mm x 8.88 mm die with 1,050,000 devices. We describe the design method of a tag memory, a data memory, and a clock generator for the high speed CCM. Our evaluation of the CCM reveals that the delay time from address signals to a hit signal is about 14 ns.

Keywords: Cache memory, Tag memory, CAM, Data memory, Clock generator

1. INTRODUCTION

The high speed 32 bit microprocessors; Gmicro/100, Gmicro/200, and Gmicro/300, being based on the TRON architecture specification, are developed to achieve high performance for three application systems.[1],[2],[3] The clock frequency of these CPUs is more than 20 MHz. And as this speed exceeds the delay time of the main memory, it is difficult for the CPUs to access the main memory without a wait state. In order to reduce this speed gap, the need for high speed cache memory is increasing. For this reason a CCM that can be used for the Gmicro family of microprocessors has been developed.[4]

In order to send a hit signal to the CPUs without a wait state, the CCM must generate the hit signal as soon as possible. This paper describes design methods of a tag memory to generate the hit signal quickly. A data memory of the CCM is accessed very fast in a zero wait state read and write. So, we present techniques of a configuration of the data memory and sense amplifiers to obtain fast access time. If a phase difference of an external clock to internal clocks in the CCM is large, it is difficult for the CCM to operate synchronously with the CPUs. The paper describes new techniques to reduce the phase difference. The paper also evaluates the CCM, and shows a very fast access time of the CCM. A result of the evaluation guarantees that the CCM can be accessed by the CPUs without a wait state.

2. ARCHITECTURAL FEATURES OF THE CCM

Table 1 gives a brief description of the CCM specifications. The CCM has three modes, G100, G200, and G300, which correspond to host microprocessors GMICRO/100, GMICRO/200, and GMICRO/300, respectively. These modes provide the best cache controller/memory for each GMICRO microprocessor to get high performance easily. The configuration of the CCM is a 4-way set associative, and the LRU (Least Recently Used) replacement algorithm is used. Because the CCM has an address monitor function, when a bus master except the host CPU modifies a data in the main memory, the data in the CCM is invalidated.

Table 1. Specifications of the CCM

Host CPUs	GMICRO/100, /200, /300
Clock frequency	20MHz
Cache size	16K bytes
Tag memory	4x256x21 bits
Block size	16 bytes
Entry	256 sets
Configuration	4 way set associative
Replacement algorithm	LRU(Least Recently Used)
Write algorithm	Write-through
Fetch algorithm	On demand

Figure 1 shows a CCM internal block diagram. There are a data memory, a tag memory, an LRU memory, and control circuits. The data memory has 16K bytes and consists of four ways; each way has 256 entries and each entry contains four words. In the CCM, one word corresponds to 32 bits.

Like the data memory, the tag memory has four ways. The tag memory stores tag address signals (A0:19) and a valid bit in Content-Addressable Memory (CAM) cells. Entry address signals (A20:27) activate one of 256 entries, and word address signals (A28:29) select one word from a block of four words. The LRU memory decides which way must be replaced. The control circuits generate signals that control the CCM.

Major features of the CCM are as follows.

1) A physical address cache

2) A zero wait state read for the GMICRO CPUs

3) A four word burst-translation in cache-miss

4) A completely synchronous operation with the GMICRO CPUs

5) Multi-cache systems can be constructed by using an address comparator

6) An instruction cache and a data cache can be selected

7) A purge and a freeze function in each way

8) Needs no change of software (in Pin mode)

9) An address monitor function

These features are available in all modes for the GMICRO CPUs. If a requested word is in the CCM (cache-hit), each CPU can access the CCM without a wait state. The CCM outputs one word in each of the three modes, however when the GMICRO/300 makes a block access, the CCM outputs four words in the G300 mode.

If a requested word is not in the CCM (cache-miss), the CCM accesses one block of four words, which contains the word the CPU wants to access, from the main memory by using a synchronous clock. A burst-translation and a non-burst-translation are available in this case. These translations can be selected at the access speed of the main memory.

Features (5), (6), and (7) are used by writing their corresponding conditions into the CCM internal registers when PINM/REGM# pin is set to "L" level (Register mode). When the PINM/REGM# pin is set to "H" level (Pin mode), it is not necessary to change software because the CCM internal registers are not used.

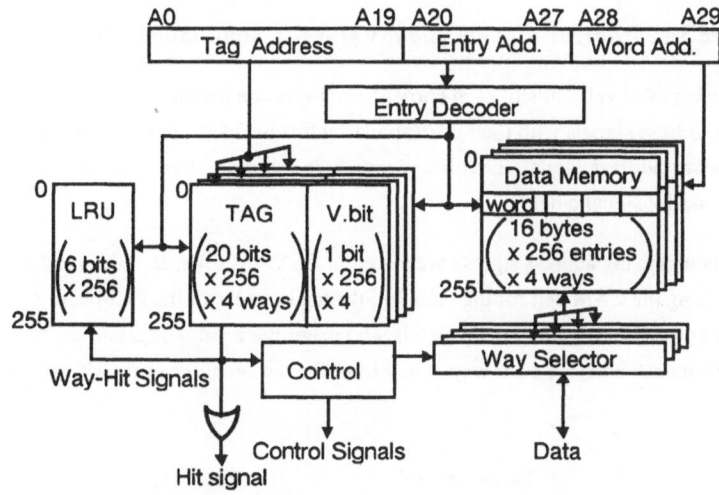

Fig. 1. Internal Block Diagram of the CCM

3. THE DESIGN METHOD OF THE HIGH SPEED CCM

In this section, we describe the design method of the tag memory, the data memory, and a clock generator for the high speed CCM.

3.1 The Design Method of the Tag Memory

The tag memory consists of four ways, and each way has 256 entries. Each entry contains CAM cells for storing the tag address signals (A0:19) and a valid bit. The tag memory compares the tag address signals with their corresponding bits in the CAM cells. To perform such a comparison at a high speed, we use the following techniques.

(1) An Asynchronous CAM

In a conventional cache system, after address signals from a microprocessor are set, they are sampled by using a clock. The tag memory compares the sampled tag address signals with their corresponding bits in comparators, and a hit signal is generated as the result of the comparison. Therefore, the tag memory in this conventional cache system consists of synchronous circuits. When address signals are sampled in a clock cycle, the tag memory do not compare them until the next clock cycle begins. Therefore the time between the sampling and the beginning of the comparison is wasted, thus leading to a longer delay time in the conventional cache system.

As shown in Fig. 2, the CAM cells, whose match line is connected to Vcc via a p-channel transistor, are used in the tag memory of the CCM. The amplitude of the match line is about 1.0 V. Using these CAM cells with the match line enables the CCM to compare the tag address signals with their corresponding bits in the CAM cells asynchronously. Therefore the CCM can eradicate the time loss arising during the comparison phase mentioned above. To use these CAM cells, area of the CCM increased by 12 percent.

(2) To Compare Tag Address Signals and a Valid Bit Simultaneously

If a tag memory has plural valid bits in each entry of each way, on generating a hit signal, the tag memory compares the tag address signals with their corresponding bits in CAM cells, and then finds out if the valid bit selected by word address signals is valid. Because the comparative processes are sequential, it is difficult to generate a hit signal quickly.

Both the valid bit and the tag address signals are stored in the CAM cells, as if the valid bit is one of the tag address signals. Using the CAM cell for the valid bit, the tag memory of the CCM compares the tag address signals with their corresponding bits in CAM cells, and examines a valid bit simultaneously, because it has only one valid bit in each entry of each way. Therefore, the tag memory of the CCM can generate the hit signal quickly.

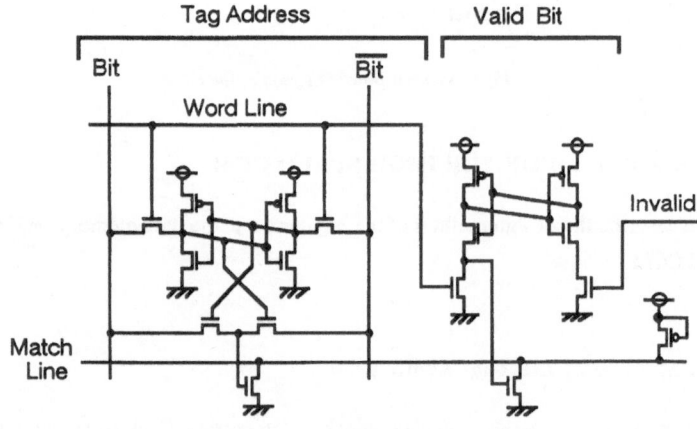

Fig. 2. CAM Cell for Tag Address and a Valid Bit

(3) Divided Bit Lines

In the tag memory of the CCM, a bit line of CAM cells is split and the sense amplifiers are configurated sequentially to get faster access time. If the bit line of the CAM cells is not divided, the capacitance of the bit line, which is connected to 256 CAM cells, is about 3.5 pF. It's very difficult to drive this bit line quickly. The bit lines therefore are divided into 8. Being divided, the bit line current can be reduced to an 1/8 and faster access time can be obtained.

In order that a hit signal be generated, all 256 match lines, that express the result of the comparison of 21 bits in CAM cells, must be joined together. As shown in Fig. 3, the 32 match lines are first joined and then connected to a pre-sense amplifier. The output of each pre-sense amplifier is then connected to a main-sense amplifier to generate a hit signal. In other words a sense line and a bit line are divided to get faster access time.

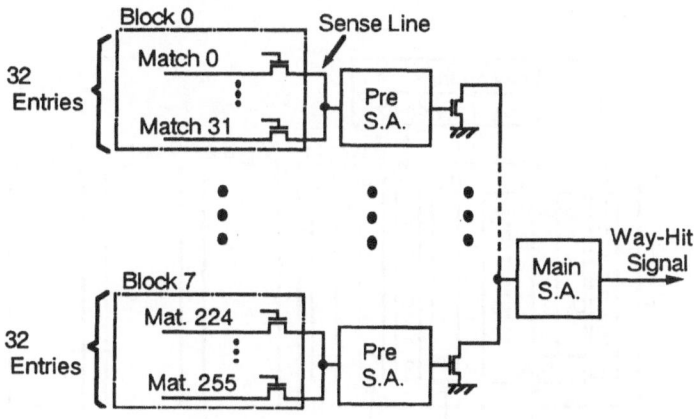

Fig.3. Divided Sense Line of Tag Memory

3.2 The Design Method for the Data Memory

The data memory of the CCM consists of four ways, each way has 256 entries and each entry contains four words, and has 16K bytes of data. The data memory stores four words of data which correspond to one tag address stored in the tag memory.

When a cache-hit occurs in a read cycle, the data in the data memory is output to a CPU. In the case of a cache-hit in a write cycle and a cache-miss in a read cycle, the data is written in the data memory. The data memory is controlled by clocked signals. In this section, the design method of the data memory is described.

(1) The Configuration of the Data Memory

Figure 4 shows the configuration of the data memory. There are four word blocks in the data memory and each word block is divided into two blocks by an entry decoder. A word line is divided into eight parts and each divided word line controls 64 memory cells. One sense amplifier is connected to four bit lines that correspond to a way-A, a way-B, a way-C, and a way-D. These bit lines are selected by control signals, which are generated by way-hit signals and internal clocks in a control circuit, and these signals control the y-selector.

The merits of the configuration of the data memory are as follows. As plural words need not be accessed simultaneously, these words in the data memory are accessed sequentially. The peak current in the data memory is reduced by using this configuration, because the number of memory cells, which are accessed simultaneously, decreases. When a block access is required, CCM reads or writes four words in the data memory sequentially. If this configuration of the data memory is adopted, the same I/O line and sense amplifier are not used in the block access. As the control circuit doesn't have to equalize and pre-charge the I/O line for every word access but only for the first word, the control circuit becomes simpler. This configuration needs no increase in area of the CCM.

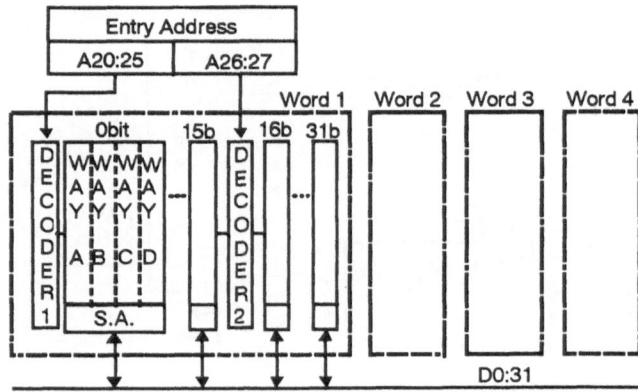

Fig. 4. Block Diagram of Data Memory

(2) Sense Amplifier Circuits

One bit of the data memory circuit is described in Fig. 5. A bit line pre-charging circuit consists of five n-channel transistors. A memory cell of the data memory consists of four n-channel transistors and two high-resistivity loads. A y-selector has two n-channel transistors whose gates are connected to a control signal generated by an internal clock and a way-hit signal, that indicates which way is selected. An I/O line pre-charging circuit consists of three p-channel transistors. A first sense amplifier whose input signals are I/O lines is a cross-coupled sense amplifier, and its outputs are connected to the inputs of the second current-mirror sense amplifier.

Because n-channel transistors are used in the bit line pre-charging circuit and p-channel transistors are used in the I/O line pre-charging circuit, the pre-charge voltage of the I/O line is higher than that of the bit line. Therefore the delay time caused by y-selector becomes small. As the pre-charge voltage of the I/O line is

Vcc, it is useful to use the cross-coupled sense amplifier. When Vcc is 5.0V, the output voltage of the cross-coupled sense amplifier is about 2.3V. In this case the current-mirror sense amplifier whose input is connected to the output signal of the cross-coupled sense amplifier operates well, because the sensing gain of the current-mirror sense amplifier is higher when the input voltage is lower.

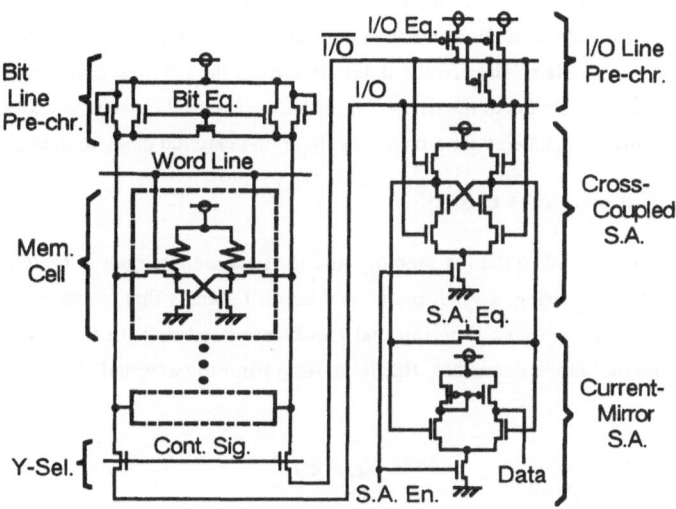

Fig. 5. Data Memory Circuit

3.3 The Design Method of the Clock Generator

As shown in Fig. 6, the 20 MHz version CCM generates two internal clocks from a 40 MHz external clock (In the G300 mode, two 20 MHz external clocks are used.). These 20 MHz internal clocks have a phase difference of 90 degrees.

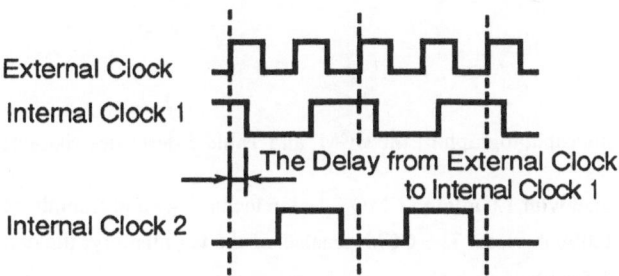

Fig. 6. External Clock and Internal Clocks of the CCM

(1) The Reduction of the Phase Difference Between the External Clock and the Internal Clocks

Figure 7 illustrates the clock generator of the CCM. In this circuit, nonoverlapping signals are generated from the external clock in a nonoverlapping signal generator. These signals input into a frequency divider that consists of two latch circuits, and divided signals that have a phase difference of 90 degrees are generated. These divided signals are sampled by the external clock and the inverted external clock, and are sent to control circuits of the CCM. Because the nonoverlapping signal generator, which has long delay time, is bypassed, it is possible to shorten the delay time from the external clock to the internal clocks. When the phase difference is reduced, the delay time from the external clock to output signals of the CCM becomes smaller. For instance, a delay time from an edge of the external clock to data signals shortens.

(2) The Wiring of the Internal Clocks

The internal clocks are not sent to the tag memory and the data memory but to the control circuits in the CCM, because, the tag memory is asynchronous and control signals that synchronize with the internal clocks are sent to the data memory. The internal clocks are used only in the control circuits. As the capacitance of the internal clock decreases, the delay time from the external clock to the internal clocks becomes shorter.

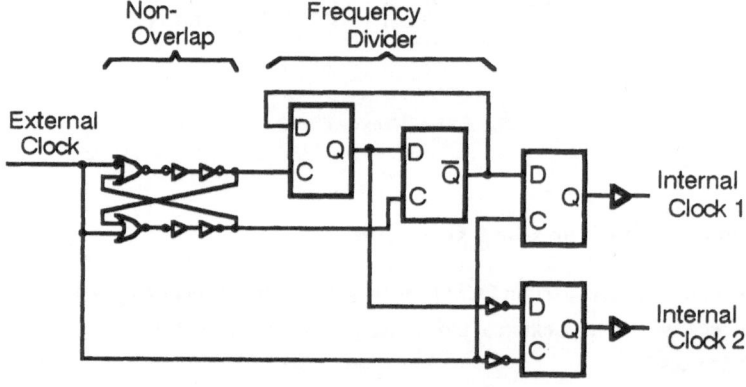

Fig. 7. Internal Clock Generator

3.4 Chip design

Photograph 1 shows a microphotograph of the CCM, and Table 2 describes characteristics of the CCM.

The CCM can be fabricated with 1.0 micron CMOS design technology and is implemented in a 9.24 mm x 8.88 mm die with 1,050,000 devices. The CCM consists of the tag memory, the data memory, the LRU memory, and the control circuits.

Details of the chip design are as follows. The address bus is wired between the tag memory and the circuit including the address pins to shorten the address bus. And the data bus is wired between the data memory and the circuit including the data pins to shorten the data bus. In order to shorten the wiring length of the hit signal, the control circuit that generates the hit signal is placed near the sense amplifier of the tag memory. A GND pin and a Vcc pin are placed in every four output buffer circuits to generate stable output signals.

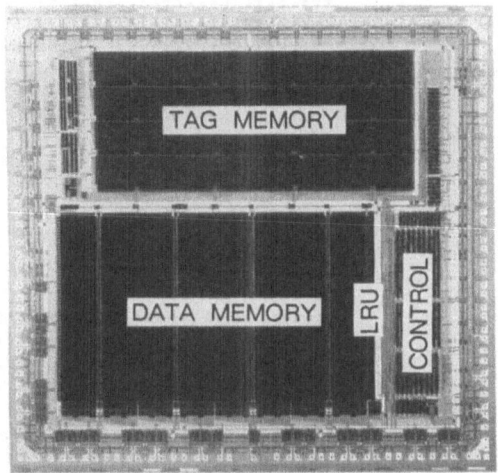

Photo. 1. Microphotograph of the CCM

Table 2. Characteristics of the CCM

Address to Hit	14ns (typical)
Devices	About 1,050,000
Die size	9.24mm x 8.88mm
Technology	1.0 micron CMOS double poly-si & double Al
Package	135pins PGA
Supply voltage	5V±5%
Power	1.5W

4. EVALUATION OF THE CCM

Figure 8 (A) shows a schmoo plot of Vcc versus delay time from address signals to a hit signal ($T_{ADD-HIT}$) at 25 °C, and the capacitance of every output signal is about 70 pF. $T_{ADD-HIT}$ is about 14 ns at Vcc=5V. Fig. 8 (B) shows a schmoo plot of Vcc versus delay time from an edge of the external clock to data signals ($T_{CLK-DATA}$) at the same condition. The edge of the external clock corresponds to the edge of a internal clock, which makes a control signal of a y-selector with a way-hit signal. $T_{CLK-DATA}$ is about 16 ns at Vcc=5V.

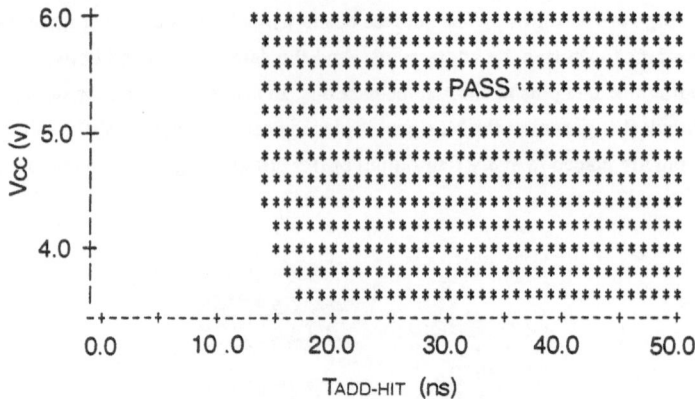

Fig. 8 (A). Schmoo plot of Vcc versus TADD-HIT

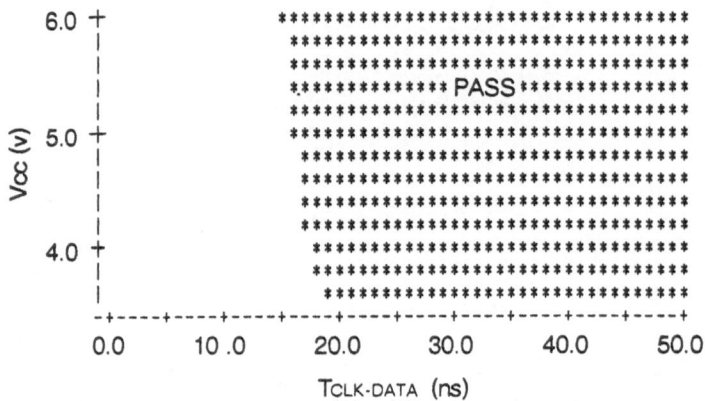

Fig. 8 (B). Schmoo plot of Vcc versus TCLK-DATA

5. CONCLUSION

This paper describes the design method of the tag memory, the data memory, and the clock generator for the high speed CCM that can be used for the GMICRO family of microprocessors. Evaluating the CCM, the delay time from address signals to a hit signal is about 14 ns and the delay time from a clock which activates a y-selector in the data memory to a data is about 16 ns. The result of the evaluation guarantees that the CCM can be accessed by GMICRO CPUs without a wait state.

6. ACKNOWLEDGEMENTS

The authors would like to thank the members of the GMICRO group, Hitachi Ltd. and Fjitsu Ltd., for their useful comments. We also wish to thank Dr. T. Enomoto, Dr. O. Tomisawa and all the engineers involved in this project at Mitsubishi Electric Corp.

REFERENCES

[1]   T. Shimizu, et al., "A 32-BIT MICROPROCESSOR BASED ON THE TRON ARCHITECTURE: DESIGN OF THE GMICRO/100," Proceedings of theThirty-third IEEE COMPUTER SOCIETY INTERNATIONAL CONFERENCE, February 1988, pp.30-33.

[2]   K. Takagi, et al., "Outline of GMICRO/200 and Memory Management Mechanism," Third Project 1987, Springer-Verlag, Tokyo, 1987, pp.258-272.

[3]   T. kitahara, et al., "The GMICRO/300 32-Bit Microprocessor," IEEE Micro, Vol.10, No.2, June 1990, pp.68-77.

[4]   H. Nakagawa, et al., "The configuration of Cache Controller/Memory (CCM) for the GMICRO family microprocessors," TRON gijyutu kenkyukai ronbunsyu Vol.3, No.1,1990, pp.29-38. (in Japanese)

Akira Yamada : He is a researcher of microprocessor peripheral group in LSI device development department (III) at LSI research and development laboratory. He joined Mitsubishi Electric Corporation in 1984. He has been engaged in the design of a 16-bit microcontroller and a cache controller/memory. He received his B.E. and M.E. degrees, both in precision engineering from Shinsyu university, Nagano, Japan in 1982 and 1984, respectively. He is a member of the Institute of Electronics, Information and Communication Engineering of Japan.

Hiromasa Nakagawa : He is a researcher of microprocessor peripheral group in LSI device development department (III) at LSI research and development laboratory. He joined Mitsubishi Electric Corporation in 1979. He has been engaged in the design of a 8-bit microcontroller, a 16-bit microcontroller and a cache controller/memory. He received his B.E. degree in electrical engineering from Hokkaido Institute of Technology, Sapporo, Japan in 1976. He received his M.E. degree in electronics engineering from Hokkaido University, Sapporo, Japan in 1979. He is a member of the Institute of Electronics, Information and Communication Engineering of Japan.

260

Masayuki Hata : He is a researcher of microprocessor peripheral group in LSI device development department (III) at LSI research and development laboratory. He joined Mitsubishi Electric Corporation in 1985. He has been engaged in the design of a 16-bit microcontroller and a cache controller/memory. He received his B.E. degree in physics from Osaka City University, osaka, Japan in 1985.

Mitsugu Satoh : He is a researcher of ASIC microprocessor group in LSI device development department (III) at LSI research and development laboratory. He joined Mitsubishi Electric Corporation in 1984. He has been engaged in the design of a 32-bit processor and a cache controller/memory. He received his B.E. degree in electrical engineering from Doshisha University, Kyoto, Japan in 1984.

Koichi Nishida : He is a manager of microprocessor peripheral group and ASIC microprocessor group in LSI device development department (III) at LSI research and development laboratory. He joined Mitsubishi Electric Corporation in 1971. He has been engaged in the design of computer terminals, the development of VLSI custom processors and a cache controller/memory. He received his B.E. degree in electronics engineering from Tokyo Denki University, Tokyo, Japan in 1971.

Above authors may be reached at : LSI Device Development Department (III), LSI Research and Development Laboratory, Mitsubishi Electric Corporation, 4-1, Mizuhara, Itami, Hyogo, 644 Japan

Toshiyuki Hiraki : He is a researcher of microcomputer engineering section D in microcomputer department at Kita-Itami works. He joined Mitsubishi Electric Corporation in 1987. Since then, he has been engaged in the design of a cache controller/memory. He received his B.E. degree in computer science from Kyoto Sangyo University, Kyoto, Japan in 1987.

Above author may be reached at : Microcomputer department D, Kita-Itami Works, Mitsubishi Electric Corporation, 4-1, Mizuhara, Itami, Hyogo, 644 Japan

The Evaluation of M32/100's Bitmap Instructions Used in the Graphic Primitive

Mamoru Sakamoto, Toru Shimizu, Kazunori Saitoh
LSI Research and Development Laboratory, Mitsubishi Electric Corporation

Abstract

Bitmap instructions of the M32/100, a 32-bit microprocessor based on the TRON architecture specification, are designed for bitmap display control. This paper describes their performance evaluation of the bitmap instructions when applied to the Graphic Primitive, which is graphic application software used in the BTRON specification operating system. The bitmap instructions can paint rectangles with a pattern 1.5 - 2 times faster and move windows 2.7 - 3.3 times faster than move instructions looped by software on a color display with 8 bits per pixel.

Keywords: M32/100, Bitmap instruction, Graphic Primitive, BTRON

1. Introduction

A GUI (Graphic User Interface) is increasing its importance and market. The computer systems in 1990s cannot do without one. Computer systems with a GUI supply higher productivity than those with a CUI (Character User Interface). In addition, GUIs are fun for users. BTRON, an operating system developed in the TRON projects, supports a GUI in itself.

However, GUIs have not spread through low-price personal computers yet. This is due to the fact that the overhead for a GUI is much for current microprocessor units (MPUs). To reduce the main MPU's load, workstations today usually have some display controllers or special graphic hardwares.

In order to support a GUI on low-price personal computers, MPUs based on the TRON architecture specification [1] have bitmap manipulation instructions, which perform the bit block transfer (BITBLT) function. They enhance the performance of bitmap display control, such as moving windows and drawing figures, without the help of special graphic hardware.

The bitmap instructions of the M32/100, a 32-bit microprocessor based on the TRON architecture specification, are 2 - 3 times faster than move instructions on a color display with 8 bits per pixel [2]. In this paper, we evaluate the performance of the bitmap instructions of the M32/100 when applied to a graphic application software used in the BTRON specification operating system, called the Graphic Primitive.

2. M32/100

The M32/100 is a general purpose, 32-bit microprocessor based on the TRON architecture specification. It is designed as a small personal workstation MPU, an embedded system controller, and a core processor of ASICs (Application Specific ICs). The M32/100 has 5-stage instruction pipeline scheme with a branch prediction mechanism and a branch target cache, and achieves two clock cycle execution of simple instructions. The M32/100 instruction set consists of move, compare, arithmetic, logical, shift, bit manipulation, fixed-length bit field manipulation, variable-length bit field (bitmap) manipulation, string, queue manipulation, jump, operating system related instructions. Among these, the bitmap instructions perform the bit block transfer function. Due to micro-operation pipelining and the optimum use of the memory bus, they execute the BITBLT functions 2 - 3 times faster than move instructions on a color display with 8 bits per pixel [2].

The bitmap instructions manipulate bit lines (or bit fields) of variable length which extend over several word boundaries. As shown in Figure 1, they read a source bit field and a destination bit field, perform a logical operation between them, and store the result in the destination bit field. Either the FORWARD or BACKWARD option is applied to control the processing direction of the bits from MSB to LSB or from LSB to MSB, respectively. The position of the bit field is specified by a base address, a bit offset , and the number of the bits.

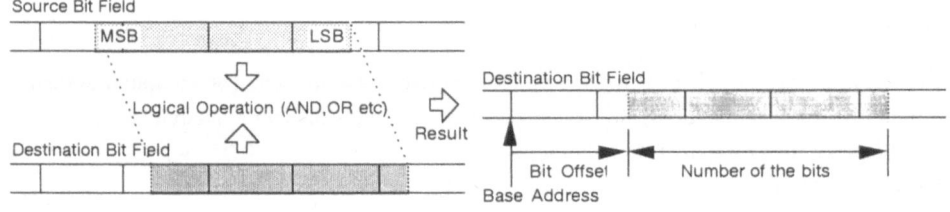

Fig.1 Function of Bitmap Instructions

The M32/100 has the following three bitmap instructions:

BVMAP   This is the most general bitmap instruction that performs one of 16 logical operations between the source and the destination bit field as shown in Figure 1.

BVCPY   This instruction is a subset of BVMAP. It only copies the source to the destination bit field.

BVPAT   This instruction fills the destination bit field with a 32-bit pattern repeatedly. It can perform one of 16 logical operations between the pattern and the destination bit field.

3. Graphic Primitive

We developed graphic application software called the Graphic Primitive. This is software that draws character fonts or many kinds of figures on the bitmap placed in the video RAMs. This software consists of basic subroutines (or primitives) generally used in various graphic applications.

The Graphic Primitive has two main types of functions: figure drawing functions and bitmap transfer functions.

3. 1 Figure Drawing Functions

The Graphic Primitive has functions to draw many kinds of figures, such as lines, rectangles, round-rectangles, circles, ovals, arcs, sectors (pie-shaped oval), chords, polygons, and spline-curves. Not only filling but also framing each figure (i.e., drawing only its frame) is possible. The width of the frame can take any number of pixels. Patterning as shown in Figure 2 is useful especially for monochrome displays and page printers. Before writing the patterned figures in the destination bitmap, a logical operation may be performed between the source (patterned figure) and the destination bitmap. For example, the exclusive-OR function is useful for drawing the 'rubber bands' in an interactive painting and drawing application.

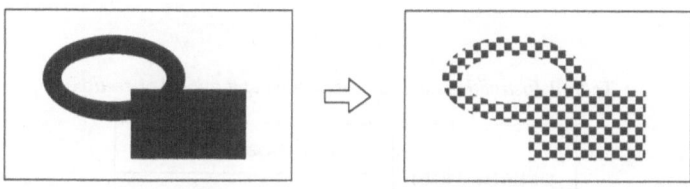

Fig. 2 Patterning

3.2. Bitmap Transfer Functions

The Graphic Primitive has functions to transfer a rectangular region, or a window, in the bitmap. Resizing or rotating the source region is also possible on transfer. A logical operation can be performed between the source and the destination. The transfer is performed correctly even when the source and the destination regions overlap. Simply copying a rectangular region is frequently used as it is a basic function of window move.

4. Implementation of the Graphic Primitive

We implemented the Graphic Primitive on an M32/100 SBC (Single Board Computer) system. The video RAM configuration in this system is made so that one pixel occupies 8 bits (1 byte) * 1 plane.

4.1. Figure Drawing Functions

Drawing a figure is done in two steps:

Step 1:   The figure is decomposed into pixels. And if necessary, they are clipped by the bitmap boundary and some of them are selected to be drawn.

Step 2:   The source data for these selected pixels are taken from the pattern. Then a logical operation is performed between these source data and the destination pixel data, and the result is stored into the destination pixels.

In our implementation, the bitmap instructions of the M32/100 are used in step 2. The bitmap instruction itself can do both patterning and a logical operation at the same time.

In order to achieve the best performance, we use the best instruction among the three bitmap instructions, according to the size of pattern and the necessity of the logical operation as shown in Table 1.

Table 1 Instructions used for patterning and logical operation

pattern width	logical operation	
	No	Yes
4 pixels	SSTR	BVPAT
other than 4	BVCPY	BVMAP

When the width of the pattern is 4 pixels (i.e., 32 bits), we use a BVPAT. One BVPAT can process one horizontal pixel line in a figure. Since the standard patterns such as BLACK 100% and Grey 50% are of 4 * 4 pixel size, it is worth while giving special treatment for these small patterns and enhancing the performance.

When the width of the pattern is other than 4 pixels, we use a BVMAP. In this case, the BVMAP is repeated to process one horizontal pixel line.

If no logical operation is necessary, we use a SSTR (Store STRing) and a BVCPY instead of the BVPAT and BVMAP respectively. The SSTR is an instruction of the M32/100 that fills word/half-word/byte strings. Since a horizontal pixel line is the same as a byte string on our video RAM configuration, we can use the SSTR to achieve better performance.

4.2. Bitmap Transfer Function

Bitmap transfer is just the same as filling the destination rectangular region with the source rectangle as the pattern. Therefore, we use a BVMAP for this. Unlike the patterning, however, bitmap transfer requires some special treatment when the source and the destination regions overlap. Namely, it is necessary to ensure that writing into the destination will not destroy the source data not yet processed. As shown in Figure 3, if the destination rectangle is to the south side of the source rectangle, we start from the southernmost horizontal pixel line and proceed to the northern pixel lines one by one. If the destination is to the north side of the source, we start and proceed in the reverse order. Furthermore, if the source pixel line and the destination pixel line overlap, we must specify the FORWARD or BACKWARD option for BVMAP as shown in Figure 4. When the destination pixel line is to the east of the source, we specify the BACKWARD option, otherwise we specify the FORWARD option.

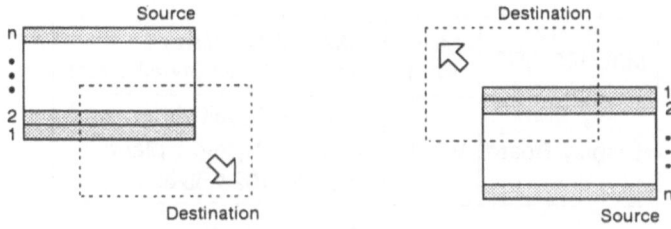

Fig. 3 Order of pixel line transfer (1,2,···, n indicates the oder)

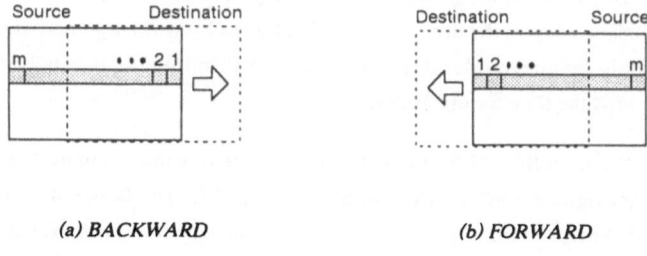

(a) BACKWARD　　　　*(b) FORWARD*

Fig. 4 Order of pixel transfer (1, 2, ···, n indicates the oder)

Table 2 Instructions used for bitmap transfer

transfer direction	logical operation	
	No	Yes
to the east	BVCPY/BACKWARD	BVMAP/BACKWARD
other than east	BVCPY/FORWARD	BVMAP/FORWARD

If no logical operation is necessary, we use a BVCPY. The bitmap instructions used for bitmap transfer is summarized in Table 2.

5. Evaluation

We timed our Graphic Primitive on an M32/100 SBC system. The outline of this M32/100 SBC system is shown in Table 3.

Table 3. The outline of the M32/SBC system

M32/100 SBC	MPU RAM	M32/100 (20 MHz) 8MByte SRAM (1wait state)
Display Board	VRAM	1 MByte (3 wait state) 1 pixel=1 Byte× 1 plane 1024 × 1024 pixel

In order to compare the four instructions shown in Table 1, we used a 4 * 4 and a 16 * 16 pixel pattern, with no logical operation and the exclusive-OR operation for each pattern. And in addition to our Graphic Primitive, we made special version of Graphic Primitive, in which loops of the MOV (MOVe) or XOR (eXclusive-OR) instructions are used for patterning instead of bitmap instructions. By the MOV and XOR instructions, we access the destination bit field word by word argument if possible. This loop is written in assembly language. Modifying the Graphic Primitive so that only the pixelization is processed, we measured the time for pixelization.

Table 4 shows the execution time of filling rectangles of several widths. Figure 5 shows the execution time of drawing other figures. Each figure is of 640 * 400 pixels. The frame of each figure is 16 pixel wide. The grey part shows the time spent for patterning. Table 5 shows the execution time of bitmap transfer. We moved the rectangle 4 pixels to the east and west and the results are shown in Table 5(a) and 5(b) respectively.

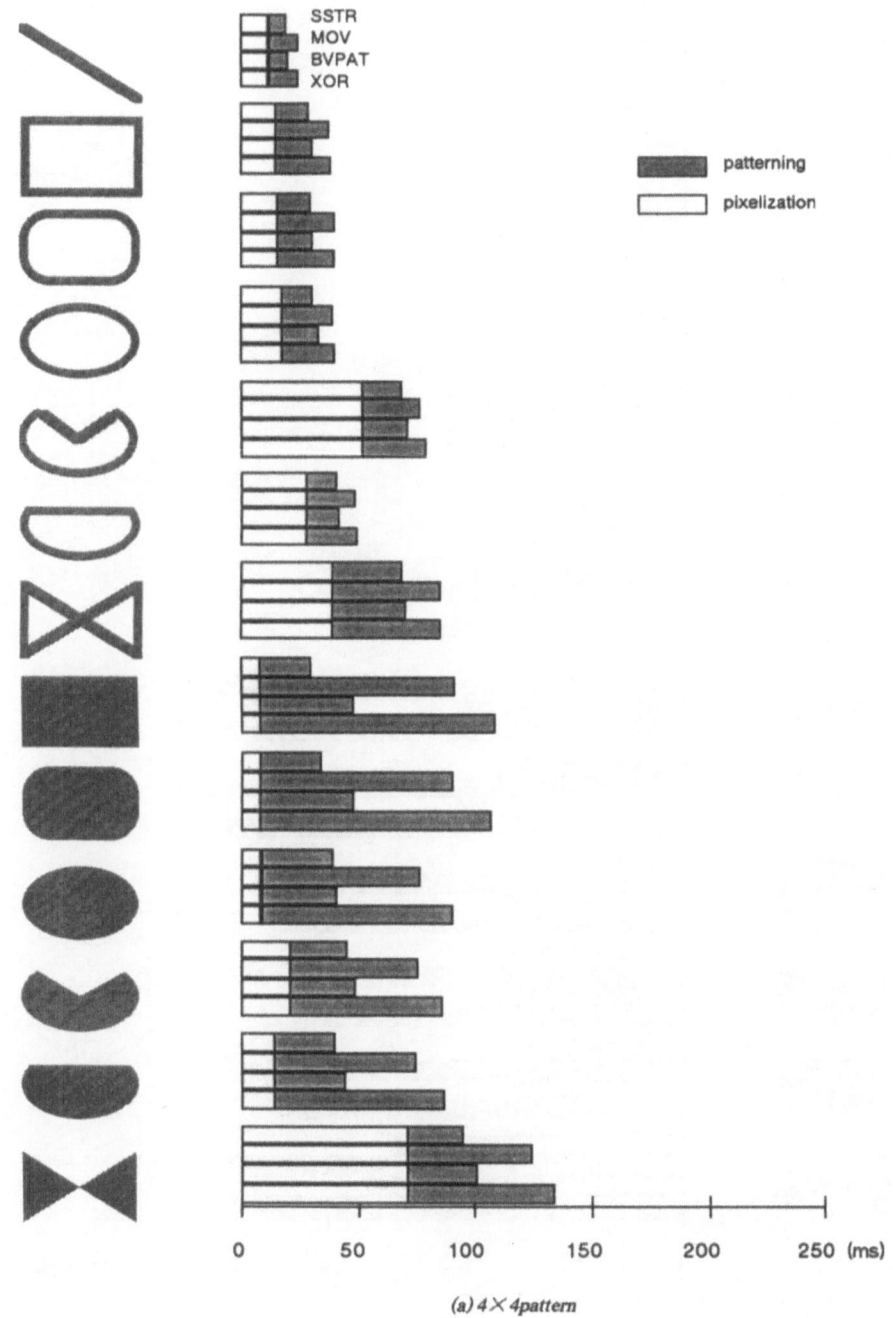

SSTR
MOV
BVPAT
XOR

patterning
pixelization

0   50   100   150   200   250 (ms)

(a) 4 × 4 pattern

Fig. 5 Execution time of drawing figure

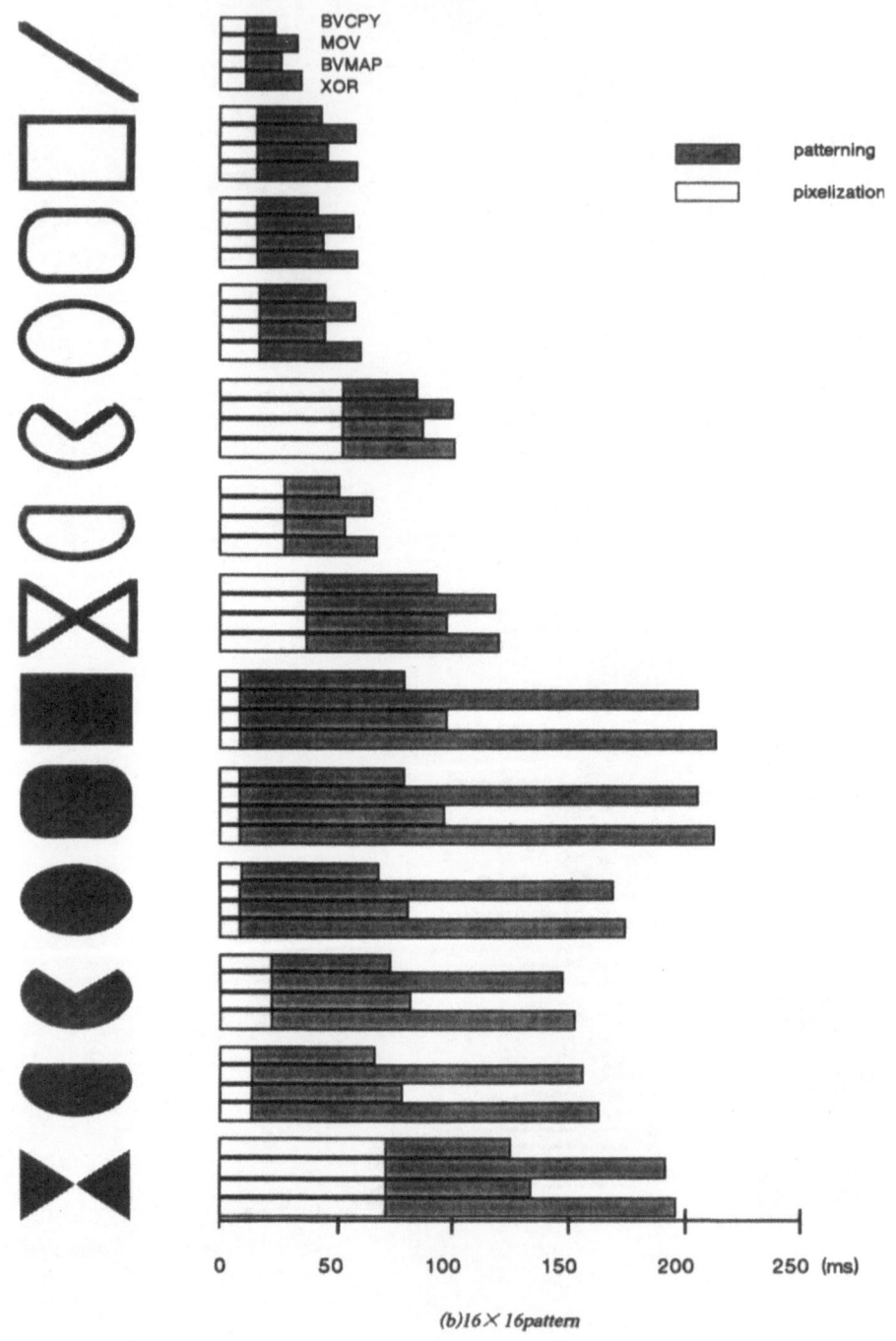

BVCPY
MOV
BVMAP
XOR

patterning
pixelization

0   50   100   150   200   250 (ms)

(b)16×16pattern

Fig. 5 Execution time of drawing figure

Table 4 Execution time of painting a rectangle

*(a) 4 * 4 pixel pattern*

Logical operation	Instruction	320×400	640×400	1024×400
No	SSTR	23.2 ms	32.4	42.5
	MOV	54.1	92.6	138.1
Yes	BVPAT	32.4	50.0	70.9
	XOR	62.9	110.3	166.8

*(b) 16 * 16 pixel pattern*

Logical operation	Instruction	320×400	640×400	1024×400
No	BVCPY	50.2 ms	82.4	120.6
	MOV	112.9	208.2	322.0
Yes	BVMAP	58.8	99.1	146.8
	XOR	116.9	215.5	333.5

Table 5 Execution time of bitmap transfer

(a) BACKWARD

Logical operation	Instruction	320×400	640×400	1024×400
No	BVCPY	18.7 ms	36.2	56.9
	MOV	61.9	120.8	190.7
Yes	BVMAP	27.5	53.8	85.1
	XOR	64.2	125.3	198.0

(b) FORWARD

Logical operation	Instruction	320×400	640×400	1024×400
No	BVCPY	18.7 ms	36.2	56.9
	MOV	50.7	98.5	155.2
Yes	BVMAP	27.4	53.7	85.0
	XOR	54.5	106.2	167.6

From the above results, we make the following comments.

- As for patterning, executing bitmap instructions is 1.5 - 2.5 times faster than looping the MOV or XOR. The longer the bit field, the faster it is.

- If the SSTR is applicable, it can achieve the highest speed. The SSTR is 1.2 - 1.8 times faster than the BVPAT for pattering.

- As for filling a figure, patterning occupies most of the total time, and executing bitmap instructions is 1.5 - 2 times faster than looping the MOV or XOR.

- As for framing a figure, the time for pixelization tends to be longer and the time for patterning tends to be shorter as compared with filling the same shape of the figure. (This is not true for a polygon since the pixelization algorithm for filling a polygon is quite different from that for framing.) Executing the BVCPY is only 1.2 times faster than looping the NOV or XOR.

- As for bitmap transfer, executing the BVCPY is 2.3 - 3.3 times faster than looping the MOV, and executing the BVMAP is 2 - 2.3 times faster than looping the XOR.

As indicated above, the bitmap instructions can improve the performance of the Graphic Primitive. In addition, if one pixel of the video RAM occupies less than 8 bits (one bit per pixel for example), their performance improvement will be bigger than obtained so far because bitmap instructions can manipulate bit fields of any length at any bit position while the MOV and XOR cannot. We are currently developing the Graphic Primitive for a video RAM of 1 bit per pixel.

6. Conclusion

The 32-bit microprocessor M32/100 has bitmap instructions to achieve high performance of BITBLT without special graphics hardware. We implemented the Graphic Primitive using them and found that they can fill a rectangle 1.5 - 2.0 times faster and move a rectangle 2.7 - 3.3 times faster than the MOV or XOR instructions.

References

[1] TRON ASSOCIATION, "SPECIFICATION OF THE CHIP BASED ON THE TRON ARCHITECTURE Ver. 1.00.00.00", TRON ASSOCIATION, 1989

[2] Toru Shimizu, Shunichi Iwata, Yuichi Saito, Toyohiko Yosida, and Kazunori Saitoh,"A 32-bit Microprocessor with High Performance Bit-map Manipulation Instructions", Proc. of ICDD, pp.406 - 409, 1989

271

Mamoru Sakamoto: He received his B.S. and M.S. degrees both in electrical engineering, from Kyoto University, Kyoto, Japan, in 1986 and 1988 He joined Mitsubishi Electric Corporation in 1988. Since then, he has been engaged in research and development of basic software for microprocessors at LSI Research and Development Laboratory.

Toru Shimizu: He received his B.S., M.S. and Ph.D. degrees, both in computer science, from University of Tokyo, Tokyo, Japan, in 1981, 1983, and 1986, respectively. He joined Mitsubishi Electric Corporation in 1986. Since then, he has been engaged in the research of VLSI microprocessor architecture and basic software for the microprocessor at LSI Research and Development Laboratory. Dr.Shimizu is a member of ACM, IEEE, the Institute of Electronics, Information and Communication Engineers of Japan, and Information Processing Society of Japan.

Kazunori Saitoh: He received his B.S. and M.S. degrees, both in electrical engineering, from Waseda University, Tokyo, Japan, in 1975 and 1977, respectively. He received Ph.D degree in electrical engineering in 1989, from Osaka University, Osaka, Japan. He joined Mitsubishi Electric Corporation in 1977. From 1977 to 1980, he was engaged in the development of CAD and electron beam lithography technology at the VLSI Cooperative Laboratory. From 1980, he has been engaged in research and development of VLSI process technologies and basic software for microprocessors at LSI Research and Development Laboratory.

Above authors may be reached at :

LSI Research and Development Laboratory
Mitsubishi Electric Corporation, 4 - 1 Mizuhara, Itami,
Hyogo, 664, Japan.

Chapter 5: CHIP (2)

Inline Procedures Boost Performance on TRON Architecture

Craig Franklin, Carl Rosenberg
Green Hills Software, Inc.

ABSTRACT

Green Hills Software, Inc. introduces Inline Procedures, an advanced optimization, for its family of four optimizing compilers (C, C++, Fortran, Pascal) for the TRON Specification Chip architecture. Both Manual and Automatic procedure inlining are implemented. Inline Procedures can be Local to one compilation or Global across multiple compilations. Inline Procedures can be mixed across all four languages, for example, a C routine can be inlined into a Fortran calling routine.

Most compilers do not implement Inline Procedures. The few compilers which do implement them often only implement Manual, Local, and single language Inline Procedures (example: C++). The advanced Green Hills Procedure Inliner confronted many design problems during implementation to remove these restrictions. We describe our solutions, with examples. We present some interesting performance measurements which show up to 35% speed improvement on standard benchmarks on the Gmicro/200 TRON Architecture microprocessor. We also show, in a methodologically sound comparison, that Green Hills compiler technology outperforms MIPS compiler technology. Finally, we give directions for further research.

Keywords

Compilers, Optimizing Compilers, Inline Procedures,
Global Register Allocation

1. Introduction To Inlining

1.1. Why Inlining?

Consider this ANSI C coding of the integer absolute value function, **abs**:

    int abs(int i) { return(i >= 0 ? i : -i); }

This could produce the following TRON Architecture code:

```
       .global    _abs
_abs: mov        @(4,sp),r0
       cmp        #0,r0
       bge        $L1
       neg        r0
$L1: rts
```

When the **abs** function is invoked, for example, by referencing **abs(j)**, where **j** is in register r3, the following TRON Architecture code is generated:

```
push     r3           ; j, the argument to abs, is in r3
bsr      _abs
```

Clearly, one would like to have the C compiler simply use the **abs** function definition to generate the following code *inline*:

```
mov      r3,r0
cmp      #0,r0
bge      $L1
neg      r0           ; r0 = abs(r3) = abs(j)
$L1:
```

Note that it takes two instructions to call the **abs** function and five instructions for the out-of-line **abs** function itself, for a total of seven instructions, compared with four instructions for the inline **abs** code.

The term *procedure inlining* or simply *inlining* refers to the process of substituting a copy of the body of a function or procedure in place of the function invocation or procedure call. The resulting code is faster, since the call/return overhead has been eliminated. In addition, the newly inlined code can often provide new opportunities for optimization which were not available when the code was out-of-line.

The ability to perform procedure inlining is a standard language feature of Ada and C++. In those languages, the **inline** keyword is used to designate procedures which are to be inlined each time they are invoked.

1.2. Inlining With Macros

Procedure inlining is not the only possible mechanism for performing such a code substitution. In C, for example, one can define the following macro:

#define abs(i) ((i) >= 0 ? (i) : -(i))

In the presence of this macro definition, **abs(-3)** would expand to ((-3) >= 0 ? (-3) : - (-3)), which an intelligent compiler can simplify to (3).

Note the use of (i) instead of i in three places in the macro definition. If (i) were replaced by i, then **abs(-j)** for example, would produce (-j >= 0 ? -j : --j), and --j has an entirely different meaning than the desired -(-j).

The problem with the macro approach is that the macro argument is copied literally to every place it appears in the macro body. Thus **abs(j++)** expands to:

(j++ >= 0 ? j++ : -j++)

But this is not the desired semantic meaning. There are two bugs. (1) The correct return value is the absolute value of the original value of **j**. What is returned here is the absolute value of the incremented value of **j**, since the test (j++ >= 0) increments **j**. (2) The correct value of **j** after the **abs** function is invoked is original **j+1**, but here the value of **j** is original **j+2**, because **j** is incremented twice by the macro-expanded **abs** function.

1.3. Inlining With Procedures

What is wanted is for the abs function to have the semantics of a procedure:

inline int abs(int i) { return (i >= 0 ? i : -i); }

This will expand **abs(j++)** into the equivalent of the following expression:

(i = j++, (i >= 0) ? i : -i))

which is what is desired. Here **i** = **j**++ first copies the argument value to **i** and then increments **j**.

But an inline procedure is considerably more powerful than a C macro. Consider:

```
inline double vector_sum(double *v, unsigned int n)
    {
    register double sum = 0.0;
    while(n-- > 0) sum += *v++;
    return(sum);
    }
```

There is no way to express this calculation as a C macro, since a C macro cannot both contain statements and also return an expression value. In addition, this inline procedure contains a new scope and declares a new variable, namely **sum**.

Thus an inline procedure has more power than a macro, has the same fast execution speed as a macro, but has the same semantics as a procedure.

Note that each argument of a procedure or function in C, C++, Fortran, or Pascal has a data type. This is not true for a macro. Thus the C macro

```
#define abs(i) ((i) >= 0 ? (i) : -(i))
```

will work equally well for **int**, **float**, or **double** arguments. The corresponding code using inline functions is:

```
inline int abs(int i) { return (i >= 0 ? i : -i); }
inline float fabs(float f) { return (f >= 0.0 ? f : -f); }
inline double dabs(double d) { return (d >= 0 ? d : -d); }
```

However, a programmer would like to simply be able to use **abs(x)** without being concerned with the data type of **x**. In C++, one can define an **overloaded** function **abs** which will select **abs**, **fabs**, or **dabs** depending on the data type of the argument. ("Overloaded" is the C++ terminology for what other languages call "generic".)

2. History Of Inlining

2.1. Fortran Statement Functions

The earliest widespread example of user-defined inlining in a high level language was the statement function feature of Fortran. A Fortran statement function is a single statement of the form:

```
function_name(arg1,arg2,...,argn) = expression
```

This defines the function **function_name** with its arguments to be the **expression**. Each argument did have an associated type, which could be declared explicitly elsewhere or typed by the implicit Fortran type rules based on the first letter of the name of the identifier. Because the arguments had types, the semantics of a statement function are like those of a function, not a macro.

2.2. Builtin Functions

Older languages such as Fortran and PL/I simply made a list of the most useful inline functions, such as ABS, MIN, and MAX, and made them *built-in* to the compiler. Except for Fortran statement functions, the user could not define his own built-in functions (unless he was a compiler writer and could modify the compiler), but this compromise was satisfactory for many years.

In Fortran, the generic functions were also builtin and user generic functions were not available. In full ANSI PL/I (but not in subset ANSI PL/I), the user had the full power to declare generic functions. However, since none of the user declared functions, whether generic or not, could be inline, a certain amount of efficiency was lost.

Newer languages like C++ and Ada permit user-defined extensions through generic functions. C++ permits operator overloading. These newer languages were designed to achieve certain goals: object oriented programming, reusable modules, and management of large programming projects. These goals mandated the new features. However, for generic functions and operator overloading (the goals) to be efficient, and therefore widely used, inlining (the implementation method) is required. Hence inline procedures were added to C++ and Ada for *efficiency*, not for fundamental design reasons. An inline procedure is no more powerful than an ordinary procedure. It is simply faster, that is, more efficient in time.

Given this history, it is possible that if compilers had implemented efficient *automatic* inline procedure expansion, than *manual* inlining, via a user keyword, would not have become so popular or widespread. A comparison with vectorizers and parallelizers might be appropriate here. Most vectorizers are automatic. Parallelizers are both manual and automatic. Historically, automatic vectorizers have been highly efficient, while automatic parallelizers have not, thus requiring manual user directives for effective parallelization.

Since Green Hills needed to implement inline procedures for C++, we naturally asked if our other languages (C, Fortran, and Pascal), could also benefit. In our implementation, all four languages share the same common procedure inliner and global optimizer. See Figure 1. Inline expansion can occur across languages, for example, an inline procedure defined in C can be expanded inline into a Fortran or Pascal program which calls it.

3. Taxonomy Of Inlining

Now that we have explored some examples, let us make a framework for describing different types of procedure inlining.

3.1. Manual Procedure Inlining

If the user knows which procedures should be inline procedures, then the procedure can be marked as inline at its definition point. This is called *manual procedure inlining*.

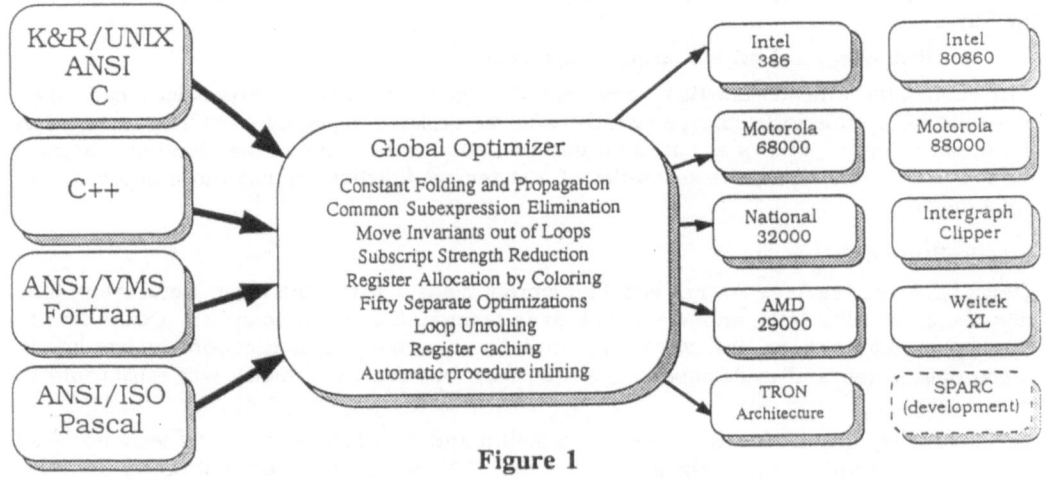

Figure 1

Example of manual procedure inlining:

```
/* This program inlines the abs function on every call.   */

#include <inline.h>   /* The inline.h include file is explained later. */
#include <stdio.h>

inline int abs(int i) {  return (i >= 0 ? i : -i);  }

void main()
    {
    printf("abs(-1) = %d, abs(0) = %d, abs(+1) = %d", abs(-1), abs(0), abs(+1));
    }
```

3.2. Manual Call Inlining

In manual procedure inlining, every call to an inline procedure is expanded. Alternatively, only some of the calls to the procedure can be marked for inline procedure expansion. This is called *manual call inlining*.

For C, C++, and Pascal, Green Hills uses a #pragma statement to implement manual call inlining. There are three relevant pragmas:

```
#pragma ghs inlinecall=p1,p2,p3
#pragma ghs noinlinecall=p1,p2,p3
#pragma ghs revertinlinecall=p1,p2,p3
```

where p1,p2, and p3 are procedure names.

The **inlinecall** pragma tells the inliner to inline calls to these procedures from now until the end of the source file.

The **noinlinecall** pragma tells the inliner not to inline calls to these procedures from now until the end of the source file.

The **revertinlinecall** pragma tells the inliner to revert the inline status of these procedures to their declared state, from now until the end of the source file. If they were declared as inline, they will be inlined. If they were not declared as inline, they will not be inlined.

Example of manual call inlining:

```
/* This program inlines the vector_sum function on some calls.      */

#include <inline.h>   /* The inline.h include file is explained later. */
#include <stdio.h>

double vector_sum(double *v, unsigned int n)
    {
    register double sum = 0.0;
    while(n-- > 0) sum += *v++;
    return(sum);
    }

void main()
    {
    double v1[10] = {  0.0, 1.0, 2.0, 3.0, 4.0, 5.0, 6.0, 7.0, 8.0, 9.0 };
    double v2[10] = {  0.0, -1.0, 2.0, -3.0, 4.0, -5.0, 6.0 };
    double sum;
```

```
#pragma ghs inlinecall=vector_sum
         sum = vector_sum(v1,10);
#pragma ghs noinlinecall=vector_sum
         printf("sum of the elements of vector v1 = %f",sum);
         printf("sum of the elements of vector v2 = %f",vector_sum(v2,7));
         }
```

Note for future reference that the inline expander in the compiler must deal with the fact that **register double sum** declaration in the **vsum** procedure could conflict with the **double sum** declaration in the **main** procedure. The inliner must be careful to distinguish them.

3.3. Automatic Procedure Inlining

Sometimes the user does not know which procedures should be inlined, and wants the compiler to decide. If the compiler analyzes the program and marks some procedures as inline, this is called *automatic procedure inlining*.

Example of automatic procedure inlining:

```
/* The Green Hills C compiler will inline the abs function on every call.  */

#include <stdio.h>

int abs(int i) { return (i >= 0 ? i : -i); }

void main()
     {
     printf("abs(-1) = %d, abs(0) = %d, abs(+1) = %d", abs(-1), abs(0), abs(+1));
     }
```

3.4. Automatic Call Inlining

The compiler can be even more sophisticated and individually mark the procedure calls, so that some but not necessarily all calls to a given procedure will be inlined. This is called *automatic call inlining*.

Example of automatic call inlining:

```
#include <stdio.h>

int factorial(int n)
     {
     printf("factorial argument = %d",n);
     return (n < 0 ? 1 : n * factorial(n-1));
     }

void print_factorial(int j)
     {
     /* these calls to factorial will be inlined */
     printf("factorial(-1) = %d", factorial(-1));
     printf("factorial( 0) = %d", factorial( 0));
     printf("factorial(+1) = %d", factorial(+1));
     printf("factorial(+2) = %d", factorial(+2));
     printf("factorial(+3) = %d", factorial(+3));

     /* this call to factorial will not be inlined */
     printf("factorial(%d) = %d",j,factorial(j));
     }
```

After inlining and optimization by the compiler, the final program looks like this:

```
#include <stdio.h>

int factorial(int n)
    {
    printf("factorial argument = %d",n);
    return (n < 0 ? 1 : n * factorial(n-1));
    }

void print_factorial(int j)
    {
    /* all of these calls to factorial were inlined completely */
        printf("factorial argument = %d",-1);
    printf("factorial(-1) = %d", factorial(-1));
        printf("factorial argument = %d",0);
    printf("factorial( 0) = %d", factorial( 0));
        printf("factorial argument = %d",1);
    printf("factorial(+1) = %d", factorial(+1));
        printf("factorial argument = %d",2);
        printf("factorial argument = %d",1);
    printf("factorial(+2) = %d", 2);
        printf("factorial argument = %d",3);
        printf("factorial argument = %d",2);
        printf("factorial argument = %d",1);
    printf("factorial(+3) = %d", 6);

    /* this call to factorial was not inlined */
    printf("factorial(%d) = %d",j,factorial(j));
    }
```

In this case, the factorial function containing the embedded **printf** call is too large to be inlined on every call. Only the calls where the argument to factorial is a constant will be inlined, because then there is a good chance of expression simplification and dead code elimination. Subsequent recursive expansion and compile time expression evaluation will compute the factorial function *at compile time* for constant arguments.

3.5. Closed Version Of An Inline Procedure

It can happen that a procedure is inlined every time it is called, but the compiler should also produce a closed (non-inlined) version of the procedure. This can happen when the address of the procedure is taken, for example, so that the procedure can be passed as an argument to another procedure. Another example is if the compiler is invoked with the debugger option (-g). Some debuggers can invoke a compiled function as part of expression evaluation, but the function code must be available in closed form.

Example of an inline procedure with a closed version also:

```
/* The Green Hills C compiler will inline the fabs function on every call. */
/* It will also make a normal version of the fabs function for the & operator.   */

#include <stdio.h>

float fabs(float f) { return (f >= 0 ? f : -f); }

void main()
    {
    float area;
    extern float romberg_integration(float (*)(float), float, float);
```

```
printf("fabs(-1.0f) = %d, abs(0.0f) = %d, abs(+1.0f) = %d", fabs(-1.0f), fabs(0.0f), fabs(+1.0f));

/* Compute the area under the curve y = fabs(x) between -1 and +1 */

area = romberg_integration(&fabs,-1.0f,+1.0f);
printf("Area of y = fabs(x) between -1 and + 1 = %f",area);
}
```

3.6. Local And Global Inlining

Sometimes an inline procedure is local to a single compilation (for example, a static inline C procedure). This is called *local procedure inlining*.

Sometimes the same inline procedure is referenced in many different source files which are compiled separately. This is called *global procedure inlining*.

3.7. Mono- And Multi-Lingual Inlining

Some compilers implement inlining only within a single language, such as C++. This is called *monolingual inlining*.

The Green Hills inliner can inline across languages. For example, the Fortran runtime library is written in C. If desired, one or more of the runtime library routines can be inlined into the Fortran calling program. This is called *multilingual inlining* or *cross-language-inlining*.

4. Classifying Inlining Implementations

Armed with our new taxonomy, we can now describe succinctly how various languages and implementations perform procedure inlining. Inlining has four dimensions: (1) manual/automatic (2) procedure/call (3) local/global (4) monolingual/multilingual. These dimensions are orthogonal, so our taxonomy can describe 16 different possible combinations.

4.1. C++ Inlining

The C++ language, for example, has manual procedure inlining. C++ does not have manual call inlining nor automatic procedure inlining. Manual procedure inlining in C++ is both local and global. C++ has manual local inlining for static procedures, and manual global inlining for the rest, although global inline procedures must be placed in an include file which is included in each separate compilation.

4.2. Ada Inlining

The Ada language has manual procedure inlining. Ada lacks both manual call inlining and automatic inlining, either automatic by procedure or automatic by call. Ada also has both local and global inlining. Both are manual by procedure, not by call.

4.3. MIPS Inlining

The MIPS Corporation compilers have extensive inlining. In our taxonomy, MIPS has manual procedure inlining, automatic procedure inlining, and automatic call inlining. Each of these is both local and global. The MIPS inliner is multilingual. The only capability MIPS lacks is manual call inlining: there is no syntax for the programmer to designate manually that some calls should be inlined and others should not. Manual inlining either inlines all calls or no calls to a given procedure. Oddly enough, the MIPS inliner does implement automatic call inlining.

However, in spite of their sophisticated analysis of inlining, the MIPS compilers perform inlining very late, during link editing. Therefore, inlined procedures do not get the benefit of all the earlier optimizations which the MIPS compilers perform.

4.4. Kuck And Associates Inlining

Kuck and Associates, Inc., of Champaign-Urbana, Illinois, produces Fortran-to-Fortran and C-to-C translators which can vectorize, parallelize, and convert from one language dialect to another. They have a complete implementation of manual and automatic, procedure and call inlining, however, they are monolingual.

They found that they absolutely needed automatic inline expansion for good performance on supercomputers of such standard benchmarks as LINPACK. The inner loop in LINPACK calls a subroutine named SAXPY (or DAXPY, in double precision), and SAXPY must be expanded inline before the other supercomputer vector optimizations can be applied.

4.5. Green Hills Inlining

Green Hills C, C++, Fortran, and Pascal compilers implement the entire inlining taxonomy: manual and automatic, procedure and call, local and global, mono- and multi-lingual.

5. Inlining Implementation Issues

The first two implementation issues are:

1) Which parts of the full inlining taxonomy will be implemented?
2) When during compilation will the inline procedure calls be expanded?

Green Hills implemented the whole taxonomy, since different parts of it seemed to be useful to different users. The Green Hills inliner implements manual procedure inlining, manual call inlining, automatic procedure inlining, automatic call inlining, local and global inlining for all cases of manual and automatic inlining, and mono-lingual and multi-lingual inlining.

We also decided to perform inline expansion as early as possible, to get the full benefit of all possible optimizations on the body of the inlined procedures. We implement inline procedure expansion immediately after lexing and parsing, before any optimization. This insures that all inline code will be optimized as completely as possible. After we implemented our early inlining strategy, we compared our inliner to the MIPS inliner, which uses a late inlining strategy. In numerous tests, the Green Hills compilers were able to perform more optimizations and more complete optimizations on inlined code because of early inlining.

Once we made these two fundamental design decisions, to implement full inlining and to inline early, we then had to address two additional issues:

3) What is the user interface?
4) What is the internal representation of inline procedures?

6. User Interface

We decided to give the user as much flexibility as possibility. The user has complete control over manual and automatic inlining, and can mix them.

6.1. Manual Procedure Inlining In C++

C++ already had the **inline** keyword, so no work was required.

6.2. Manual Procedure Inlining In ANSI C

Here is how we added the **inline** keyword to C, using the same syntax as for C++. In order to conform to ANSI C, all new keywords must begin with a double underscore, so **inline** is not a valid ANSI keyword, but _ _inline is. Therefore, we implemented the _ _inline keyword, and also created a new include file named inline.h, which contains one line:

```
#define inline _ _inline
```

By adding the statement **#include <inline.h>** to the top of the program being compiled, the user can use the **inline** keyword rather than the ugly _ _inline keyword.

By requiring the ANSI C user to include **inline.h** early in the source file being compiled, we achieved complete compatibility between C and C++ without violating the ANSI C Standard.

6.3. Manual Procedure Inlining In ANSI Pascal

Since our Pascal compiler has a builtin C preprocessor, we were able to use the same implementation strategy for ANSI Pascal as we used for ANSI C. We added the _ _inline keyword, which is enabled by a compiler option. When the option is disabled, the keyword is an ordinary identifier. In this way, we maintain conformance to the ANSI and ISO Level 1 Pascal standards. We also added the same inline.h file we used for C, which defines **inline** as _ _inline, so the user can use the **inline** keyword.

6.4. Manual Procedure Inlining In Fortran

For Fortran, we had previously implemented almost all of the VAX/VMS Fortran extensions, including the OPTIONS statement for FUNCTIONs and SUBROUTINEs. This gave us a natural place to add the inline designator, so we did. The syntax is:

OPTIONS/INLINE

immediately before a SUBROUTINE or FUNCTION statement.

6.5. Manual Procedure Inlining On The Compiler Command Line

In addition to this form of manual procedure inlining using the **inline** keyword or option in the program source, we also permitted manual procedure inlining to be specified on the compiler command line:

cc -OI=abs,min,max csource.c

This will cause the compiler to know beforehand that invocations of **abs**, **min**, and **max** are to be expanded. The definitions of these functions are expected to be found in the source file(s) being compiled.

6.6. User Interface For Automatic Inlining

For automatic inlining, it is useful if the compiler can see the entire program, that is, everything that the linker would see. To do this, the user lists all the source programs on a single compiler command line, together with the -OI option:

cc -OI csource1.c csource2.c fortransource1.f pascalsource1.p

In effect, -OI, without a list of inline procedure names, directs the compiler to identify and inline any procedures that it thinks it should. These options can be combined, that is,

cc -OI=abs,min,max -OI csource1.c

is a legal command line. It tells the compiler to manually inline three procedures: abs and min and max. In addition, it tells the compiler to automatically inline any other procedures in the source file for which that would be appropriate.

The compiler will perform two passes over the entire source. The purpose of the first pass is to determine automatically which procedures or calls are to be inlined, and to mark them with the internal equivalent of the manual procedure and call inline directives. The second pass is normal compilation, but the compiler has access to the definitions of all the inline routines (from the first pass), since it may be doing multi-lingual global inlining.

7. Internal Representation

Since we inline immediately after lexing and parsing, the internal representation of a procedure is the internal tree for the procedure, together with its internal symbol table. In order to implement global inlining, we need to save this internal representation in a file between separate compilations. Therefore, we devised a pair of routines which convert internal trees and symbol tables to an external representation and back again reliably. Because we are using the same internal trees for inlining as the rest of the compiler uses for all other transformations, we had at our disposal the tree printing tools and other tree management utilities, which were a great help.

7.1. The .l Files

In the initial implementation of automatic global inlining, Pass 1 of the inliner constructed a giant database which contained all procedure definitions from all the source files. Pass 2 then performed normal compilation of each source file, and consulted the database on each call, to see if inline expansion should be performed.

The problem with this approach is that it did not mesh well with Unix *make* files. All .o files depended on the giant database, which in turn depended on all the .c files. Even a one character change in one source file would trigger a total rebuild. A better design was needed.

The solution we adopted was to split the giant database into pieces, with each piece corresponding to an input source file. Each piece had a .l suffix. (The .l suffix stands for "library"; the more natural .i suffix was already in use by others.) Pass 1 of the inliner now transforms each input .c file into a .l file. Pass 2 of the inliner then transforms each .l file into a .o file. So now if a source file changes, only the corresponding .l and .o files are affected.

This rule is similar to having a Unix *make* file in which the .h file dependencies are not recorded, lest a change to one .h file force a complete rebuild. It is up to the user to decide if a change to a .h file, or in the case of the inliner, a .c file, requires an total rebuild. If so, the rebuild must be performed manually, for example, by deleting all .l and .o files and then running make. However, Unix *make* handles the dependencies among .c, .l, and .o files cleanly.

There is one interesting design question: why run Pass 2 on the .l files? Why not run Pass 2, which is very similar to an ordinary compile step, on the original .c files? Clearly, if everything worked perfectly, these operations would be identical. However, there is a philosophical issue here. The bodies of the inline procedures are being retrieved from the .l files. If we retrieved the calling procedures from the original .c files, there would be an opportunity for an inconsistency between the .c file and the corresponding .l file.

Here are possible sources of an inconsistency between the .c file and the corresponding .l file. With large software projects such as a compiler, with 100,000 source lines or larger, the .c source files are often being changed by many different programmers. If the compiler were to read from source files and inline from .l files, the two versions of each file would need to be kept absolutely synchronized. Scale up to a 1,000,000 source line project, such as a phone switch, with 50 to 100 programmers, such synchronization might become nearly impossible. But the compiler can just as easily read .l files. as .c files, thus completely avoiding the problem. If you want a guaranteed consistent compilation, just make sure the .l files don't change during compilation, which is a much easier task.

A second reason has to do with consistency of compilation. Various compiler checks are actually done by compiler tree modifications, which would be saved in the inline .l file. In addition to worrying about the source files being kept absolutely synchronized, the programmer would need to make sure he was using the same options on reading the this potential inconsistency is avoided simply by having the compiler always read the .l file.

A third reason has to do with compiler consistency; one could have the program produce one tree when the compiler read the .c source file, and another, different tree if an older, slightly different compiler version was used to create the .l file. Usually this is not serious, but potentially undesirable. Again, it is easily avoided by always using the .l files as the intermediate stage of the compilation.

Thus by always using the .l files, we enhance the reliability of the process.

In addition, we think that the .l files are a natural repository for feedback information from an execution profiler. This would tell the compiler the preferred direction for branches, which loops were executed most often, etc., enabling the compiler to allocate machine resources to the program more effectively.

8. Implementation Difficulties

The full implementation of inline procedures took two years, during which we learned exactly why prior implementors had not tried to implement full inlining.

8.1. Runaway Recursive Inline Expansion

We first implemented a tree copy routine, to perform the actual expansion of inline procedure bodies. The routine to copy the internal tree was written first, and has not changed very much. The problems mostly lie in other areas.

However, there was one interesting problem. Consider the following C routine:

inline int factorial(int n) { return ((n <= 1) ? 1 : n * factorial(n-1)); }

If we naively apply inline expansion to **factorial(i)**, then the compiler will go into an infinite loop. Therefore, we need to keep track of recursive inline expansion, whether direct or indirect, as we copy the tree. When we reach a depth limit, we refuse to expand any more copies. The default compiler depth limit is 2, but it can be set to any level between 1 and 16. Note that the inline expansion depth does not depend on the names of the called procedures. A calls A calls A calls A has a depth of 4. A calls B calls C calls D also has a depth of 4.

The depth limit prevents infinite recursion, that is, it prevents incorrect behavior. Separate from the depth limit is a strategy for recursive inline expansion, that is, how deep should we expand to generate good code. After examining many programs, we decided on the following strategy: each time an inline procedure P is referenced, expand it. This expansion may cause further inline expansion. If this subsequent expansion ever calls P again, then for the second reference to P, *do not* expand it. In effect, there are two copies of P. The first one is inline. The second one is not. This strategy rule can be turned off, in favor of the depth rule above. Note that the strategy rule only applies "vertically" as opposed to "horizontally". Suppose a procedure calls P 10 times. Then all 10 calls to P will be expanded inline, since these calls are "horizontal".

8.2. Symbol Name Conflict

The first difficulty is in copying the symbol table. As mentioned above, if the inline procedure has a symbol with the same name as the procedure containing the call, there will be a symbol conflict. What we do is to copy the symbol if there is no conflict (to assist user debugging), but if there is a conflict, we make a new symbol with no name. In either case, when we copy the tree, we make the references to the symbol table point to the newly copied symbol.

8.3. Static Variable Semantic Problem

There is a semantic difficulty with **static** variables in C. For example, consider the following procedure, which simply counts how many times it has been called, and returns that value:

```
int count_calls()
    {
    static int count=0;
    return (++count);
    }
```

If we inline this procedure by naive copying, we will create multiple copies of the declaration

static int count=0;

But the semantics of the **count_calls** function require that all these copies refer to one and only one variable, so that the same semantics will be observed when the procedure is inlined as the procedure had when it was not inlined.

We have solved this problem, but it's a little tricky. There are several cases:

- There is only a single compilation
- There are multiple compilations
  - The inline procedure is static
  - The inline procedure is not static

8.3.1. Single Compilation With An Inlined Static Variable

If we are performing a single compilation, which may be indicated by the **-OI** option on the command line, the inliner takes the static variable in the inline procedure and makes a single static variable with global scope (a global static variable) to which all the inlined copies of the inline procedure refer. Since each local inline static variable has been transformed into a global static variable, the program semantics are preserved. As we discussed above, in the section on Symbol Name Conflict, if the name of the new global static variable would not conflict with any other name, then we leave the name alone (to assist user debugging), but if there is a conflict, we cause the new symbol to have no name. In either case, we redirect the references from the old local static symbol to the new global static symbol. We preserve the semantic meaning of the program but we gain the efficiency of inline code.

8.3.2. Multiple Compilation With An Inlined Static Variable In A Static Inline Procedure

If there are multiple separate compilations, then there are multiple separate copies of the local static variable **count**. However, since the inline procedure is itself static, it is semantically correct to have multiple copies of the local static variable **count**, one copy per separate compilation. Again, for each compilation, the inliner transforms the local static variable **count** into a global static variable to which all the inlined copies of the inline procedure **count_calls** in a given compilation refer.

8.3.3. Multiple Compilation With An Inlined Static Variable In A Non-Static Inline Procedure

In the case that the **count_calls** procedure is not itself **static**, we know that the name **count_calls** is unique in what ANSI C calls *file scope*, that is, the scope of all external names in the program. We can also take advantage of the fact that in ANSI C, names beginning with a double underscore are reserved for use by the compiler. Using these tools, we can transform the above into:

```
int __count_calls_count=0; /* initialize global variable to 0 */

int count_calls()
    {
    extern int __count_calls_count;
    return (++__count_calls_count);
    }
```

The **static** variable **count** has now been renamed into the **extern** variable __count_calls_count. This name is unique within the file scope, by construction, since **count_calls** was unique, and since the newly constructed name cannot conflict with any user name (because it begins with a double underscore, which is reserved for the compiler). Thus we can now give the correct semantics for the inline expansion, across separate compilations, of the C function **count_calls**.

Similar remarks apply to C++, Fortran, and Pascal, which have similar rules about unique external names and procedures.

This design solution does have one remaining problem: we can no longer access the variable **count** with the debugger, since it has been renamed. However, it is possible to modify the debugger to handle this case.

8.4. Assembler Overflow

The initial implementation of inline procedures was manual and local. This required that an inline procedure be defined before it was referenced. We simply retained the internal tree and symbol table for all inline procedures, and copied them both to the call site. However, when we considered implementing automatic inlining, it was clear that we needed a two pass compiler: the first pass needed to examine the entire program to see which procedures should be inlined, and the second pass would perform the actual compilation of all source files, emitting one gigantic assembly language file as output. The first thing we noticed after we implemented this design is that we often produced several megabytes of assembler source as a single output file. This large assembler source file could crash some Unix assemblers. Our solution was to extend our own proprietary assembler to handle such large input files reliably.

8.5. Optimization Problem With Fortran Static Variables

There were other problems. After the inliner had been working well for some months on C programs, we tried it on some Fortran source code. The inliner worked, but performance measurements showed that the inline code was slower than the original. Why? It seems that the Green Hills Fortran compiler takes care to promote Fortran scalar static variables to registers when it can. This speeds up most Fortran programs considerably. However, when the inliner was used, the Fortran optimizer could no longer assume that the inlined static variables were local (not referenced by any other subroutine), so it could not promote them to registers. So they ran slower. The solution was for the inliner to examine the procedure to be inlined before expanding it, to locate the static variables that might be register candidates, and mark them as such. After inlining, the Fortran optimizer could use the mark to do at least as well as before.

8.6. Automatic Inline Strategy

There is another set of important implementation issues: what strategy should the automatic inliner use? How should it identify procedures to be marked as inline? Should it stop at automatic procedure inlining, or is there some additional benefit from automatic call inlining? If so, how should the inline calls be distinguished?

Here are our answers to these questions. Define a procedure as "small" if the number of operators in the tree which represents the body of the procedure does not exceed a certain threshold. Define a procedure as "medium size" if it is not "small" but the number of operators in the tree which represents the body of the procedure does not exceed a certain larger threshold.

When the **-OI** option is used on the compiler command line, then the automatic inliner is invoked. It processes the entire set of source routines which also appear on the command line. Usually, this is the entire set of source files for a whole program, not counting library routines. In some sense, the compiler has as much information about the final program as the linker does. The compiler first processes all of the input source files as pass 1. Then it analyzes what it has found. It constructs a spanning tree from the **main** procedure, and marks all procedures in the tree. Those which are not marked are never called. Of course, X could call Y which calls Z, but if no one calls X, then all three are never marked. Since they are not marked, they are deleted.

Now the global inline strategy module performs both automatic procedure inlining and automatic call inlining: if a procedure is never called, we delete it; if it is called once, we mark it as inline; if it is called several times, but is small, we mark it as inline. This is a reasonably simple, yet very powerful automatic inline strategy.

We recently extended the Green Hills inliner strategy module to analyze two more cases: (1) If a procedure is medium size, as defined above, but it is often called with all constant arguments, then we mark the procedure as inline. In this context, "often" means that the number of calls with all constant arguments is at least 2/3 of the total number of calls to that procedure. (2) If a procedure is medium size, then for those calls which have at least one constant argument, we perform automatic call inlining. The hope is that the constant argument, upon inline expansion, will present opportunities for constant folding, code deletion from **if** or **switch** statements with a constant expression, etc.

9. Inlining Performance

We have measured the performance of the Green Hills inliner carefully with two different tests. The first test was to measure the same standard benchmarks with and without inlining for the TRON Architecture. The second test was to take the published benchmarks used by MIPS and measure them on a similar architecture using the Green Hills compilers.

9.1. Green Hills Inline TRON Code Versus Out-Of-Line TRON Code

We have measured the effect of inlining on standard benchmarks on the TRON architecture. Figure 2 shows the results on a 20 MHz Gmicro/200 TRON Architecture Unix V.3.2 system with zero wait-state memory on the Dhrystone, single precision Whetstone, double precision Whetstone, single precision Linpack and double precision Linpack benchmarks.

Note that inlining produced a performance boost of 60% on Dhrystone and more than 100% on both single and double precision Whetstone. However, it produced almost no improvement on Linpack, aside from eliminating the call overhead.

9.2. Green Hills Inliner Versus MIPS Inliner

We also attempted to compare the Green Hills compilers with the MIPS compilers, to see which company had better compiler technology. The Green Hills inliner was crucial to this comparison, since the MIPS inliner is the major factor in MIPS compiler performance. Such a comparison is methodologically difficult, since Green Hills compilers produce code for ten different architectures but not MIPS, while MIPS compilers produce code only for the MIPS architecture.

We addressed this methodological question by selecting from our supported targets the one which was closest to the MIPS architecture: like the MIPS architecture, it is a RISC architecture, only Load and Store instructions access memory, all instructions are 32 bits with three operands, most integer ALU instructions execute in one cycle, instruction execution is pipelined, it has 31 integer registers of 32 bits each, and the cache organization, size, hit cost, miss cost, and replacement algorithms are either neutral or favor MIPS.

Our goal was to run a series of benchmark experiments in which the dominant difference in performance was the compiler technology, not the underlying hardware.

The reference architecture was a Motorola 88000. In general, where there are differences, they favor MIPS. For example, MIPS has a one clock load latency on a cache hit, while the M88000 has a two clock latency.

Now it is a truism in the benchmark world that he who chooses the benchmarks, wins. If we had chosen our own benchmarks, we would have selected those which used optimizations we had that MIPS lacked, and easily won the contest. So we didn't do that. We wanted to know objectively which company had the best compiler technology. So we used the MIPS published benchmarks. These are the programs that MIPS feels they do the best on. Figures 3 and 4 give the results: Green Hills compilers outperform MIPS compilers in methodologically comparable environments. For Figure 3, the Motorola system is 20 MHz and the MIPS system is 16.67 MHz, so the numbers must be rescaled. For Figure 4, both systems are at 25 MHz. After rescaling Figure 3, Green Hills beats MIPS in both cases.

Perhaps more interesting is the relative optimization provided by the inliner: Figures 2 and 3 show that inlining can sometimes produce more improvement than all the other optimizations combined. However, as the Linpack benchmark in Figure 2 and the Queens and Quick benchmarks in Figure 3 show, sometimes inlining gives little or no improvement. For Linpack, only the call overhead is saved.

Standard Benchmarks

Program	No Opt No Inline	Full Opt No Inline	Full Opt Inline	Inline % Change
Dhrystone 1.1	7989	9823	15673	60%
Single Whetstone	2732	3110	6974	124%
Double Whetstone	2248	2685	6053	125%
Single Linpack	0.32 MFlops	0.39 MFlops	0.40 MFlops	2%
Double Linpack	0.28 MFlops	0.33 MFlops	0.34 MFlops	3%

20 MHz Gmicro/200, 0 Wait States

Figure 2

Stanford Composite Benchmarks
(All times in milliseconds)

Manufacturer System CPU Speed Compiler	Opus Personal Mainframe/8000 Motorola 88000 20 MHz Green Hills			Digital Equipment Corp. Decstation 3100 MIPS R/3000 16.67 MHz MIPS		
Program	No Opt No Inline	Full Opt No Inline	Full Opt Inline	No Opt No Inline	Full Opt No Inline	Full Opt Inline
Perm	115	113	97	174	157	157
Towers	193	123	79	247	185	174
Queens	81	58	58	153	123	123
Intmm	109	40	39	232	110	108
Mm	127	62	60	228	89	87
Puzzle	1092	376	377	1274	624	626
Quick	95	66	66	174	94	95
Bubble	228	65	65	223	123	124
Tree	247	224	203	273	206	203
FFT	219	123	106	314	192	181

Figure 3

Standard Benchmarks

	Avalon	MIPS
Manufacturer	Avalon	MIPS
System	AP/30	R/3000
CPU	Motorola 88000	MIPS R/3000
Speed	25 MHz	25 MHz
Compiler	Green Hills	MIPS
Program	Full Opt Inline	Full Opt Inline
Dhrystone 1.1	71,022	45,000
Single Whetstone	49,000,000	17,000,000
Double Whetstone	20,000,000	13,600,000

Figure 4

10. Future Enhancements

Clearly there is more that can be done. Here are some possible directions for future development, listed in the order in which we plan to investigate them:

(1) We think that the .l files are a natural place to put profiling data from measuring actual execution, so the compiler can learn which conditional branch directions are more likely, which loops are executed most often, which variables are dynamically used most, and so on. Some researchers have claimed that branch prediction feedback is useful for trace scheduling, while others dispute this. We would like to measure it and see for ourselves.

(2) We believe that our early inlining strategy has proven its worth, and could be extended to perform some of the functions now done by advanced linkers. For example, the MIPS linker performs inter-procedural register allocation. So does an experimental DEC linker. We think that late register allocation has the same problems as late inlining, and we think that extending our global inliner to perform inter-procedure register allocation early, during compilation rather than during linking, would be an interesting experiment. The only resolution to the debate is to implement it and measure it, just as we have done for early versus late inlining.

11. Summary

We presented an overview of and a taxonomy for procedure inlining. Using this taxonomy, we described a complete implementation of procedure inlining. We discussed some of the problems we faced and how we solved them, both with the external user interface and with the internal implementation. Our performance numbers with and without inlining on a TRON architecture show clearly that procedure inlining delivers a substantial performance improvement. Our methodologically sound performance comparison with MIPS indicate that Green Hills compiler technology is superior. Finally, we outlined a future research program.

Acknowledgements

The authors would like to acknowledge the founders of Green Hills Software: Dan O'Dowd, President and Carl Rosenberg, Vice-President of Reseach And Development, who created the compiler technology described here. In particular, Mr. Rosenberg designed and helped implement the Procedure Inliner. Mike Haden retargeted the Green Hills C, C++, Fortran and Pascal compilers to the Gmicro, as well as the Assembler, Linker, Librarian, and Debugger. He also produced Figure 2. Carl Rosenberg produced Figure 3. Dan O'Dowd produced Figure 4.

We would also like to thank Dr. Ken Sakamura of Tokyo University for creating an interesting architecture as a target for our efforts, and also Mitsubishi, Hitachi, and Fujitsu for their implementations of that architecture. We would like to express our gratitude to Mr. Haruyasu Ito of Fujitsu, who has been our guide during the past two years of development. We owe a special debt to Mr. Norihiko Ito of Hitachi, who first introduced Green Hills to the TRON architecture in 1986 and who has worked with us since then to make this project a success.

References

[1] Sakamura, K., "TRON VLSI CPU: Concepts and Architecture," TRON Project 1987, Springer-Verlag, pp. 199-238.

[2] Sakamura, K., "Architecture of the TRON VLSI CPU," IEEE Micro, Volume 7, Number 2, pp. 17-31, April, 1987.

Craig Franklin has been Vice-President of Marketing for Green Hills Software, Inc. since 1986.

After graduating with a BS in Mathematics from Stanford university in 1966, Mr. Franklin spent two years on the Apollo program at North American Rockwell, five years at MIT on the Multics project, five years at Data General in charge of PL/I, and five years as President of his own company, Carolina Software.

For thirteen years, Mr. Franklin was a member of ANSI PL/I Standards Committee X3J1, where he helped to produce X3.53-1976 (ISO 6160) ANSI Standard For Programming Language PL/I and X3.74-1987 ANSI Standard For Programming Language PL/I General Purpose Subset (ISO 6522 Programming Language – General Purpose PL/I).

Mr. Franklin has produced ten commercially successful compilers, in ten tries, for languages including PL/I, Fortran, C, Pascal, Basic, and SAS for organizations including MIT, Data General, Plessey, Brandeis University, SAS Institute, Digital Research, and Microtec Research.

Carl Rosenberg is Vice-President of Research And Development for Green Hills Software.

From 1975 to 1978, Mr. Rosenberg was a consultant to the NASA/Ames Research Center and to National Semiconductor, responsible for obtaining, maintaining, and upgrading a wide variety of compilers and other software tools. In 1978, Mr. Rosenberg helped develop one of the first 8086 compilers for Siemens AG, and was responsible for continuing development until 1980. Mr. Rosenberg joined National Semiconductor in 1980 to implement the VAX and NS32000 code generators as part of the Pascal Compiler Development Group. In 1982, he co-founded Green Hills Software.

Craig Franklin may be reached at Green Hills Software, Inc., 510 Castillo Street, Santa Barbara, California 93101, USA. Tel: (805) 965-6044, Fax: (805) 965-6343.

After 1 February 1991, Carl Rosenberg may be reached at Green Hills Software, Inc., Oasys Division, One Cranberry Hill, Lexington, MA 02173 USA. Tel: (617) 890-7889, Fax: (617) 890-4644.

A Forth Kernel for Gmicro[1]

Henry Neugass
Microsystems Consultant

ABSTRACT

Forth is an interactive language that is especially adapted to hardware/software development on embedded processors. This paper describes a Forth kernel implementation for Gmicro/200, describes the use of Forth as a development tool, and discusses Forth characteristics with respect to the TRON framework.

Keywords: Forth, Gmicro, embedded processing, software development

1. INTRODUCTION

Forth is an interactive, extensible, ROMable, object-oriented language originally developed for the process-control environment. The Forth kernel described in this paper comprises approximately the minimum set of predefined Forth language constructs necessary to do useful work.

There are several good reasons for porting Forth to the Gmicro series:

- The Gmicro family has two members that are specifically designed for embedded processing, the classification that has superseded "process-control." The Gmicro/100 addresses lower-end applications and the Gmicro/200 is aimed at the higher-end. These devices represent the future of 32-bit embedded processing.

- The Gmicro family is designed to meet the TRON specifications, and TRON provides the blueprint for the future standardization, internationalization, and democritization of computer systems [1].

- Porting a language to a new machine is a very good way to become familiar with the architecture.

---

[1]Gmicro is a trademark of Gmicro Group for the TRON Specification Microprocessor.

What can Forth contribute to Gmicro and TRON?

Forth is an *open* language. Because of its nature, and because it is in the public domain, the entire structure and method of the language is available for inspection and alteration.

Forth is a *flexible* language. Forth depends on very few assumptions about its use. Forth imposes few rules on programmers, and, in general, each of the rules may be changed if it is not appropriate to the application.

Forth is a *direct* language. Development in Forth is done from the bottom-up. This means that programmers can check each primitive operation, immediately and directly, before continuing to higher levels of abstraction.

Viewed broadly, Forth has some similarities to the TRON interface description and executable specification language model TULS (TRON UNIVERSAL LANGUAGE SYSTEM). TULS is described [2] as an interactive language whose description may be dynamically changed. TULS allows "editing, interpreting, and compiling in its own environment." These are also characteristics of Forth.

2. FORTH COMPONENTS

A Forth system is a *dictionary* of *Forth words*, each of which may be interactively executed or compiled to build definitions of new Forth words. Forth words share some characteristics of subroutines and are referenced by name.

2.1 Forth code words

CPU-specific machine code routines, *Forth code words,* perform elementary logic functions, arithmetic operations, search procedures, and time-critical work such as interrupt service. In Forth systems configured with a native assembler, users may define code words in-line. Otherwise, code words are constructed during the cross-assembly phase of cross-compiling a new Forth system image, as described in this paper.

A trivial Forth code word is the one that defines a 32-bit integer add for Gmicro/Forth, the word "+":

```
CODE +
  r0 pop
  r1 pop
  r1 r0 add
  r0 push
  NEXT
END-CODE
```

This example shows several characteristics of Forth: There are few restrictions on identifier tokens. Arguments and return values of Forth words are almost always passed on the stack. Forth uses "Reverse-Polish" postfix notation. Code words are concluded, not by a subroutine return, but by the function symbolized here by the macro NEXT, which references the low-level address interpreter of Forth.

2.2 High-Level Forth

Forth code words support a larger group of Forth words which are written in the Forth language. High-level Forth code is generally CPU-independent, except for a few system-specific I/O and initialization routines.

For example, the trivial Forth word "1+" increments the value on the top of the stack and is defined as follows:

```
: 1+
  1
  +
;
```

Words defined in this manner, programmed in Forth, are known for brevity as *colon definitions*. In this definition, the ":" (colon) and ";" (semicolon) characters are shorthand for the functions *define* and *end-define*. The "+" is a reference to the code word defined just above. In more conventional terms this definition may be expressed:

```
define 1+
[as]
1 +
end-define
```

(Defining such a word may make sense only in terms of the resulting economy-of-reference: the operation is specified, in compiled form, by a single word-length execution address. For increased execution speed, the word "1+" may be defined as a Forth code word like "+"; the reference cost is the same, and the choice of these alternatives is up to the programmer.)

The resident Forth Compiler adds each new definition to the dictionary, as illustrated in *Fig. 1*.

It is axiomatic in Forth practice that a new definition be tested immediately. Typing a number places its value on the stack; the "." (period) operator pops and displays the value on the stack top. With these operations, the definition of "1+" can be tested at the terminal:

```
5 1+ . 6 ok
```

In this case, the definition is correct, and Forth responds with the new value and its prompt, "ok".

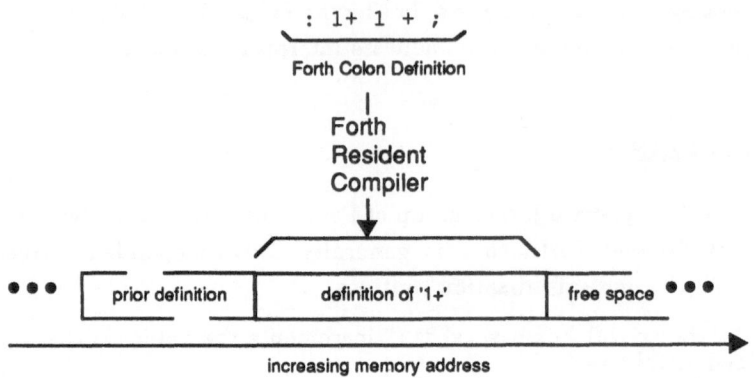

Fig. 1   Resident Forth Compiler Operation

2.3 The Forth System

The components of a typical complete Forth system, excluding buffers and stacks, are illustrated in *Fig. 2*:

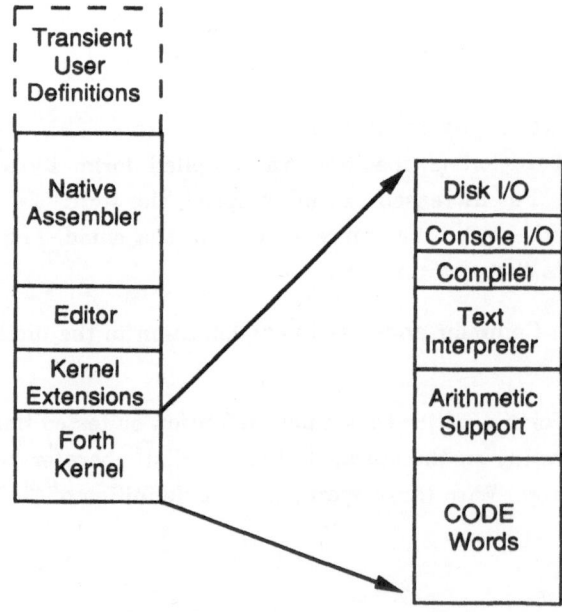

Fig. 2   Forth System Elements

New definitions, such as the definition of "1+" described above, extend the dictionary into a transient storage area. The set of pre-existing definitions often includes an editor and a native assembler. Both the editor and the assembler are written in Forth and execute within the Forth environment. All existing definitions, including those implementing the text interpreter and the compiler, may be replaced by re-definition.

A full explanation of the Forth language is beyond the scope of this paper. See reference [3] for more information.

3. PORTING THE FORTH KERNEL

Forth has been ported to processors ranging from microcontrollers to mainframes.

The target in this case was the Gmicro/200 microprocessor on the Hitachi H32SBC, a VME-bus board equipped with EMS (Executive Monitor System) firmware. EMS and board peripheral devices provide asynchronous serial (RS-232) hex-record transfer capabilities, which were used to transfer code images from the development host.

The development host was a DOS-based 80386 operating at 25 Mhz.

3.1 Kernel Description

A run-able Forth system image is a memory-resident data structure —a linked list— containing the code routines and the compiled form of the high-level Forth code. Each list node contains a name count, a name string, linkage information, the address of executable code that characterizes the specific node type, and machine code or a list of high-level execution addresses corresponding to a high-level language construct. *Figure 3* shows the node corresponding to a high-level Forth word:

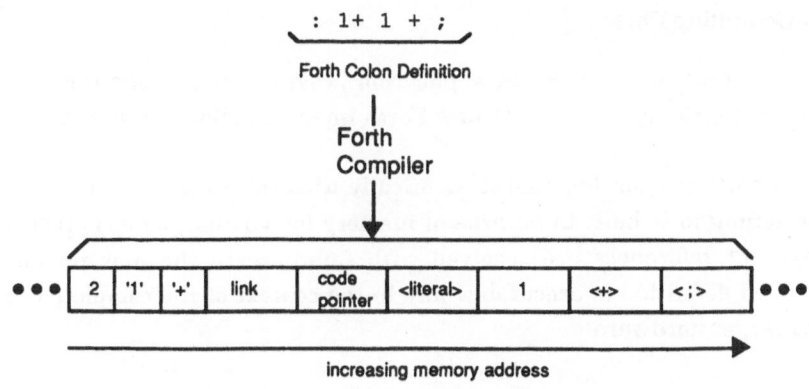

Fig. 3   *High-Level Definition Node Contents*

Besides the list structure, there is also a base record in a fixed format that contains initialization instructions and data, as well as the address interpreter engine of Forth. In other words, there is a great deal of internal structure to Forth.

3.2 Porting the kernel

Developing Forth for a new CPU requires coding some 80 Forth code words, which, in the case of the Gmicro/200, average about 24 bytes each in length. Among these, the longest routines are about 160 bytes long, and some are very short. These numbers are fairly representative of the task of porting Forth to a typical 16- or 32-bit processor.

In addition to changes to processor-specific code words, porting the kernel requires changes to a few high-level definitions, for example, to the definitions of words supporting console input/output in the H32SBC/EMS environment.

3.3 The Gmicro/200 Kernel

The Gmicro/200 Forth source code was derived from the source for a Hitachi H8/532 Forth also developed by the author. Although the H8/532 is not specifically a TRON-standard device, the architectures and instruction sets are quite similar. Porting the source code required little more than register reassignments and substituting explicit coding for special features of the H8/532 instruction set that are unavailable on the Gmicro/200.

The assembly-language instructions used in the Gmicro/Forth kernel were chosen from those that are common to Gmicro/100, Gmicro/200, and Gmicro/300. Portability among these devices should be automatic.

3.4 Cross-Compiling Forth

A Forth Cross-Compiler is a Forth application program that builds the code and data structures that make up an entirely new Forth image, as shown in *Fig. 4*.

The Cross-Compiler operates almost identically with the resident compiler except that each new definition is built in an area of memory (or virtual memory) reserved for the new image, all references are resolved with reference to the new image, and each cross-compiled definition is executable only in the context of the completed image, after loading to target hardware.

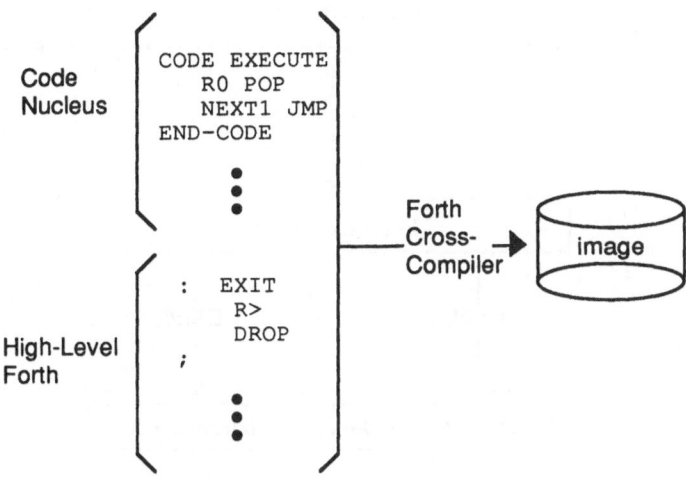

Fig. 4   Cross-Compiler Function

In this case, the Forth cross-compiler used had been intended for 8-bit and 16-bit targets and required some modification for building a 32-bit image. Also, since the Gmicro architecture requires instructions to start on an even address, the cross-compiler had to be modified to byte-pad the data structure as necessary.

A Forth Cross-Compiler is customized for each target CPU with a Cross-Assembler module capable of producing machine-specific object code in a format compatible with the Forth environment.

3.5 Forth Cross-Assembler

It is moderately difficult to write a native assembler on an existing Forth system, but it is markedly more difficult to write a Forth Cross-Assembler for a new CPU. To avoid this problem, it is possible to invoke a conventional cross-assembler from the Forth environment.

For this work the Forth cross-compiler was modified to operate normally until it needed to assemble a code routine at a specific offset in the object image. At this point it spawns, via an EXEC call, a DOS interface program, coded in C, passing a name designator and a code offset. The interface program in turn invokes a conventional cross-assembler and linker as summarized in *Fig. 5:*

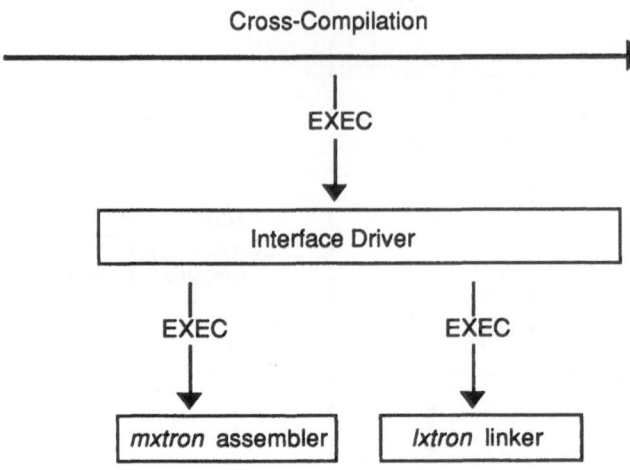

Fig. 5   *Spawning the assembler and linker*

Source code for each routine is maintained in a separate file. Object code is transferred back to the Forth environment through a common file. The tools used for this purpose were the Green Hills Software *mxtron* assembler and *lxtron* linker, respectively.

As it turned out, all the code routines assembled by this method were position-independent and did not requiring linking to a specific address. However, the link-to-address mechanism was retained for the sake of generality.

3.6 Forth Register Model

Forth requires an Interpreter Pointer, which maintains the current target of the low-level address interpreter, and two stack pointers. The Gmicro/200 register assignments are shown in *Fig. 6*.

Registers R0 through R5 are used by Forth code words to implement primitives. Registers R6 through R10 are not assigned. R11 is used to store and retrieve address interpreter return points (the "Return Stack"). The address interpreter pointer (IP) is stored in R12. R13 is reserved for use as a context pointer. R14, the frame pointer, is not currently used, but is reserved. R15, the Hardware stack pointer, is also used for the Forth parameter stack (PS), which is used to pass values among Forth words.

To give some perspective on register use, references to R0 and R1 comprise about 60% of the bulk register use among the low-level Forth code words. References to R2, R3, R4, and R5 make up only about 13%. The use of R15-relative addressing could probably reduce the latter frequency to almost zero. Forth is very sparing of resources.

301

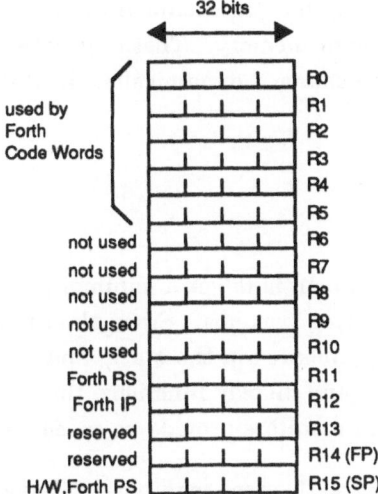

Fig. 6   Gmicro / Forth Register Assignments

3.7 Memory Model

The EMS monitor supports both physical and logical address space modes of the Gmicro device. For the purpose of this work, a logical address space starting at address zero was chosen. (This happened to correspond to physical address 0.) The Forth image was constrained, for convenience, to lie within a 64k byte area. The resulting memory map is shown in *Fig. 7*.

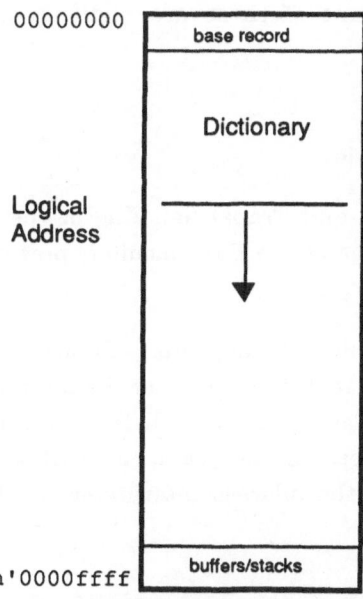

Fig. 7   Forth Memory Map under EMS

The standard Forth memory map has the dictionary growing toward high memory and places buffers and stacks in high memory. These allocations are usually specified at cross-compile time but may be changed dynamically. In this case, there was plenty of room in the 64K allocation.

4. KERNEL DEBUGGING

The usual strategy for porting Forth is to get a minimal portion of Forth operating and to interactively test the remaining portions. Since almost all of Forth is composed of routines that communicate arguments via the stack, and because Forth itself provides convenient stack manipulation and display functions, this is usually the most practical approach. Most debuggers and monitors provide no specific stack-oriented functions.

The debugging process starts with cross-loading the image produced by the cross-compiler. The first steps are to verify the placements and linkages of the fixed portions of the Forth data structure, and then to check that the Forth address interpreter is functioning correctly. This is usually done using a native monitor/debugger or an in-circuit emulator.

The next step is to check the mechanism for storing, and later retrieving, address interpreter return points, that is, verifying that the "Return Stack" is working correctly.

By this point, assuming that console I/O is operating, Forth is often able to respond to some keyboard commands. The balance of the system is debugged by using the Forth text interpreter, in tandem with a native monitor/debugger, to check specific Forth mechanisms. The most important of these are dictionary search words, math operators, and the compiler.

4.1 EIT handling and the EMS monitor

The EIT (Exceptions, Interrupts, and Traps) handling of the Gmicro architecture, coupled with the complete facilities of the EMS monitor, provided a very productive initial debugging environment.

The EMS monitor implements execution breakpoints —through traps or via the Gmicro hardware— which are useful for debugging details of the machine code portion of the Forth kernel. However, most of Forth consists of lists of execution pointers that are processed by the address interpreter. In these cases, instruction breaks are much less useful. Placing a breakpoint in the address interpreter can be effective, but this approach is usually tedious.

The Self-Debug Operand Breakpoint function of the Gmicro device, on the other hand, provides the best possible facilities for early testing of a Forth kernel. It is a matter of isolating a specific execution pointer and commanding EMS to place an Operand Breakpoint at the indicated memory address. When that breakpoint is reached, the EMS monitor is used to examine registers, the Parameter Stack, and the few static data structures used by Forth.

The exception-handling facilities of the Gmicro processor provide unparalleled stability in the early stages of debugging. The device detects odd-address instruction fetches, zero-divides, address-translation violations, and invalid instructions —among other errors— and the EMS monitor reports the error type and location. The hardware exception detection facilities are so efficient that there were no cases during development in which the image was damaged by run-away execution.

4.2 EMS Monitor Calls

In addition to debugging tools, the EMS monitor provided console I/O functions for the initial versions of the Forth kernel, namely

- Console serial port initialization
- Console Character Output
- Console Character Input
- Console Input Status

As soon as the characteristics of the hardware became more clear, references to these EMS monitor routines were eliminated in favor of direct Forth access to the console port hardware.

5. HOST INTERFACE KERNEL ADDITIONS

The Gmicro/Forth kernel was originally equipped with one I/O device, the console. The first addition to the kernel was an interface to access mass storage on the host computer, which also acted as a console terminal. This interface illustrates Forth programming techniques.

5.1 A Simple Serial Interface

The console terminal is a PC, running a terminal-emulation program. A host interface/terminal emulation program implemented in Forth on the host computer was modified to interleave block I/O with console communications. Similarly, the standard

Forth disk I/O definitions in Gmicro/Forth were modified to route mass storage access through the console port.

To obtain a specific logical disk block, the Gmicro/Forth user types, for example,

```
100 BLOCK
```

and Gmicro/Forth returns the address of a buffer containing the data from logical disk block 100. "BLOCK" is the standard Forth word for accessing mass storage.

5.2 Host Interface Implementation

The implementation of this interface was direct and economical. First, Gmicro/Forth sends a one-byte control message leader to the host Forth terminal emulator, signaling that the following message has special meaning and is not intended for the console display. Then Gmicro/FORTH sends the ASCII string

```
100 SEND-BLOCK<null>
```

The host Forth system simply collects the null-terminated text. When the message is complete, the host Forth system *interprets* this command string, using a duplicate invocation of its standard text interpreter. "SEND-BLOCK" is a Forth application word, defined on the host, that arranges for the requested block to be transmitted to Gmicro/Forth.

5.3 Extending Host and Target

Beyond the physical layer protocol, this "host interpret" interface mechanism is completely general, that is, Gmicro/Forth can access any function on the host Forth system including the Forth compiler, to extend the host Forth system.

For example, if the host interpret mechanism alone exists on the host, Gmicro/Forth can define the operation of the word "SEND-BLOCK" on the host as follows:

```
: SEND-BLOCK BLOCK DUP BPB + SWAP DO I C@ >COM1 LOOP ;
```

(In this construction,

"`:`" means "define the following token"

"BLOCK" is the standard mass storage access function

"DUP BPB + SWAP" sets up arguments for the DO loop

"DO ... LOOP" contains elements to be repeated

"I C@" obtains a byte from the block

">COM1" transmits the byte

";" concludes the definition

resulting in a new host language element, SEND-BLOCK. Each of these tokens used within the definition are pre-defined in the host Forth kernel.)

This example lacks error detection support and protocol details, but it is adequate for prototyping work.

The extensibility property is symmetric, that is, the host Forth can also extend Gmicro/Forth by a similar mechanism.

5.4 Using Forth Objects for Communications Support

On the Gmicro/Forth side of the interface, the SEND-BLOCK command is generated by a member of a class of host-access commands, each member of which contains a name by which it is invoked, a pointer to the command string data, and an execution pointer to code which formats and transmits the message. The Gmicro/Forth commands

```
" SEND-BLOCK" HCMND:   Host-Send-Block
```

generate a new Gmicro/Forth word, "Host-Send-Block," which can be invoked whenever block data is required, for example, as follows:

```
100 Host-Send-Block
```

In response, Gmicro/Forth sends a leader character, the string "100", the string "SEND-BLOCK", and a null to the host. The value "100" is obtained directly from the invocation. The string "SEND-BLOCK" is obtained from the definition of "Host-Send-Block". The protocol details are obtained from the definition of the entire class, HCMND:, which is as follows:

```
: HCMD:
<BUILDS
    '
DOES>
    @
    1 Send-Host-Command
;
```

(In this construction,

   ":" means "define the following token"

   "<BUILDS" precedes instructions for making the class instance

   "," stores the string address when the instance is built

   "DOES>" precedes object-associated instructions

   "@" obtains the string address

   "1 Send-Host-Command" sends single-parameter commands

   ";" concludes the definition

resulting in a new host language class, "HCMD:". Each of these tokens are pre-defined in the Gmicro/Forth and all, with the exception of Send-Host-Command, are part of the Forth kernel.)

This construct may be used to create additional host interface commands, each of which sends a parameter and a string to the host.

5.5 Characteristics of the Host Interface

No portion of this host interface represents any special new technology.

Postscript[2], a printer-hosted Forth variant, is an example of a sophisticated method for sharing a serial link to transfer both data and formatting commands from a host computer to a laser printer. In some cases, the formatting commands take the form of language extensions.

More importantly —especially for new systems development— the host interface described above was implemented in a few hours, under prototype conditions, without full hardware or monitor documentation. Memory use was in the small hundreds of bytes on both the development host and the Gmicro/200 target.

---

[2] PostScript is a trademark of Adobe Systems, Inc.

6. RESULTS

The resulting Forth system image is about 15K bytes in size. The porting effort took a total of about 3 weeks of intensive work.

The efficiency of the address interpreter and other low-level functions was benchmark tested by nesting a null DO loop within another loop. Gmicro/Forth executed at a rate of about 200K inner loops loops per second. For comparison, an optimized 16-bit Forth executes the same test at a rate of about 330K inner loops per second on a 25 MHz 80386. (The clock rate of the Gmicro/200 on the H32SBC was, in this case, 16 Mhz.)

The address interpreter performs a double-indirect jump to executable code, as shown in *Fig. 8:*

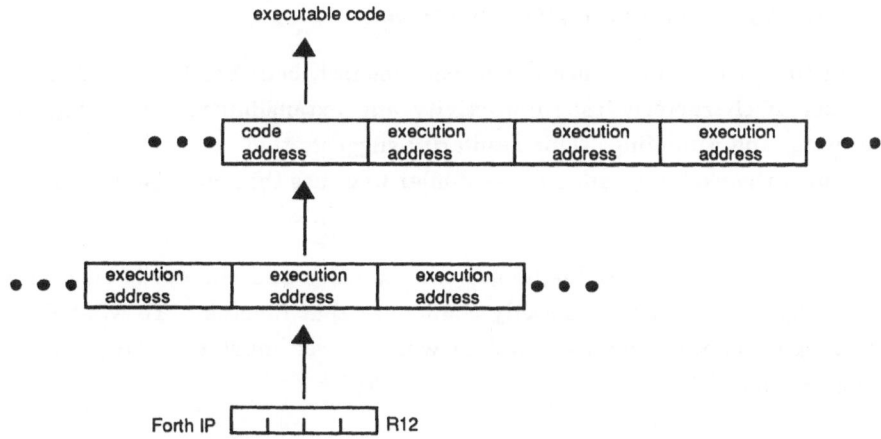

Fig. 8   Address interpreter

In the process, the interpreter pointer must be increased to point to the next 32-bit execution address. The initial implementation of the address interpreter was:

```
mov.w      @r12,r0        ; fetch @ I.P.
add        #4,r12         ; advance I.P.
mov.w      @r0,r1         ; fetch code address
jmp        @r1            ; jump to code
```

Using Extension-Mode addressing, this was recoded as

```
add        #4,r12         ; advance I.P.
jmp @(@(@(r12,-4)))       ; jump to code
```

which resulted in more compact code but no significant change in the speed benchmark described above. More efficient execution of extended-mode addressing would have a very significant effect on the speed of Gmicro/Forth.

7. DISCUSSION

Forth has evolved pragmatically, with emphases on interactions among the human user, the application, and the hardware. The common thread through the history of Forth has been to increase the access of the programmer to all aspects of system function.

7.1 Comparing TRON TULS and Forth

The TRON TULS model is fully comprehensive: it is designed to support all possible interactions among system components in an HFDS (Highly Functional Distributed System), namely, human-with-human, human-with-application, application-with-application, application-with-system, and so on.

Although the goals of Forth are much more modest, both Forth and TULS envision a unique set of characteristics: interactivity and extensibility, with integral editing, interpreting, and compiling. This similarity suggests that issues faced in the practice of Forth over the past 15 years may be similar to issues that must be faced in the TRON project.

For example: Programming languages enforce rules and standards on programmers. The property of extensibility directly challenges that function. To what degree is an extension part of the language, and to what degree must the extension follow the language standards?

7.2 TACL, Forth, and dynamic adaptation

The design philosophy of TULS, with its implementation, TACL (TRON APPLICATION CONTROL-FLOW LANGUAGE) [4] [5] clearly recognizes the need for dynamically adapting programming tools in an HFDS.

(It might also be added that as system size and complexity increase, the need for access to system functions at all levels increases. Further, it is increasingly important that users be able to combine these functions in ways that are unanticipated in the original system design.)

Bottom-up implementation is a fundamental form of dynamic adaptation in programming tools. Forth encourages —almost requires— programmers to test each Forth word as it is defined. In practical terms, this usually increases productivity, improves software component quality, and reduces reliance on after-the-fact debugging. On the other hand, each test a programmer performs entails a certain amount of risk.

Within the relatively limited scope of most Forth applications, this risk can usually be contained. Within the virtually unlimited scope of a highly distributed system, the extent of the risk may not be so easy to evaluate.

8. CONCLUSIONS

This paper describes an implementation of Forth for the Gmicro/200.

Forth in an open language, and because it is of such modest size, it may be completely understood —and ported— by a single individual.

Forth shares some characteristics of the TRON TULS language model and its implementation, TACL. Some of the issues associated with an interactive, extensible language may also be common.

ACKNOWLEDGEMENTS

The author wishes to thank Hitachi Micro Systems, Inc., San Jose, CA (USA) for technical aid and encouragement; Green Hills Software, Inc., Santa Barbara, CA (USA) for the use of its Gmicro software development tools; and Jerry Boutelle, Nautilus Systems, Santa Cruz, CA (USA) for the Cross-Compiler.

REFERENCES

[1]   Hitachi H32 Microprocessor Family description.

[2]   K. Sakamura, TULS: TRON Universal Language System, TRON Project 1988 (Proc. of Fifth TRON Project Symposium), Springer-Verlag, 1988, pp. 3-18.

[3]   L. Brodie, Starting Forth, Prentice-Hall, Englewood Cliffs, NJ, 1981.

[4]   K. Sakamura, TACL: TRON Application Control-flow Language, TRON Project 1988 (Proc. of Fifth TRON Project Symposium), Springer-Verlag, 1988, pp. 79-91.

[5]   N. Koshizuka, H. Takada, M. Saito, Y. Saito, and K. Sakamura, Implementation Issues of the TACL/TULS Language System on BTRON, TRON Project 1989 (Proc. of Sixth TRON Project Symposium), Springer-Verlag, 1989, pp. 113-130.

Henry Neugass is an independent consultant. He received a BA in Psychology from UCLA in 1973 and an MS in Scientific Instrumentation from the University of California, Santa Barbara, in 1975.

The author may be reached at 1179 Grand Street, Redwood City, CA 94061 (USA).

The GMICRO Microprocessor and the AT&T UNIX* Operating System

Cathleen Reiher, William P. Taylor
INTERACTIVE Systems Corporation

ABSTRACT

GMICRO* is a family of high-performance microprocessors based on the TRON architecture specification. INTERACTIVE Systems Corporation designed and developed the port of AT&T's UNIX System V Release 3 to the GMICRO/200. This was the first UNIX System port to the GMICRO family of microprocessors. INTERACTIVE Systems Corporation has ported various versions of the UNIX operating system to a wide variety of hardware architectures.

Although most of the UNIX operating system is portable, much of the kernel depends on the hardware architecture to assist in memory management; exception, interrupt, and trap (EIT) handling; the system call interface; signal transmission; and C run-time startup routines. The software generation system and commands that depend on kernel data structures needed to be modified to take advantage of the GMICRO/200's features.

The paper discusses some of the methods INTERACTIVE used to develop the UNIX System for the GMICRO. It also discusses the advantages that the GMICRO brings to the development of the UNIX System software, particularly in the areas of memory management support, process management support, EIT support, and programming language support.

Keywords: UNIX System, GMICRO/200 microprocessor, software development, operating system

1. INTRODUCTION

Three members of the GMICRO Group (Fujitsu Ltd., Hitachi Ltd., and Mitsubishi Electric Corp.) designed a microprocessor based on the TRON architecture specification [1], [2] called the GMICRO. The GMICRO family of microprocessors consists of the GMICRO/100, the GMICRO/200, and the GMICRO/300. These members of the GMICRO Group asked INTERACTIVE Systems Corporation to port a version of AT&T's UNIX System V Release 3 to the GMICRO/200.

INTERACTIVE Systems Corporation has years of experience in porting various versions of the AT&T UNIX System to a number of architectures, including various Intel*, Motorola*, and RISC processors. This experience enables the INTERACTIVE designers and developers to determine the difficulty of a port. The development team at INTERACTIVE found that the GMICRO/200 offered a number of advantages that made the hardware-dependent portions of the port (especially the memory management and the software generation system) relatively easy to implement.

*The following trademarks shown as registered are registered in the United States and other countries:

UNIX is a registered trademark of UNIX System Laboratories, Inc.
GMICRO is a trademark of GMICRO Group for the TRON specification microprocessors.
Intel is a registered trademark of Intel Corporation.
386 is a trademark of Intel Corporation.
VP/ix is a trademark of INTERACTIVE Systems Corporation and Phoenix Technologies, Ltd.
IBM is a registered trademark of International Business Machines Corporation.
Motorola is a registered trademark of Motorola Corporation.

INTERACTIVE employed some innovative methods to develop the UNIX System for the GMICRO, such as creating a standalone software platform to study the hardware, provide a bootstrap, maintain the system, and debug kernels. INTERACTIVE was able to take advantage of the GMICRO/200 features to implement the machine dependent portions of the UNIX operating system.

This paper discusses the specific features of the GMICRO/200 that eased the UNIX System port. It also presents some comparisons with UNIX Systems designed for other architectures that showcase the advantages of the GMICRO architecture.

This paper contains the following sections:

Section 2 gives a brief and general description of the UNIX operating system.

Section 3 gives a brief description of the features the GMICRO microprocessor provides in the areas of memory management, process management, EITs, and programming languages.

Section 4 describes how particular GMICRO features were employed in the porting of the UNIX System. This section contains four subsections that discuss memory management, process management, EITs, and programming languages. Each subsection first defines its subject (such as memory management), then describes how it applies to the UNIX System and how some specific GMICRO/200 features eased its implementation.

Section 5 describes the features of the GMICRO architecture that were not fully utilized for the UNIX System port.

2. THE UNIX OPERATING SYSTEM

The UNIX operating system for the GMICRO Single Board Computer (SBC) System [3] is based on the UNIX Time Sharing Operating System (System V Release 3.1) [4], [5] developed at AT&T Bell Laboratories. Fujitsu, Hitachi, and Mitsubishi requested that INTERACTIVE provide them with a UNIX System based on System V, and the INTERACTIVE developers chose release 3.1 because it was the most stable version of the UNIX System at the time the work was started.

The UNIX operating system is a computer industry standard, general-purpose system primarily used on high-end microprocessors. The system is an interactive, multi-tasking system that allows many users to run programs simultaneously. Two reasons for the UNIX System's popularity are its portability to new architectures and its support of standards. Indeed, the IEEE POSIX standard is derived in large part from the UNIX System.

Most of the UNIX System kernel and all of the associated programs are written in C. The UNIX System has been ported to a wide range of computers from microprocessors (such as the GMICRO and Intel 386), to mainframes (such as the IBM* 370 series), and to supercomputers (such as the Cray 2). The UNIX System source code can be purchased from AT&T and modified to meet specific requirements.

Software developers find the UNIX System environment especially useful because of its powerful tools. For example, users can write programs called *shell scripts*, which use the language of the command interpreter with existing UNIX System programs as subroutines.

The UNIX community is also working toward standardizing the UNIX operating system to provide a high-quality user and programmer interface that marries features from the System V and Berkeley UNIX variants. Since the UNIX System is such a popular operating system, Fujitsu, Hitachi, and Mitsubishi felt that porting it to the GMICRO/200 would help the GMICRO architecture increase its popularity.

The UNIX System consists of two basic parts: the *kernel* and *user code*. The kernel is the nucleus of the operating system that provides low-level primitive services that support user access to system resources and manage the resources on behalf of the user processes, as well as the operating system. The kernel size varies depending upon the software features it supports, but the basic GMICRO kernel is approximately 225 kilobytes in size, exclusive of optional networking-related code.

The user environment is a large set of diverse programs that consists of three basic parts: the *file system*, which provides a hierarchical method of data handling that makes it easy to store and access information; the *shells*, which are interactive programs that interpret and execute user commands; and the *commands*, which are programs that users execute to edit text, develop software tools, and exchange information with other users.

The system designers and developers attempted to keep as much of the AT&T System V Release 3 UNIX kernel and commands intact, so as to keep the UNIX System port close to the industry standard and to conform to the System V Interface Definition (SVID). About 90-95% of the 600,000 lines of UNIX System source code is directly portable to various architectures. The remaining 5-10% of the UNIX System needs differing levels of modification to enable it to run on a different architecture, like the GMICRO/200 microprocessor.

Figure 1 illustrates a simplified model of the UNIX System. Each of the concentric circles represents one portion of the system: the kernel, the shell, and the user programs. The user programs are the software generation system, the text processing tools, the information management tools, and so on. The arrows indicate that communication is occurring between the kernel and the user programs. The shell is the user interface and command interpreter for the UNIX System.

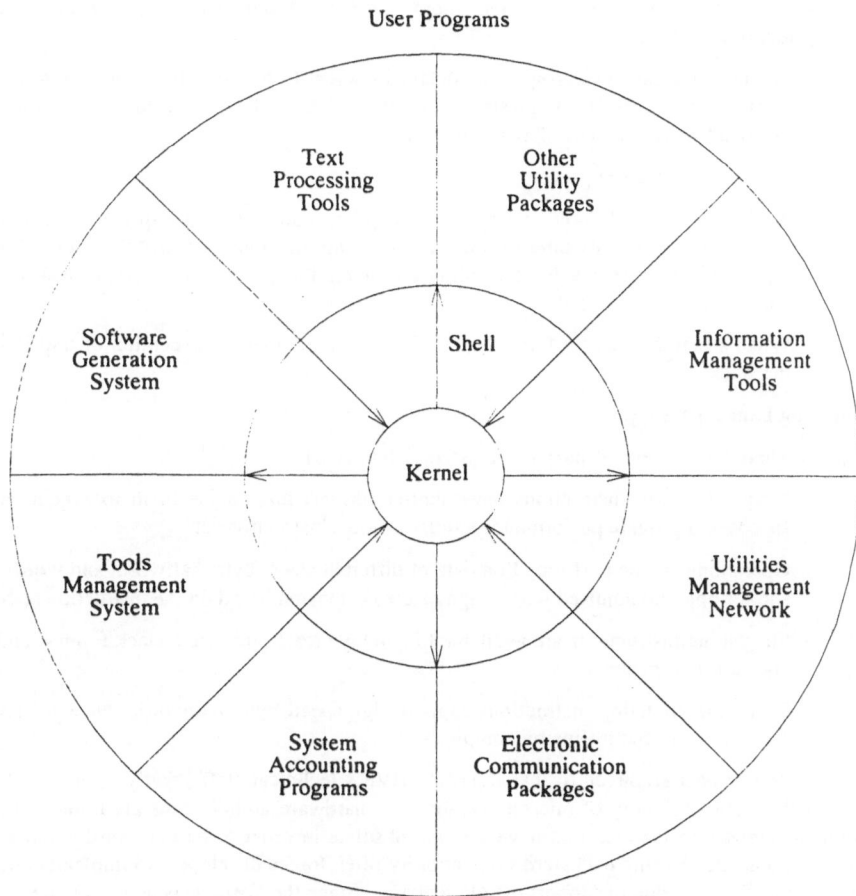

Figure 1. Simplified Model of the UNIX System

3. THE GMICRO ARCHITECTURE

The GMICRO/200 is a high-performance, general-purpose 32-bit microprocessor with advantageous features such as on-chip memory management, distributed on-chip caches, and an advanced pipeline architecture. This section briefly describes the GMICRO features, while section 4 describes how the UNIX System uses them. Some of these features simplified the task of porting the UNIX System to the GMICRO SBC:

Memory Management Support

- The GMICRO/200 supports virtual memory. It is divided into shared and unshared *regions*. Each region is further subdivided into *sections* that are made up of *pages*. While the page size is static (4K bytes), the section size can vary between 64K and 4M bytes. Page tables and section tables can vary between 64 bytes and 4K bytes, which saves memory when tables are short.

- The GMICRO/200 has four levels of protection in the form of rings, with the innermost ring having the highest level of protection and the outermost ring having the lowest level of protection.

Process Management Support

- The *ldctx* (load context) and *stctx* (store context) instructions quickly save and restore context information.

- The use of delayed interrupts and delayed context traps simplify the handling of multiple external interrupts and requests, respectively. These delayed features store the context-independent and context-dependent requests.

Exception, Interrupt, and Trap Support

- An EIT vector table holds entries for exception, interrupt, and trap handler routines. An EIT event uses one of three formats for stacking information about the event. Events are assigned one of 16 levels (depending on their priority) and an interrupt mask identifying which levels are enabled.

- When a memory access fails, detailed information about the exception or trap is saved on the stack.

Programming Language Support

- There are 16 general-purpose registers (R0 to R15).

- Frequently used instructions have shorter formats that enable them to execute at higher speeds and provide performance similar to RISC instruction set.

- Operations can be performed on data of different sizes (byte, halfword, and word) with the shorter operand adjusted with a sign or zero extension based on the instruction opcode.

- Subroutine instructions are available to quickly create and delete stack frames, and to save and restore registers.

- String manipulation instructions support high-speed byte, halfword, and word processing and can be placed in-line by compilers.

One aspect of the GMICRO architecture that INTERACTIVE's technical staff greatly appreciated was the "newness" of the GMICRO family of microprocessors. As hardware architectures are refined, it is necessary to continue supporting features that have become obsolete in order to be backward-compatible with previous generations. Supporting backward-compatibility often forces developers to implement needlessly complicated and inefficient code to support the old features. Since the GMICRO is new, INTERACTIVE was able to take full advantage of the architecture.

4. PORTING ADVANTAGES OFFERED BY GMICRO

INTERACTIVE began the UNIX System porting effort by designing and implementing a standalone system. The standalone system provides a bootstrap for loading the UNIX System kernel (which was being ported in parallel with the standalone system development), a kernel debugger, and utilities needed for system installation and maintenance. The standalone system provides a simple environment for learning about new hardware and for debugging a new software generation system (C compiler, assembler, and so on). Testing the standalone system itself was simplified by the debugging capabilities and I/O support subroutines provided by the GMICRO SBC's firmware. Through this standalone testing and through reading the hardware manuals [6], [7], the development team was able to find GMICRO/200 features that would facilitate and improve the UNIX System port.

Most of the GMICRO architecture features INTERACTIVE used in the UNIX port are used in the kernel. Another significant piece of software that benefited from the GMICRO's architectural features is the kernel debugger, which is the system analog of the UNIX System user-level debugger (sdb(1)). Although kdb does not offer a source code debugging environment, it does provide most of the features one expects of an interactive debugger such as the ability to inspect and modify hardware registers and counters, the ability to set and clear breakpoints and to single-step through individual machine instructions, the ability to distinguish between physical and virtual addresses, the ability to produce formatted displays of kernel data structures in response to user-defined commands, a complete expression evaluator, and a disassembler.

This section provides information on how the GMICRO features eased the porting of the UNIX System. The subjects discussed are memory management, process management, EITs, and programming languages. Each subject is defined and shown how it applies to the UNIX System. Each section explains how INTERACTIVE used the various GMICRO features to the advantage of the port.

4.1 Memory Management Support

Memory management is vital to support the concept of virtual memory. Virtual memory allows the operating system to provide users with much larger address spaces than physical main memory alone would permit, by swapping pages of memory to and from disk. Hardware must provide the mechanisms for translating addresses, while the operating system software must decide which pages remain in memory and which migrate to disk. When a process tries to access a page that has been moved to disk, a page fault occurs, and the operating system must move the requested page into main memory.

The UNIX System depends on virtual memory and the swapping of pages from memory to disk. The UNIX System memory management swaps out both individual pages and entire processes under the control of the scheduler in order to maintain a pool of free pages to use in resolving page faults. Each user process has several different memory regions that can share the following attributes: read-only, read-write, shared, and unshared. The kernel itself also contains multiple data regions that cannot be read by any user process. The kernel may write any segment except its own text segment, which contains kernel executable code.

Table 1 lists the GMICRO instructions that deal with memory management. Some of the instructions listed were used in the UNIX System port. Along with the instructions that were used in the UNIX System port, Table 1 also lists some features that were not used.

The acs, jrng, and rrng instructions interface with the four-level ring protection scheme provided by the GMICRO. Since the UNIX System implementation only used portions of the ring protection scheme, those instructions were not used. The ldp and stp instructions can be very useful for loading to and storing from physical addresses on some systems. The UNIX System, however, has always had a simple method for accessing physical addresses by allocating a range of virtual addresses that map all possible physical addresses. Therefore, the ldp and stp instructions were not needed.

The GMICRO virtual memory space is divided into shared and unshared regions. The UNIX System memory management also divides its virtual memory area into shared and unshared regions, so it was much easier to design the software to take advantage of the hardware than it would have been with processors that support memory management in a different way.

TABLE 1. Memory Management Features

GMICRO Instruction	Function	UNIX System Features
acs	Test Access Right	Not Used
movpa	Move Physical Address	Kernel Debugger, Bootstrap, I/O using DMA
ldate	Load Address Translation Table Entry	Memory Management
state	Store Address Translation Table Entry	Memory Management
ldp	Load to Physical Address	Not Used
stp	Store From Physical Address	Not Used
ptlb	Purge Translation Lookaside Buffer	Memory Management
pstlb	Purge Specified Translation Lookaside Buffer Entries	Memory Management
jrng	Jump to Ring	Not Used
rrng	Return to Previous Ring	Not Used

Memory space is divided into sections that can be further divided into pages. While the page size is static (4K bytes), the section size can vary between 64K and 4M bytes. The GMICRO lets both section tables and page tables vary in size from 64 bytes to 4K bytes, but section tables are always sized at 2K bytes in the UNIX System.

Cutting tables down to the essential size saves memory and shortens table searches. Each process has two section tables available, one in the shared region of the memory and the other in the unshared region. The section table in the unshared region is part of the u-block, and specific to each distinct process. A single section table in the shared region is shared by all processes (see section 4.2).

The address translation mode is disabled when the kernel is being booted and when the kernel debugger is being used. These features require that address translation be mapped directly to the physical memory, which simplified software testing in the early stages of the port. Being able to run without address translation provided a firm foundation for the kernel debugger (*kdb*).

The *movpa* instruction is used in those instances when the address translation is disabled. It performs translation from a virtual to a physical memory address based on a specified translation context. Normally, when the UNIX System is running, virtual memory is used by enabling address translation. When the kernel is not in control of the system (when the standalone system or *kdb* is running), however, virtual memory is not available, so physical memory must be accessed directly.

The memory management unshared address translation was simple for *kdb*, because of the *movpa* address translation instruction on the GMICRO. Other architectures require a more complicated and slower process (looking through all the memory management tables, deciding whether an address is valid, and so on) to translate an address. The GMICRO can perform address translation in one instruction, using the unshared address translation base (UATB) as its only memory management argument. The simplicity of using this instruction made it easy to provide a *kdb* enhancement to allow for the examination of any arbitrary UNIX System process, which is a powerful debugging capability.

The GMICRO/200 provides four levels of protection in the form of rings: the innermost ring having the highest level of protection, and the outermost ring having the lowest. Currently, only two of the rings are used by the UNIX System, the innermost (ring 0) for all kernel processing, and the outermost (ring 3) for user-level processing. User processes cannot be allowed to write into the kernel memory space or into each other's memory spaces. The two rings used by the UNIX System on the GMICRO provide the necessary protections.

4.2 Process Management Support

Process management permits multiple processes to share the resources of the system at the same time. The hardware and the software participate in a complicated and highly cooperative effort to interrupt processes using the processor, schedule the processes, and assign priorities to the processes waiting to use the processor.

User programs obtain system services by entering the kernel and performing the functions for themselves. The executing process is divided into two parts, the *user code* and its *system code*, which is the process' own (logical) copy of the kernel.

The processes execute in one of two different modes, *kernel mode* or *user mode*. Switching between these modes is referred to as a *state change*. A *process switch* occurs when one process relinquishes control of the CPU, allowing another process to take control.

State changes can happen many times during execution, but process switches only occur when the current process cannot or may not continue executing (e.g., while waiting for an I/O operation to complete, or when the CPU time slice allocated to the process has expired).

Table 2 lists the GMICRO instructions that deal with process management. These instructions were used in the UNIX System port.

TABLE 2. Process Management Features

GMICRO Instruction	Function	UNIX System Features
ldc	Load Control Register	Kernel
stc	Store Control Register	Kernel
ldctx	Load Context	Kernel
stctx	Store Context	Kernel

The *ldctx* and *stctx* instructions facilitate the switching of processes, which is a feature of any multiprocessing operating system. Process switching is used so that each process will get its fair share of the CPU's time, since the CPU can be used by only one process at a time. The kernel manages the CPU's usage by scheduling processes to use it on a priority basis. Processes usually switch in and out of the CPU a number of times before they are completed.

The kernel uses two data structures to store information about active processes: the *process table* and the *u-block*. The process table stores information related to all processes that must be available when they're inactive (asleep or suspended), including the process priority, status flags, and the pending signal array. The u-block, on the other hand, stores information related to a process when it is active, such as open file descriptors, the stack to use when executing in kernel mode, and the root and current working directories. Since the u-block is only needed when the process is active, it can be swapped to disk when the process is inactive.

Delayed interrupts simplify the handling of multiple external interrupts and system calls by allowing drivers to defer non-critical interrupt processing by triggering a lower priority interrupt that is delayed until no higher priority interrupts are pending. Delayed interrupts are used by the serial communications drivers to support input at high baud rates. These are used for processing of serial I/O data that need not be performed at the high priority interrupt level.

The delayed context trap feature is used as an effective method for generating user program profiles. A delayed context trap is initiated by the clock interrupt handler when the interrupted user process is being profiled. When interrupt processing completes, the delayed context trap occurs, allowing for sampling of the user program counter. User program profiling is helpful when trying to determine where code can be optimized, etc.

4.3 Exception, Interrupt, and Trap Support

Exceptions, interrupts, and traps are events that cause the processor to stop executing the current instruction stream and begin executing another stream to handle the event. *Exceptions* are events that occur when there is a hardware or a program error. *Interrupts* are usually requests for service from I/O devices such as keyboards, printers, or disks. *Traps* are events requested by a program or exceptions that the processor handles when an instruction completes.

Normally, the UNIX System handles all EITs in the kernel. When the kernel debugger is running, some EITs are handled by *kdb*, transferring control from the kernel. They are also used to enter and exit the UNIX System kernel for privileged processing.

Table 3 lists the GMICRO instructions that deal with exceptions, interrupts, and traps. These instructions were used in the UNIX System port.

TABLE 3. Exception, Interrupt, and Trap Features

GMICRO Instruction	Function	UNIX System Features
trapa	Trap Always	Debugger Breakpoints, System Calls
reit	Return from Exception, Interrupt, or Trap Handler	Kernel Debugger, Kernel
wait	Set Interrupt Mask and Wait	Kernel (Idle Loop)

The EIT vector table holds entries for many handler routines, with three information-stacking formats, and up to 16 levels of interrupt masking. EITs are the means of transition from user mode to kernel mode. The vector number indicates the type of EIT that occurs. EIT's are identified in three basic groups: system calls, traps, and interrupts. The vectors provide a convenient and clean method for handling EITs; most architectures do not deal with EITs in this manner.

On the GMICRO, EITs can be processed by handlers that run with or without address translation enabled. The information that is stacked during an EIT event can be placed on either the ring 0 stack or the interrupt stack. This powerful feature simplified implementation of the kernel debugger, which uses physical mode addressing and the interrupt stack, while the kernel uses virtual mode addressing and the ring 0 stack.

The CPU saves detailed error information on the stack when an exception or trap involves memory access. The information saved includes address translation information, the access type, and sometimes address and data. The fact that the EIT vector number is automatically saved on the stack is a convenience not offered by some architectures. The error information that is saved helps to determine how to handle particular EIT events. Some RISC processors do not offer this type of automatic detailed error information. Instead, instructions must be issued to gather the error information from various locations in order to determine how to handle an EIT event.

The GMICRO *wait* instruction provides the UNIX System with a simple, one-instruction idle loop.

4.4 Programming Language Support

Most programming done by users is in a high-level programming language, such as C. Architectures can support programming languages by providing instructions that perform tasks usually required by high-level languages, such as string manipulation and loading of multiple registers. Another useful feature is when opcodes of the most common instructions have signed and unsigned variants and allow operands of different sizes. Providing these types of instructions makes compilation of high-level languages easier and leads to faster execution of programs.

Since most of the UNIX operating system is written in the C language, it makes sense that C is the programming language of choice on UNIX Systems. The INTERACTIVE development team implemented a complete C programming environment for the GMICRO.

Table 4 lists the GMICRO instructions that support high-level programming languages. These instructions were used in the UNIX System port.

TABLE 4. High-level Programming Language Features

GMICRO Instruction	Function	UNIX System Features
ldm	Load Multiple Registers	Kernel, Standalone System, Library Routines
stm	Store Multiple Registers	Kernel, Standalone System, Library Routines
smov	Copy String	Copy and String Library Routines
scmp	Compare String	Copy and String Library Routines
ssch	Search String	Copy and String Library Routines
sstr	Fill String	Copy and String Library Routines
bfextu	Extract Bit Field with Possible Zero Extension	C Compiler
bfinsu	Insert Bit Field with Possible Zero Extension	C Compiler

The INTERACTIVE developers used the multiple register instructions (*ldm* and *stm*) extensively throughout the kernel, libraries, and standalone system. These instructions allow multiple registers to be loaded and stored in one instruction, rather than having to load and store each register one at a time.

The string-manipulation instructions (*smov*, *ssch*, *scmp*, and *sstr*) provided a simple implementation for the copy and string-manipulation routines found in the various libraries. The developers chose to code particular routines in assembly language using these instructions rather than in C, because the assembly language would run faster. Given the string-manipulation instructions provided with the GMICRO, the *str*()* library routines were obvious candidates for hand coding. The *smov* instruction was used for structure assignment in C.

The use of the string instructions enabled the developers to produce simpler and shorter code than they would have been able to produce on a microprocessor that did not have these instructions. For example, the *strcmp()* routine for GMICRO looks like this:

```
        .export  _strcmp
_strcmp:
        ldm      @(4,sp),(r0,r1)  ; get s1 and s2
        cmp      r0,r1
        beq      done
        mov      #0,r2            ; go until mismatch or
        mov      #0,r3            ; .. a byte is 0
        scmp/eq.b
        beq      done
        mov      @(-1,r0).b,r0
        sub      @(-1,r1).b,r0
        rts
done:   mov      #0,r0
        rts
```

An equivalent routine for the Intel 386 takes about twice the number of lines as the GMICRO version, and uses a loop construction instead of a single compare instruction. In addition to being shorter, the GMICRO routine is easier to read and understand than the one produced for the 386; and hence easier to debug.

The bit field instructions (*bfextu* and *bfinsu*) were not used directly in the operating system, but are generated by INTERACTIVE's C compiler. The *bfextu* and *bfinsu* instructions are used for C language bit fields that are always unsigned values.

There are 16 general registers available on the GMICRO. Within a high-level language function, registers R0 through R3 are volatile, registers R4 through R13 are non-volatile (register variables), R14 is the frame pointer, and R15 is the stack pointer. Having this many general registers is a luxury not offered by older CISC microprocessor architectures.

The GMICRO provides a short format for frequently used instruction types. INTERACTIVE's assembler looks at the operands of particular instructions and determines which format of the instruction to issue. There is a table that outlines some criteria for determining which formats to use, but most of the work is done through a sophisticated branching mechanism.

Signed and unsigned operations work on data of different sizes (byte, halfword, and word). Any time the C compiler sees an instruction dealing with operands of different sizes, it can translate it into one assembly instruction. For example, the operation:

```
int i;
unsigned short u;
. . .
        i += u;
. . .
```

translates on the GMICRO to:

```
addu  @u.h,@i.w
```

while it needs two instructions on the Intel 386:

```
movzwl u,%eax
addl   %eax,i
```

GMICRO subroutine instructions can quickly create and delete stack frames and save and restore general registers. The *enter* instruction creates a stack frame and saves selected registers onto the stack. The *exitd* instruction restores the register information and returns from the routine.

5. PORTING MISMATCHES WITH THE GMICRO

The GMICRO microprocessor offered many features that eased the UNIX System porting task, but there were also a few features that were not used in the UNIX System porting task, and some features that were not used to the extent they might have been.

5.1 Four-level Ring Protection

The GMICRO provides memory protection by arranging four levels of protection in four concentric circles. The closer the rings are to the center, the more privileged they are. Since the UNIX System has two levels of protection (system and user), only two of the GMICRO ring levels were used. The developers used the inner ring (ring 0) to support the system level and the outer ring (ring 3) to support the user level. The two middle rings were not used for the UNIX System port, though they might be useful when trying to emulate other operating systems, like BTRON. INTERACTIVE UNIX provides a similar type of operating system emulation for DOS via the VP/ix* utility, which runs on the Intel 386.

The GMICRO provides the *jrng* and *rrng* instructions to transfer control from one ring to another. These instructions are a natural choice for implementing system calls, but they were not used in the UNIX System port. The *jrng* instruction generates a stack frame that differs from those generated by EIT events, which was undesirable because it would require the kernel to handle both the EIT stack frame and the *jrng* stack frame. Instead, the *trapa* instruction was used for system calls because it causes an EIT event, generating an EIT stack frame. Thus, the kernel only needs to support a single stack frame format.

The two unused protection rings that the GMICRO provides are unavailable to the UNIX System user; the *jrng* and *rrng* instructions are illegal instructions, as they are not supported. These rings could be used on a UNIX System, but they would require kernel support not provided in the current implementation.

5.2 Queue Manipulation Instructions

Queues provide a convenient way to construct and maintain ordered lists of items. The GMICRO supports three powerful queue instructions (*qins*, *qdel*, and *qsch*) that allow the insertion of an item into a queue, the deletion of an item from a queue, and the search for an item in a queue, respectively.

Though the UNIX System uses queues (most notably the kernel scheduler queue), it was not possible to take advantage of the GMICRO queue manipulation instructions. The port did not use the queue instructions mainly because they do not equate to any primitives in the C language. It is difficult to map a sequence of C queue manipulation instructions to just one assembly instruction and the overhead for a procedure call would negate any performance advantage. Pointers are widely used in C. Queues are created in C by using pointers. It would be difficult, if not impossible, for the C compiler to tell when to insert the queue instructions and when to just leave the pointers as they are. There are also no UNIX System kernel assembly language functions or library functions that can take advantage of these powerful instructions. These queue manipulation instructions might be useful with programs that are written mostly in assembly language, or in a high-level language containing queuing primitives.

5.3 Floating Point Coprocessor

The GMICRO supports an IEEE-compatible Floating Point coprocessor, or FPU. When the UNIX System kernel switches execution from one process to the next, all state information must be saved for the old process and restored for the new one. Floating point state information contains as much as 300 bytes, more than half of the total state information. The developers discovered a way to circumvent the need to repeatedly save and restore the floating point state for most process switches.

The coprocessor identity field (*cpid*) of the process status word (PSW) allows the kernel to recognize processes that use the FPU. When a process accesses the FPU for the first time (detected by a coprocessor disconnection exception), it is marked as a floating point process, and only then does its floating point state information get saved and restored. This happens at process switch time. Since most UNIX System commands do not use floating point, this performance improvement usually manifests itself at process switching time.

SUMMARY

The INTERACTIVE development team greatly appreciated the advantages offered by the GMICRO/200 processor. The GMICRO/200 is a powerful processor that is well-suited to supporting the UNIX operating system. Many of the approaches taken by the GMICRO/200 designers in the areas of memory management, process management, EIT, and programming language support are similar to those taken by the UNIX operating system, thus easing the task of designers and developers, and letting the designers use powerful GMICRO instructions to make the system more efficient.

Advances in the semiconductor industry have made it attractive to produce multiprocessor systems. The UNIX System has been ported to some multiprocessor systems in the past, and standards are actively being developed. The GMICRO provides the necessary features for multiprocessor systems, such as instructions with bus lock and write-through caches. Such a multiprocessor system would be a very powerful computer. A UNIX System for a GMICRO multiprocessor would be an interesting area for future development.

Table 5 summarizes the GMICRO instructions and where they were used in the UNIX System implementation on the GMICRO/200.

TABLE 5. GMICRO Features Used by the UNIX System

GMICRO Instruction	Function	UNIX System Features
movpa	Move Physical Address	Kernel Debugger, Bootstrap, I/O using DMA
ldate	Load Address Translation Table Entry	Memory Management
state	Store Address Translation Table Entry	Memory Management
ptlb	Purge Translation Lookaside Buffer	Memory Management
pstlb	Purge Specified Translation Lookaside Buffer Entries	Memory Management
ldc	Load Control Register	Kernel
stc	Store Control Register	Kernel
ldctx	Load Context	Kernel
stctx	Store Context	Kernel
trapa	Trap Always	Debugger Breakpoints, System Calls
reit	Return from Exception, Interrupt, or Trap Handler	Kernel Debugger, Kernel
wait	Set Interrupt Mask and Wait	Kernel (Idle Loop)
ldm	Load Multiple Registers	Kernel, Standalone System, Library Routines
stm	Store Multiple Registers	Kernel, Standalone System, Library Routines
smov	Copy String	Copy and String Library Routines
scmp	Compare String	Copy and String Library Routines
ssch	Search String	Copy and String Library Routines
sstr	Fill String	Copy and String Library Routines
bfextu	Extract Bit Field with Possible Zero Extension	C Compiler
bfinsu	Insert Bit Field with Possible Zero Extension	C Compiler

ACKNOWLEDGEMENTS

The authors would like to thank the developers, integrators, testers, and documentation writers at INTERACTIVE Systems Corporation who worked hard to port the UNIX System to the GMICRO/200. We would also like to thank Larry Phillips and Fred Simmons of INTERACTIVE and William Homan of HMSI for keeping us on track. Thanks also to Peter Reiher for his assistance in reviewing early drafts of this paper and to Steve Zucker for his thorough review. We would especially like to thank Fujitsu, Hitachi, and Mitsubishi for creating the GMICRO/200, and giving us the opportunity to port the UNIX System to their microprocessor.

REFERENCES

[1] K. Sakamura, "Architecture of the TRON VLSI CPU," *IEEE Micro*, Vol. 7, No. 2, pp. 17-31, April 1987.

[2] K. Sakamura, "TRON VLSI CPU: Concepts and Architecture," *TRON Project 1987*, Springer-Verlag, Tokyo, pp. 200-308, 1987.

[3] *Design Specification: UNIX System V Release 3 for the GMICRO Single Board Computer System*, INTERACTIVE Systems Corporation, December 1988.

[4] *UNIX System V Release 3 System Administrator's Guide*, AT&T, 1987.

[5] *UNIX System V Release 3 Programmer's Guide*, AT&T, 1987.

[6] *Hitachi 32-bit Microprocessor H32/200 Operation and Architecture Manual*, Hitachi, Ltd., December 1987.

[7] *Hitachi 32-bit Microprocessor H32/200 Programming Manual*, Hitachi, Ltd., December 1987.

324

Cathleen Reiher is a Member of the Technical Staff at INTERACTIVE Systems Corporation. After graduating with a B.A. in Linguistics from the University of California at Los Angeles in 1982, Ms. Reiher spent three years as a member of the technical publications department at INTERACTIVE. In 1986, she spent the fall semester teaching English at Fudan University in Shanghai, People's Republic of China, and returned to INTERACTIVE in 1987.

William P. Taylor has been a Principle Member of the Technical Staff for INTERACTIVE Systems Corporation since 1985. Prior to joining INTERACTIVE Systems Corporation he worked at Lawrence Livermore National Laboratory and at Quotron Systems, Inc. Mr. Taylor received his B.S. in Computer Science from the University of California at Berkeley in 1975 and his M.S. in Computer Science from the University of California at Davis in 1977.

The authors may be reached at INTERACTIVE Systems Corporation, 2401 Colorado Avenue, Third Floor, Santa Monica, California, 90404, USA.

SRM32: Implementation of Symbolic ROM Monitor on GMICRO F32 Series

Yoshitaka Kimura, Hiroshi Shida, Shigeru Sasaki
FUJITSU DEVICES INC.

Haruyasu Ito
FUJITSU LIMITED

ABSTRACT

This paper describes the implementation of the Symbolic ROM Monitor for GMICRO F32 series (hereinafter called SRM32) which interfaces to the architecture of the GMICRO F32 series CPU.

SRM32 is a symbolic debugger which operates user programs on the target system (hereinafter called the target) using the GMICRO F32 series CPU based on TRON specifications in realtime and directly uses symbols of the source program.

The GMICRO F32 series CPU provides a self-debug support function by which enable debuggers to be effectively created. By utilizing the best effort of this self-debug support function, SRM32 provides the function of step execution of programs and various types of break function.

This paper outlines SRM32 first and then describes the method of using the architecture of the GMICRO F32 series CPU. Finally, this paper describes examples of SRM32 implementation and possible future developments.

Keywords: Symbolic Debugger, Exception Interrupt Trap(EIT), EIT Vector Base(EITVB), Return from EIT handler(REIT), Self debug Trap.

1. INTRODUCTION

1.1 Configuration of SRM32

Figure 1 shows the configuration of SRM32 operation.

SRM32 consists of the SRM32 host, operating on the host system (hereinafter called the host), and the SRM32 monitor, operating on the target.

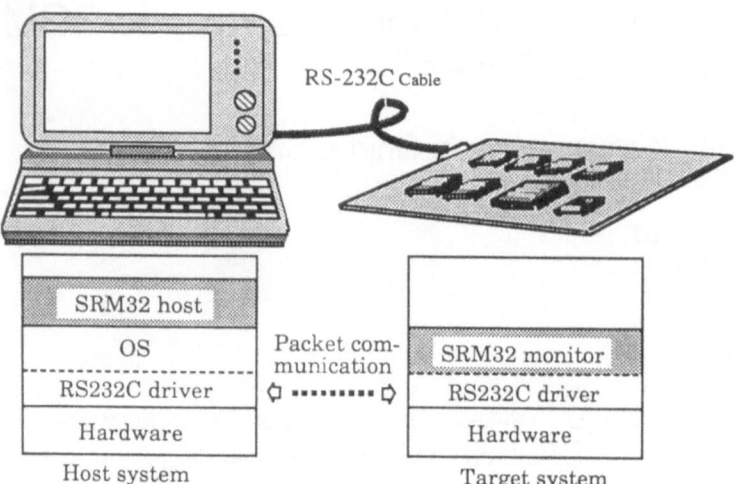

SRM32 host			
OS	Packet com-	SRM32 monitor	
RS232C driver	munication	RS232C driver	
Hardware		Hardware	
Host system		Target system	

Figure 1 Configuration of SRM32 operation

The host requires approximately 400 KB of memory and operates under the control of the host operating system. The monitor requires approximately 24 KB of ROM and approximately 4 KB of RAM. In addition to these areas, the monitor requires an RS232C communication port, as well as the driver for the port.

The SRM32 host controls all man-machine interfaces and analyzes commands entered by the users. It also uses packet communication and requests the monitor to execute the entered commands through the communication port.
The monitor executes the requested command and returns the execution result to the host. After receiving the result, the host processes the data and displays it.

Thus the SRM32 host and the monitor cooperate to execute a command.

The communication between the host and monitor is only made through the RS232C port.

Therefore, the host can be implemented in any personal computers and workstations having an RS232C interface, and the monitor can be implemented in various targets. The internal structure of the SRM32 was designed considering this implementation. Currently, the host is implemented in machines which work under MS-DOS, MS OS/2[1], and SunOS[2].

Figure 2 shows an example of SRM32 memory map.

---

[1] MS-DOS and MS OS/2 are registered trademarks of Microsoft Corporation, U.S.A.

[2] SunOS is a registered trademark of Sun Microsystems Corporation.

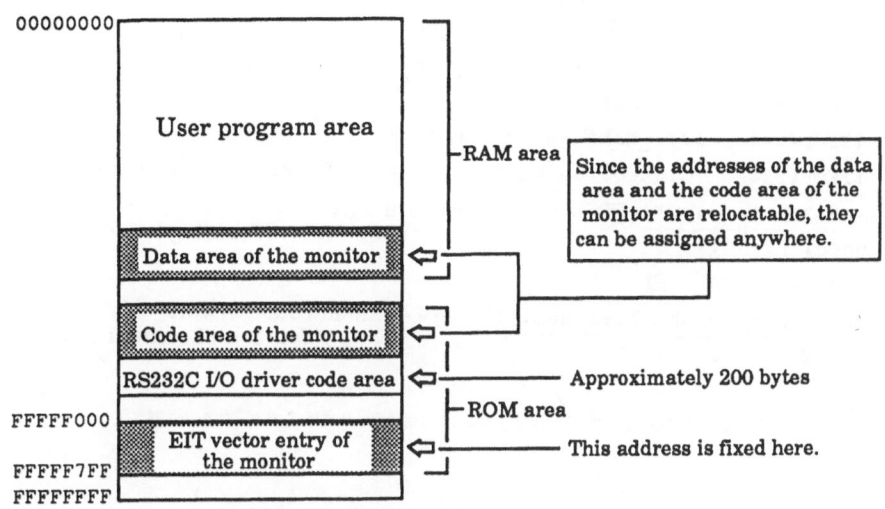

Figure 2 Example of SRM32 memory map

1.2 Features

This paragraph shortly describes the features of SRM32.

(a) Symbolic debug

By storing the symbol information at the host side, SRM32 can perform a symbolic debug function using symbols included in a source program written in assembler or C.

Laptop-type computers or notebook-type computers can be used as the host. In appearance, SRM32 is the same as stand alone debugger (ROM monitor or ROM debugger) using the dumb terminal for the console. However, if a debugger uses the dumb terminal, the debugger in ROM has to handle all the debug operations and the dumb terminal is used only to display the results on the screen. This restricts memory and communication speed and causes difficulty of the implementation for handling symbols.

To solve such problems, SRM32 adopts a low-cost, compact personal computer or workstation as a console in place of the dumb terminal. Besides, each command operation is prepared at the host side as much as possible, while the minimum required functions are performed at the target side.

Therefore, SRM32 can support symbolic debug function using source program symbols, as well as the regular debug function based on program address and register value.

```
SRM32>s 4⏎    ----- Execution of 4-line step
%TEMP#903    if( intrs( ptr ) == ERROR )   /* intro set */
%TEMP#941 intrs( ptr)
%TEMP#944    if( _dskflag == OFF )   {
%TEMP#948    _disktbl.unitnam = *( ptr + UTNAP );/* unit name set */
SRM32>m !  dskflag⏎ ----- Reference of data
                              (The content of dskflag is 1.)
00001001   01
00001002   00  .⏎
SRM32>m !  disktbl.secnum, 1⏎ ----- Modification of data
                                     (Set disktbl.secnum to 1.)
SRM32>
```

Figure 3 Sampled debug image of program written in C language

Also, since SRM32 allows various operations on the host, such as programming, compiling, assembling and linking, a series of operations in addition to debugging can be executed in the host computer.

Figure 3 shows the debug image of the program written in C.

(b) Support for EIT processing

The SRM32 monitors an EIT event generated during the execution of a user program.

(c) Various break functions

The SRM32 supports the following breaks: breaks (two) caused by the instruction break register, breaks (two[*1]) caused by the operand break register, and software breaks (16) caused by the exclusive "RIE" instruction. In addition, SRM32 supports a break caused by calling SRM32 directly from the user program. It also supports a forced break as an optional function by the abort switch on the target system.

(d) Support of registered space

SRM32 supports all logical, physical and control spaces in the CPU.

(e) Stub function support

While a user program is being executed, SRM32 can tentatively execute another user program or command. SRM32 contains 16 stub points and can support functions such as replacement of an undefined routine, batch processing, snap shot, and so on.

[*1] Only one break point is supported by GMICRO 200.

(f) Interruption release

No interrupt is possessed by the SRM32. The SRM32 releases all of the interrupts executed by the CPU for the user.

(g) Indication of system fault information

For the GMICRO 200/300 , information on system faults that occurred while debugging can be identified by using the function provided by the CPU.

(h) Program load/save

The SRM32 can download object programs created in the host (in load module format) to the target RAM via the RS232C interface. On the other way around the SRM32 can save object programs (memory images) on the target into the host as files.

1.3 SRM32 Commands

The SRM32 command structure was designed to be compatible with other debuggers for the GMICRO᠈ software simulator (hereinafter referred to as the simulator) and host emulator (ICE) (hereinafter referred to as the emulator). In addition, this command structure supports command name changes, command additions, and command macros, so that SRM32 can support self debugging of the operating system based on the ITRON specifications. Table 1 lists the 56 commands that SRM32 supports.

2. SRM32 IMPLEMENTATION

2.1 SRM32 Operating Environment

SRM32 is operated in the environment as follows :

1) Ring level   0
2) Operation mode   Physical mode
3) Stack in use   Interrupt stack (SPI)

The TRON specification based CPU provides a four-stage memory protection function according to the ring level. A low-order ring level cannot access a high-order ring level. Only when the ring level is set to 0, the CPU privileged instructions are used or all registers are accessed. Since a debugger must be able to access all registers, SRM32 is operated at the ring level of 0.

The SRM32 is operated in the physical mode. For details, see Support Method between Logical and Physical Areas.

Table 1 SRM32 commands

Function		Command name abbreviation	Function		Command name abbreviation
Break			**Register operation (CPU, FPU)**		
	Instruction break	BI		Display and setup of register	R
	Operand break	BO			
	Software break	BSI	**File operation**		
Program execution				Program load	LD
	Continuous execution	G		Program save	SV
	Continuous execution with instruction break	GBI		Content verification between file and memory	VF
	Step execution	S			
	Execution of step around	SA	**Symbol operation**		
Assemble				Scope display	SCP
	1-line assemble	A		Symbol display	SY
	Disassemble	DA		Addition and deletion of symbol	CS
				Symbol value reset	ES
Memory operation			**Utility**		
	Display	D		OS command execution	!
	Change	M		Submit processing	SBT
	Comparison	CMP		Setup and display of screen output mode	EC
	Initialization	FIL		Prompt setup	SPP
	Block transfer	MOV		Specification of command execution history file	LOG
	Data search	SCH		Command help	H
				Calculation function	V
Equipment				Indication of comment	;
	Setup and display of debug level	DL		End of SRM32	EX
	Setup of subroutine execution environment	CE	**Control command**		
	Replacement of command	DF		IF command	IF
	Setup and display of radix	RA		REPEAT command	REPEAT
	Deletion and display and simulated set up instruction	SB		WHILE command	WHILE
	Display of character string and formula	PRT	**Disk operation**		
	Changes of display of address translation table	MTT		Disk read	RD
	Display and initialization of timer value	TI		Disk write	WD
	Setup and display of execution mode	EM		Disk format	FD
	Logical address check	AC		Disk check	CD
	Copy of EIT vector	VC		Disk boot	BD
	Change of EIT and JRNG vector display	VS		Disk boot image write	BWD
	Display of system fault information	ST			
	Environment initialization	INIT			
	Register initialization	IR			

The TRON specification based CPU provides stack pointers SP0, SP1, SP2, and SP3 and interruption stack pointer SPI. They are arranged according to ring level. Stack pointers SP0 and SPI are used by the program operated at the ring level of 0. However, SRM32 uses SPI, because of the correlation between system programs such as the OS and the debugger. Therefore, SP0 to SP3 can be used freely by the user, but SPI is shared with the user.

2.2 User Programs Notification

Since SRM32 is operated at the ring level of 0, in the dispatch operation to the user program, both the ring level and the PC are required to switch.

Although the TRON specification CPU has various instructions which change the PC such as jump instruction, jump subroutine instruction, return subroutine instruction, trap instruction, and jump ring instruction, these instructions cannot switch the ring from high-order level to low-order level.

The following two types of instruction allow the ring to be switched from the high-order level to low order level: "RRNG: Return from internal RiNG" instruction, and "REIT:Return from EIT handler" instruction which is a return instruction from EIT.

Out of user's PSW information stored in the stack, only PSH and RNG information are reflected to PSW in the "RRNG"instruction. Therefore SRM32 notifies the user program using the "REIT" instruction.

Control can be transferred to the user program in the following sequence: setup of the user program information for execution in a dummy stack frame for the "REIT" instruction that the SRM32 has created in the user SPI, specification of instruction reexecution type for reserved instruction exception at the EITINF[*1] in the stack frame, execution of the "REIT" instruction, and then branching to the address specified by the PC (start address of the user program) on the dummy SPI. Figure 4 shows a dispatch image of the control to the user program.

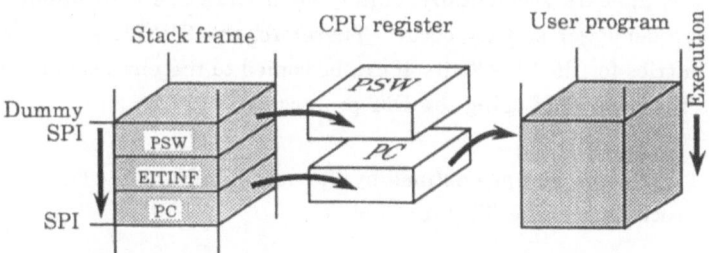

Figure 4 User program notification(Use of REIT instruction)

[*1] EITINF indicates EIT information.

2.3 Processing of EIT(Exception, Interrupt, Trap)

The TRON specification based CPU can provide several EIT tables and determines which EIT table is to be used, according to the EITVB[*2] register.

Figure 5 shows the operation flow of the TRON specification based CPU from occurrence of an EIT event to the processing program.

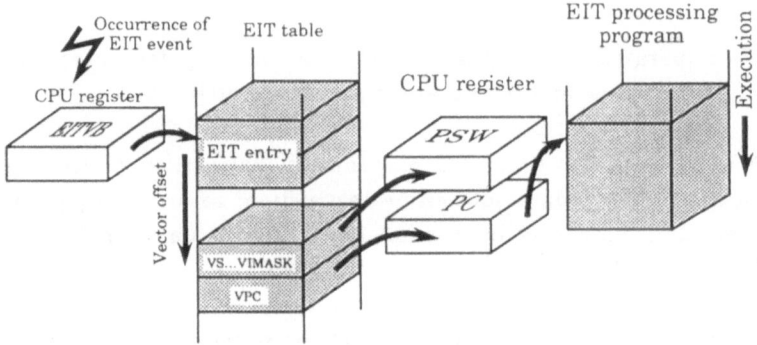

Figure 5 Flow of EIT processing

Because the ordinary CPU can provide only one EIT table, EIT entry used by the debugger can't be used by user, therefore, EIT can't be fully supported by self-debugger. However, the SRM32 fully supports the EIT processing by making full use of the CPU functions. SRM32 has its own EIT table. This table is used when SRM32 is performing the operation. The entries of the EIT handler for the SRM32 are set in this table. Upon dispatch to the user program, the EIT table address is set in the EITVB as well. This allows SRM32 to define EIT processing independently from the user program.

The number of EIT entries is 255 and user programs don't always guarantee to define all the entries strictly. Many users strongly request definition of the EIT processing in later processes according to their needs. Furthermore, there is a case where an EIT, that is not expected to occur, appears accidentally. Many such EITs are convenient if they can be monitored by the debugger as they occur. Therefore, the SRM32 supports a function by which the EIT entries for the SRM32 itself can be copied to the entries of the user EIT table. Figure 6 shows the method of using the EIT processing.

The user uses EIT entries that are defined by the user him/herself. The user can leave the undefined EIT processing to the SRM32.

[*2] EITVB indicates EIT vector base register.

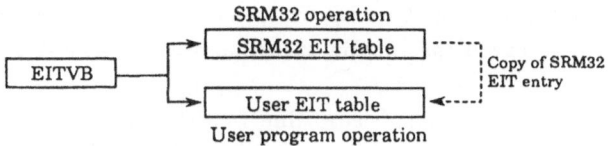

Figure 6 Use of SRM32 EIT processing program

```
SRM32>G ⏎
EIT 17: Bus access exception
(FORMAT)  Format No:1 EIT type:4 EIT vector:11
(PSW)     SM:0 RNG:0 AT:0 DB:0 IMASK:0 PRNG:0 CPIO:0 F:0 X:0 V:0 L:0 M:0 Z:0
(PC)      00002398
(EXPC)    00002398
(IOINF)   NWR:0 ATEL:0 ATEC:0 NAT:1 BL:0 RD:1 BAT:0 SIZ:4
(ERADOR)  FFC00000
(ERDATA)  000000CE
SRM32>
```

Figure 7 Screen output when EIT (Bus Access Exception) occurs

If an EIT occurs, the SRM32 outputs detailed information to the host display to indicate occurrence of an EIT and awaits a command. Figure 7 shows a sample display output when a bus access interrupt occurs. Support of this function enables faults contained in the user programs to be rapidly found and investigated.

2.4 Software Breaks

Software breaks are supported by intentionally embedding an instruction to generate an EIT event at an address to break and making the CPU execute this address.

Although the ordinary CPU uses the software interrupt instruction ("SWI" or "INT" instruction etc.) to achieve this software break, the SRM32 uses an instruction, which is common to the TRON specification based CPU, called "RIE:raise Reserved Instruction Exception." This generates the reserved instruction exception.

This "RIE" instruction is designed to implement the self debugger and advantages such that all entries of the CPU internal interruptions are released to the user, compared with the existing "SWI" and "INT" instructions.

Factors to generate the reserved instruction exception are not limited to execution of the "RIE" instruction. If a reserved instruction exception occurs, SRM32 checks the cause of the occurrence.

If a reserved instruction exception occurs due to the "RIE" instruction, the SRM32 executes a software break and outputs a message indicating the processing. If a reserved instruction exception occurs due to other factors, the SRM32 outputs the normal EIT (reserved instruction exception) information and awaits command entry.

2.5 Support Procedure of Logical and Physical Spaces

The TRON specification based CPU provides a mode in which it operates using physical addresses and a mode in which it operates using logical addresses. According to the user programs, both physical address mode (hereinafter called physical mode) and logical address mode (hereinafter called logical mode) can be used.

Therefore, the debugger must support both logical mode and physical mode.

To offer this function, it is assumed that the debugger operates in logical mode when a user program is executed in logical mode, and in the physical mode when the user program is executed in physical mode. However, this causes the address translation table to be shared and results in an increase in restrictions on the debugger's functions. Since the TRON specification based CPU provides the "MOVPA: Move Physical Address" instruction, which converts a logical address into a physical address, the SRM32 can support both modes by converting a logical address into a physical address using the "MOVPA" instruction internally. Figure 8 shows the processing image of a logical address.

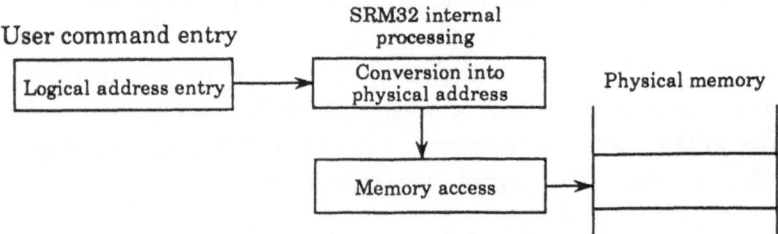

Figure 8   Logical address processing

3. EFFECTIVE USE OF GMICRO F32 SERIES DEBUG SUPPORT

Compared with ordinary CPUs, the GMICRO F32 series CPU provides more powerful debugging support.

This chapter describes the contents of this debugging support and how to effectively use the function with the SRM32.

3.1 Debug Support Function

The GMICRO F32 series CPU supports debugging of the user program by generating the self debug trap intentionally.
The following two conditions enable the self debug trap.

1) The debug mode bit (DB) of the processor status register must be set to 1.
   PSW: [| DB |]

2) The applicable bit of the debug control register must be set to 1.

The self debug trap does not occur unless the above two conditions are satisfied.

The debug register is described below. As shown in Figure 9, the debug registers are divided into the following three types: debug control registers, instruction break registers and operand break registers. In the GMICRO F32/100,/200,/300 , there are slight difference in the debug registers.

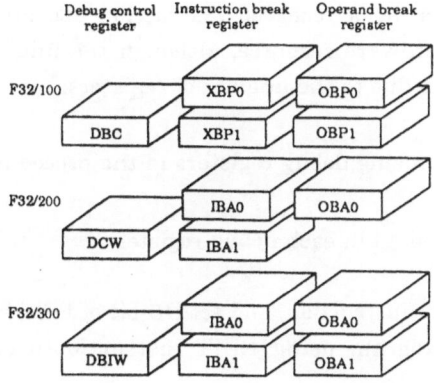

Figure 9 Configurationof GMICRO F32 Series debug register

1) Debug Control Registers (DBC, DCW, DBIW)
   These registers set up the debug conditions. When the self debug trap occurs, the events are reflected to these registers.

2) Instruction Break Register(IBA0/1, XBP0/1)

When the address set in these registers is matched with the execution address (PC) of the instruction and the instruction is executed, the self debug trap occurs. The GMICRO F32/100, /200 and /300 contain two registers respectively.

3) Operand Break Registers (OBA0/1, OBP0/1)

When the instruction accesses an operand at the address set by these registers, the (operand access) self debug trap occurs. The GMICRO F32/200 provides one register, while the GMICRO F32/100 and /300 provide two registers.

The following functions can be offered by using these registers.
   1) One-step execution
   2) Instruction break at the specified address
   3) Operand access break at the specified address

Together with these functions, the following functions can be offered.
   1) Instruction break of the program in ROM
   2) Individual operand break at memory read or write

3.2 Utilization of Debug Support Function in SRM32

SRM32 offeres single step program execution, instruction break, and operand break, utilizing these internal registers as mentioned above.

Another break method, such as software break, is offered by setting "RIE"instruction at specified address and generating a reserved instruction exception. Therefore, software break is not restricted by hardware resource, although the number of instruction break and operand break are limited due to the number of registers.

SRM32 offeres break function using debug registers in the procedure as shown below:

   1) Set an address and a data in each debug register
   2) Set user context
   3) Form a stack for REIT instruction, and set DB-bit of PSW in the stack to "1"
   4) Dispatch to user program using REIT instruction(user program is executed debug mode)
   5) Execution of user program
   6) Generate a self debug trap
   7) Output the respective messages and break

Thus, break functions, which used to be offered only by an emulator, can be offered very easily by utilizing GMICRO F32 series CPU's debug support function.

4. COMPARISON WITH OTHER DEBUG TOOLS

The GMICRO F32 series provides a simulator, an emulator, and self-debuggers (EMS[*1] and SRM32) which operate in the target. They are used to debug user programs. All these debuggers have both advantages and disadvantages. So each debugger is used depending on the debug phase respectively.

At first we compare the SRM32 with the simulator and the emulator, and then discuss the difference between the SRM32 and the EMS, which are both self-debuggers.

The simulator allows the host computer to simulate CPU operation using software and the program can be debugged to a certain degree, even if the actual target system is not existing. Although the simulator is very convenient at early stages of software development, it cannot be used for realtime debugging.

The emulator solves this problem. Because the emulator executes the program representatively of the CPU in the target system, it provides advanced functions such as realtime debugging. However, the emulator is very expensive and is difficult to connect to the hardware (physically). It is also difficult to perform each type of setup that depends on the target system. The more the frequency goes up, the more sensitive the emulator operation becomes due to the length of interface cable and other factors. That is, the emulator is largely restricted by operation and maintenance after the software has been completely developed.

The SRM32 covers those areas where the emulator is not good at. The price is low. All the targets can install the SRM32. The interfacing for the communication is only by an RS232C cable. And SRM32 can be kept in the target as a maintenance monitor even after the software development is completed. However, the SRM32 is inferior to the emulator in terms of functions provided.

Table 2 shows the differences between the simulator, the emulator and the SRM32, from the viewpoint of program types which can be debugged.

Table 2 Programs that can be debugged by different debuggers

Program type	SRM32	Emulator	Simulator
Interruption processing program	O	O	Δ
Device driver	Δ	O	×
Initialization program	Δ	O	Δ
Program other than the above	O	O	O

O : Debug allowed
Δ : Debug allowed except for a part of the program
× : Debug not allowed

[*1] EMS is the shortened form of Executive Monitor System.

4.1 Differences from the Viewpoint of Programs that can be Debugged

Since the simulator performs all the process in the host, interrupts are not fully supported. The simulator is marked with Δ for debugging the interrupt program. Besides, for the initialization program, the simulator can support a memory initialization program only, but cannot support I/O and other initialization programs. This program is therefore marked with Δ.

Although the SRM32 is considered to be basically capable of debugging all programs, it cannot debug programs that do not guarantee the operation of the SRM32, i.e., the initialization program for the RS232C port that the SRM32 uses for communication with the host and the device driver for this port. The initialization program is therefore marked with Δ.

Because the emulator monitors the CPU by hardware and controls CPU operation from an external circuit, it can debug all programs.

4.2 Difference between Debug Tools from the Viewpoints of Characteristics and Price

Table 3 shows the difference of debug tools from the viewpoint of their characteristics, price and so on.

Table 3 Total comparison of debuggers

Item	SRM32	Emulator	Simulator
Realtime debug	Possible*1	Possible	Not allowed
Price	Less expensive	Expensive	Less expensive
Physical connection	RS232C cable only	Complexed due to insertion and extraction of the CPU, connectionof the CPU cable, etc.	Unnecessary
Area of installation	Target only	Target and emulator	Unnecessary
Target system	Necessary	Necessary (Can debug to some degrees without the target system.)	Unnecessary
Mounting in the target system/maintenance	Possible	Not allowed	Not allowed
Application to multiple debug sets	Comparatively easy	Difficult	— — —

*1 Because the SRM32 must execute an internal routine, an internal small overhead is incurred when an execution break occurs in the program.

Although the emulator is excellent from the viewpoint of program debugging, the SRM32 is excellent from the viewpoint of price / performance ratio.

Besides, since the SRM32 can be physically connected to other equipment easily and takes up little space, it can be handled easily in general.

If the above three types of debug tools are to be used effectively, they should be used as follows: the simulator is used at a level where the target is not provided or at the program unit debug / test level; the emulator is used when the hardware debug of the target is taken place or completed or to confirm the basic operation of the program when the program connection test is performed; the SRM32 is used when multiple targets are provided or when the operation test of the program is performed or the program is in execution.

4.3 Comparison between SRM32 and EMS

EMS is a self-debugger on GMICRO's SBC specified with VME bus. It requires a dumb terminal for console input / output in addition to SBC. Table 4 shows differences between SRM32 and EMS from the viewpoint of configuration and debugging capability.

Table 4 Comparison of configuration and debug ability

Item		SRM32	EMS
Implementation on various targets		Possible	Impossible
Required memory size	target	ROM:24KB RAM:4KB	ROM:256KB RAM:96KB
	host	About 400KB	---- ---- ----
Required hardware except target		Host system	Dumb terminal
C language source code level debugging		Possible	Impossible
Symbolic debugging		Possible	Impossible
Means of program loading (except host system)		Disk system	Disk system & Ethernet
Comparison of execution commands	step execution	Possible	Possible
	execution of step around*1	Possible	Impossible
	stub execution*2	Possible	Impossible
	instruction/operand break	Possible	Possible

*1: Execution of step around means executing subroutine jump instruction as one step.
*2: Stub execution means function of simulated execution.

As shown in Table 4, EMS almost satisfies functions of assembler level debugger, but it doesn't have the capability of C language source code level debugging, and also it's only for SBC. EMS can't be implemented on another target systems.

The development purpose of SRM32 is to overcome some weak points of EMS, and offer low priced, portable C language source code level debugger for GMICRO F32 series.

5. EXAMPLE OF SRM32 IMPLEMENTATION

The host and the SRM32 monitor are portable. The following implementation example assumes that the notebook-type MS-DOS personal computer FMR-50NB1 is used as the host, the F32/200 evaluation board, which contains GMICRO F32 CPU as well as bunch of family peripheral LSIs, is used as the target. Table 5 shows the specifications of the F32/200 evaluation board. Photo 1 shows the implement sample of SRM32.

Table 5 Specifications of F32/200 evaluation board

Item	Specifications
CPU	• F32/200 20 MHz • Data bus/address bus 32 bits
CPG	• F32/200 clock pulse generator
FPU	• F32/FPU 20 MHz Coprocessor mode
IRC	• F32/IRC IRH operation
TAGM	• F32 tag memory 1024 entries x 2 ways
DMAC	• F32/DMAC subchannel mode
Cache memory	• 8 KB Write through method
UART	• 8251 compatible products x 2 (MB89371)
TIMER	• 8254 compatible product
RAM	• DRAM 1 MB
ROM	• EPROM 128 KB

Photo 1 Implement sample of SRM32

a) Host

Figure 10 shows the configuration of the host to implement.

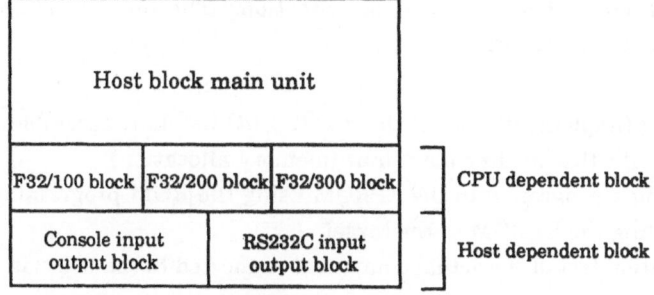

Figure 10 Configuration of SRM32 host

To enhance the portability, the SRM32 host is written in C. By modifying the console input output block and RS232C input output block as shown on Fig11 depending on the host OS, the implementation on another host can be done. The flow of actual operations is shown below.

1) Creation of keyboard I/O block and RS232C I/O block (coding and compilation)
2) Link with the host main unit
3) Connection of the target equipped with the SRM32 monitor block to the host via the RS232C interface
4) Actual operation test of the equipment

In addition, the host is developed using standard I/O functions only. This allows the equipment adopting the same operating system to be operated as the host. For example, in case of personal computers, all the PCs which work under MS-DOS can handle this host role.

The host is unified for all GMICRO F32 series CPUs, F32/100, /200, /300. The CPU type is determined when the SRM32 is activated. If the CPU-dependent block is expanded, an additional high-order CPU of GMICRO can be easily supported.

b) Monitor

As shown in Figure 1, the monitor block is divided into the monitor main unit and the RS232C driver, i.e., the target dependent block. Implementation on another target is done simply by rewriting this RS232C driver.

Although the F32/200 evaluation board mentioned above uses MB89371 which is an 8251 compatible product as an RS232C UART device, the GMICRO 100 SBC, based on the VME base specification uses M5M8251, and the GMICRO 200 SBC and GMICRO 300 SBC use HD64941. Implementation to the monitor was easily done because their specifications are not very different from the 8251 specification. The flow of actual operations for implementation is shown below.

1) Coding (implementation) of the RS232C I/O handler, assemble
2) Link with the monitor main unit (memory allocation)
3) Writing a program into the EPROM using the ROM programmer, and then installing the EPROM in the target
4) Operation test of the actual equipment connected to the host via the RS232C cable

The monitor block is written in C as far as possible as in the case of the host block to increase the implementation capability. However, the register operation block and EIT handler are written in assembler.
Actually, implementation of the above host requires changing approximately 30 steps, and implementation of the monitor requires changing approximately 20 steps.

As mentioned above, the SRM32 is excellent in implementation and has been operated with the GMICRO F32 SBC board based on the VME bus specification and GMICRO F32 training tools. Photo 1 shows a sample implementation of the SRM32 on a notebook-type personal computer and F32/200 evaluation board. Because no emulator is used, the debug environment is very simple and saves space.

6. FUTURE DEVELOPMENTS

Personal computers and work stations have already used the SRM32, and the GMICRO F32/100,/200,/300 are completely supported. In addition, the symbolic debug functions have been offered. As the next step, an enhancement of C source code level debug function and multi--window support are now going on. The multi-window operating environment is planned to be supported by MS OS/2 and SunOS. A high-order CPU of GMICRO F32 series is also to be supported. Figure 11 shows a screen image of the multi-window environment in SunOS.

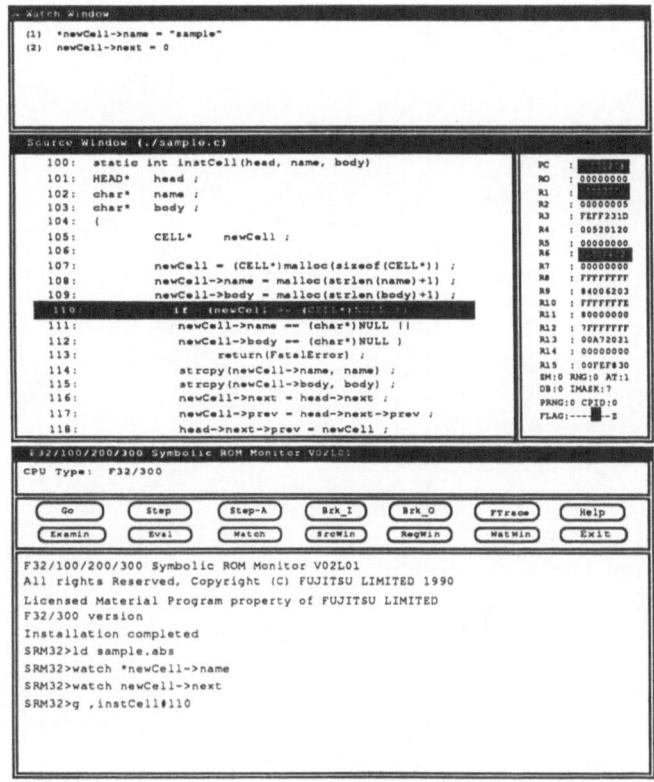

Figure 11 SRM32 Multi-window screen image

ACKNOWLEDGMENTS

The authors would like to thank the members of the simulator/emulator development group for their support with the GMICRO F32 series and all people concerned for their valuable suggestions and cooperation in the development of the SRM32, also appreciate the contribution of Richard Jensen, Makoto Awaga, who reviewed this paper.

REFERENCES

[1] "GMICRO F32/300 MB92301 32bit Microprocessor Users Manual," FUJITSU LIMITED 1990

[2] "GMICRO F32/200 MB92201 32bit Microprocessor Operation Architecture Manual," FUJITSU LIMITED 1988

[3] "GMICRO F32/200 MB92201 32bit Microprocessor Programming Manual," FUJITSU LIMITED 1988

[4] "GMICRO F32/100 MB92101 32bit Microprocessor Users Manual" FUJITSU LIMITED 1990

[5] "GMICRO F32 series Symbolic ROM Monitor Users Manual," FUJITSU LIMITED 1990

Yoshitaka Kimura is a software engineer of Microcomputer Development Department of FUJITSU DEVICES INC. He joined FUJITSU DEVICES INC., after graduating from the University of Nihon Industrial in 1984. He has been engaged in the development of support software for microcomputers.

Hiroshi Shida is a software engineer of Microcomputer Development Department of FUJITSU DEVICES INC. He joined FUJITSU DEVICES INC., after graduating from the University of Electronics and Communications in 1984. He has been engaged in the development of support software for microcomputers.

Shigeru Sasaki is a software engineer of Microcomputer Development Department of FUJITSU DEVICES INC. He joined FUJITSU DEVICES INC., after graduating from the Nihon University in 1989. He has been engaged in the development of support software for microcomputers.

Above authors may be reached at: Microcomputer Development Department, FUJITSU DEVICES INC. 1812-10, Kosugi Fujitsu Building Shimonumabe Nakahara-ku Kawasaki, 211 Japan

Haruyasu Ito is a manager of Microprocessor Development Department of FUJITSU LIMITED. He joined FUJITSU, after graduating from Yokohama City University in 1971. He has been engaged in the development of support software for microcomputers.

Above author may be reached at: Microprocessor Development Department, FUJITSU LIMITED, 1015 Kamikodanaka, Nakahara-ku Kawasaki, 211 Japan

Performance Evaluation of TOXBUS

Katsuyuki Okada
NTT Communication Switching Laboratories

Matao Itoh, Seijun Fukuda
FUJITSU LIMITED

Takashi Hirosawa
Oki Electric Industry Co.,Ltd.

Tohru Utsumi
Toshiba Corporation

Keiko Yoshioka
Hitachi Limited

Yuji Tanigawa
Matsushita Electronics Corporation

Koji Hirano
Mitsubishi Electric Corporation

ABSTRACT

The TRON-specification extended bus (TOXBUS) is a system bus developed for the constructing high performance, tightly coupled multiprocessor systems and fault tolerant systems.

This paper analyzes and evaluates TOXBUS's split transfer by using software simulator and reports its performance and reliability.

We recognized the system throughput increased by using this transfer method. And we added copyback cache coherency control signal to TOXBUS in order to build a system having a copyback cache.

We are also investigating of implementation of a function for early detection and notification of bus signal fault, an isolation function for an obstruction extension inhibiting. In addition, we studied a redundant structure for signals.

A compact bus with few signals which can be extended to 64 bits can be realized.

Thus, this bus will contribute to future communications systems and information processing systems.

Keywords: Synchronous transfer, Split transfer, Cache coherency protocol, Compactness of Implementation, Fault-tolerant system

1. INTRODUCTION

The functions of TOXBUS, such as split transfer, copyback cache coherency control protocol, compactness and reliability are discussed. The simulation results and evaluations of split transfer are given.

At present, VMEbus[*1] or MultibusII[*2] is generally used as a system bus. We predicted that construction of an advanced multiprocessor system bus using these buses would be extremely difficult, however, and began studying the use of clock synchronous split transfer to give the system bus better transfer capability.

Thus, we have promoted the study of system bus specifications that would enable the realization of advanced multiprocessor systems and fault tolerant systems.

In the process of analyzing and evaluating TOXBUS may points in which is superior to conventional system buses were found. We named this system bus, TOXBUS.

The system bus greatly affects the performance of a multiprocessor system consisting of many processors, memories, and I/O controllers. Although processor performance has improved due to advances in LSI technology, if the transfer capability of the system bus is not improved, the system performance will not improve. Therefore, to construct a high performance multiprocessor system, a system bus that can resolve the above shortcomings must be developed. For example, when developing a copyback cache controlled multiprocessor system or fault tolerant system, a system bus should support these functions. Additionally, in order to ensure compatibility with function units (processors, memories, and I/O controllers connected to the system bus), the specifications of the system bus must be standardized. In other words, if a function unit is made to connect to a standardized system bus, then it may be used in other systems as well, with the result that a system can be conducted efficiently.

The characteristics of TOXBUS are stated below.

2. CHARACTERISTICS

Figure 1 shows configuration example of tightly coupled multiprocessor system.In this figure, several function units (processors, shared memories, and I/O controllers) are connected to TOXBUS via the system bus interface.

It is evident that the information transfer over TOXBUS increases proportionally with the number of function units that are connected. One of the characteristics of TOXBUS which contrives to solve this problem and the reason why it so affects the problem is explained below.

[*1]: VMEbus is IEEE-P1014 standard bus

[*2]: MultibusII is IEEE-P1296 standard bus

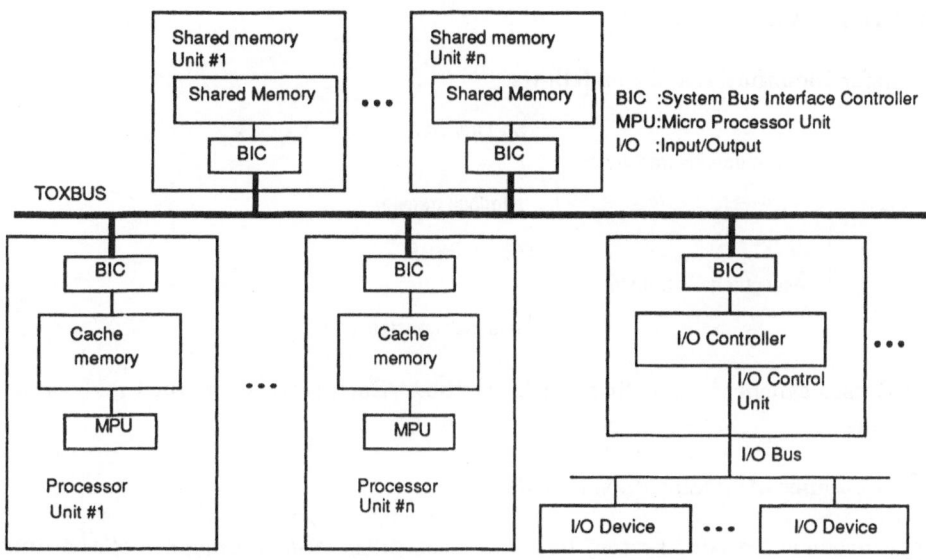

Fig.1 Configuration example of tightly coupled Multiprocessor system

(a) Improved transfer capability

    1) Implementation of synchronous transfer by a high speed clock

    2) Efficient use of the system bus, thus enabling the implementation of split transfer to increase throughput

(b) Copyback cache support function

    Support of copyback cache coherency control

(c) Compact implementation

    Reduction of signals. Also can handle 64 bit addresses and data.

(d) Fault tolerance

    1) To prevent the extension of a fault throughout the system, the function unit where the fault occurred is isolated (Isolation function)

    2) Duplicate structure of control signal lines

3. IMPROVED TRANSFER CAPABILITY

In this section, method of bus transfer and performance evaluation, number of transmission buffers required for shared memories will be discussed.

3.1 BUS TRANSFER

Bus transfer combinations are as follows.

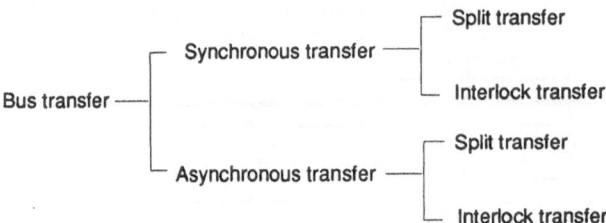

TOXBUS uses synchronous split transfer method. Each transfer method is discussed in detail below.

(a) Predominance of synchronous transfer

In a synchronous transfer system bus, the clock phase and frequencies of the function units connected to the bus are the same.

In an asynchronous bus, each function units do not operate at the same clock. To overcome this, an acknowledge signal transmitted or received between function units is checked.

Therefore, it may be judged that the transfer capability is greater in a synchronous transfer bus.

(b) Predominance of split transfer

In a split transfer system bus, after the transmit unit orders a command/address/data, the system bus is released. Then, the use of system bus is obtained when the receive unit is ready to answer, and the transmit unit is answered. While the system bus is released, another function unit may use it. Fig 2 shows the concept for the split transfer.

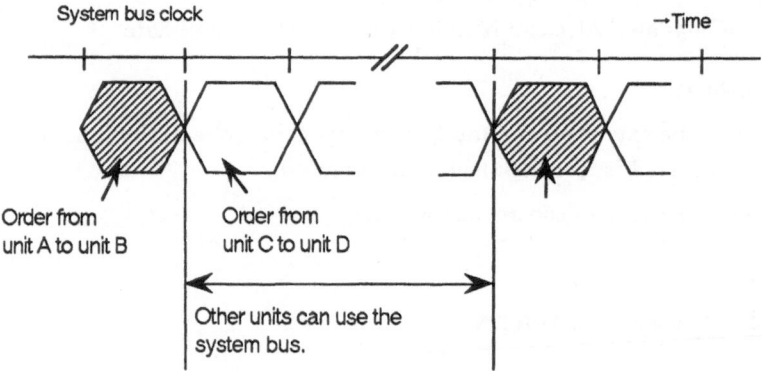

Fig.2 Concept for the split transfer

In an interlock transfer system bus, the transmit unit which has acquired the use of the bus retains it until an order is transmitted and an answer is received.

Therefore, it can be judged that the transfer efficiency of a split transfer is better. Especially when the time period until the receiving unit answers is long or in a multiprocessor system where the traffic is great, a big difference is discernible.

However, before beginning evaluating split transfer, we assured that is also has a drawback, which is as follows.

   1) Function units require a buffer to hold order/answer information
   2) When answering, the system bus is required once again, and the process of acquiring the bus slows the answering.

These assumptions were made in vain. Regarding 1) the advance of LSI technology and 2) Our analysis, evaluation result mentioned 3.2 .

The details of performance analysis and evaluation are as follows.

3.2 ANALYSIS AND EVALUATION OF TRANSFER PERFORMANCE

In this section, the result of analysis using software simulator (GPSS) and comparison evaluation of split transfer and interlock transfer targeted for tightly coupled multiprocessor system is discussed.

(a) System structure condition for analysis

As shown in Figure 1, the objective is a tightly coupled multiprocessor system with processors and one shared memory. However, the I/O controller is excepted from analysis and evaluation as the frequency with which it uses the bus is low.

1) System Bus
Figure 3 shows the read/write transfer sequence of the analyzed TOXBUS. The order command C_O in the figure consists of 32 bits and comprises of the category of transfer, read/write indication, and the receiving function unit number.

Specifically, the address is 32 bit, the system bus width is 64 bit and a multiplexed transfer is need for command/address/data.
The transfer content or transfer sequence of interlock transfer is the same as specified in Figure 3, the only difference being in the retention of system bus during the interval between order and answer. Therefore, a figure of transfer sequence for interlock transfer is omitted.

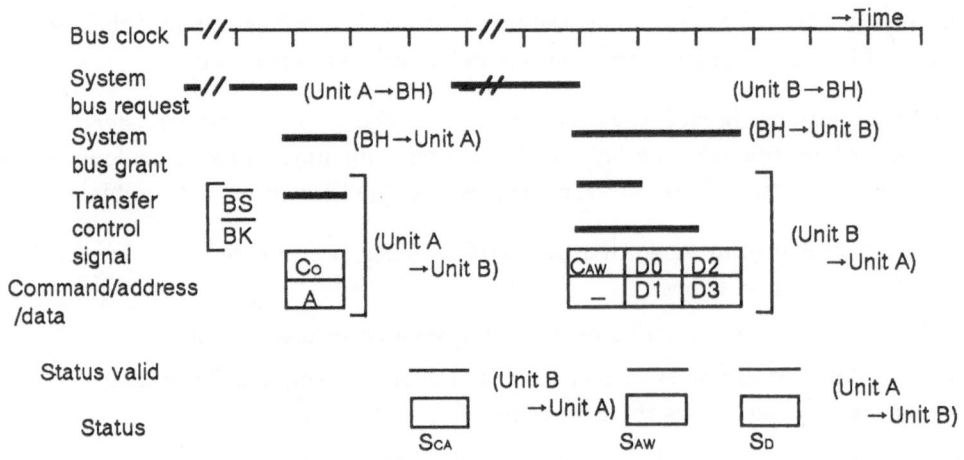

1) Data read transfer sequence

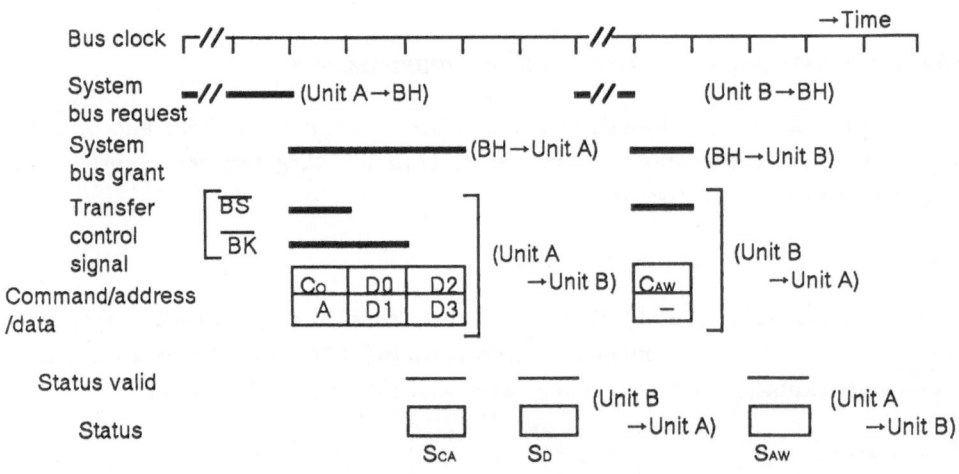

2) Data write transfer sequence

Co : Order command,   CAW : Answer command
A   : Address, D : Data, S : Status, BH : Bus handler
Unit A : Processor
Unit B : Memory

Fig.3 System bus transfer sequence

2) Processor

A processor with a write-through cache memory executes read/write in 4 byte units. During read, if a cache miss hit occurs, the processor copies 16 byte of data from the shared memory to the cache.

Also, when the microprocessor (MPU) transmits a write data to the system bus interface control block (BIC) of a function unit attached to it, it is interpreted as a condition to conclude the write. Afterwards, the MPU executes the next instruction. The BIC contains a transmit buffer for temporarily storing the write data. Therefore, the MPU does not have a cache or store buffer.

3) Queue Model

Figure 4 shows a queue model of split transfer. The shared memory control circuit (including BIC) has a FIFO (First In First Out) finite length buffer (queue) where processing is done in the transfer receiving order. When the shared memory buffer is full, bus transfer is retried.

Bus arbiter consists of two infinite length FIFO buffers (queues) for order and answer. Bus arbiter begins processing the FIFO buffer for answer first, and when the answer buffer is empty, the order buffer is processed. This is in order to shorten the read time, and to avoid the increase of the number of retry processing when the FIFO buffers of shared memory are full.

The queue model for interlock is omitted.

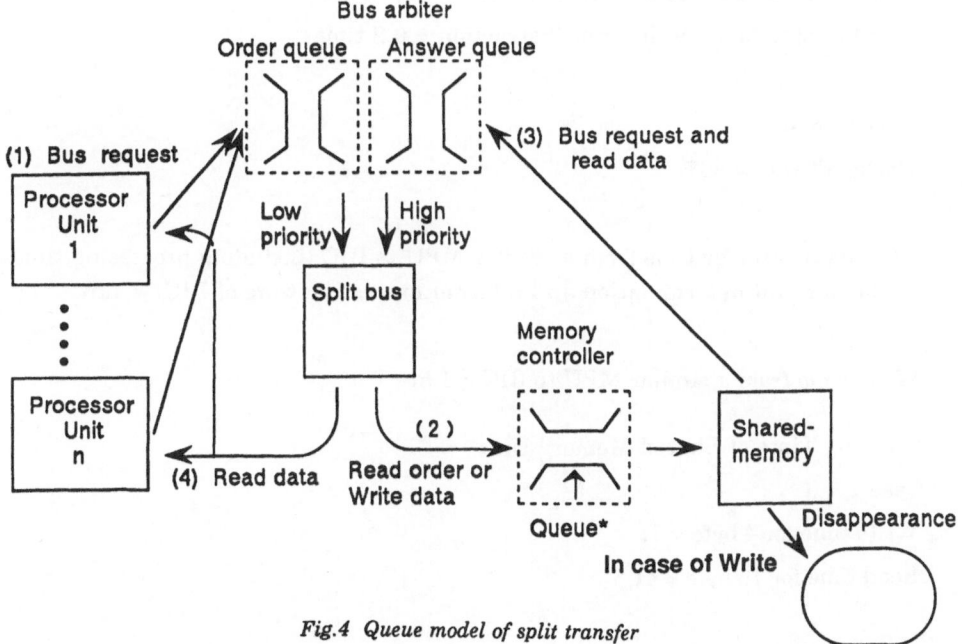

Fig.4 Queue model of split transfer

354

(b) Evaluation Condition

1) System bus related

- clock cycle time (τ) of system bus. This is the time required to transfer eight byte of information. Here, τ=100ns [2]

- transfer time over the system bus
  write (data 4 byte) = 2τ
  read of order (no data) = 1τ
  read of answer (data 16 byte) = 3τ
  Arbitration time (Non-wait) = 1τ

2) Processor Related

- When cache hit is assumed to be 100%, the average time for instruction execution processing
  E_0 (Instruction execution, processing time is exponentially distributed) = 3.75τ

- The frequency of memory access
  Average interval between memory accesses = $E_0/1.5$
  Number of memory reads per instruction = 1.3 times
  Number of memory writes per instruction = 0.2 times

- Cache memory
  Cache hit rate = 90%

- Read data transfer time from a similar MPU to BIC (including processing time of cache miss hit determination and internal processing time of BIC) = 1.5τ

- Write time from a similar MPU to BIC = 1.5τ

3) Processing Time of Shared Memory Unit
  - Case 1
  Write time for 4 byte = 1τ
  Read time for 16 byte = 4τ

- Case 2

 Write time for 4 byte = 2τ

 Read time for 16 byte = 8τ

- Case 3

 Write time for 4 byte = 0.5τ

 Read time for 16 byte = 2τ

(c) Analysis and evaluation of system performance

When four buffers are set for the shared memory (refer to 3.3), Figure 5 shows the relationship between the number of processors and the throughput of the multiprocessor system for both the split transfer and interlock transfer.

Figure 6(i) shows the relationship between the number of processors and system bus usage, and Figure 6(ii) shows the relationship between the number of processors and the shared memory usage.

From these figures, the following can be stated.

1) For interlock transfer, the throughput of the system does not saturate until four processors. Whereas for split transfer, the system throughput does not saturate until eight processors. With eight or more processors, in case of split transfer, the system throughput is 80-90% higher than that of interlock transfer.

2) With two processors, the system throughput of interlock transfer is slightly greater than that of split transfer. This is because the system bus usage is low and therefore the advantage of split transfer is last, and also because the answer is delayed due to arbitration required twice. However, the difference is small. Split transfer may be said to be useful for single processor to multiprocessor systems.

3.3 NUMBER OF BUFFERS REQUIRED BY THE SHARED MEMORY

Here, the relationship between the number of buffers required by the shared memory targeted for a tightly coupled multiprocessor system shown in Figure 1 and system throughput using the analysis and evaluation results obtained by using software simulator (GPSS) will be discussed.

The conditions of the examining model are the same as 3.2(a) and the evaluation conditions are the same as 3.2(b). Figure 7 shows the relationship between the number of buffers required by the shared memory and system throughput. From this figure, the following may be said.

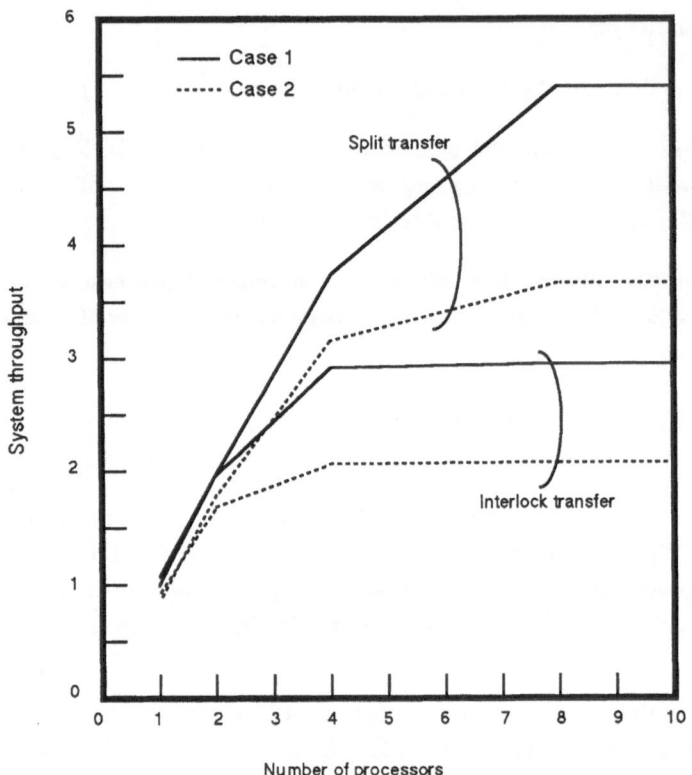

	4 byte write time in shared memory	16 byte read time in shared memory
⎯ Case 1	τ	4τ
┈ Case 2	2τ	8τ

τ : Bus transfer cycle

Factors : Buffer length in shared memory = 4
When number of processors = 1 in split
transfer, system throughput is 1.0

Fig.5 Number of processors vs. system throughput

357

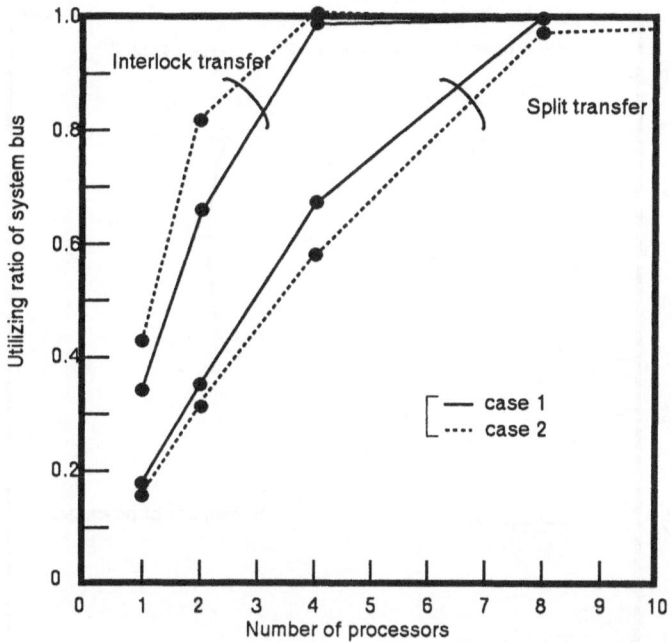

Fig.6 (i) Utilizing ratio of system bus

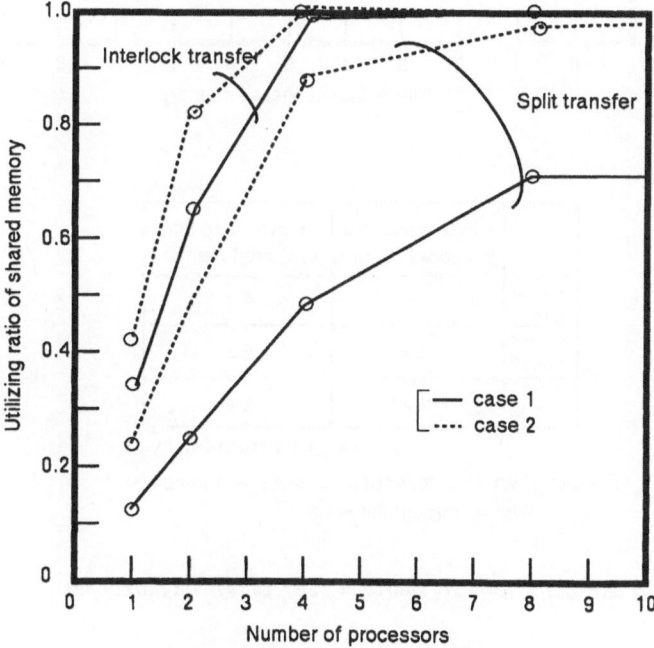

Fig.6 (ii) Utilizing ratio of shared memory

Fig.6 Utilizing ratio of system bus and shared memory

358

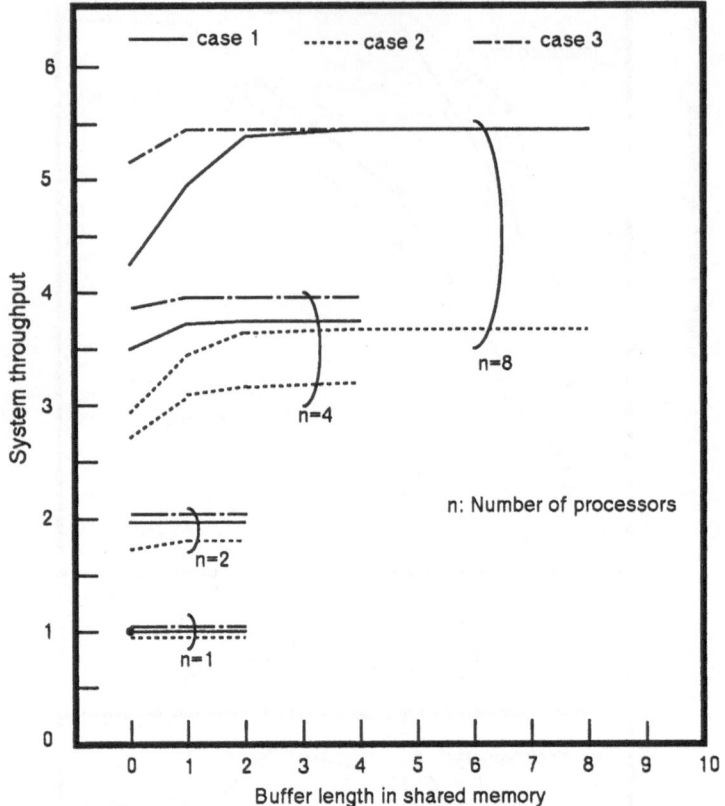

	4 byte write time in shared memory	16 byte read time in shared memory
case1	τ	4τ
case2	2τ	8τ
case3	0.5τ	2τ

τ : Bus transfer cycle

Factors : When number of processors = 1 in case 1,
System throughput = 1.0

Fig.7 Buffer length of shared memory vs. system thtrouhput

1) The system throughput increases as the number of buffers of the shared memory are increased. This is because the number of retries when the buffer is full decreases. When the number of processors is great and the read/write time of shared memory is long, having 1 buffer rather than 0 buffer can have a great effect. In this figure, in case 1 and system throughput is 10-20% higher.

2) When buffer of shared memory are increased to more than 2-4, then without depending on the number of processors, the system throughput saturates. If the performance of shared memory is inferior to system bus is assumed, then as many shared memory buffers are required as the number of processors. However, the performance of existing shared memories is not so low and therefore even though the number of buffers is small, it does not affect the throughput.

3) Compared to the system throughput difference of Case 1 and Case 2, the difference between Case 1 and Case 3 is small. This is because even if high speed read/write of shared memory is assumed, if the number of processors increases, system bus usage saturates, and system throughput is limited.

4. COPYBACK CACHE COHERENCE

For multiprocessor systems with cache memory, it is extremely important to develop a system such that contradictions do not occur in data stored in each processor's cache. Various coherency control protocols are therefore recommended [3].

When write-through protocol, an extremely simple consistency control protocol, updates cache data, shared memory data is also updated through the system bus. At the same time, other processors receive data and addresses updated by the cache.

If the same address exists in that cache, the cache data is invalidated. It is not necessary to add new signals to the system bus in order to implement write-through protocol. Further, implementing write-through protocol is easy and fault correction is relatively simple.

Since, however, shared memory is accessed when writing with write-through protocol, the traffic in that part of the system bus increases.

Copyback protocol reduces the write frequency. When cache data is rewritten, copyback protocol does not immediately update shared memory data.

In this protocol, however, a mismatch occurs when the same address exists in cache data and shared memory data. When using this protocol, therefore, new signals which notify the system bus of mismatches are required.

In the following sections, we would like to propose some new functions necessary for the copyback cache protocol system bus. In order to be able to construct an inexpensive and simple system, out proposal makes it possible to mix copyback and write-through protocols.

4.1 VARIOUS COPYBACK CACHE DATA STATUSES

For the control of copyback cache data statuses, the following two general methods exist.

1) Control of three statuses

- Invalid status (I): data is not registered.
- Shared & Unmodified status (SU): registered data is shared between multiple processors and shared memory.
- Exclusive & Modified status (EM): registered data exists in only one cache.

Figure 8 (i) shows status transition diagrams and transition factors.

2) Control of four statuses

In addition to the three statuses above, the following is added.

- Exclusive & Unmodified status (EU): registered data is shared only between one processor and shared memory.

Figure. 8 (ii) shows this status transition diagram and transition factors.

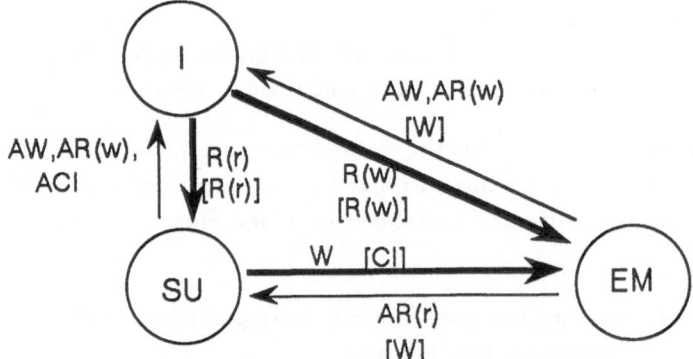

Fig .8 (i) Three-status management of cache data

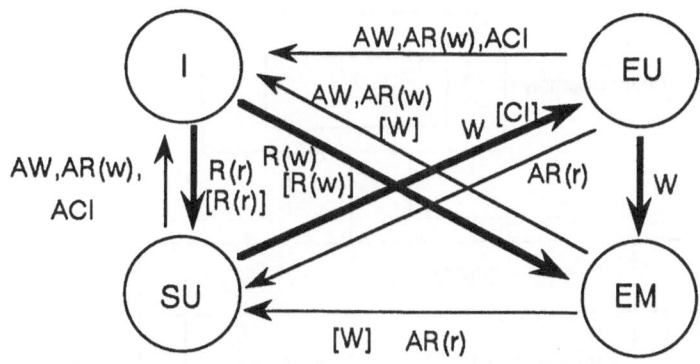

Fig.8 (ii) Four-status management of cache data

Status transition factor
1) Event in its own processor
R(r) : Read caused by a read miss, R(w) : Read caused by a write miss
W : Write, CI : Cache Invalidation
2) Event in another processor or I/O controller
AR(r) : Another's Read caused by a read miss, AR(w) : Another's Read caused by a write miss
AW : Another's Write ACI : Another's Cache Invalidation
[ ] : Transfer type
——— : Accessing from its own processor
——— : Accessing from another processor

Fig.8 Management of cache data

4.2 NEWLY-ESTABLISHED TRANSIENT STATUS

When using copyback protocol, the split transfer system bus has problems which give rise to processing contradictions, as is shown in Figure 9 and explained below.

1) Processor #0 requests modified data read to shared memory. Modified data read means that read data is immediately rewritten in the processor.

2) After processor #0 orders until shared memory answers, processor #1 requests access to the same data.

3) Shared memory answers to processor #0.

4) Shared memory answers to processor #1.

5) Processor #0 rewrites the answered data.

As a result, the data of processors #0 and #1 are mismatched.

As a countermeasure, it is suggested that the cache coherency control protocol already in the transient status is necessary [4]. Based on this, we defined the midway access status characteristic of the split transfer as a transient status which shows the status transition in progress in the TOXBUS.

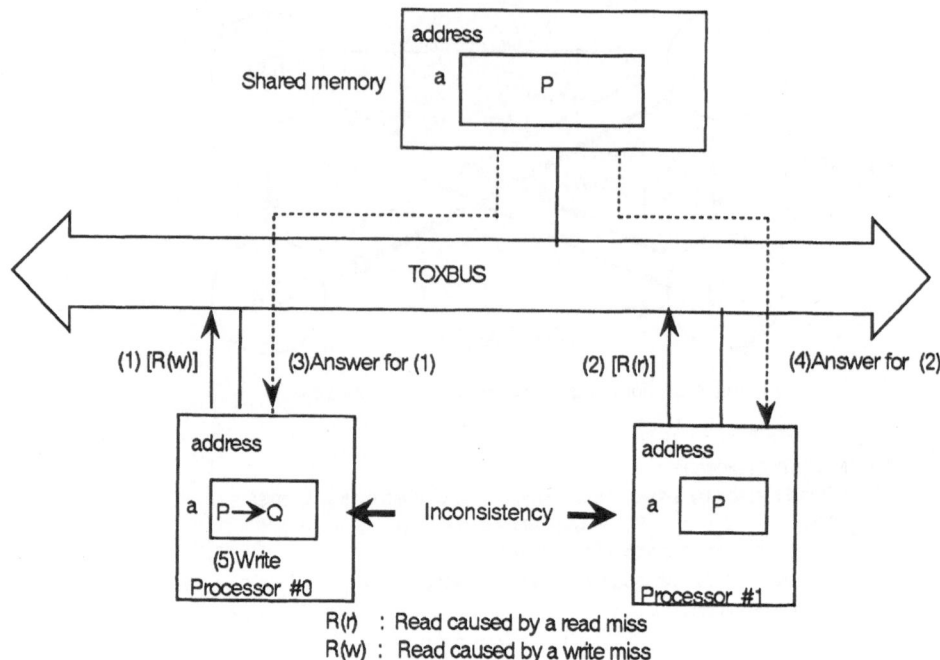

R(r) : Read caused by a read miss
R(w) : Read caused by a write miss

Fig.9   Example of inconsistency

4.3 COPYBACK CACHE COHERENCY CONTROL PROTOCOL

Figure 10 shows the copyback cache coherency control protocol for the TOXBUS. Control is executed by seven cache data statuses including the transient status. The netted portions of the diagram are stable statuses of cache data in memory; the remaining areas are transient.

In an attempt to reduce the number of system bus cycles used, the invalidated command (CI) in the diagram has been established to execute cache purge processing for only one cycle of the system bus.

(a) RETRY signal

Updated data in the copyback cache may sometimes exists in the cache of another processor without existing in shared memory. In such a case, to prevent access of shared memory, the TOXBUS has a RETRY signal which the processor containing the updated data (EM status data) asserts.

Figure 11 shows an example of cache coherency control processing by the RETRY signal. When the RETRY signal is asserted, shared memory refuses access from

363

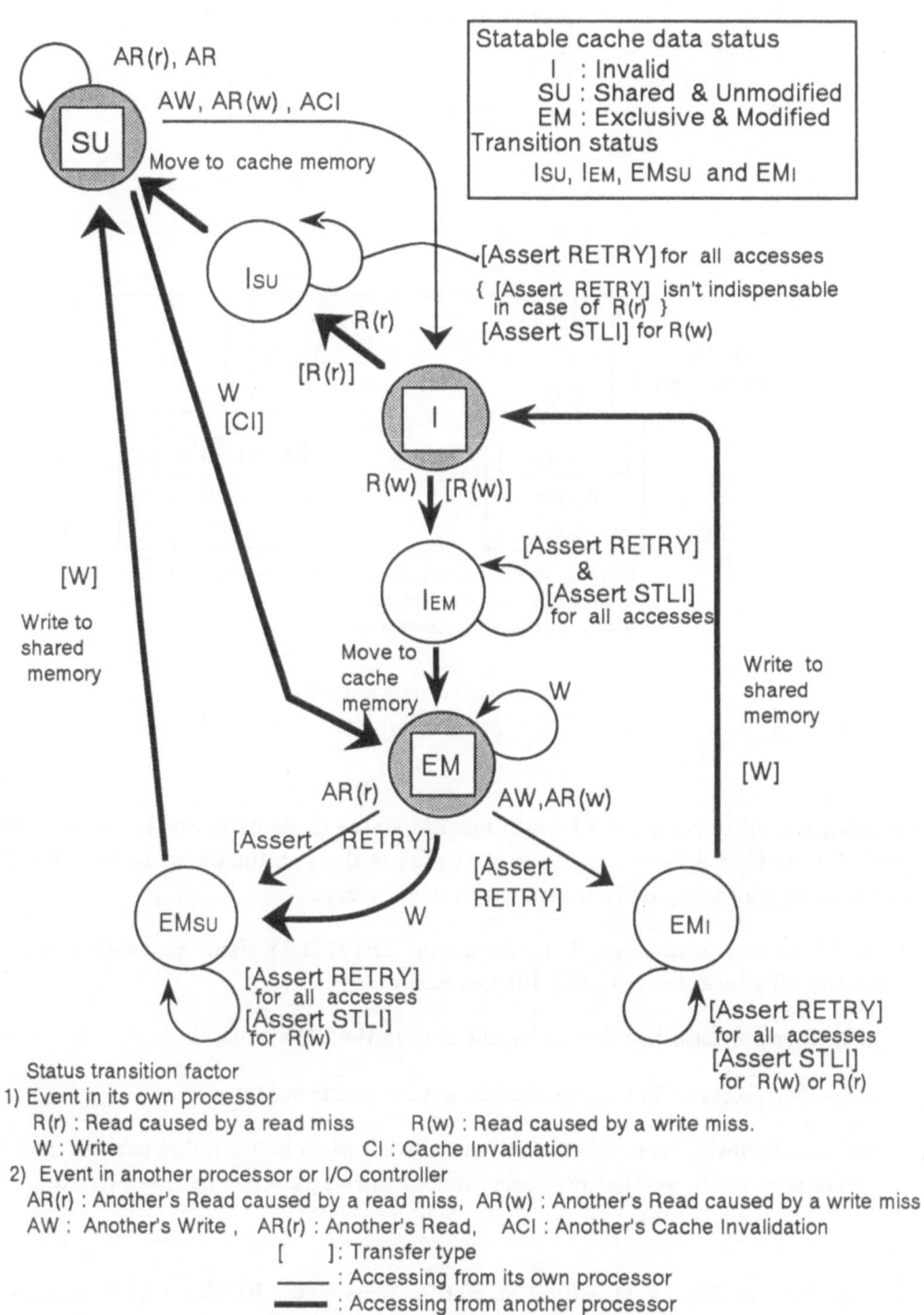

Statable cache data status
 I : Invalid
 SU : Shared & Unmodified
 EM : Exclusive & Modified
Transition status
 I_{SU}, I_{EM}, EM_{SU} and EM_I

AR(r), AR
AW, AR(w), ACI

SU

Move to cache memory

I_{SU}

[Assert RETRY] for all accesses
{ [Assert RETRY] isn't indispensable
  in case of R(r) }
[Assert STLI] for R(w)

R(r)
[R(r)]

W
[CI]

I

R(w) [R(w)]

[W]

Write to
shared
memory

I_{EM}

[Assert RETRY]
&
[Assert STLI]
for all accesses

Move to
cache
memory

W

EM

Write to
shared
memory

[W]

AR(r)

[Assert RETRY]

AW,AR(w)

[Assert
RETRY]

EM_{SU}

W

EM_I

[Assert RETRY]
for all accesses
[Assert STLI]
for R(w)

[Assert RETRY]
for all accesses
[Assert STLI]
for R(w) or R(r)

Status transition factor
1) Event in its own processor
   R(r) : Read caused by a read miss   R(w) : Read caused by a write miss.
   W : Write   CI : Cache Invalidation
2) Event in another processor or I/O controller
   AR(r) : Another's Read caused by a read miss, AR(w) : Another's Read caused by a write miss
   AW : Another's Write , AR(r) : Another's Read,   ACI : Another's Cache Invalidation
                    [   ] : Transfer type
                    ⎯⎯ : Accessing from its own processor
                    ▅▅▅ : Accessing from another processor

Fig.10 Copyback Cache Coherency Protocol

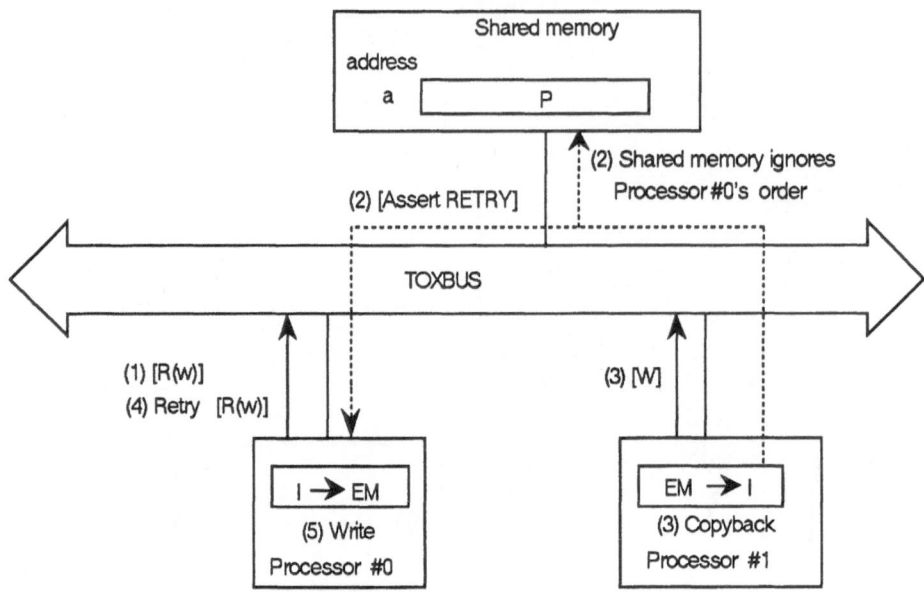

Fig.11 Example of retry protocol

processor #0. After processor #1 which has EM status cache data, copybacks EM status cache data to shared memory, processor #1 goes to the I status (Refer to Fig. 10). The processor #0 which originally transmitted retries access.

Cache coherence is made possible by the above. The RETRY signal noted above asserts in the following cases (refer to Fig. 10), i.e., when

1) another processor has accessed cache data in the EM status

2) another processor has accessed cache data in the transient status

3) the cache invalid command has been received, when buffer full, a parity error, etc. have occurred in another processor, and when re-access has been requested.

As explained in Figure 11 with EM status cache data, RETRY signal processing (processor #0) is repeatedly executed until processor #1 copybacks cache data to shared memory. By so doing, the system bus traffic greatly increases and the access time for processor #0 lengthens.

As one countermeasure to this, there is a protocol which directly transfers EM status cache data between processors. When this occurs, each cache converts to the SU status and the condition of shared memory is set to steal the cache data. The following problems exists with this protocol.

1) Since shared memory steals cache data transferred between caches data, receive verification to the transmitting processor is not answered. Thus, when shared memory produces a receive error, error correction is difficult.

2) Receive decision logic of shared memory becomes complicated.

As a countermeasure, we used the protocol stealing cache data when EM status cache data are copybacked to shared memory, thereby reducing system bus traffic. When processor #0 does not copyback even after a fixed time, processor #1 re-accesses shared memory. With this method, even if processor #1 which originally transmitted cache data fails, data contradictions do not occur.

As shown in Figure 12, even when steal is executed, problems characteristic of the split bus occur, as follows.

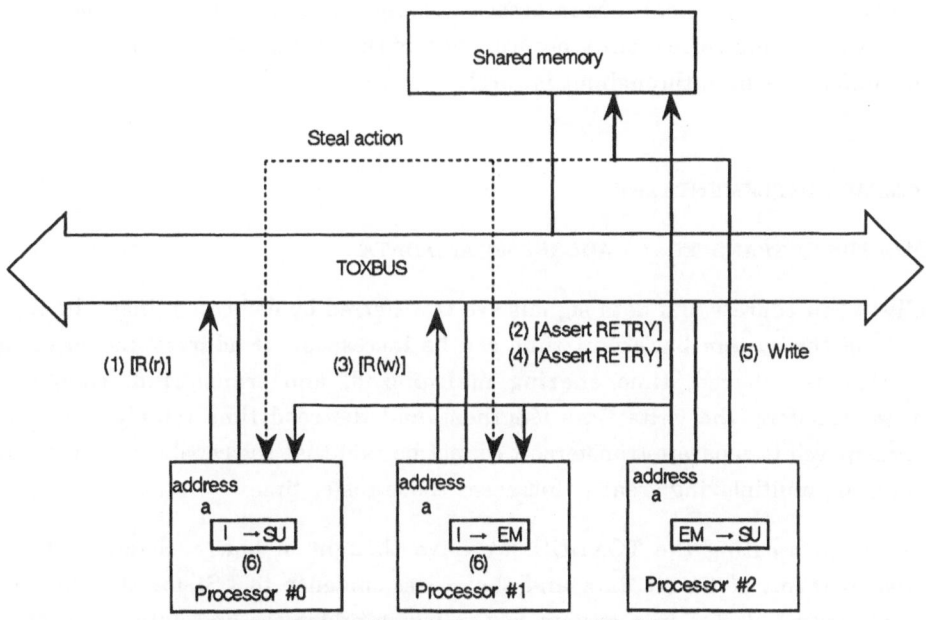

Fig.12 Example of contradiction in stealing

1) Processor #0 reads miss, and reads shared memory.

2) Since processor #2 has the most recent cache data, it asserts the RETRY signal.

3) Processor #1 writes miss the same address processor #0 tries to read, and reads shared memory. The most recent cache data, however, is not yet copied back to the shared memory by processor #2.

4) Since processor #2 has the most recent cache data, it asserts the RETRY signal.

5) Processor #2 copies back the most recent cache data to shared memory, at which time, processors#0 and #1 steal the data which processor #2 is copying back.

6) The cache data of processor #0 goes to the SU status, and the cache data of processor #1 is rewritten and goes to the EM status. This is the kind of contradiction which occurs.

To avoid this kind of contradiction, the TOXBUS has a STLI (Steal Inhibit) signal. The STLI signal is asserted in the following cases (Refer to Fig. 10), i.e., when

1) another processor accesses to transfer wait cache data in the I_{EM} status

2) another processor reads the cache by write miss hit to transfer wait cache data in a transient status other than the I_{EM} status (including the case in Fig. 12).

The STLI signal asserts only when access to transient status cache data is executed. Since, however, this infrequently occurs, even if the system throughput has a signal which inhibits stealing, throughput is rarely reduced.

5. COMPACT IMPLEMENTATION

5.1 MULTIPLEX TRANSFERS OF ADDRESSES AND DATA

Usually, when address and data signals are transferred by dedicated lines, the transfer quantity of the system bus's unit time can be increased. If address and data signal conductors are shared, time sharing multiplexed, and transferred, compared to separate transfers, the write time lengthens and the read time remains unchanged. Thus, compared to separate transfers, it cannot be said that the capability to transfer by time sharing multiplexing greatly increases the transfer time.

Therefore, in creating the TOXBUS, we have thought of how each address/data is handled in terms of 64 bit data and the correspondence to LSI for the system bus interface control block. In a system bus in which addresses and data are separated, however, this LSI might prove complicated.

Therefore, reducing the number of bus signals without greatly reducing the transfer capability is the essential point. For TOXBUS specifications, then, we selected a bandwidth of eight byte and a time sharing multiplexed transfer of addresses and data (refer to Fig. 3).

5.2 CONTROL SIGNALS (COMMANDS) SHARING DATA LINES

The two following system bus control signal configurations exist.

1) With leased signal conductors control information
2) With shared control signal conductors and data lines to reduce the number of signal conductors

According to 1), the following control signals which must have leased lines exist.

1) System bus priority control signal
2) Control signal indicating address or data transfer start and completion
3) Transfer result notify signal coexisting with addresses and data for high-speed
4) Parity signal to increase reliability

With these, signals for compensating transfer information such as types of access, read/write indicators, the number of transfer byte, etc., can share data lines

Based on this kind of thinking, we made the control signal conductors which must be leased the necessary minimum limit. Commands, then, are that control information which shares data lines.

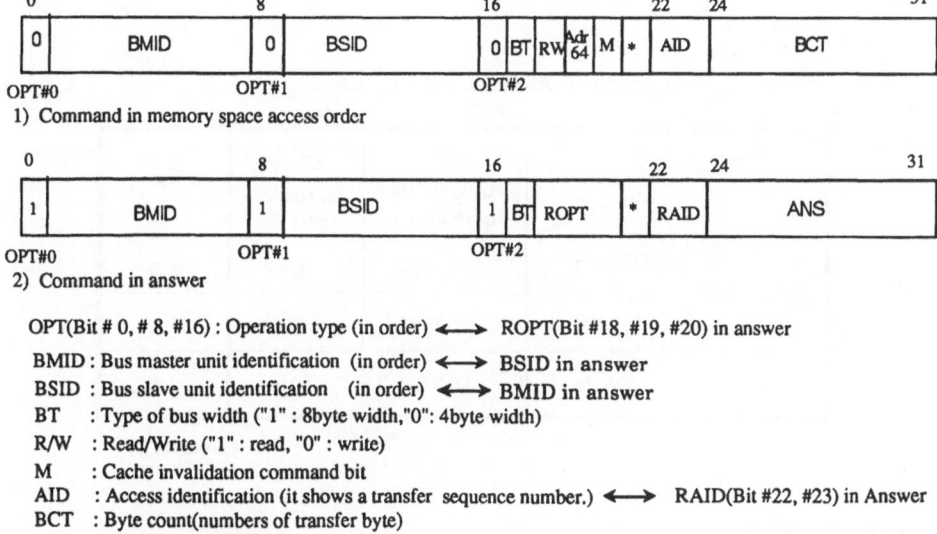

Fig.13 Command format

Figure 13 shows TOXBUS commands. Commands have ID numbers for control information about types of bus access, read/write indicators, etc., and for transmit/receive function units, and are configured with 32 bits.

By providing commands in the above way, a system bus with few signal conductors (TOXBUS) could be realized.

5.3 COMPACT IMPLEMENTATION EVALUATION

What can be generally said is that when signal conductors are increased, the transfer quantity of the system bus's unit time increases. To carry out LSI of the system bus interface control and to easily construct the system, however, it is important to reduce the number of system bus signal conductors.

As a means to evaluate the system bus compact mounting, in addition to the total number of signal conductors, we used the unit time system bus throughput (T)/the number of signal conductors (S).

Based on this method of evaluation, we compared the TOXBUS to an existent standard system bus. Table 1 shows the results of this evaluation.

If the transfer capability of the two system buses were equal, we would expect the value of T/S to be large. Since the total number of signals is relatively small and the value of T/S large, the TOXBUS is a very compact system bus.

Table 1 Evaluation of compactness

		(T) Throughput of bus transfer	(S) Number of signal	T ÷ S
Synchronous	TOXBUS	80 MB/s	88	0.9
	Multibus II	40 *MB/s	64	0.6
Asynchronous	VME bus	19 *MB/s	106	0.2

*cf. Reference [5]

6. FAULT TOLERANCE

Functions which support fault tolerance are divided into the following three classifications.

1) fault detection, 2) prevention of fault extension, and 3) fault correction and diagnosis support

In this section, we will explain the characteristics implemented in he TOXBUS about these three functions.

6.1 FAULT DETECTION FUNCTION

To detect 1 bit errors in signals, the TOXBUS has parity bits whose addresses, data, and control lines are in 1-byte units. In this section, we will discuss in detail fault detection functions of control signals which cannot be handled by parity.

(a) Granting error correction code status

As shown in Figure 3, status is the information notifying the result of a data transfer returned to the function unit which originally transmitted after two cycles of a command transfer. Not only is parity granted to the status, but the following problems also occur. This will be explained using exclusive control of a memory area as an example.

For a processor to release a leased memory area, when a write indicating the release is executed, the occurrence of a parity error in the status is assumed. In this case, since it is unclear whether or not the write has been normally terminated, a rewrite must be attempted using a hardware or software RETRY.

If, however, the first write terminates normally and the shared locked memory area is released, a contradiction in the processing will occur either after another processor verifies the locked area and writes, or if the first processor rewrites and releases the locked area.

In order to understand even from the above examples, only a parity check for a status is insufficient. Thus, we also are investigating of providing a 1 bit error correction command (ECC code) for the statuses of the TOXBUS.

(b) Locked signal fault detection function

The function unit which transmitted data continuously asserts a locked signal until an answer is received. As a result, the unit transmitting the answer cannot answer the parity for which locked signals are included in the group of transfer control signals when answering.

Thus, a special detection function is required to check for locked signal faults.

We investigated a simple way to verify, without increasing the number of signal conductors, whether or not the receiving unit has normally received a locked signal. As a result, we provided TOXBUS statuses with a code indicating the normal reception of locked signals.

(c) Signal duplex configuration

One control signal conductor's error causes processing contradictions in the whole system. So we also examined a duplex configuration of a one bit error correcting for each separate signal. In this section, we will consider the case in which

the RETRY signal in copyback cache is not normally received.

Suppose that the data one processor is trying to read exists in the EM status in another processor's cache. In such a case, if shared memory cannot receive the RETRY signal, it cannot cancel that read order. So the unit which originally transmitted the data receives an answer to the read order from shared memory, resulting in contradictions.

We created these spare signals-RETRY, STLI, and so on. In other words, there is a pair of signals for each signal. When a mismatch occurs between the signal conductors of a pair, each signal's combination is defined as shown in Table 2. Their purpose is to gain a stable advantage when mismatches occur.

With the STLI signal, for example, if the above mismatch occurs, cache coherence is maintained because the receiving side does not steal the data. We prescribed this signal conductor as an optional signal, however, and decided to reduce the number of signals in a system which does not request fault tolerance.

Table 2 Judge of mismatch types

	BS *1	AS *1	Low reliability	High reliability
RETRY STLI	0	1	0 *2	0 *2
	0	0		1
	1	1	1	1
	1	0		1

*1 BS : Basic signal   AS:Additional signal
BS and AS are a pair of sinals for high reliability.
*2 0: Regard as negation   1: Regard as assertion

6.2 FAULT EXTENSION PREVENTION FUNCTION

Faults occurring in one function unit may extend other function units through the system bus. In order to prevent this, we examined a function (isolation function) which would deny access to the system from a unit in which a fault had occurred.

The TOXBUS isolation function is explained as follows.

If a fault is detected in a function unit and notified to the bus handler, the bus handler does not return the use enabled signal to that function unit. Neither does the bus handler return the status transmission enabled signal to the unit in which the fault has occurred.

By using the above function, any signal from a function unit in which a fault has occurred can be electrically intercepted, thereby preventing the fault from having any extension on the system bus.

6.3 FAULT PROCESSING AND DIAGNOSTIC SUPPORT FUNCTION

(a) Statuses

The system bus is the common transfer path within the system and the point at which the system's reliability is determined. The TOXBUS considers this reliability, and at the transfer of an error, the receive function unit subdivides the error content, and immediately returns it to the original transmitter as a status. By so doing, the function unit which originally transmits can execute an analysis and diagnosis of the error content. The status is that which notifies the data line fault which occurs when an order and answer are transmitted. In the TOXBUS, data lines occupy a separate, special bus.

(b) Serial bus

When an error occurs in a system bus, each function unit must transmit and diagnose the information for other function units. Thus, the TOXBUS prescribes a serial bus with a low number of signals.

7. CONCLUSION

As stated earlier, the TOXBUS is a system bus with a high transfer capability which uses synchronous split transfer. This bus system can handle a copyback cache coherence and a conventional 64 bit configuration. Further, even though the TOXBUS incorporates multiple functions, it is a compact implementation system bus requiring few signal conductors and one in which LSI of the bus interface is certain to prove feasible. Therefore, we could say that the TOXBUS is a system bus which can accommodate conventional high-speed systems. For TOXBUS details, we hope reading "TOXBUS Specifications" published by the TRON Association.

ACKNOWLEDGEMENTS

We would like to especially thank Dr. Ken Sakamura, Assistant Professor of the University of Tokyo, for his helpful comments and guidance during our investigation of the TOXBUS specifications.

REFERENCES

[1] Paul L.Borrill :"Micro Standards Special Feature: A comparison of 32-bit buses," IEEE MICRO, p.71-79, Dec. 1985.

[2] Hidetaka Satoh, Norio Matsui, Katsuyuki Okada:"ANALYSIS OF HIGH SPEED BUS LINES IN PRINTED CIRCUIT BOARDS," IEEE International Electronic Manufacturing Technology Symposium,   1989.

[3] Archibald J., Baer J.L. :"Cache Coherence Protocols," Trans. Comput., Vol.4, No.4, Nov. 1986.

[4] Akira MORI, Masanori HIRANO : "Cache Coherency Protocol for Tightly Coupled Multiprocessor with split Bus," National Convention of The IECE of Japan, D-120, 1990.

[5] H.kirrmann : "Micro Standard - Reported on the Paris MultibusII meeting," IEEE MICRO pp.82-89. Aug. 1985.

Katsuyuki Okada is a senior research engineer at NTT Communication Switching Laboratories. Since joining the company in 1975, he has been engaged in the research and development of processor systems for electronic switching systems, and in the research of digital communication network configurations. He received the B.S.degree from the Osaka University in 1975. He is a member of IEICE and IPSJ.

Above author may be reached at : NTT Communication Switching Laboratories, 9-11, Midori-cho 3-chome, Musashino-shi, Tokyo, 180 Japan.

Matao Itoh received the B.S. in electrical engineering from the University of Tokyo in 1970. He is a manager of Gmicro/300 design group.

Seijun Fukuda received the B.S. in department of pure and applied science from the University of Tokyo in 1987. He has been engaged in Gmicro/300 logic design group.

Above author may be reached at : Third Design Department First LSI division,. FUJITSU LIMITED. 1015,Kamikodanaka, Nakahara-ku, Kawasaki, 211 Japan.

Takashi Hirosawa is an assistant manager of Switching Systems Engineering section in Switching Systems Engineering department, Switching Systems Engineering Division, Telecommunication group at Oki Electric Industry Co.,Ltd. He joined the company in 1981 after graduating from Tohoku University in Sendai. Since then, he has been engaged in the development of basic hardware system of super-minicomputer. He is a member of IPSJ.

Above author may be reached at : Oki Electric Industry Co.,Ltd. B23 1-3, Nakase, Tchiba pref. 262-01 Japan.

Tohru Utsumi received the B.S. from Kobe University, in 1985. He joined TOSHIBA Corporation in 1985. Since then he has been engaged in development of TRON specification VLSI at Semi-conductor Device Engineering Laboratory. He is a member of IPSJ.

Above author may be reached at : TOSHIBA Corporation, 580-1 Horikawa-cho Saiwai-ku, Kawasaki, 210 Japan.

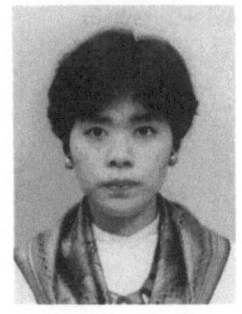

Keiko Yoshioka joined Hitachi, Ltd in 1984 and now an Engineer in the Microcomputer System Engineering Dept. at the Semiconductor Design & Development Center of Hitachi's Semiconductor Division. She is currency engaged in research and development of single board computer for microprocessors. She received the B.S. in electric engineering from the Science University of Tokyo in 1984.

Above author may be reached at : Hitachi, Ltd. Semiconductor Design & Development Center, 20-1 Josuihoncho 5 chome kodaiira-shi. Tokyo 187 Japan.

Yuji Tanigawa was born in Aichi, Japan, on December 20, 1956. He received the B.S. and M.S. degrees in electric Engineering from university of Osaka Prefecture, Osaka in 1979 and 1981 respectively. In 1981 he joined the micro processor design Group at the Matsushita Electric Industrial Co.,Ltd. From 1981-1984 he worked on the design of a time shared dual microprocessor. From 1985-1988 he worked on the the design of a parallel computer system. From 1989-1990 he worked on the support of 32-bit microprocessor at Matsushita Electronics Corporation.

Above author may be reached at : Matsushita Electric Industrial Co.,Ltd, 1, Koutari-Yakimachi, Nagaokakyoshi, Kyoto 617 Japan

Koji Hirano received the B.S. degree, in information physics, from Hiroshima University, Hiroshima Japan, 1984. He joined Mitsubishi Electric Corporation in 1984. Since then, he has been engaged in research and development of VLSI microprocessor architecture and application hardware system at LSI Research and Development Laboratory.

Above author may be reached at : LSI R & D Laboratory, Mitsubishi Electric Corporation, 4-1 Mizuhara, Itami, Hyogo, 664, Japan

Appendix: Additional Contributions

Realtime OS TR90
Based on Micro-ITRON Specification

Katsuyasu Yamada, Shuji Takanashi
Toshiba Corporation

Yukio Okada, Michio Tamura
Toshiba Microelectronics Corporation

ABSTRACT

The TR90 is a realtime operating system based on micro-ITRON
specifications. Toshiba has implemented it on the original 8-bit
single-chip microcomputer. The micro-ITRON specification is
supported up to the level 3. This paper describes the functions,
implementation, an application and performance of the TR90.

Keywords:TR90, Micro-ITRON, realtime operating system, TLCS-90,
8-bit microcontroller

1.Introduction

The TR90 is a realtime operating system based on micro-ITRON
specifications, and runs on Toshiba's TLCS-90 microcontrollor.
The TLCS-90 is a CMOS high-functional 8-bit original single-chip
microcontrollor for embedded-system applications. As basic
functions, the minimum instruction execution time is 320ns at
12.5MHz, and the highly orthogonal instruction set consists of
163 basic instructions. This includes multiplication and
division, 16-bit arithmetic instructions, and instructions of bit
operation. Its mnemonics are upward compatible with the
TLCS-Z80(*) processor. It also provides 10 internal/4 external
interrupts, and 11 channel micro DMA functions. For the
TMP90C840A of TLCS-90 series, the memory size is expandable up to
8K bytes for the built-in ROM, 256 bytes for the built-in RAM,
64K bytes for the program memory, and 1M bytes for the data
memory. Table 1 shows additional features, Table 2 the basic
instructions, and Figure 1 the memory map and registers. Table
3 indicates the execution time for basic instructions.

Table 1 TLCS-90 Features

8-bit A/D converter:6 analog inputs
General-purpose serial interface
   (asynchronous, I/O interface mode)
Multi-function 16-bit timer/event counter
   (PPG output mode, measurement of frequency and
    pulse range, and measurable time difference)
Four 8-bit timer
   (PWM output mode, capable of PPG output mode)
2-channel stepping motor control board
Standby, watchdog timer function

(*)Z80 is a registered trademark of Zilog Corporation.

Table 2 Instructions (TMP90C840)

LD	MUL	LDW	DIV	PUSH	INCW	POP	DECW	LDA	RLCA	EX	RLC	EXX
RRCA	LDI	RRC	LDIR	RLA	LDD	RL	LDDR	RRA	CPI	RR	CPIR	SLAA
CPD	SLA	CPDR	SRAA	ADD	SRA	ADC	SLLA	SUB	SLL	SBC	SRLA	AND
SRL	OR	RLD	XOR	RRD	CP	BIT	INC	RES	DEC	SET	INCX	TSET
DECX	JP	DAA	JR	CPL	JRL	NEG	CALL	LDAR	CALR	CCF	DJNZ	SCF
RET	RCF	RETI	NOP	HALT	DI	SWI	EI					

Table 3 Basic Instruction Execution Speed

Instruction process	State numbers	Instruction process	State numbers
R $\rightarrow$ R (8/16bit)	2,4/4,6	RXR $\rightarrow$ R (8/16bit)	18/192
@R $\rightarrow$ R	6/8	CMP (R,R)	4/8
R±R $\rightarrow$ R	4/8		
R±@R $\rightarrow$ R	6/8	PUSH/POP	8/10

(@R indicates a register indirect addressing mode.)

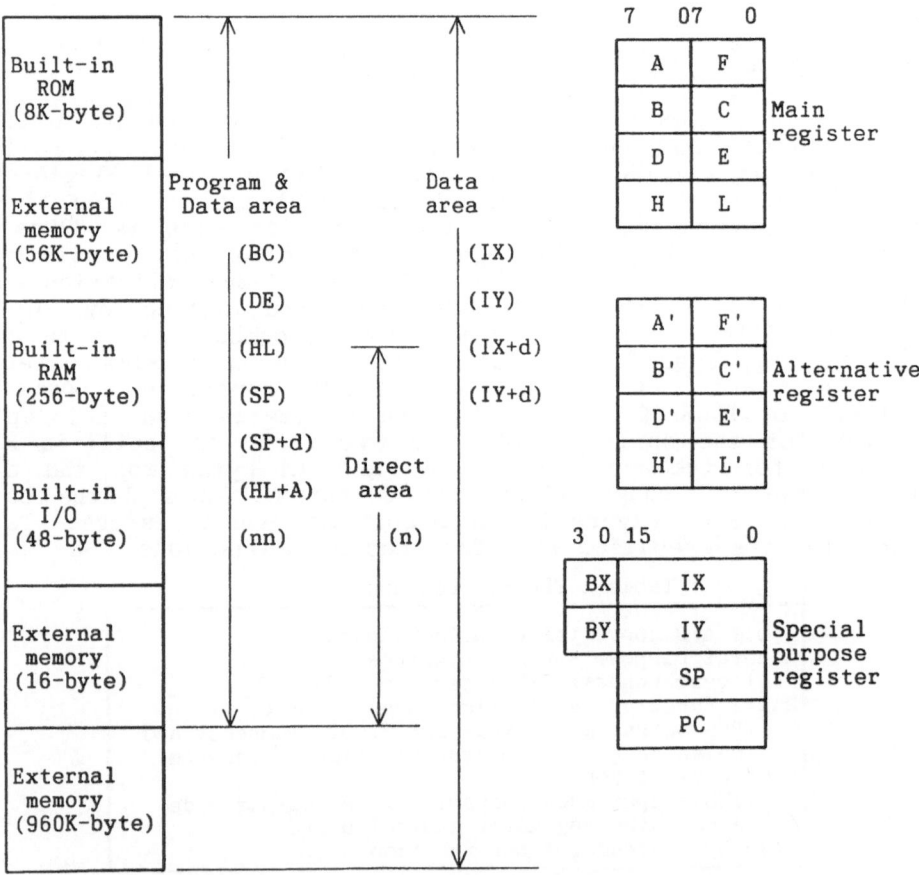

Figure 1 Structures of Memory Map and Registers (TMP90C840AN)

2. TR90 Design Philosophy

TR90 Functions

The micro-ITRON specification is designed for single-chip microcomputers with the limited ROM and RAM capacity. It has a beneficial effect on all aspects of program development, including training, productivity, standardization, maintenance, and ease of accommodating system upgrades. For the memory efficiency of the TLCS-90, Toshiba has developed a micro-ITRON specification OS for the TLCS-90 series. It improves the efficiency of application program development.

When we designed the TR90, we considered the RAM capacity, the ROM capacity and its performance essential. Usually a RAM space is more limited than a ROM space. Thus, the priority of a RAM space is higher than that of a ROM space. There is a trade-off between a performance and a code size. Therefore we had to develop several versions. In order to save a RAM space, we adopted thread-type tables in the OS. We can save one byte per entry. The TLCS-90 series microcontroller has alternative registers other than main registers. To save a RAM space, user tasks must be designed so as not to use the alternative registers. Then we can save the alternative register space. And system calls are made as subroutines.

In order to improve its performance, we used each task's stack as its TCB, and paid attentions to ratios between access times to registers and memories.

Language Interface

The TR90 is written by assembly language for the TLCS-90. For the C language, it supports the C compiler available by Toshiba, which is developed exclusively for the TLCS-90 microcontroller. We have designed the TR90 to link with the C compiler.

Debugger

We have the TLCS-90 emulator for the TLCS-90 series microcomputer in order to develop application systems. Therefore it is natural to build the TR90 debugger into the emulator, and to use the following composition (Figure 2) with the TLCS-90 emulator for debugging TR90 application software. For the efficiency of the application program development, both the debugger commands and the commands specified from the real time operating system, could be used intermixedly at the same time. Therefore we designed such debugger.

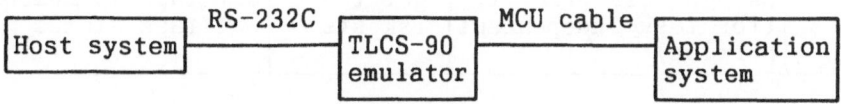

Figure 2 Composition of the TR90 Debugger

3.TR90 Functions

The TR90 fully utilizes the capabilities of the 8-bit microcomputer TLCS-90 series. The TR90 covers three levels of micro-ITRON specifications. Figure 3 shows the system structures.

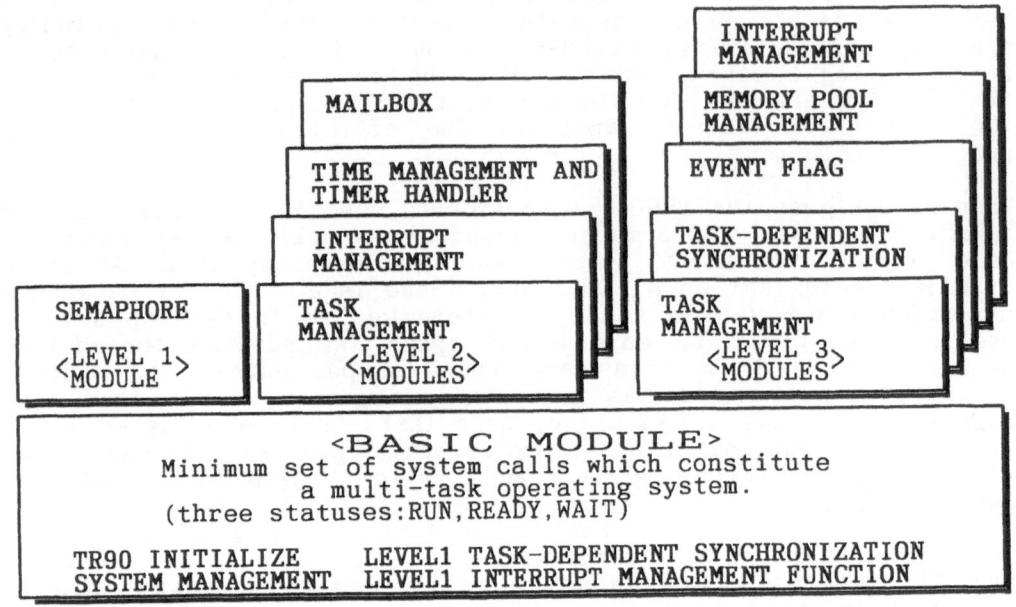

Figure 3 TR90 Structures

3.1.Task management functions

The maximum value of the task id (non-negative integer) is 127 and is assigned statically at the system activation. For the task priority, it provides 15 levels. For task states, it provides run, ready, wait, wait-suspend, suspend, and dormant states. Table 4 shows the system calls for the task management.

Table 4 Task management functions

System call	Function	System call	Function
sta_tsk	Start task	rot_rdq	Rotate ready queue
ext_tsk	Exit task	irot_rdq	Rotate ready queue
ter_tsk	Terminate task		(for task-independent
chg_pri	Change task priority		portion)
ichg_pri	Change task priority	get_tid	Get task ID number
	(for task-independent	tsk_sts	Get task status
	portion)		

3.2.Task-dependent synchronization functions

Without using synchronous communication functions, the TR90 transits task states, and takes synchronous timing between tasks. Such functions include transitions to suspend, resume, and wait states, or wakeup from the wait state. The memorized request number is 15 times the maximum. Table 5 shows the system calls for the task-dependent synchronization.

Table 5 Task-dependent synchronization functions

System call	Function	System call	Function
sus_tsk	Suspend task	wai_tsk	Wait for wakeup task
isus_tsk	Suspend task (for task-independent portion)	wup_tsk	Wake up task
		iwup_tsk	Wake up task (for task-independent portion)
rsm_tsk	Resume task		
irsm_tsk	Resume task (for task-independent portion)	can_wup	Cancel wakeup task
slp_tsk	Sleep task		

3.3.Synchronization and communication functions

Synchronization/communication functions support event flags, semaphores, and mailboxes. For the event flag, one event signifies one byte and the maximum number of event flags is 255. The semaphore is a counting type and its maximum counting value is 255. The maximum acceptable number is 255, which is set at system activation. The maximum acceptable number of the mailbox is 255 and it is also set at system activation. Table 6 shows the system calls for the synchronization/communicaion functions.

Table 6 Synchronization and communication functions

System call	Function	System call	Function
set_flg	Set event flag (word)	sig_sem	Signal semaphore
iset_flg	Set event flag (word) (for task-independent portion)	isig_sem	Signal semaphore (for task-independent portion)
clr_flg	Clear event flag (word)	wai_sem	Wait on semaphore
		preq_sem	Poll and request semaphore
wai_flg	Wait event flag (word)	snd_msg	Send message to mailbox
pol_flg	Poll event flag (word)	isnd_msg	Send message to mailbox (for task-independent portion)
rcv_msg	Receive message from mailbox		
prcv_msg	Poll and receive message from mailbox		

3.4.Memory pool management functions

The memory area available for a dynamic use is made up of 255 memory pools. The maximum value of one memory block is 65535. Table 7 shows the system calls for the memory pool management.

Table 7 Memory pool management functions

System call	Function	System call	Function
pget_blk	Poll and get memory block	rel_blk	Release memory block

3.5.Time management and timer handler functions

The time management sets and reads the system clock. The TLCS-90 series microcontroller uses four 8-bit timers as its hardware timer. Two of these are utilized as a 16-bit timer. The interrupt frequency of the hardware timer is from 1 to 65535 microseconds and is set at system activation. Table 8 shows the system calls for the time management.

Table 8 Time management and timer handler functions

System call	Function	System call	Function
set_tim	Set time	get_tim	Get time

3.6.Interrupt management functions

Table 9 Interrupt vectors

Order	Types	Interrupt request elements	Vector
1	NMI	SWI command	10H
2	NMI	NMI (NM I pin input)	18H
3	NMI	INTWDT (Watchdog)	20H
4	MI	INT0 (External input)	28H
5	MI	INTT0 (Timer 0)	30H
6	MI	INTT1 (Timer 1)	38H
7	MI	INTT2 (Timer 2)	40H
8	MI	INTT3 (Timer 3)	48H
9	MI	INTT4 (Timer 4)	50H
10	MI	INT1 (External input)	58H
11	MI	INTT5 (Timer 5)	60H
12	MI	INT2 (External input)	68H
13	MI	INTRX (Serial receiving completed)	70H
14	MI	INTTX (Serial transmitting completed)	78H

*:INTAD(A/D converter) is selectable as software.

The user may create and register the interrupt program (interrupt handler) at any time (statically at system activation). However, the correspondence is set up beforehand between the interrupt elements and the value of the interrupt vectors (see Table 9). The general-purpose interrupt indicates the interrupt handler from which the user registers the specified vector value to the address. The interrupt vector value is assigned from 10H in an 8-byte unit. Table 10 shows the system calls for the interrupt management.

Table 10 Interrupt management functions

System call	Function	System call	Function
ret_int	Return from interrupt handler	chg_ims	Change interrupt mask
ret_wup	Return and wakeup task	ims_sts	Get interrupt mask status

3.7. System management functions

Table 11 shows the system calls for the system management.

Table 11 System management functions

System call	Function	
get_ver	Get version number	

3.8. TR90 Debugger Functions

The TR90 debugger features a display of the operating system's status, a trace, a real time execution, and an issue of system calls. Figure 4 shows the flowchart of the debugger processing. The commands for the TR90 debugger contain tasks, event flags, ready queues, semaphores, mailboxes, and memory pools. Table 12 shows the list of the commands.

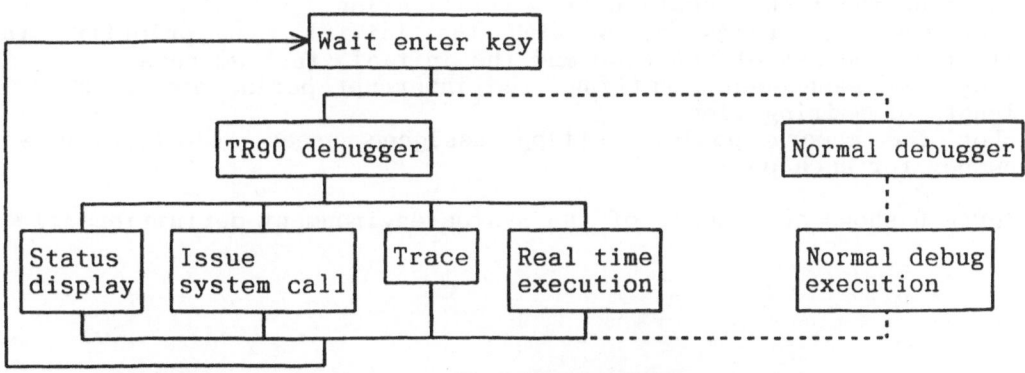

Figure 4 Flowchart of the TR90 Debugger Processing

Table 12 Debugger Commands

Commands	Explanations
DE	Display event flag status
DEM	Display event flag status in comparison mode
DM	Display mailbox status
DR	Display ready queue status
DS	Display semaphore status
TDI	Display timer status
DB	Display memory pool status
DT	Display task
G	Execute user's program
RK	Set/Display/Cancel break point
SC	Issue system call
T	Trace system call

4.System Design

4.1.System Design

When activating the system, first, the application program should include the interrupt handler written in either the assembler or C language. Then, the system environment definition file is written for linking the basic unit of the operating system with other required modules. Figure 5 indicates the flowchart of the entire system.

4.2.System Environment Definition

The system environment definition file limits the specification levels and defines the system parameters such as:
 -Setting levels corresponding to the micro-ITRON
 -Selecting to use the TR90 debugger
 -Setting the interrupt vector table
 -Setting the number for tasks, priorities, memory pools, mailboxes, event flags and semaphores
 -Setting the task execution at initialization
 -For the task register, setting the initial task priority, the starting address of the code and the initial stack address
 -For time management, setting the interrupt period and a multiple length of waiting time
 -For the memory pools, setting assigned areas, block size and number for each pool

Figure 6 shows an example of the system environment definition file.

385

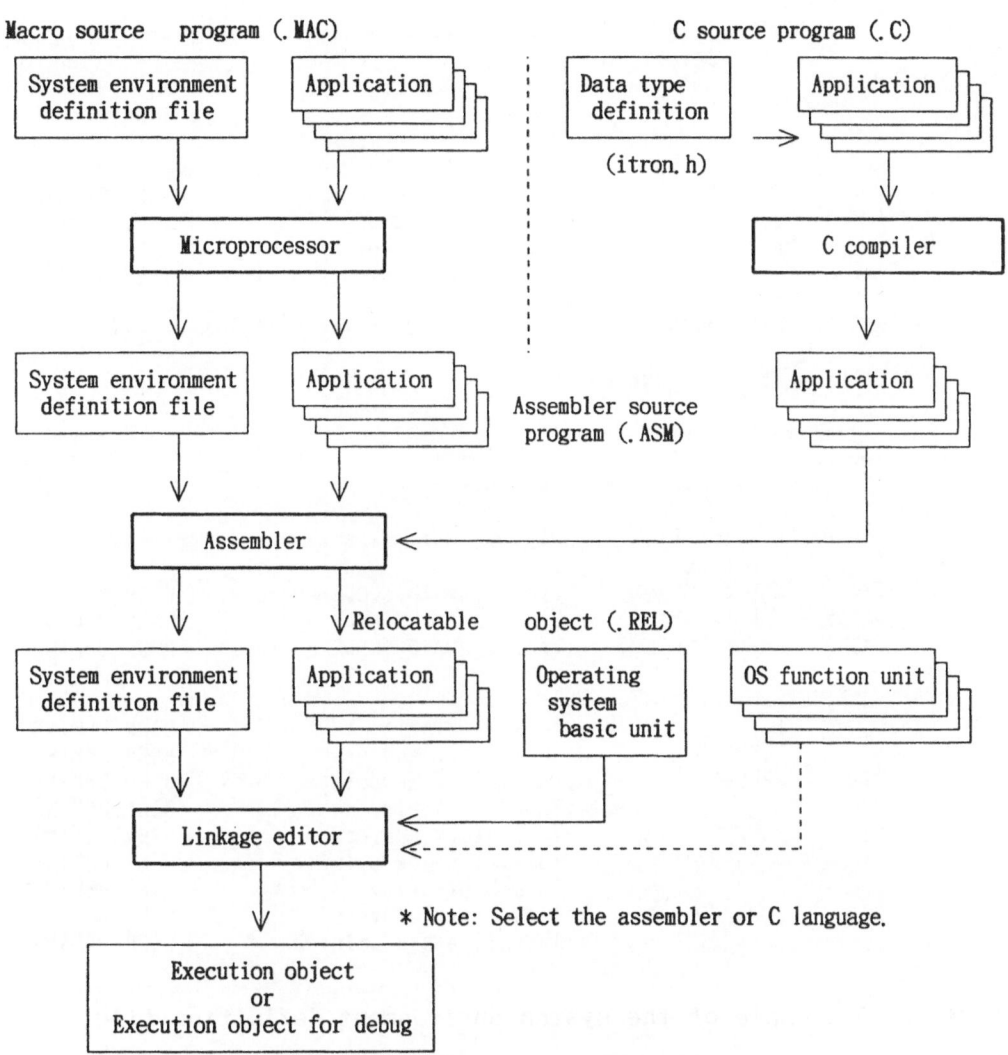

Figure 5 System Design Flowchart

```
; ***** USER DESCRIPTION DATA (START) *********************************
                   *** Definition ***
TASKNO   EQU    3                ;Task number              --USER DEFINE--
PRITY    EQU    3                ;Priority                 --USER DEFINE--
MPLNO    EQU    2                ;Memory pool number       --USER DEFINE--
POOL     EQU    140              ;Memory pool assigned area --USER DEFINE--
MAILNO   EQU    3                ;Mailbox number           --USER DEFINE--
EVFLG    EQU    3                ;Event flag number        --USER DEFINE--
SMPHNO   EQU    3                ;Semaphore number         --USER DEFINE--
RUNID    EQU    1                ;Initial execution task ID --USER DEFINE--
CLOCK    EQU    10               ;CLOCK (MHz)              --USER DEFINE--
; ***** USER DESCRIPTION DATA (END) ***********************************

         CSEG   REL    DROMTBL


         *************************************
         ***       ROM area table        ***
         *************************************

; ***** USER DESCRIPTION DATA (START) *********************************
; ***      User define module      ***
         EXTRN  CSEG(,USR1CD)    ;User task ID1(CODE address) --USER DEFINE--
         EXTRN  CSEG(,USR2CD)    ;User task ID2(CODE address) --USER DEFINE--
         EXTRN  CSEG(,USR3CD)    ;User task ID3(CODE address) --USER DEFINE--

;        Task definition table (TDT)
TDT:     DB     1                ;Task 1 priority          --USER DEFINE--
         DW     ,USR1CD          ;Task start address       --USER DEFINE--
         DW     0FFC0H           ;Initial stack pointer    --USER DEFINE--
         DB     2                ;Task 2 priority          --USER DEFINE--
         DW     ,USR2CD          ;Task start address       --USER DEFINE--
         DW     0FF80H           ;Initial stack pointer    --USER DEFINE--
         DB     3                ;Task 3 priority          --USER DEFINE--
         DW     ,USR3CD          ;Task start address       --USER DEFINE--
         DW     0FF40H           ;Initail stack pointer    --USER DEFINE--
```

Figure 6 Example of the system environment definition file

5.Example of TR90 Application

Elevator control simulation

We have applied the TR90 to an elevator control simulation. Due to screen space's limitations, the simulation is designed with four cages for 8 floors. Elevators are controlled under a specific logic by inputting the parameters in terms of both the period of passenger use and the passenger occurrence probability. The result is simulated on a display by calculating the average waiting time at each floor. Changing the logic for controlling the elevator makes various simulations.

Process Outline

The outline of the simulation process is indicated in Figure 7 and
is explained below. The system calls used are event flags, mailboxes
and semaphores for synchronization and communication functions. In
addition, system calls are also used for task management functions
and task-dependent synchronization functions.

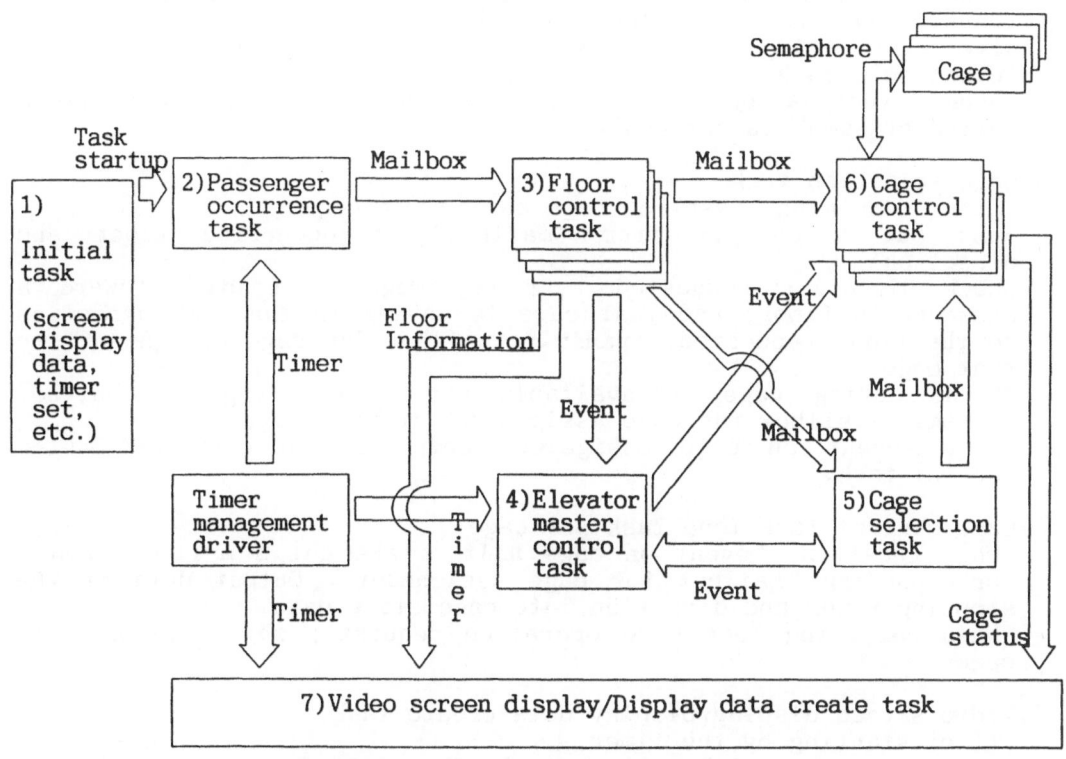

Figure 7 Process Outline

1)Initial task
  *Initialize various fixed data.
  *Start up all tasks.

2)Passenger occurrence task
  *After starting by the timer,
  Set data on the period of passenger use and the percentage of
  passenger use at each floor.
  Transmit to "mailbox for passenger use per floor".

3)Floor control task (one task per floor)
  *After receiving from "mailbox for passenger use per floor",
  Transmit to "mailbox for waiting passengers per floor".
  Create "event times floor button pressed".

Transmit to "mailbox for occurring floor and direction".
Output numbers of waiting passengers to "information table per floor".

4)Elevator master control task
*After starting by the timer,
If "event times floor button pressed" is generated,
For cage selection task, issue "event on cage assignment request". Wait for "event on cage assignment complete" to be transmitted from cage selection task.
After generating "event on cage assignment complete", issue "event on cage halt" to cage control task.
Issue "event on operation request", even if "event times floor button pressed" is not generated.

5)Cage selection task
*After receiving "event on cage assignment request",
Take out a mailbox from "mailbox for occurring floor and direction".
Check direction requested. If any cage is heading toward a passenger's floor, and that cage is moving in the same direction to the floor requested, transmit "mailbox for cage assignment" to that cage.
If no moving cage is available and when a cage is halted, transmit "mailbox for cage assignment" to that cage.
Issue "event on cage assignment complete" to elevator master control task.

6)Cage control task (one task per cage)
*When receiving "event on cage halt", take out a mailbox from a corresponding "mailbox for cage assignment". Output data of the stopping floor and direction into cage state data.
*When receiving "event on operation request", shift to the next cage.

7)Video screen display/Display data create task
*After starting by the timer,
Output contents of "cage state data" and "information table per floor" onto the video.

Table 13 shows an example of the simulation output.

Table 13 Example of the Simulation Output

Floor	Period of use	Occurrence probability	Average waiting time
8	10sec	0.25	5sec
7	50sec	0.50	6sec
6	55sec	0.50	5sec
5	30sec	0.75	6sec
4	50sec	0.25	6sec
3	35sec	0.50	5sec
2	20sec	0.75	7sec
1	15sec	0.50	6sec

6.Evaluation of the TR90

Code Size

The code size of the operating system basic module is 1.3K bytes, and that of the entire TR90 is 5.4K byte.

Performance

We have several performance data. They are measured by the TLCS-90 realtime emulator. The maximum non-interrupt time when a task is woken up by wup_tsk, is 65 microseconds at 12.5MHz. The maximum task changeover time that is, the time from the withdrawal of the context of an old task to completion of the following: selection of a new task, load of a new context and transfer of control, is 55 microseconds at 12.5MHz.

7.Conclusion

The TR90, the real time operating system based on micro-ITRON level 3 specifications, has been developed for an 8-bit single-chip microcomputer TLCS-90 series for embedded system control. The·code size of the operating system is a minimum structure of 1.3K bytes, which operates on a 256-byte RAM including user tasks.

Acknowledgements

We would like to express our deep gratitude to Professor Ken Sakamura, of Tokyo University, and also to the staff members concerned for guiding us in developing the TR90.

Katsuyasu Yamada:He received B.S. degree, in mathematics, from Tokyo Science Institute, Tokyo, in 1968. He joined Toshiba Corporation in 1968. From 1968 to 1983 he was engaged in software development of mainframe computers. Since then, he has been engaged in software development of microcomputer. He is a senior specialist of microcomputer systems & software section, Microcomputer Systems Marketing & Engineering Department, Integrated Circuit Division.

Shuji Takanashi:He received B.S. and M.S. degrees, both in mathematics, from Osaka University, Osaka, Japan, in 1977 and 1979, respectively. From 1979 to 1982, as a doctor-candidate, he was engaged in research on Differentail Algebra in Osaka University. He joined Toshiba Corporation in 1982. From 1982 to 1990, he was engaged in research and development of VLSI and CAD. Since then, he has been engaged in software development of microcomputer.

Yukio Okada:He received B.S. degree, in electric communication technology, from Tokyo Denki University, Tokyo, Japan, in 1987. He joined Toshiba Microelectronics Corporation in 1987. Since then, he has been engaged in microcomputer software design at System Design Department IV.

Michio Tamura:He received B.S. degree, in environmental technology, from Saitama Industrial College, Saitama, Japan, in 1982. He joined Toshiba Microelectronics Corporation in 1982. From 1982 to 1986, he was engaged in research and development of basic software for 16-bit microprocessors at Microcomputer Software Design Section. From 1986, he has been engaged in research and development of realtime OS.

Above authors may be reached at:Microcomputer Systems Marketing & Engineering Department, Integrated Circuit Division, Semiconductor Group, Toshiba Corporation.
Semiconductor System Enginnering Center
580-1,Horikawa-cho, Saiwai-ku, Kawasaki, 210, Japan

Communication Terminal for Heterogeneous Network Based on BTRON HMI

Nobuyuki Enoki, Hideyuki Oka, Aki Yoneda, Makoto Ando
Kansai Information and Communications Research Laboratories,
Matsushita Electric Industrial Co., Ltd.

ABSTRACT

Recently, many kinds of computer network services in UNIX workstations and personal computers have become popular. However, the users have to learn a lot of knowledges to use them and there are many differences on each operation of the network services.

In this paper, for solving these problem, we propose that the BTRON1 specification HMI will be used for accessing other network systems and the communication software should be programmed by using "hostcap".

We have implemented mail/news reader, which are examples of our proposals, for the other network using the BTRON1 specification HMI. And we have realized the Intelligent Terminal, which is a mechanism to make communication software with a good graphical user interfaces communication software, on the BTRON1 specification OS.

Keywords: Network communication software, Electric mail/news, Hostcap, Graphical user interface, Intelligent terminal

1 Introduction

Recently, many UNIX workstations and personal computers have been equipped in companies or laboratories. The computer environment is very popular so that each user in the office or the laboratory have one computer. Users want to use computer resources more efficiency, and to communicate with others. Therefore each computer needs to have various kind of network communication equipments and becomes popular. Many communication software are developed so as to use the network communication equipment.

However, there is one problem that an amount of network communication software which have an easy and a friendly interface for end users is very little. Because many communication software are developed and are popularised by software engineers who are computer and software experts. And, basically, operations of almost communication software consist of character commands. The another problem is that operations of each network communication software depend on the corresponding network, so there are many different operations for end users. And then, the end users have to remember many operations of each communication software for communicating with a lot of people and collecting information from many resources.

Indeed, there is an electric mail as network wide applications. For example, on the UNIX system, there are many differences in the operations acoording to difference of the system version. And also, operation manners of the communication software on the UNIX workstation are different with operation manners on the personal computer.

In this paper, we have two proposal. At first, for developing an easy and a friendly user interface's communication software, we propose that the BTRON1 specification HMI is a suitable interface for the network communication software which has a good graphical user interface.

Next proposal, we develop a network communication software by using "hostcap" so that users may use the communication software as same operation among the each network. This new idea "hostcap", which is a point of this paper, is explained in detail later. The "hostcap" is a kind of file which is consisted of translation rules of BTRON1 specification HMI to the host machine's commands for accessing the each network. If we use the "hostcap" for programming applications of network communication software, the end users are able to use the network communication software without consiousness of host machine's difference.

For solving the network communication software's problems, we focus on the electric mail/news as a network-wide service in this paper, and we have implemented some communicating applications using the BTRON1 specification HMI and the mechanism of "hostcap". The applications are called BMail and BNews. And then, we have also implemented BTRON1 specification Intelligent Terminal mechanism whose purpose is to develop a good graphical user interface's applications by using the "hostcap", easily. The each application is explained later. After all, the BTRON1 specification HMI is efficient for the network communication software and the "hostcap" is very useful for accessing many kinds of networks.

2 Machine Specifications

In this paper, the machines what we use have following specifications.

1. Workstation BE series (Made by Matsushita Electric Industrial Co., Ltd.)

CPU	80386(25MHz)
Memory	12 MB
Disk	170 MB
Software	BE-OS:Unix Sytem V R3.2+4.3BSD

2. BTRON1 specification experimental machine

CPU	80386SX(16MHz)
Memory	3 MB
Disk	40 MB
Software	BTRON1 specification OS

These machines can communicate with each other using a RS232C communication port. The workstation has a Ethernet port and can communicate with other workstations by using the Ethernet port.

3 Hostcap

In this chapter, we describe the "hostcap" that is a new idea in this paper for accessing several other networks with the BTRON1 specification HMI.

3.1 Abstract of Hostcap

The "hostcap" file consists of translation rules between the BTRON1 specification HMI and the command set of the target host machine for accessing other systems. The translation rules are included some entries corresponding to each host machine's operation or procedure.

For example we have described a general operating flow for using electric mail system. And, as shown in figure 1, We have divided the general operating flow into each operation for using the electric mail. And each operation is treated as one operation entry in the "hostcap" file.

The objective of the "hostcap" file is description of command sequence corresponding to each operations and each supported host machine.

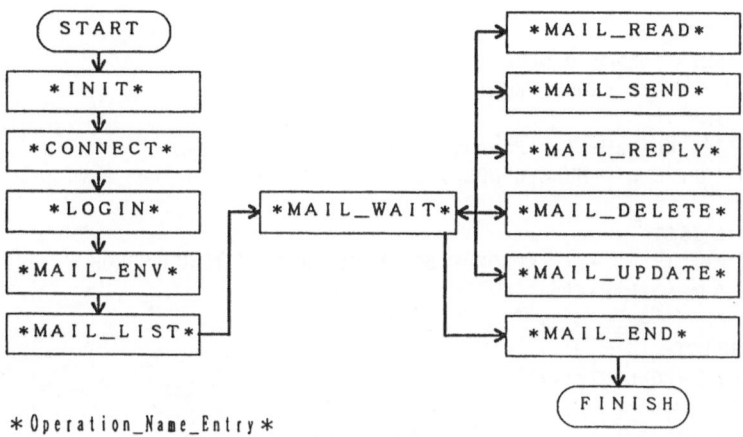

Figure 1: Flow of electric mail reader

When some operations on the BTRON1 specification OS are occured, an application executes commands corresponded to host name entry which is set this time. An application refferes entry of operation, some command sequences, from the "hostcap" file by using host name entry and operation name entry.

For example, when user opens a mail box, which is displayed like a virtual object on the BTRON1 specification experimental machine, the mail application executes some operation entries, which are *INIT*, *CONNECT, *LOGIN, *MAIL_ENV* and *MAIL_LIST*. Another example, when user send an electric mail, the mail application executes *MAIL_SEND* entry.

Therefore, we can use the network communication services without consiousness of host machine's difference.

3.2 A structure of the "hostcap" file

A format of the "hostcap" file and a part of "hostcap" example is shown as figure 2.

```
1   ;; Comments
2   ;; The hostcap formats as follow:
3   ;; (HostNameEntry
4   ;;     (OperationNameEntry
5   ;;       ((TranslationCommand-1)
6   ;;        (TranslationCommand-2)
7   ;;              :
8   ;;        (TranslationCommand-N))))
9   ;; TranslationCommand formats as follows:
10  ;; (SendMessage ReceiveMessage WaitTime ReceiveDataFormat)
11
12  ;; For BE workstation.
13  (BE
14    (*CONNECT*
15      (('RET' ''>>'' 0 NULL)
16       (''connect $HOST_NAME'' ''login:'' 0 NULL)))
17    (*LOGIN*
18      ((''$USER_NAME'' ''Passwd:'' 0 NULL)
19       (''$PASSWD'' NULL 5 NULL)))
20              :
21    (*MAIL_LIST*
22      ((''mailx -N -f'' $PROMPT 30 $NEW[N|U|SPACE]$NUM $FROM ...))))
23  ;; For Sun workstation.
24  (SUN
25    (*CONNECT*
26      (''BE *CONNECT*''))
27              :
28    (*MAIL_LIST*
29      ((''/usr/ucb/mail -N -f'' $PROMPT 30 $NEW[N|U|SPACE]$NUM $FROM ...))))
30  ;; For NiftyServe.
31  (NIFTY
32   (*CONNECT*
33     ((''ATDP$HOST_NAME'' NULL 30 NULL)
34      (''00+.'' ''-->'' 1 NULL)
35      (''SVC'' ''-->'' 1 NULL)))
36   (*LOGIN*
37     ((''$USER_NAME'' ''-->'' 1 NULL)
38      (''$PASSWD'' NULL 20 NULL)))
39   (*MAIL_LIST*
40     ((''READ'' ''>'' 10 #FORMAT#))))
```

Figure 2: A format of hostcap

As shown in figure 2, the "hostcap" file consists a set of host name entry. And, each host name entry includes a set of operation name entry, before described. Each operation name entry consists of some fields, which are sending commands, a receiving response, a waiting time out interval and a format of receiving data. We prepare the host name entries and operation name entries corresponding to services and host machines.

When we want to add or support a new host machine, we make and add the entry for new host machine in the "hostcap". And when we want to add a new services, we prepare some operation name entries. Then, we can support a new machine and we can make an application for a new service using new "hostcap" file. And, for complementing the translation rules in the "hostcap", the personal information data, for example account name, password and so on, are stored in another file.

3.3 Example of hostcap

Now, we prepare the host name entries are "BE", "SUN" and "NIFTY". The entry "BE" is indicated "BE" workstation, that is an UNIX host machine made by Matsushita Electric Industrial Co., Ltd. The entry "SUN" is indicated "SUN" workstation, that is an UNIX host machine made by Sun Microsystems Co., Ltd.. The entry "NIFTY" is indicated "NiftyServe" network communication services for personal computer users.

4 Applications

We have described the "hostcap" in the last chapter. And we try to make some applications by using the "hostcap".

We choose an electric mail/news systems as network wide applications. We have implemented some network service applications for accessing some other networks with the BTRON1 specification HMI. Also, we have thought that the BTRON1 specification HMI is used an intelligent network communication terminal.

In this chapter, we describe about electric mail/news readers called BMail/BNews and Intelligent Terminal by using "hostcap" mechanism on the BTRON1 specification OS.

4.1 BMail

In this section, we describe about the **BMail** which is an electric mail reader on the BTRON1 specification OS to be able to read some other host machine's electric mail.

4.1.1 Abstract of BMail

The **BMail** which is based on BTRON1 specification OS is an electric mail reader for reading on the UNIX host machine or the network host machine of personal computers.

Traditionally, for reading an electric mail, the users connect UNIX system or access from terminal. And the users do the procedure of login to the own account and typed some commands for reading an electric mail on the each host machine. For only reading the electric mail, the operations on each host machine are different from the other host machine's one. Therefore, almost users can not operate some host machine's electric mail.

So, by using the **BMail** we connect to one of the host machine which is supported by the "hostcap" from the BTRON1 specification system as a terminal. The host machines which are prepared the entry in the "hostcap" file are "BE" workstation, "Sun" workstation and "NiftyServe" which is the network for personal computers. We can read and send an electric mail on each system with the BTRON1 specification HMI.

4.1.2 Features of BMail

Summarization of the **BMail** features is following.

1. We can read the other network's electric mail with operation of the BTRON1 specification HMI.

   We can read the other network's electric mail with same operation of the BTRON1 specification real object/virtual object file system.

   In the **BMail** system, electric mails of the other host machine is displayed like the virtual object of the BTRON1 specification as shown in figure 3. Each the BTRON1 specification operation in the **BMail** is corresponded to action of electric mail reader on each host machine. (See figure 4.)

2. We can transfer an electric mail data in the **BMail** to the BTRON1 specification basic editors.

   A part or all of an electric mail data are able to paste the basic editor of the BTRON1 specification by "cut & paste" operation. It is easy to translate an electric mail data on the other network's host machine to BTRON1 specification TAD data by only mouse operation.

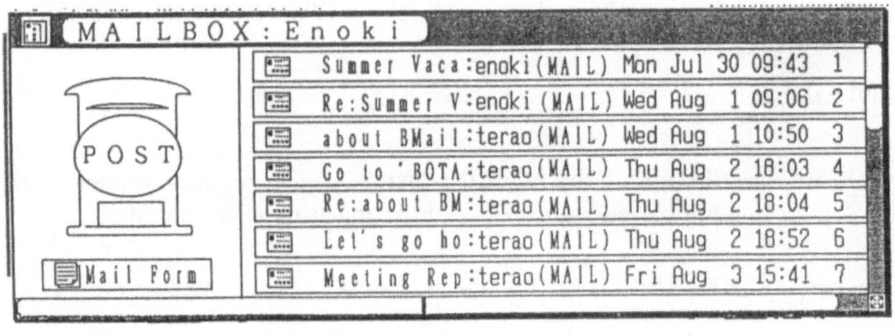

Figure 3: Display screen of BMail

action	operation
read a message (or open)	double click at the pictgram by pointing device or select sub-menu the "display" in the execution menu.
quit a mail (or close)	double click at the pictgram by pointing device or select sub-menu the "quit" in the execution menu.
send a reply message	select sub-menu the "reply" in the execution menu.
delete a mail	select sub-menu the "delete" in the execution menu or push the "delete" key.
send a message	paste a document to the application.
down load a message	move a mail like a virtual object to another window.

Figure 4: Table of the BMail operation

3. We can send the electric mail from the **BMail** user to the other network's users.

We can send the messages, which are written by the BTRON1 specification basic editor, from the **BMail** user to other network's users easily. First in the **BMail**, the BTRON1 specification TAD data are translated the ASCII text data. And the translated the ASCII data are sent by using network's host machine commands.

4. Also we can send the multi-media message to the other **BMail** user through the other network.

When it is clear that a message receiver is used the **BMail** on the BTRON1 specification system, we can exchange a TAD data with adding predefined identification. By using other network, we can send the documents which is written by BTRON1 specification basic editor.

To send the multi-media documents, the **BMail** sends the multi-media mail with predefined identification from the BTRON1 specification experimental machine to the host machine by using binary transfer routine. And the **BMail** executes host machine's mail sending command. To receive the multi-media documents, the **BMail** judges that the receive message is multi-media mail by the predefined identification. When the message has judged multi-media document, the **BMail** has received and displayed the multi-media documents on the screen of BTRON1 specification experimental machine.

5. We can classify the mail automatically by **BMail**.

The received electric mails are classified some cabinets with given rules by the BMail. These classification rules are sender addresses, time, date, title and so on.

This classification is like the real object/virtual object file system of the BTRON1 specification. The message on the network host machine are displayed virtual object in the BTRON1 specification file system. After all, we can see that those mail messages are classified automatically.

4.1.3 Implementation of BMail

In this section, we describe about the **BMail** implementation. We developed the **BMail** which is a prototype application of an electric mail reader on the BTRON1 specification system. The **BMail** have been programed by using the "hostcap". We support the following host machines, the "BE" workstation on the UNIX based system V, the "SUN" workstation on the UNIX based 4.3BSD and the "NiftyServe" network which is one of the famouns commercial network for personal computers in Japan. Now we have these machine's "hostcap" entries. We have used the mail commands which are supported standardly in each host machine.

When we set a host name entry of the "hostcap", the **BMail** gets the translation rules corresponding to the given host name entry from the "hostcap" file. So, if we change the host name entry, we can access the other network's host machine.

In the **BMail**, personal information data, a host name entry, an account name and so on, is stored as one of records in the real object of BTRON1 specification. And, the **BMail** reads the record, uses the host name entry and execute mail services.

4.1.4 Compare with other mail readers

There are some other systems as same as **BMail**'s purpose. Most of them is for the Machintosh by Apple Co. Ltd.. Some examples explain below.

1. Navigator

    The "Navigator" is an application for accessing a computer network "CompuServe", one of the famous network in America. It can only access the "CompuServe" network. The user sets up all thing to do at the "CompuServe" himself before accessing that. Then, he starts "Navigator" and wait until finishing. After that his mail is stored in his Machintosh and treat easily by "Navigator". The user reads his mails and replays some mail. The "Navigator" sends them appropriately at the next access.

2. CONNECT

    In the network "CONNECT", there is an easy application to use network communication. It is only for Machintosh user as same as "Navigator" before described. One of the features is to be able to send non-text data, graphic data, figure data and etc..

The "Navigator" is only to access the network of "Compuserve" for Machintosh. And also, in case of the "CONNECT", it can't be access any networks except the "CONNECT" by using Machintosh.

There are some problem that most of applications specificate one special network. They are not available to use same operation on the general computer communication networks and the UNIX network.

In the **BMail**, when we add a new host name entry, we can use an electric mail on a new computer network. Also, data exchanging between other networks is easy because all of documents in the BTRON1 specification are structured with format of TAD.

4.2   BNews

In this section, we describe **BNews** which is a news reader application program and which treats articles of the UNIX network news using BTRON1 specification human machine interface. The network news is one of the famous message exchange systems in the UNIX world.

4.2.1   About the UNIX network news system

We describe the UNIX network news system below. The UNIX network news system is used as broadcasting some messages among many people.

Someone logins a UNIX machine, and posts a message (called a article). The posted article is transmitted to other UNIX machines by using communication lines such as Ethernet or RS232C. Thus articles are transmitted one after another, and stored in the disks of each machine. The articles are classified and stored into the news groups. The news groups have a hierarchic structure using the UNIX hierarchic file system. Before posting an article, we select the news group suited for that article. And when reading articles, we select the news group which we interested in.

A news reader program has following functions in news system which runs above procedure.

- displaying active news groups list

- selecting a news group

- displaying articles list in a selected news group

- displaying article

- unsubscribing news groups

- followuping the selected article

- posting a new article

- replying the selected article

4.2.2   Features of BNews

We show the example of **BNews** display screen on figure 5.

In the UNIX network news system, news groups have hierarchic structure. **BNews** display each hierarchic news group as a virtual object. In news groups, there are articles or there are lower news groups. In case there are articles into news groups, when we open such virtual object which means a news group, there are articles into a window. In case there are lower news groups into news groups, when we open such virtual object which means a news group, there are another virtual objects which means lower news groups into a window.

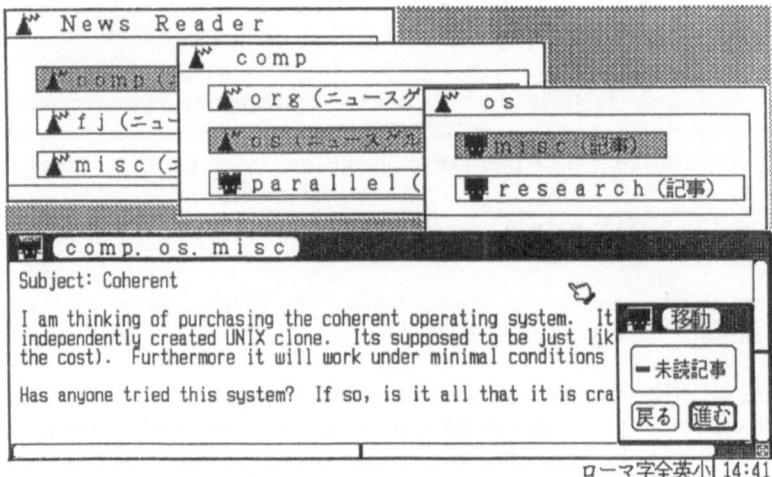

Figure 5: display screen of BNews

In other words we can display news groups, select news groups and read articles in the network news using same method of the file operation with BTRON1 specification real/virtual object maneger.

4.2.3   Implementation of BNews (Method of connecting to news system)

In **BNews** system, when we execute program, first we login a UNIX machine which is described in a hostname entry of "hostcap" on the BTRON1 specification experimental machine. Then **BNews** do the following command for the UNIX machine.
% telnet nntp_server_name nntp
The 'nntp_server_name' means the hostname which is described in a nntp_server entry of "hostcap" on the BTRON1 specification experimental machine, and which is stored network news articles. The 'nntp' means the port number of nntp (Network News Transfer Protocol)[1]. So **BNews** connects to the news server machine using nntp, and accesses the network news system. The nntp defines the commands and these responces, we can access network news system without consciousness of UNIX version's difference. Then if UNIX machines support the nntp, we do'nt have to consider about machine difference. So we can connect **BNews** to many machines.

4.2.4   Implementation of BNews (Method of news groups management)

BNews creates the news group management table on the BTRON1 specification experimental machine, which has data of the news group structure in the news server machine, when **BNews** connects to the news server machine for the first time. Because the data of news group structure in the news server machine is not so often updated. We show the news group management table of **BNews** on figure6. And we show the link state of the news group management table on figure7.

---

[1] Refer to RFC977.

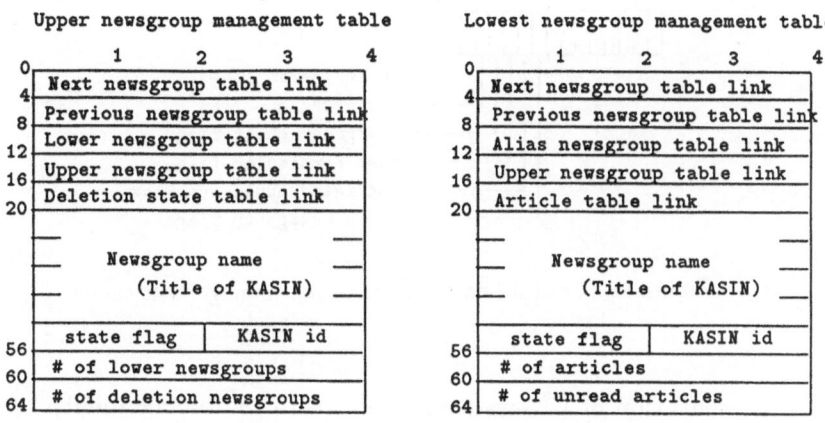

Figure 6: The news group management table

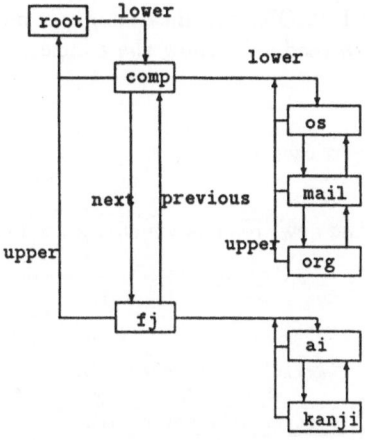

Figure 7: The linkage of news group management tables

The first five pointers in the news group management table are used for creating link state of the news group management table in figure7. There are links for the forward/backward relation, the upper/lower relation, deletion state and aliase state. The forward/backward relation links and the upper/lower relation links represent a logical relation of news groups.

The deletion state links are used in order to make news group unsubscribed, which the user don't want to read. The aliase state links are used in order to display news group into easy access area, which the user access very often. These pointers describe memory address, because these tables are loaded from the executing real object. We show the state flag of the news group management table on figure8.

The state flag shows the state of the news group state. When the user gives a instruction for**BNews**, these tables are updated by using nntp and getting some date from news server machine.

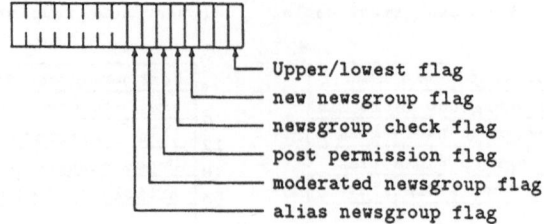

Figure 8: The state flag in news group management tables

4.2.5 Implementation of BNews (Method of articles management)

The data about read articles or unread articles are updated one after another, while articles are read. In the UNIX machines the data about read articles or unread articles are updated in local system and with individuals.(It means each login name.) So in **BNews** the article management tables are on the BTRON1 specification experimental machine and updated one after another, while articles are read. We show the article management table of **BNews** on figure 9.

4.2.6 Compare with other news readers

We show comparison between the news readers which are used generally in UNIX and **BNews**. (See figure 10.)

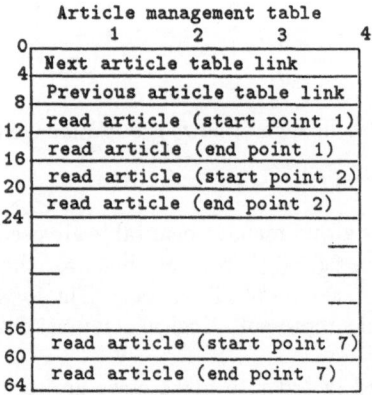

Figure 9: The article management table

program	readnews	rn	vn	gnus	BNews
select news groups	no	command	arguments	on screen	on screen
posting	no	no	no	yes	yes
follow,reply,cancel	yes	yes	yes	yes	yes
header list	no	yes	yes	yes	yes
search articles	no	command	arguments	sort	yes
read again	no	command	no	yes	yes
collect articles	no	no	no	no	yes
Human interface	character	character	character	character	graphical

Figure 10: The Compare with other news readers

4.3 BTRON1 specification Intelligent Terminal

In this section, we describe BTRON1 specification Intelligent Terminal. This system is consisted of an application software on the BTRON1 specification experimental machine, some definition files on the UNIX system and some executive commands on the UNIX system. Using this system, we can enter the data using a BTRON1 specification HMI, and process the data by the UNIX system.

4.3.1 Abstract of BTRON1 specification Intelligent Terminal

BTRON1 specification Intelligent Terminal is connected to the UNIX system as a terminal for input/output data using a BTRON1 specification HMI.

The UNIX system depends on the BTRON1 specification system for entering the data, and doesn't concern with it. While users enter the data to the BTRON1 specification system, the BTRON1 specification system doesn't communicate the UNIX system. After that, the BTRON1 specification system transmites the data to the UNIX system and ask the UNIX system to prosess the data.

The BTRON1 specification system connected to the UNIX system is loaded with the data definition file and the screen definition file from the UNIX system, which are prepared beforehand, and, according to the contents of the definition files, constructs the screen for input/output of data.

After transmitting the data, the BTRON1 specification system executes the UNIX command which is prepared beforehand to process the data.

Redefining these definition files and the UNIX commands, we can construct another data management system without reconstructing the program itself running in the BTRON1 specification experimental machine.

4.3.2 HMI of BTRON1 specification Intelligent Terminal

Summerization of HMI of BTRON1 specification Intelligent Terminal is as follows briefly. (see figure 11)

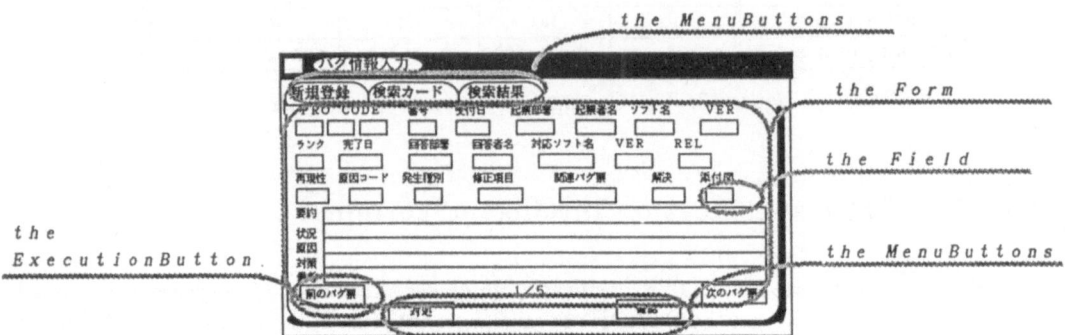

Figure 11: The screen form.

The screen of BTRON1 specification Intelligent Terminal is consisted of following parts.

1. Field

   Field is used for input data. Several kinds of Fields are supported

   (e.g.) numeral type, character type, string type.

2. Form

   Form is a unit of screen consisted of some Fields.

3. MenuButton

   When this button is clicked, the Form linked by the button is displayed.

4. ExecutionButton

   When the ExecutionButton is clicked, data of Fields designated by the ExecutionButton are transmitted to the UNIX system as a UNIX file and the UNIX command designated by the ExecutionButton is executed to process the UNIX file.

   The file consisted of the return value is created by the UNIX command. That file is transmited to the BTRON1 specification experimental machine, and the return value is displayed in the BTRON1 specification experimental machine, if necessary.

Combining above-mentioned parts, we can make the screen for input/output of data. Users can enter the data by unified HMI method using the BTRON1 specification parts manager.

4.3.3 Inplementation of BTRON1 specification Intelligent Terminal

Summerization of the flow of this system is as follows briefly. (see figure 12)

1. The BTRON1 specification experimental machine is connected to the UNIX system as a terminal. Several BTRON1 specification experimental machines are connected to a UNIX system.

2. The BTRON1 specification system connected to the UNIX system is loaded with the data definition file and the screen definition file from the UNIX system, and according to the contents of the definition files, constructs the screen for input/output of data.

3. Users enter and edit the data using a BTRON1 specification HMI.

4. Clicking the ExecutionButton, input data is transmited to the UNIX system as a UNIX file.

5. The UNIX command designated by the ExecutionButton is executed to process the UNIX file.

6. After command execution, if some value are returned, they are transmitted to the BTRON1 specification experimental machine and displayed.

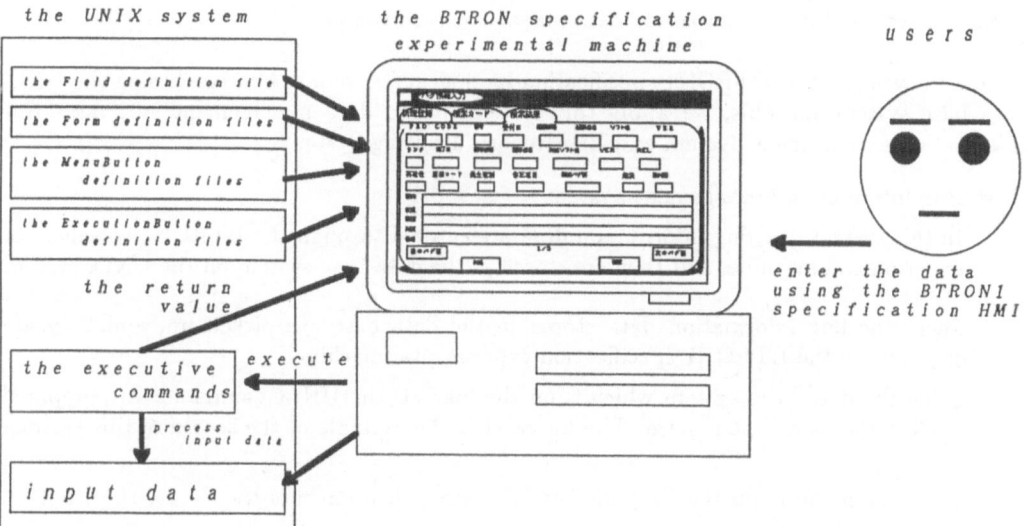

Figure 12: The data flow model.

Followings must be defined in the UNIX systems.

1. Field definition file

   This file defines the types of data to be entered through each Fields. (For example, the types are for text or for figure.)

2. ExecutionButton definition file

   This file defines the attributes of ExecutionButton. The attribute of ExecutionButton is consisted of the name of UNIX command, identifyer for transmitted Form, and so on.

3. Form definition file

   This files defines construction of Form. This defines what parts are constructing the Form also defines where these parts are located.

4. Menu definition file

   These files define attribute of MenuButton. When MenuButton is clicked, the Form linked by the button is displayed.

5. Executive commands

   These commands are executed as UNIX command when ExecutionButton is clicked. They take on processing data. So, the application software on the BTRON1 specification system takes on input/output of data.

Making above-mentioned parts, and combining them, BTRON1 specification Intelligent Terminal behaves as if it were an adhoc data management software.

We have developed this BTRON1 specification Intelligent Terminal. And combining the UNIX data base system and this, we apply this system to two data management systems - Bug Information Management System and Bug Reports Printing System.

- Bug Information Management System

  In this system, the bug information data are entered through the BTRON1 specification experimental machine, and they are stored in the data base system on the UNIX system.

  Then, the bug information data stored in the data base are picked up, and they are displayed in the BTRON1 specification experimental machine.

  Using the data base system which is on the market, the UNIX commands are prepared to treat the data base system. The figure 11 is the example of the screen of this system.

  This system sums up the bug information data , then outputs the data , the result of summing up.

4.3.4 Applicability of this system

One of the features of this system is to separate entering the data from processing the data perfectly, the former taken on a terminal (the BRON1 specification experimental machine), the latter taken on the host computer (the UNIX computer). Then, the host computer designates the types of data which are necessary to process the data, and doesn't concern with entering the data. On the otherhand, the terminal doesn't concern with processing the data which the terminal enters. Therefore, the host computer can be connected to every terminal which is used for entering the data designated by the host computer. This time, the terminal were developed on the BTRON1 specification experimental machine. We can do it not only on the BTRON1 specification experimental machine, but on another machine such as Machintosh or a MS-DOS machine. Then, using several kinds of the terminal, we can enter the data with each terminal's HMI. And we can use another computer as the host. This time, we use the UNIX computer as the host. However, we can do it on the another machine which prepare the definition files and execution commands.

5 conclusion

In this paper, we have proposed that the "hostcap" mechanism is very useful for accessing other network on the BTRON1 specification. We have developed some applications, BMail, BNews by using the "hostcap". And we have developed that one Intelligent Terminal system has implemented on the BTRON1 specification experimental machine.

We have explained the "hostcap" file format before. Also, we think that the "hostcap" file is described another format like a TACL.

Some future researches are remained.

- Applicability of hostcap
  In this paper, we target a UNIX environment and one network for personal computer. We will inspect applicability of hostcap in some other environments, some personal computer networks, ISDN services, inner-corporated networks etc..
- How to display the different network's messages at the same time
  We will develop that an electric message from one networks and another message from another networks can be seen same time in the same window display.

References

[1] Feinler, J., O.J.Jacobsen, and M.Stahl: *DDN Protocol Handbook Volume Two, DARPA Internet Protocols*, DDN Network Information Center, SRI International, Menlo Park, California, December 1985.

[2] N.I.F. Corporation:*NIFTY-Serve Access Guide Version 2 (in Japanease)*, N.I.F. Corporation, Chiyoda-ku, Tokyo, 1989.

[3] TRON Association *BTRON1 Specification, Software Specification*, TRON Association, Minato-ku, Tokyo, 1990.

Nobuyuki Enoki is an engineer in Kansai Information and Communications Research laboratories of Matsushita Electric Industrial Co., Ltd. (MEI), Osaka, Japan. He received B.E. and M.E. degrees in information science from Hiroshima University, Hiroshima, Japan, in 1986 and 1988, respectively. He has been engaged in the research and development of computer operating system and computer. He is a member of the IPSJ and the IEICEJ.

Hideyuki Oka is an engineer in Kansai Information and Communications Research laboratories of Matsushita Electric Industrial Co., Ltd. (MEI), Osaka, Japan. He received B.E. and M.E. degrees in electric communication science from Waseda University, Tokyo, Japan, in 1983 and 1985, respectively. He has been engaged in the research and development of computer operating system and computer communication. He is a member of the IEICEJ.

Aki Yoneda is an engineer in Kansai Information and Communications Research laboratories of Matsushita Electric Industrial Co., Ltd. (MEI), Osaka, Japan. He received B.E. degree in mechanical engineering from Waseda University, Tokyo, Japan, in 1989, respectively. He has been engaged in the research and development of computer operating system and computer communication.

Makoto Ando is an engineer in Kansai Information and Communications Research laboratories of Matsushita Electric Industrial Co., Ltd. (MEI), Osaka, Japan. He received B.E. and M.E. degrees in information engineering from Osaka University, Osaka, Japan, in 1980 and 1982, respectively. He has been engaged in the research and development of operating system and computer. He is a member of the IPSJ.

Above authors may be reached at: Matsushita Electric Industrial Co., Ltd. KANSAI Information and Communications Research Laboratories, 1006, Kadoma, Kadoma-shi, Osaka, 571, Japan

Pitfalls on the Road to Portability

James D. Mooney
West Virginia University

ABSTRACT

This paper considers some problems which may arise in the quest for software portability, especially those relating to the system interface, and evaluates the CTRON specification to determine if these problems may be avoided.

The literature on portability is reviewed, especially case studies describing porting experience. The portability-related tasks performed by several classes of software developers and implementors are examined. These considerations lead to identification of four potential problem areas: subsets, specification level, range and performance guarantees, and language bindings.

The CTRON specification is then examined in relation to these problem areas, and several recommendations are stated.

Keywords: CTRON, Pitfalls, Portability

1. INTRODUCTION

1.1 Portability Concepts

The objective of CTRON is to define a set of system interfaces to improve the portability of higher level software. The goal of this paper is to identify some pitfalls that may obstruct the development of portable software, and to examine the ways in which CTRON may avoid these pitfalls. As a prelude, we must first establish what we mean by portability. The following summary will provide a framework for this discussion.

There are many possible definitions for software portability. In a recent article (Mooney 1990) I have proposed the following definition:

> *An application is portable across a class of environments to the degree that the effort required to transport and adapt it to a new environment in the class is less than the effort of redevelopment.*

This definition focuses on applications, but it may also be applied to portability of extended OS modules. The definition points out the distinction between physical movement of software and adaptation to the needs of each environment. It also emphasizes that portability is a matter of degree. We will adopt it as a working definition for this paper.

The term *environment* is used to refer collectively to the total collection of software and hardware with which a program interacts in a particular installation. The alternate term *platform* is also commonly used for this purpose.

Two distinct types of portability are usually considered for software modules. A program that can be transported in its executable form to a new environment, and executed without change, exhibits *binary portability*. This is only possible if the CPU architecture and certain other system elements are identical across the two environments. Although simplest by far for programmers and users, binary portability can only be achieved within a very narrow range of environments.

Source portability exists if the source files for the program can be transported to a new environment, and executed after being recompiled with a suitable compiler. If necessary, these files can be modified and adapted before compiling, but the modifications should be limited and straightforward.

There are also issues of data portability, and portability of users, programmers, training, and documentation. These issues are important but we will not consider them further in this discussion.

An application program interacts with its environment through a set of interfaces. A typical set of application program interfaces is shown in *Fig. 1*. This model may be applied also to extended OS modules. In this diagram direct interfaces are shown by solid lines, and indirect interfaces are shown by dashed lines. Note the central role of the operating system in most of the program interfaces.

This view represents a program during execution, and does not reflect the interfaces derived from other program representations during development. In particular, the language in which a program is written, and any intermediate representations used, form important additional interfaces.

The interfaces used by an application collectively define its view of the environment. If the interfaces are consistent across environments, portability will be achieved even though the system components may differ.

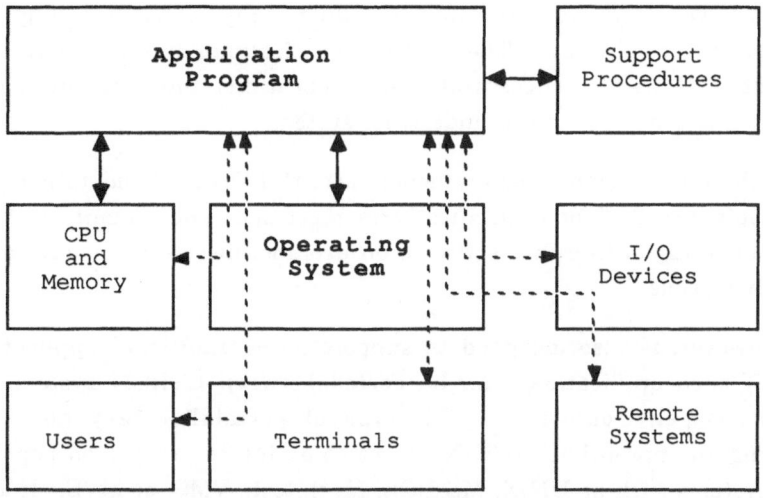

Fig. 1 -- Application Program Interfaces

1.2 Portability and CTRON

In the previous section we outlined a framework for discussion of portability in general. Let us next consider how that framework is related to CTRON.

The CTRON Specification (TRON 1989) is intended to enhance portability by defining a standard interface to a wide range of operating system services. Low level interfaces are provided by the Basic OS modules (BOS), consisting of the Kernel and I/O Control. Higher level interfaces are provided by the Extended OS modules (EOS).

CTRON is intended to support portability across various hardware environments, including heterogenous systems in a network, so source portability is the only realistic goal.

CTRON supports portability at two distinct interface levels. The Basic OS interface supports the movement of portable EOS modules across different BOS environments. The EOS interfaces in turn (together with the BOS) support application portability.

The complete CTRON interface is so large that few systems could provide support for every function; moreover, few applications or EOS modules require more than a small subset of the functions defined. For this reason various subsets and optional configurations are defined for CTRON, and most implementations will support only a subset of the total specification.

The target application classes for CTRON systems include switching and communication, information processing, and workstation applications. Some of these applications have special requirements including high performance, high reliability, and hard realtime constraints. The CTRON specification defines mechanisms to meet these needs. However, successful implementations must include appropriate performance guarantees from the underlying system.

Because of these performance requirements, most CTRON implementations will consist of system software designed specifically to meet the requirements of the CTRON interface. Layering of interface software on existing, dissimilar operating systems is not normally feasible.

CTRON, however, is also designed to support more traditional applications. It is beneficial if such applications can be ported between CTRON systems and other general-purpose environments. This type of portability may be enhanced by implementing an appropriate CTRON subset as an interface layer on popular existing operating systems such as UNIX, MS-DOS, Macintosh, VMS, or MVS. If this is done, applications designed to use the CTRON interface may run both in "pure" CTRON environments and on more traditional systems.

To enable portable program development, any system interface standard must include language bindings which specify the syntax and (possibly modified) semantics for accessing the defined services within the context of suitable programming languages. CTRON includes complete language bindings for three languages: C, Ada, and CHILL.

1.3 Goals of the Paper

This paper is concerned with the process of achieving software portability, and with the role of the system interface in supporting that goal. Particular emphasis will be placed on the portability characteristics of the CTRON interface. We will begin with a brief survey of the available literature on portability, to see what lessons may be learned. In light of this experience, we will try to identify the principal activities related to portability that may occur in the course of the development and use of software systems, and the persons who perform these activities.

We will then consider some key steps that occur during each of these activities, and the difficulties that may occur during each of these steps, especially problems due to the characteristics of the system interface specification. CTRON will be assessed to determine how well it avoids these difficulties. Based on this assessment, some recommendations for future refinement of CTRON will be made.

The paper is necessarily limited in scope. Many issues that are important to the overall goal of portability will not be discussed. Some of these include physical transportation of programs, media formats, data formats, documentation, and training.

2. LEARNING FROM EXPERIENCE

2.1 Overview of the Literature

The literature on software portability is limited, but some worthwhile lessons can be learned from it. There are a few textbooks, chapters, surveys, and course notes which focus on portability. Foundation work is contained in the course notes by Poole and Waite (1975) and the full advanced course edited by Brown (1977). Textbooks on software portability include those by Wallis (1982), Dahlstrand (1984), and LeCarme and Pellisier-Gart (1986). Chapters on portability have appeared in software engineering texts (Sommerville 1989, Ch. 17) and operating system texts (Lane and Mooney 1989, Ch. 20).

A recent survey of strategies for supporting portability is presented by the author (Mooney 1990).

Although some of the works cited propose some theoretical concepts, formal theories and methodologies for portability are still lacking. Furthermore, no systematic experimental studies have been reported. Much of the useful information in the literature is gained, instead, from individual experience reports and case studies.

A few authors have collected portability guidelines based on extended experience. Waite (1975) presents guidelines for the physical distribution of portable software. Tanenbaum *et al* (1978) identify a large number of potential barriers to software portability. Many of the issues raised by Tanenbaum are most applicable to older mainframe environments and not relevant to CTRON. However, this paper lists a number of subtle problems that can arise when assumptions are made about the structure and behavior of file systems and I/O devices in various environments. The actual structures found on different systems often do not conform to these assumptions.

A few common system interfaces have been proposed besides the TRON series. All of these have somewhat different goals than CTRON, but similarities exist in specific areas. Hall *et al* (1980) proposed a "virtual operating system" with a set of UNIX-like primitives. Other primitive sets have been proposed for special functional areas including distributed I/O (Cheriton 1987) and robotics (Schwan 1987).

IEEE Standard 1003.1 (POSIX) presents a more detailed UNIX-like interface which is being widely adopted (IEEE 1988). An appendix to the standard contains some of the rationale for its design. IEEE Standard 855 (MOSI) proposes a program interface for small computer systems (IEEE 1990). Some explanations for the design of MOSI are given in two articles by the author (Mooney 1985, Mooney 1986). In addition, proprietary interfaces have been standardized for the operating systems of several vendors.

A number of case studies exist which discuss both porting of existing software and designing software for portability. Classes of software ported include applications, compilers, and operating systems. We will examine some of these studies in the rest of this section.

2.2 Porting Applications

Case studies of actual porting of applications are very relevant to CTRON, but reports of this type in the open literature are rare. A few examples include TeX (Zabala 1981), the CHEF editor (Peck 1981), and WordPerfect (Blackham 1988). Curiously, all of these are text processors of various types. These programs involve no concurrency or high performance requirements, and access few services not defined within their chosen programming language. Thus they represent relatively simple cases for portability. Reports of the porting of more complex applications have not been found.

The TeX text processing system was written in Pascal and is implemented in a wide range of medium and large environments. TeX is a file processing system which normally operates in batch mode. Difficulties in porting TeX arose primarily from the limitations of standard Pascal, and the free use of nonstandard extensions in the original design. Other problems arose from limits on program size, data structure sizes, or value ranges. TeX is a very large program.

CHEF is an interactive editor similar to UNIX *ed* written in BCPL. It was ported to several large and small environments. The designers favor use of a single source file with conditional compilation to adapt the file for each system type. Conditional compilation is also used to select optional features which may be omitted to save memory space.

WordPerfect is a word processor written in assembly language, which has been implemented (by the designer) on many microcomputers. Modular structure is used to enhance portability by allowing suitable modules to be selected for each environment.

2.3 Porting Compilers

The porting of compilers is important to our study primarily as an example of application porting. Examples of compilers that have been ported include UNIX PCC (Johnson 1978), UCSD Pascal (Campbell 1983), and Tanenbaum's Amsterdam Compiler Kit (Tanenbaum 1983). However, most descriptions concern *retargeting* of compilers, which is a change of function rather than adaptation to a new environment.

UCSD Pascal is ported as a complete user environment; this is similar to the porting of operating systems, and is considered in the next section.

2.4 Porting Operating Systems

The greatest number of reports available on software porting concern the porting of operating systems. If the operating system itself can be ported to the desired target environments, then the subsequent porting of applications is greatly simplified.

Porting operating systems raises some problems quite different from porting applications. The operating system must interact intimately with its hardware environment, and the interesting cases are those in which the hardware is significantly different. This experience is relevant to the porting of CTRON Extended OS components.

A number of operating systems have been designed (or redesigned) with portabilitiy as a definite goal. These include UNIX (Johnson 1978), MACH (Rashid 1988), THOTH (Cheriton 1979), PICK (Cook 1984), MUSS (Theaker 1979), and TRIPOS (Richards 1979). Other operating systems that have been ported to dissimilar processors include SOLO (Powell 1979) and OS/6 (Snow 1978).

Some adaptation of portable operating systems is inevitable due to the differing hardware which the OS must control. In most cases, a modular organization is used, with a few modules (e.g. device drivers, memory manager, interrupt manager) to be rewritten for each environment. A few systems (MUSS, THOTH, and UCSD Pascal) are written in (or compiled to) a "machine language" for a common abstract machine. An interpreter for this machine must be written for each environment. This approach can lead to great inefficiency unless the machine language is carefully chosen.

3. WHO CARES ABOUT PORTABILITY (AND WHY)?

Everyone agrees that portability is desirable, but to clearly understand the reasons for its importance, let's examine portability issues from the viewpoint of specific classes of people involved with software design and use. There are at least five groups who may have specific goals with respect to portability. These groups form a hierarchy, as shown in *Fig. 2*. The objectives of each group are supported by the groups that follow.

The following list identifies the five groups that form this hierarchy, and summarizes the portability goals for each group.

1) **Users**: those who use applications and systems as tools to accomplish useful work.

   GOAL: to have a wide range of application software available in each environment at reasonable cost, and to be able to use consistent software in different environments.

2) **Application Installers**: those who install applications in specific environments.

   GOAL: to port existing applications to specific new environments.

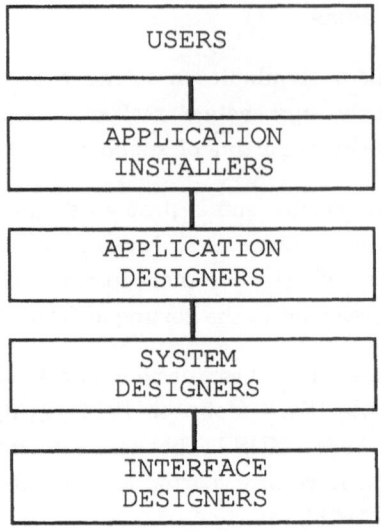

Fig. 2 -- A Portability Support Hierarchy

3) **Application Designers**: those who design and develop applications.

GOAL: to design applications which can be easily ported among different environments.

4) **System Designers:** those who design and develop system software to support the needs of applications.

GOAL: to provide mechanisms and interfaces for specific new or existing environments which facilitate porting of applications.

5) **Interface Designers**: those who design standard interfaces to be used between applications and system components.

GOAL: to design system interfaces providing effective support for higher-level software portability.

Except for users, the goal for each category is to complete a definite activity. This activity involves a series of steps, and is supported by a particular collection of resources. We will examine in more detail the activities carried out by the three central groups: application installers, application designers, and system designers. In each case we will try to list the resources that are generally available, and the distinct steps that seem most important in order to attain the desired portability goals. The author and many readers of this paper fall into the category of interface designers, the final group; alas, the procedures for this group are not so well defined.

4. THE APPLICATION INSTALLER

The installer of an application normally has the following resources available:

1) application source and data files.

2) designer's documentation.

3) system hardware, software and documentation, including OS and compilers.

With these resources the installer must carry out the following tasks:

1) **Ensure support for all necessary interfaces**, with suitable configurations, in the target environment. Port supporting software if necessary.

2) **Perform any necessary adaptation** due to interface differences or desired behavior differences.

3) **Compile** revised source files with a compiler targeted for the new environment. Also adapt data files as necessary.

4) **Install** executable program and data files in the new environment.

These tasks will be aided or hindered by the characteristics of the interface elements in the target environment. Before we consider the problems that may arise, let's examine the other classes of developers.

5. THE APPLICATION DESIGNER

The application designer typically works with the following resources:

1) application specification.

2) language definitions.

3) applicable standard interface specifications.

The process of designing a portable application will include these tasks:

1) **Identify environment characteristics required** by the planned application. These may include graphic user interfaces, realtime response, high-capacity storage, etc.

2) **Select programming language(s)** suitable for the application and widely available for the appropriate environments.

3) **Identify additional services and resources required** that are not defined within the chosen language(s). As far as possible, avoid those that are likely to be unavailable on many target systems.

4) **Identify interface standards** or specifications which define access mechanisms

for the required services and resources, and which are or can be implemented in most of the suitable environments.

5) **Design and develop the application.** Use only standard features of the chosen language. Use the structures defined by the chosen interface specifications, with suitable language bindings. Rely on guarantees of performance, accuracy, value ranges, etc., only if provided by the chosen specifications.

6) **Isolate system dependencies** that remain due to interfaces not fully defined by any standard, or variations desirable for different classes of environments. Use modular design, data abstraction, and selective compilation as required.

7) **Document** all assumptions about suitable environments. Document known system dependencies and suitable methods of adaptation.

6. THE SYSTEM DESIGNER

The principal resources available for those wishing to design and implement a system interface to support portability, or a system containing such interfaces, are:

1) system software and documentation.

2) interface standards and specifications.

The system designer must perform the following tasks:

1) **Identify services and capabilities** which can be supported by the existing or planned system.

2.) **Identify application classes** which are likely candidates for porting to this system.

.3) **Identify services and resources** which may be required by such portable applications.

4) **Identify interface standards** which may define common access mechanisms for the required services and resources.

5) **Design access mechanisms** and interface structures for the identified services and resources, using the appropriate standards as far as possible.

6) **Implement and document** the interface and/or the system.

The concept of *application profiles*, which is now evolving in standards groups, may be helpful in characterizing both suitable application classes, and standards appropriate for each class.

7. WHAT SOFTWARE WILL BE PORTED TO CTRON ENVIRONMENTS?

CTRON provides an interface standard to support system implementors and application designers in the context of suitable system types and application classes. To assess

CTRON's potential to support portability, we must consider the type of software which may be ported to CTRON environments. The principal software classes expected to operate in CTRON environments (TRON 1989) are:

1) Extended OS components.

2) Higher level support software.

3) Real time applications.

4) General applications.

Extended OS components (e.g. file management, communication control, human-machine interface) will be ported to environments supporting the Basic OS (kernel and I/O).

Higher level support and interface software will be ported to environments including both the Basic OS and EOS components.

Communication and switching applications will be ported to environments including both the Basic OS and EOS components, and possibly higher level interfaces as well. These applications may be distributed and may have hard requirements for reliability, performance, and realtime response which must be met on all target systems.

General workstation and information processing applications will be ported to environments including both the Basic OS and EOS components, and possibly higher level interfaces. These applications may be distributed but will have less stringent performance requirements.

8. HOW WILL CTRON IMPLEMENTATIONS DIFFER?

Although all CTRON implementations are expected to follow a common specification, they will, of course, not be identical. It is the differences among these environments that can lead to problems of portability. Likely differences among CTRON environments include the following:

1. Different CTRON subsets will be implemented.

2. Nonstandard extensions may be included.

3. Performance (speed, storage capacity) and cost will vary among systems.

4. Not every system will support the same data ranges, provide the same resource capacity, or guarantee the same timing accuracy.

5. Environments will differ in reliability and fault tolerance.

Consideration of these differences will also help us to recognize some likely pitfalls.

9. WHERE ARE THE PITFALLS?

We are now prepared to try to identify some pitfalls for the portability-related activities we have considered. Review of the portability literature has been of limited help in finding barriers to portability that may be caused by the system interface. The case studies in application porting have relied primarily on services accessible through the standard definition of a programming language. This of course emphasizes the importance of the language in any system designed for portability; it also reminds us that more difficult problems are faced by applications requiring facilities which are not covered by the common language definitions.

Many of the tasks faced by designers and installers require decisions based on a good knowledge of program requirements and expectations. If this information is not available in a suitable form, portability will suffer.

Each of the viewpoints we have considered has generated a list of tasks related to portability goals. For each task, some pitfalls may be identified which could obstruct the effort to achieve the benefits of portability. These pitfalls are summarized in *Table 1*.

Some of the pitfalls in this table concern the inherent nature of specific application or system designs, such as providing unusual timing mechanisms or relying on a specialized graphic user interface. These are certainly barriers to portability, but they cannot be overcome by interface standards.

The remaining pitfalls are focused around a fairly small set of critical concerns. These pitfalls may be avoided, or at least made less dangerous, by good interface design. They fall primarily into four categories:

1.) **Too many subsets**. If many subsets are allowed, many environments may not support an adequate subset for a specific application.

2) **Wrong level of specification**. An interface standard may specify details such as data formats or specific algorithms which are not generally important to application designers, but which may not be supportable by some systems. This reduces the set of acceptable target environments.

Alternately, the standard may be silent or incomplete on some details even though reasonable specifications could be designed. As a result, system implementors will introduce arbitrary differences, and additional adaptation may be required for each system.

3) **Missing guarantees**. The standard may fail to specify information such as the maximum error for timing measurements or the minimum range for numerical data types. System implementors will not know what criteria should be met, and application designers will not know what guarantees can be relied on.

TASK	PITFALLS
APPLICATION INSTALLER	
Ensure interface support	Missing functions or inconsistent structure due to lack of standard or too many choices
Perform adaptation	May need extensive adaptation due to interface mismatches
Compile and install	Possible differences in language or language binding
APPLICATION DESIGNER	
Identify environment features	May choose to rely on features available in few environments
Select languages	Language may lack effective bindings to needed interface standards
Identify additional services	May choose to rely on services which lack standard interfaces
Identify interface standards	No standard or too many standards for some interfaces
Design and develop	Standards may be incomplete; guarantees for value ranges, resource capacities, or performance may be inadequate or missing
Isolate system dependencies	Remaining dependencies may be numerous and difficult to isolate
Document	Too many variations to document effectively
SYSTEM IMPLEMENTOR	
Identify system capabilities	Capabilities may differ unnecessarily from those of similar systems
Identify application classes	No clear match between system and application classes
Identify application requirements	Requirements not well specified
Identify standards	Standards may be missing, incomplete, or incompatible with system design
Design access mechanisms	Mechanisms may not provide expected structure or semantics due to incomplete specifications
Implement and document	Documentation may not provide full guidance for installer

Table 1 -- Portability tasks and their pitfalls

4) **No satisfactory language binding**. If there is no standard language binding at all for the language of the application, all accesses to the system interface may have to be rewritten for each environment, defeating most of the purpose of the standard.

If the language binding is not well integrated into the language, programmers will ignore the binding and perhaps the underlying interface as well. Instead they will devise nonstandard alternatives.

10. ASSESSMENT OF CTRON

The previous section identified some dangerous pitfalls. Now we can consider how well these pitfalls are avoided in the present CTRON specification.

1) **Number of subsets:** CTRON is so large that subsets are necessary. Perhaps this size is an obstacle in itself. Small systems cannot support all functions, and many classes of applications require only a small subset. The number of permitted subsets in the kernel is well controlled. Current work (Shibagaki 1990) is propagating subset control to other modules. In some cases there remains a large number of optional modules, which is undesirable but may not be possible to avoid.

2) **Level of specification:** The CTRON specification is very detailed in most cases. This is generally reasonable since most CTRON systems will be designed especially to support CTRON. However, it may be an obstacle to implementing an acceptable subset in some existing environments.

CTRON identifies elements that cannot easily be specified, especially those in the architecture-dependent interface. Adaptation is required, but this adaptation will be easier since the necessary functions are identified. More detail could be added here as suitable models evolve.

3) **Range and performance guarantees:** The CTRON language-independent specification gives no minimum value ranges for interface data types. Other interface standards do define such minimum values. Some more explicit value ranges are specified in the language bindings, but this is not the appropriate place for them.

CTRON also includes few performance guarantees except for cyclical task scheduling. These guarantees may be difficult to provide, but are especially important for an interface intended to support realtime applications.

The evolving fault-tolerance interface may help where high reliability is required.

4) **Language binding:** The CTRON specification includes full language bindings for C, Ada, and CHILL. C and Ada are widely used today for general purpose applications, and CHILL is designed especially for communication software. These languages are probably the most appropriate choices.

The language bindings now defined are simple and direct transcriptions of the functions defined in the body of the standard. This is an obvious approach, but it does not consider the programming style conventions widely used in each language. This problem is most serious for the Ada binding, and may cause it to be avoided or changed by experienced Ada programmers.

11. RECOMMENDATIONS

Based on the assessment in the previous section, I will conclude by proposing a few guidelines for further development of the CTRON specifications:

1) **Ensure only a limited number of subsets** throughout the specification. Where possible, identify the higher-level software classes which each allowable subset is intended to support.

2) **Consider removing some functions** or function groups if they seem unnecessary for portable software.

3) **Review the level of specification** to avoid unnecessary detail such as specific algorithms, parameter encodings, etc.

4) **Define a minimum range of values** for numerical types, and identify parameters requiring long or short ranges. These definitions should occur in the language-independent specification, not in the language bindings.

5) **Develop a method for providing guarantees** of timing accuracy, reliability, etc., at least within implementations where these guarantees might be important.

6) **Review the language bindings** for conformance to accepted practice and style in each language. This is especially important for the Ada language.

REFERENCES

Blackham, G., Building Software for Portability. *Dr. Dobb's Journal of Software Tools,* Vol. 13, No. 12, Dec. 1988, pp. 18-26.

Brown, P.J. (ed.), *Software Portability,* Cambridge University Press, Cambridge, England 1977.

Campbell, F., The Portable UCSD Pascal System, *Microprocessors and Microsystems,* Vol. 7, No. 8, Oct. 1983, pp. 394-398.

Cheriton, D.R., Thoth, a Portable Real-Time Operating System, *Comm. of the ACM,* Vol. 22, No. 2, Feb. 1979, pp. 105-115.

Cheriton, D.R., UIO: A Uniform I/O System Interface for Distributed Systems, *ACM Trans. on Computer Systems,* Vol. 5, No. 1, Feb. 1987, pp. 12-46.

Cook, R., and J. Brandon, The PICK Operating System, Part 2: System Control, *Byte*, Vol. 9, No. 12, Nov. 1984, pp. 132 ff.

Dahlstrand, I., *Software Portability and Standards*, Ellis Horwood, Chichester, England,1984.

IEEE Std 1003.1-1988, *Standard Portable Operating System Interface for Computer Environments*. IEEE Press, Piscataway, N.J., 1988.

IEEE Std 855-1990, *Standard Specification for Microprocessor Operating System Interfaces*. IEEE Press, Piscataway N.J., 1990.

Johnson, S.C., and D.M. Ritchie,Portability of C Programs and the UNIX System, *Bell Systems Technical Journal*, Vol. 57, No. 6, Part II, July-Aug. 1978, pp. 2021-2048.

Lane, M., and J. Mooney, *A Practical Approach to Operating Systems,* PWS-Kent, Boston, Mass. 1989.

LeCarme, O., and M. Pellissier Gart, *Software Portability*. McGraw-Hill, New York, 1986.

Mooney, J., *The MOSI Standard for Operating System Interfaces: Implementation and Use*. Tech. Rept. 85-1, Dept. of Statistics and Comp. Sci., West Virginia Univ., Morgantown, W.V., 1985.

Mooney, J., Lessons from the MOSI Project, *Computer Standards and Interfaces*, Vol. 5, 1986, pp. 201-210.

Mooney, J., Strategies for Supporting Application Portability, *IEEE Computer,* Vol. 23, No. 11, Nov. 1990, pp. 59-70.

Peck, J.E.L., and M. A. MacLean, The Construction of a Portable Editor, *Software -- Practice and Experience,* Vol. 11, 1981, pp. 479-489.

Poole, P.C., and W. M. Waite, Portability and Adaptability, in *Software Engineering: an Advanced Course,* Springer-Verlag, Berlin, 1975 (reprinted from 1973 edition).

Powell, M.S., Experience of Transporting and Using the SOLO Operating System, *Software -- Practice and Experience*, Vol. 9, No. 7, July 1979, pp. 561-569.

Rashid, R., *et al*, Machine-Independent Virtual Memory Management for Paged Uniprocessor and Multiprocessor Architectures, *IEEE Trans. Computers*, Vol. 37, No. 8 Aug. 1988, pp. 896-907.

Richards, M., TRIPOS -- A Portable Operating System for Minicomputers, *Software -- Practice and Experience*, Vol. 9, No. 7, July 1979, pp. 513-526.

425

Schwan, K., *et al*, High-Performance Operating System Primitives for Robotics and Real-Time Control Systems, *ACM Trans. on Computer Systems,* Vol. 5, No. 3, Aug. 1987, pp. 189-231.

Shibagaki, H., and T. Wasano, OS Interface Subsetting, *Proc. of the First Software Portability Symposium*, TRON Association, 1990, pp. 97-113.

Sommerville, I., *Software Engineering* (3rd ed). Addison-Wesley, Wokingham, England, 1989.

Snow, C.R., An Exercise in the Transportation of an Operating System, *Software -- Practice and Experience*, Vol. 8, No. 1, 1978, pp. 41-50.

Tanenbaum, A.S., *et al*, Guidelines for Software Portability, *Software -- Practice and Experience*, Vol. 8, No. 6, 1978, pp. 681-698.

Tanenbaum, A.S., *et al*, A Practical Tool Kit for Making Portable Compilers, *Comm. of the ACM,* Vol. 26, No. 9, Sep. 1983, pp. 654-660.

Theaker, C.J., and G.R. Frank, MUSS -- A Portable Operating System, *Software -- Practice and Experience*, Vol. 9, No. 8, Aug. 1979, pp. 633-643.

TRON Association, Original CTRON Specification Series, Vol. 1: Outline of CTRON, Ohmsha Ltd., Tokyo, 1989.

Waite, W.M., Hints on Distributing Portable Software, *Software -- Practice and Experience*, Vol. 5, 1975, pp. 295-308.

Wallis, P.J.L., *Portable Programming*. John Wiley & Sons, 1982.

Zabala, I., Some Feedback from PTEX Installations, *TUGBoat* (newsletter of the TeX Users Group), Vol. 2, No. 2, 1981, pp. 16-19.

James D. Mooney is an associate professor in the Department of Statistics and Computer Science, West Virginia University. He received the B.S. degree from the University of Notre Dame in 1968, and the M.Sc. and Ph.D. degrees from The Ohio State University in 1969 and 1977, all in electrical engineering. At West Virginia University he teaches courses in operating systems and computer architecture. He is coauthor of an operating system textbook. He chairs IEEE standards working group 855, which developed the MOSI standard, and contributes to various other standardization activities.

The above author may be reached at: Dept. of Statistics and Computer Science, West Virginia University, Morgantown, WV 26506, USA.

Realization of the Micro-CTRON Kernel under pSOS+

Alfred Chao
Software Components Group, Inc.

Abstract: The CTRON micro-kernel is well-suited for a wide range of embedded systems with hard real-time requirements. This paper discusses the results of an implementation of the CTRON micro-kernel, using as a foundation pSOS+, a field-proven, high-performance operating system.

Keywords: pSOS+, CTRON micro-kernel, deterministic behavior, hardware independence, system-analyzer.

1. cpSOS+: CTRON ON A pSOS+ FOUNDATION

An implementation of the micro-kernel subset of CTRON was realized under pSOS+, a high-performance real-time operating system kernel with a collection of support components. For the initial adaptation, the 68020/030 was selected as the target processor. Moreover, in order to provide an integrated debug capability for cpSOS+ users, this effort included an adaptation of the pROBE+ system analyzer. The capabilities of cpROBE+ are described under Section 4.

The design objective for cpSOS+ was to minimize changes to the pSOS+ kernel, in order to preserve as much of the proven reliability of the existing code as possible. This target was met quite easily and successfully. Including testing and QA, the adaptation of pSOS+ to CTRON took less than three months. The resulting implementation was achieved substantially through a transformation layer, mapping CTRON system call conventions into pSOS+ call conventions. This approach was made possible by the fact that pSOS+ provides a rich complement of capabilities that is a superset of those required under the CTRON specification. For the selected 68020/030 architecture, cpSOS+ requires a scant 14 kilobytes of code space: 12 kilobytes for pSOS+, and less than 2 kilobytes for the transformation layer.

Whereas some performance degradation may be expected from such a methodology, the actual benchmark measurements show this overhead to be well under 10% for nearly all comparable functions. We feel that this is a reasonable price to pay in exchange for assured reliability.

2. SOME BENCHMARK RESULTS

Table 1 shows a number of benchmark results for cpSOS+. Execution and measurement are performed on a MC68020 clocked at 16.7 Mhz, with 0 wait states. Measurement path always starts with the system trap entry and ends with return from the system, either in the same calling task or, in the case of a call that results in a task switch, in another task. Not all CTRON call timings are presented, since some system services, e.g. CRE_TSK or GET_BID, are typically not in time-sensitive paths.

In cpSOS+ most time-critical system calls run in constant time. The data for all of the system calls listed in this document are fixed, worst-case numbers, regardless of system state (*e.g.* number of active tasks, message boxes, etc.).

Table 1: cpSOS+ Performance Metrics

GENERAL TIMING DATA		TIME (uS)
INTERRUPT LATENCY		< 8.0
TASK CONTEXT SWITCH		30.0
SERVICE CALL TIMING		*TIME (uS)*
STA_TSK		57.0
SUS_TSK	RETURNS TO CALLER	40.0
RSM_TSK	TARGET TASK READIED, RETURNS TO CALLER	45.2
	TARGET TASK PREEMPTS CALLER	75.5
SLP_TSK	CALLER WAITS, SWITCHES TASK	74.1
WUP_TSK	TARGET TASK READIED, RETURNS TO CALLER	48.5
	TARGET TASK PREEMPTS CALLER	78.6
SND_MSG	QUEUE EMPTY	39.5
	DQ'ED TASK MADE READY	42.4
	DQ'ED TASK PREEMPTS CALLER	73.4
REL_MSG	MESSAGE AVAILABLE	38.7
	CALLER WAITS (FIFO), SWITCHES TASK	81.8
SET_EVF	SETS & RETURNS TO CALLER	25.6
	TARGET TASK READIED, RETURNS TO CALLER	46.5
	TARGET TASK PREEMPTS CALLER	76.2
WAI_EVF	EVENTS AVAILABLE	24.5
	CALLER WAITS, SWITCHES TASK	68.3
ALC_MEM		49.8
FRE_MEM		56.0
INTERRUPT OPERTIONS		*TIME (uS)*
RETURN TO NESTED LEVEL		4.8
RETURN TO INTERRUPTED TASK		17.0
RETURN TO PREEMPTING TASK		47.0

3. DIFFERENCES BETWEEN CTRON AND pSOS+

Thankfully, there are more similarities than differences between CTRON and pSOS+; otherwise, the implementation would have posed more difficulties. Nevertheless, in the subsections to follow, certain differences between the CTRON micro-kernel specification and pSOS+ will be discussed, in some cases as they relate to implementation, in other cases as commentaries on the relative merits of the two system specifications.

3.1 DETERMINISTIC BEHAVIOR

pSOS+ uses constant-time algorithms on almost all operations that could be in a time-critical path in the user's application. For example, all operations on the ready list -- insertion (scheduling), removal and dispatching, are constant-time. cpSOS+ inherits this behavior with respect to task execution levels, which we have limited to 256 levels. However, the secondary priority-level specification cannot be implemented in constant-time, at least not reasonably or with any degree of efficiency, due to the excessive memory needed to implement the requisite structures. Therefore, for applications which demand deterministic behavior, tasks will need to be assigned to separate execution levels.

In another case, under memory allocation, we constrained the memory pool allocation_unit to powers of two in order to achieve constant-time allocation and de-allocation.

3.2 MONOCHROMATIC MEMORY

In advanced applications, there are often several types of memory -- fast vs. slow, volatile vs. non-volatile, local vs. globally-accessible, single vs. dual-ported, etc. In other words, memory often come in several *colors*. Yet, under CTRON, the user has no means of conveying this color information to the cre_mpl call. It assumes that all memory pools shall be created equal, *i.e.* monochromatic. In this respect, we believe CTRON is deficient.

Under pSOS+, the equivalent rn_create call allows the caller to specify the address of the memory region being created. In this way, the initialization or supervisory portion of an application can initially bring any number of memory areas of varying colors under management as regions. From these, the rest of the application can allocate and create sub-regions of the specific color. This is a more flexible and viable paradigm. Unfortunately, we did not see a way of providing a similar capability within the CTRON specification.

3.3 TASK MANAGEMENT

In a complete CTRON operating environment, the cre_tsk call is likely to be invoked by an executive program in a context wherein the task's stack would be furnished via some means, *e.g.* the virtual memory manager. However, in a scaled-down, self-contained system wherein such higher-level facilities are not available, CTRON does not seem to provide any means to specify the size of a new task's stack. Since this is an important parameter that should be controllable by the user, cpSOS+ opted to use the user_work_area parameter under the cre_tsk call to supply the task's stack size requirement to the kernel. This is not strictly in compliance with the CTRON specification.

Similarly, CTRON provides no means to declare certain processor-dependent attributes to the cre_tsk call; for example whether the task uses any available co-processors, or the privilege state in which the task should run. Under pSOS+, we have an all-purpose *flag* parameter to which we assign such processor-specific characteristics. Unfortunately for cpSOS+, we had no choice but to default such attributes.

One major area of difference between pSOS+ and CTRON lies in the task exit/termination services. Whereas pSOS+ contains only two calls, t_delete and t_restart, CTRON provides a total of six such related calls. However, we were able to emulate all six calls, in some cases relying on the pSOS+ asynchronous signals and service routines to implement task exit routines.

4. SYSTEM DEBUG AND ANALYSIS SUPPORT

In order to provide an integrated debug capability for users of cpSOS+, we adapted the pROBE+ system analyzer to conform to the cpSOS+ interface. In addition to the standard debug capabilites, cpROBE+ provides the user with visibility and control at the CTRON kernel level. Included are *query* commands to examine all CTRON objects, *break* options on system-level activities such as task state transitions, and *profiling* of system activities. Some examples of these capabilities are shown on the next page.

5. CONCLUSIONS

This project showed that it is possible to implement the CTRON micro-kernel on top of an operating system with a sufficiently rich set of capabilities. This approach has the benefits of preserving proven, reliable code, and at the same time achieving comparable performance.

```
cpROBE+>QT      /* Query Task */

 Name      TID     Xlev Prio Status   Susp?      Parameters            Ticks
----------------------------------------------------------------------------
'..ZZ' -#00010000  FF   00   Ready
'..00' -#00020000  05   55   Qwait      Q = '..MB' -#00050000   00000023
'..RM' -#00030000  11   11   Ewait     EV = '..E1' -#00060000   00000007
'..AC' -#00040000  22   22 Running



cpROBE+>QQ '..MX'      /* Query Message Box */

 Name      QID      TQ Len     MQ Len    MQ Limit     Mgb      Qtype
----------------------------------------------------------------------------
'..MX' -#00090000  00000000  00000002  00000006    00000003    FIFO
----------------------------------------------------------------------------
Task Queue:
----------------------------------------------------------------------------
Message Queue: Msg Addr     Msg Size
               0001E300     00000004
               00288800     00000010



cpROBE+>QE      /* Query All Event Flags */

 Name      EID      Pending    Wanted        By Task        Clr  Logic
----------------------------------------------------------------------------
'..E1' -#00060000  00000000  00000033    '..RM'- #00030000   Yes   Or
'..E2' -#00070000  00000000



cpROBE+>QR #0      /* Query Memory Pool Id 0 */

                                    Unit    Free    Largest  TQ
 Name      ID     Address  Length   Size    Bytes   Contig   Len  Wait By
----------------------------------------------------------------------------
'RN#0' -#00000000 00003000 00003E38 00000100 00000800 00000800 0000  No  Fi
----------------------------------------------------------------------------
Task Queue:
----------------------------------------------------------------------------
Unit Usage:  Start Address    Length       Status

             00003000        00002538     In Use
             00005538        00000100     Header
             00005638        00000800      Free
             00005E38        00000A00     In Use
             00006838        00000400     In Use
             00006C38        00000100     In Use
             00006D38        00000200     In Use
```

Alfred Chao: The president and founder of Software Components Group, Inc., a supplier of real-time operating systems and development environments based in San Jose, California, USA. Mr. Chao was the principal architect of the pSOS+ collection of OS components. He received both his BS and MS degrees from the Massachusetts Institute of Technology, Cambridge, Massachusetts, in 1975.

The above author may be reached at:
Software Components Group
1731 Technology Drive
San Jose, CA 95110
U.S.A.
fax: (408) 437-0711

List of Contributors

Index of Keywords